VCs
of the
SECOND
WORLD WAR

by

John Frayn Turner

Pen & Sword
MILITARY

First published in Great Britain in 2004 by
Pen & Sword Military
an imprint of
Pen & Sword Books Ltd
47 Church Street
Barnsley
South Yorkshire
S70 2AS

ISBN 1 84415 067 4

A CIP catalogue record for this book is
available from the British Library

Typeset in 11/12 Centaur by
Phoenix Typesetting, Auldgirth, Dumfriesshire

Printed and bound in England by
CPI UK

Pen & Sword Books Ltd incorporates the imprints of Pen & Sword Aviation, Pen &
Sword Maritime, Pen & Sword Military, Wharncliffe Local History, Pen & Sword
Select, Pen & Sword Military Classics and Leo Cooper.

For a complete list of Pen & Sword titles please contact
PEN & SWORD BOOKS LIMITED
47 Church Street, Barnsley, South Yorkshire, S70 2AS, England
E-mail: enquiries@pen-and-sword.co.uk
Website: www.pen-and-sword.co.uk

CONTENTS

ACKNOWLEDGEMENTS

I would like to thank the staff of the Reference Library of the Imperial War Museum for their help. I have also received assistance in the past from the Press Office of the Ministry of Defence.

I wish to express my sincere gratitude for permission to reproduce or adapt accounts of actions from the following: *The Regimental History of the Royal Hampshire Regiment* (Gale and Polden Ltd.) which conveys the courage of Major Herbert Wallace Le Patourel, Captain Richard Wakeford, and Lieutenant Gerard Ross Norton; *The War in Malaya* by Lieutenant General A.E. Percival (Eyre and Spottiswoode Ltd.), describing how Brigadier Arthur Edward Cummings won the VC; Captain R.E.D. Ryder, VC, RN, who wrote his own account of *The Attack on St Nazaire* (John Murray); Captain G.B. Stanning, DSO, RN, for his narrative of Narvik; C.E.T. Warren and James Benson, authors of *Above Us the Waves* (George G. Harrap and Co. Ltd.); *The Ship Busters* by Ralph Barker (Chatto and Windus) on Flying Officer Kenneth Campbell; and finally *No. 5 Bomber Group, RAF* by W.J. Lawrence (Faber and Faber) for details of the action for which Group Captain Leonard Cheshire was awarded the Victoria Cross.

John Frayn Turner

CHAPTER ONE

The Battle of Narvik

BERNARD WARBURTON-LEE

The Germans invaded Norway in April 1940 and captured the port of Narvik almost at once. British warships were already lying off the Norwegian coast when the Admiralty immediately flashed orders to Captain Warburton-Lee of the destroyer HMS *Hardy*: 'Take three ships and attack Narvik'. The youthful Warburton-Lee, or Wash as he was always known, chose the fast H-class destroyers *Hotspur*, *Havock* and *Hunter* to help him execute this dangerous duty.

The *Hardy* arrived off Tranoy by Vest Fjord and Wash sent a boat ashore to ask local Norwegians what they knew of the enemy. The locals told them that German warships and U-boats were at Narvik. Despite this news, Wash told his officers: 'I'm attacking at dawn.' Meanwhile, *Hardy* steamed up and down the side of Vest Fjord so as not to give away their intentions to anyone spotting them.

At midnight it was snowing hard. Another destroyer, the *Hostile* had joined the four already there. They altered course to turn up Narvik Fjord. The flotilla of five destroyers edged on, through thickening snow, nearer and nearer to Narvik. They met no enemy. It was then 04.30 hours in an Arctic fjord as they glided like ghosts towards Narvik harbour. An unreal silence and more snow.

The port was still half a mile off. *Hardy* went in alone. With engines stopped, she just floated forward. Suddenly someone said: 'There they are.' Two enemy destroyers lay alongside each other right in the middle of the harbour —with bows turned to the town.

Warburton-Lee ordered: 'Fire four torpedoes.' Then he made twenty knots to take them out of range of retaliation. They saw more destroyers at the quay. One of the torpedoes hit a merchant ship astern of the destroyers. Then came an explosion erupting from the direction of the destroyers. It meant that magazines must have been hit.

As *Hardy* turned out of the harbour, they fired three more torpedoes in the general direction of the others, and emerged with only one left.

Hardy kept close to the entrance to the harbour in case anything tried to leave. She circled in front of the entrance for the second time, firing her guns at enemy flashes when they lit the snow-backed port behind the ships. Heavier gunfire came from Narvik now —from the probably damaged destroyers. Wash was anxious to find out what damage had been inflicted, as they had heard many

I

louder explosions since the first batch earlier. But they could see nothing of the result.

Not only heavy guns aimed at them now. As *Hardy* crossed the entrance to the southward, torpedoes tore through the fjord towards her. Some came very near, too close for comfort, and one actually seemed to go underneath the ship. Lieutenant Geoffrey Stanning counted six torpedoes, but others saw more and said three went under the vessel. However, none of them hit, nor did they explode. They could be heard from the deck of *Hardy* as they went ashore on the beach opposite, whirring weirdly, mechanically, as they tried to scramble up the sand. Each of the five H-class destroyers took a turn at the entrance to the harbour, then finally they all withdrew.

Wash asked the others for details of damage or casualties, and how many torpedoes they had left.

'No damage, no casualties,' came back the signals. And *Hostile* said she still had a full load of torpedoes.

Mansell told Wash that *Hardy* had a small hole in the after-funnel, and confirmed that three torpedoes had gone under them. Every one was in high spirits. The second stage of the battle was over, and still no damage had been sustained. All enemy guns seemed to have ceased fire fairly early in this latter attack; perhaps all opposition had been silenced.

Wash called in his officers. 'What do you think about things now?' he wanted to know. 'What's it to be —withdraw or go in again?'

All the while that they had been considering the latest situation, the *Hardy* was steaming slowly down-fjord. When the Captain made up his mind, they were a way from the harbour entrance. He turned her round, and at first the entrance could not be found again —just as it had eluded them before the initial assault. Then they saw the old fishing-boat near the wooden pier. Soon they were at the entrance. The harbour looked in a chaotic state, but it was difficult to discover the damage from previous attacks. Now at any rate they saw that the supposedly British ship near the entrance had been sunk, with her stern pointing mountain-wards, high out of the water.

Then there came a terrible shock.

Wash suddenly sighted three enemy warships heading straight towards them from the direction of Rombaks Fjord. He took them to be a cruiser and two destroyers —and gave the order: 'Engage.'

Hardy opened fire on them at the simultaneous second that they attacked. Visibility had increased only a matter of minutes before —or the flotilla might have collided with the three enemy vessels. Whether the first was a cruiser or leader destroyer, it certainly looked larger than the others.

Wash thought quickly after the first exchange of salvos. Then he ordered the signal to withdraw —a red Very light —at thirty knots.

Clark protested that *Hardy* was hitting them, and wanted to stay. But before another word was possible two more ships appeared ahead.

Cross said: 'Birminghams.'

They were four miles off and looked like our own cruisers. But Stanning snatched up his glasses and caught sight of hoods on their funnels.

'Not ours,' he said tersely. Then he thumbed through the pages of the *Janes* which was on the bridge. 'Large German destroyers,' he added with animation.

That clinched it. They were in a tight corner. The two Germans ahead turned sharply to port and opened fire. *Hardy* engaged them both, leaving the other three to her rear ships. It must have been at this moment, when *Hardy* was taking on the two ahead and Wash wanted the others to tackle the three remaining, that he made the last signal of his life:

'Keep on engaging the enemy . . .'

Hardy made a report about the strength of the enemy. She was being hit by now, and damage was done. The firing was uncomfortably accurate. Stanning felt several hits forward, then a tremendous tearing explosion on the bridge. Most of them were there.

Stanning was stunned for the second. He was thrown into the air, then fell on the gyro compass, near the Asdic set. Cross had been at his desk; Clark on the starboard side of the bridge forward; Wash by the Asdic set; Gordon-Smith behind the gyro compass. Torps was about too. Stanning felt as if he had been carrying a tray of china and dropped the lot.

He came to. Wash was lying on his back, breathing, but with a ghastly gash in the side of his face and another on his body. The pilot lay on his face, down the step from the compass platform. He was kicking. Stanning thought that the bridge had suddenly become very dirty. A strong smell of cordite fumes hung in the air, both compasses were broken, and the chart table could not be seen.

Stanning felt a surge of loneliness; it seemed as if he must be the only one alive in the ship. Yet the vessel still steamed at speed, making for the southern shore.

'If I don't do something quickly we'll be on the bricks.'

He hailed the wheelhouse, received no answer, and came to the conclusion he would have to go down there himself. He must have had his weight on the right foot, for as he put his left foot to the deck he found he could not walk on it. He recalled the terrific jerk of the explosion. He hopped across the bridge. On the way he rolled the pilot over on his back in the narrow alley by the torpedo control, and left him as comfortable as he could.

He slid down to the wheelhouse, which was in a shambles, and saw debris of clothes and belongings but no bodies, certainly not the coxswain's. Stanning wrenched the wheel to starboard to try to stop the ship being beached. He was surprised to find it to be working. The ship had been darkened so there was nowhere to look out to see what effect the wheel was having; but luckily the iron cover of the centre square window was hanging free, and by pushing it open he could peer through. *Hardy* had answered the helm so efficiently that she was swinging fast to starboard and the enemy. Stanning put some port wheel on and had another look. For a couple of minutes or so he went on steering the ship down the fjord, having to hop to the square window, lift up the flap, and look out at intervals to get an idea of direction.

While he was still steering, Able Seaman Smale appeared in the doorway.

'All right, are you, Smale? Come and take the wheel, so I can get back to the compass platform.'

3

Stanning was glad to see the seaman, especially as he knew him to be utterly reliable. As soon as he reached the platform he realized that something would have to be done within the next minute or so —for the ship was nearly abreast of the German destroyers. Stanning saw that both numbers one and two guns were out of action, although some of the after-guns seemed still to be firing.

The question was whether to try and rush past the Germans or ram them.

'Probably the proper thing,' Stanning thought to himself. Then he remembered about the other ships and hurried over to the starboard side of the bridge to try and see what was happening to them. He never saw them, for just as he got to that side a whole salvo seemed to strike the engine room and the boilers. A cloud of steam spurted and spluttered. The *Hardy* began to slow down, Stanning assumed the entire engine room must have been obliterated —but actually only one man was wounded by that particular salvo. Steam must have been emitted in so many places at once that no one had been hurt by it escaping under pressure.

But Stanning did not know all that, nor could he believe that there were more than a score of survivors aboard all the ship. No one could be sent to see what had happened. Another decision had to be made. What should he do with the ship? He decided to put her ashore. It seemed the obvious and only thing to do.

In a matter of seconds all the various pros and cons flitted through his brain. He tried to weigh them fairly. Calm thought was not easy. 'The ship is certainly no more use as a fighting unit, and few people can still be alive. All right; one point in favour of beaching her. But it is wrong to put a ship ashore in enemy territory, where the Germans might be able to get at some of the secret gear and the ciphers. One-all. What should I do? I don't know how to sink the ship myself. Even if I did, I couldn't possibly cope, with this wretched foot.' To remind him, it suddenly gave a twist of pain. 'I ought to be able to destroy most of the secret stuff with Smale's help. The Germans will take some time to get to the ship ashore —longer than if she were drifting about the fjord which is all she's fit for now. Poor old *Hardy*.'

Not a second could be lost. The ship was losing speed quickly now, and Stanning wanted to reach a group of houses a few hundred yards inland. There was the prospect of shelter. As he put the port wheel over to turn the *Hardy* gently in towards the shore, one of the houses was hit by a shell and set on fire. The ship glided to the shallows and grounded unbelievably gently. People at the back of the bridge began to come to life again. Several signalmen scrambled up as Stanning returned to the bridge.

He knew he must destroy the ciphers and the AS cabinet and bridge set. He still did not know that almost all the officers were alive. Heppel had defiantly gone off to fire his last torpedo at the enemy. Stanning got up the flag lockers and called some sailors by name to come and help him. Then he sent the Chief Stoker off to find Mr McCracken and help him throw the safes aft into the oil tank outside the Captain's cabin.

'Pope!' Stanning shouted to one of the midshipmen, 'go and get the ciphers out of the chart-house, shove them in the weighted bag, and chuck them overboard as far aft as you can.'

4

Mansell came up to Stanning. 'The Asdic cabinet's been blown out of the ship.' He confirmed later that the set on the bridge had been destroyed.

Up on the bridge the doctor was attending to the pilot.

'The telegraphist in radio control on the bridge was pinned in, but Pope levered the place open and let him out,' Mansell told Stanning. 'What are we going to do now?' he asked. Then answering himself: 'I want to get the motor-boat out.'

They both went down on the starboard side, but the after-thread of the davit was twisted and they could not turn the boat out.

Stanning looked up and saw the pilot coming down from the bridge alone, seriously wounded but just able to walk. He sat down beside Stanning, lit a cigarette. Stanning had to go on unreeling. A moment later the pilot suddenly began choking. Stanning thought he must be dying, for he lay quite still. The lieutenant got someone to put him in the narrow cross passage.

Mansell suggested a Carley float for taking the wounded ashore. The enemy were shelling the ship and shore spasmodically. Several shells hit the beach near those of the crew who were already ashore and filing up the enemy beach in a thin black stream. The shelling of the ship intensified. They decided to abandon her at once. Stanning went aft between the torpedo tubes and took off his oilskins. A shell burst on the 'Chief's seat' abaft the after-funnel. This must have been what killed the chief stoker . . .

Stanning was scared now. He jumped into the sea fully dressed except for his oilskins. His first urgent concern was to swim clear of the ship and avoid the shells. The water was icy. He tried to comfort himself that there was not much of him above water to hit. He had blown up his rubber lifebelt and found he was swimming quite well. Much sooner than he expected he touched ground only about fifty yards inshore from the ship. He could not wade in and had to finish the journey on his stomach.

All the others had got ashore by now. Stanning realized he was being left behind and could not catch up with the others. He shouted to two torpedo-men ahead, and they dropped back to help him. He still had 100 yards of foreshore to negotiate, covered with rocks and pools. 'Just the place for a child to play,' he thought. The pain from his injured foot was agonizing. Even with the two men's help he felt he would never make it, and told them to push ahead again. Somehow they got Stanning to dry land, or snow-clad shore. At the top of the beach a path fifty yards long to the road lay waist deep in snow. They supported Stanning between them and at last they reached the road. They trudged along it, and another path deep in a drift, then finally reached a wooden house.

The three of them groped inside. They saw dozens of men, a stench of bodies, the tang of burnt cordite, the dankness of soaked clothes. The early arrivals had dressed themselves in the clothes and bedclothes of the owners, Mrs Christiansen and her daughter. The two women were now downstairs tearing the curtains from the windows, ripping up the carpets and rugs to wrap the shivering sailors in; they ransacked their larder for food and gave almost every one a slice of bread and butter.

Stanning and his two sailors merged into the rest of the room. The company stayed like this for some minutes, sorting themselves out, talking things over. The first shock of the ship's loss was now over. They were beginning to think what it had meant, who was alive —and who dead.

Stanning's foot got more and more painful. Someone cut his boot off, and the foot swelled up like a football. He hobbled over to Dr Waind.

Then Geoffrey Stanning plucked up courage to ask the question which had been worrying him most:

'What happened to Wash?' He looked straight into Waind's eyes, waiting to tell from them whether hope still survived.

'He was almost dead before he left the ship, old chap, but they got him on to the Carley float. He died on the way . . .'

Stanning was silent for a second. Five words, like his signal: 'Keep on engaging the enemy.'

Waind went on: 'Guns and Flags must have been killed outright.'

'Thanks for telling me', said Stanning. Then he sent a message to Heppel to go back to the ship, fetch the pilot, and make sure that all the books in the Captain's cabin aft were destroyed.

They were in a peculiar position and obviously could not stay indefinitely crowded in the house which the Christiansens had now abandoned to them. Yet no one was fit to go far, and many had no boots. They really expected the Germans to send a party ashore from one of their destroyers to take them prisoner, or else get a detachment from Narvik to go by road. But nothing seemed to be happening yet. Stanning sat outside the house, as it was fairly warm now. He could speak German so he thought he could best negotiate with any enemy. At the moment he sat down, he saw —and heard —an explosion somewhere down the fjord. A column of black smoke shot high above the mountains. Although he did not know it then, *Hostile* was torpedoing *Rauenfels*. Nor did he or the others discover that *Hunter* was badly damaged and that a few minutes afterwards *Hotspur* herself was hit and her steering gear jammed; she was heading for *Hunter* at the time and rammed the other destroyer fair and square, bowling her over.

Meanwhile, *Hardy* was burning forward, and her small ammunition exploded intermittently, echoing in bursts across the beach and fjord. On the other side of the fjord, Stanning could just make out through the trees a German destroyer ashore as the *Hardy* was, with no sign of life near her.

Then someone shouted, pointing to the *Hardy*. 'Look, a man walking about on the forecastle. Must be either the pilot or a missing stoker.'

Stanning knew the shape of the man. It was the pilot. He was still alive. He hoped Heppel had got back to the ship by now and would bring him ashore.

A lorry and a car drew up outside the house. Stanning was sure they would contain Germans. But a small man in spectacles hurried up the snowy path. He proved to be a doctor.

'You ought to put some more clothes on,' he told Stanning, who was drying himself and his gear in the sun, 'and I'll get you to hospital. I've got a cottage hospital about fifteen miles away, at Ballangen. I can take all your wounded.'

The worst cases were taken out to the lorry, which whisked them away to Ballangen. After ages, it seemed, they heard the lorry returning. Stanning longed to go to hospital as his foot was aching almost unbearably. Heppel was seen on his way ashore with the pilot. A dozen of them got into the lorry —all the wounded that were left —and then the pilot appeared. He was put into the vehicle carefully, and though still a terrible sight, once more smoked a cigarette contentedly. The Germans could not kill him. Even Stanning never expected to see him again. The pilot lay on the floor of the van, with his feet against the rear door, as they bumped along the snowy road. An hour passed before Ballangen came into view. Beyond the village they turned into a square three-storey building which was the hospital. A comforting aroma of antiseptic suggested they would be in good hands. They were told that the worst cases must go on to Harstad, a better-equipped hospital.

Stanning looked down at his watch from habit. It registered 7.12 —the minute he had jumped from the *Hardy*. Wash must have gone about the same time. The pain from Stanning's foot seared through him. The doctor did not see him till about four, nearly nine hours after the battle. Then he had morphine and sank into his first sleep for four nights.

Four days of confusion followed for Stanning, under morphine. On Saturday morning, Heppel and Torps told him of a plan to get away via Tranoy. Almost as they spoke, a colossal crash heralded the opening of an attack on a German destroyer in Ballangen Bay. *Warspite* it was, in the fight. That evening Heppel rushed back into Stanning's room with the news that he had been on board *Ivanhoe*, and that he was taking the unwounded aboard that same night. The wounded would follow the next day. So about 10.00 on Sunday, 14 April, Stanning and some others were transferred into the lorry, driven down to the little pier, and put into *Ivanhoe*'s boat. Thence to *Ivanhoe*, to *Warspite*, *Woolwich* and the hospital carrier, *The Isle of Jersey*.

It was not until Stanning finally returned to Aberdeen that he heard the full facts of the Battle of Narvik.

Hardy and the other destroyers of the flotilla caused havoc to numerous supply ships and transports lying in harbour and repeatedly hit two enemy destroyers there, too, one of which blew up. In the words of the official Admiralty communique; HMS *Hardy* later engaged three large destroyers. The bridge of the *Hardy* was hit and reduced to a shambles, and Captain Warburton-Lee was mortally wounded.

The odds were against Warburton-Lee from the beginning, but he had not complained. His duty was done.

CHAPTER TWO

Glowworm versus *Hipper*

GERARD ROOPE

Before the battle of Narvik, Lieutenant Commander Gerard Broadmead Roope won his VC. But the story of HMS *Glowworm* only came to light five years later. Thus although the epic action was in fact the first naval engagement of the war to result in recognition by a Victoria Cross, the actual award came as one of the last of the war, instead of the first.

Glowworm (1,345 tons) was one of the destroyers playing a part in the self-same operation as *Hardy* and her H-class consorts. Her fight occurred forty-eight hours earlier than the Narvik epic.

The last *Hardy* heard of *Glowworm* before her own battles was when the G-class destroyer was escorting the battlecruiser *Renown*. During 7 April, a man was washed overboard in the heavy flow of the North Sea. The weather worsened hourly, and in her efforts to find him, she lost touch with the main British force. With the weather becoming increasingly impossible, Roope, as commanding officer of *Glowworm.*, reduced speed to eight knots. Then her gyro compass failed and she had to steer by magnetic compass.

Daybreak, 8 April 1940, saw her trying to rendezvous with another force in the operation. But she was never to find that force.

Suddenly *Glowworm* sighted an unidentified destroyer. Immediately the British ship challenged her. The reply came back that she was Swedish. Then she opened fire. Thirty seconds later, still in seas as savage as any the oceans over, *Glowworm* sighted a second destroyer, and there began a gallant fight against odds.

The battle rapidly developed into a slamming match, with all three destroyers manoeuvring at full speed despite the sea —and firing with all guns. The sea began to take a toll, before the enemy did. Soon, *Glowworm*'s director control tower was flooded out by the raging seas, which were hurling the ship about. Two men went overboard, and several were injured by the relentless rolling. But they scored a hit on the leading enemy destroyer. *Glowworm* escaped being hit, although she continued on the attack all the time. Then came a brief respite.

The Germans broke off the action, although already outnumbering *Glowworm* two to one. They were obviously trying to tempt her on to something more powerful. Roope knew this, but decided it was his duty to follow them to find out what big ships the Germans had at sea. He hoped to shadow them and report their

8

movements, since this could provide vital information for British forces throughout the North Sea and Norway areas, in view of the impending operation.

Glowworm sailed on. A few minutes later, the German heavy cruiser *Admiral Hipper* hove in sight. The *Hipper*, 10,000 tons against the *Glowworm*'s 1,345. The *Hipper*, with eight 8-inch, twelve 4·7-inch, and twelve 37-mm guns against the destroyer's four 4·7-inch guns. Weather conditions made shadowing out of the question –and from that moment all those aboard the *Glowworm* knew what her fate, and perhaps their own, would be.

Roope's one aim now was to inflict as much damage as possible on the enemy before being sunk. It was as certain as that. The battle began.

Long before *Glowworm*'s guns were within range, the *Hipper* poured 8-inch shells at the destroyer, hitting her mercilessly, like a heavyweight matched against a light-weight.

Glowworm was game. She made smoke to avoid the attack, and then began to close with the cruiser. The second she was within range, Lieutenant Robert Ramsay fired her torpedoes.

Meanwhile, the destroyer began to blaze. One of her four guns was already out of action. Her range-finder was hit, her speed reduced. Then the upper yard of her mast collapsed across the siren wires. Her sirens screeched unheeded in the blaze of battle.

Roope realized nothing could be gained by prolonging the fight at this range. Then it was that he decided to ram the *Admiral Hipper*. Going in under a storm of fire from all *Hipper*'s guns, and the terrible staccato sound of machine guns, he steered straight for the starboard side. A ghastly crunch signified the destroyer's bows crumpling against the cruiser's armour plating. Men fell to the deck in a welter of water, blood, flame, and smoke. Some staggered up again. Others did not.

Roope managed to draw *Glowworm* to 400 yards away from the cruiser and then opened fire once more. He scored a hit.

But the *Glowworm*'s bows were badly stoved in. A shell passed through the wheel-house. Another burst right in the transmitting station, killing most of the crew and all the staff of the wireless office on the spot. A third entered the ship under the torpedo tubes, crossed the whole width of the vessel, and burst against the forward bulkhead of the Captain's cabin. At the time, the cabin was being used as a first-aid station.

The same shell made a huge hole in the ship's side abreast the engine room. Another wrecked the after superstructure. Roope, so far, was unhurt. As *Glowworm* heeled over to starboard, he gave the order: 'Abandon ship.'

Ramsay was with him on the bridge.

'Go and get some timber and anything else that floats,' he shouted to Ramsay above the noise all around them.

Hardly any one seemed to be unwounded. Ramsay helped heave the timber over for people to cling to in the water –if they ever got there. Lifebelts were put on the injured in the hope that they would float.

Roope came down. He was the only other survivor from the bridge besides Ramsay. Engine Room Artificer Gregg rushed up to them.

'I've been down to the boiler room and let off steam, sir, so there'll be no explosion.'

'Good, Gregg.'

As they scrambled overboard the *Glowworm* capsized. She floated bottom up for a few moments, and then sank.

Ramsay swam clear. He was conscious of dots of men, heads and shoulders encircled in lifebelts, groping, struggling; and others splashing, moaning . . .

The *Admiral Hipper* stopped engines, put out a boat, and picked up survivors; but Roope was not among them, though he had been seen in the water.

Ramsay was taken before the Captain, who told him that the ramming had damaged one set of *Hipper's* torpedo tubes, flooded two compartments, and put her fresh water system out of commission. The prisoners were taken to Trondheim, but then the *Hipper* had to go to Germany for repairs in dry dock.

Only thirty-one out of the complement of 149 survived. Roope and 117 others died in an ice-cold sea.

CHAPTER THREE

Trawler at Namsos

RICHARD STANNARD

Namsos in Norway was the setting for the VC to follow Warburton-Lee's. The campaign in Norway was not one of our successes of the war, and the Navy was called in to evacuate troops from several points, of which Namsos was one. Lieutenant Richard Been Stannard, RNR, commanded HM Trawler *Arab*. A merchant seaman, he wore the interwoven gold rings of the Royal Naval Reserve on the arm of his jacket: rings dulled by endless exposure to the elements.

It was late in April 1940 when he took *Arab* towards Namsos. Somehow, together with other ships, he had to secure sufficient standing there to be able to take as many troops away as possible. A few weeks afterwards he would be doing the same thing at Dunkirk. But, in his own words, Dunkirk 'was a picnic compared to the hell of Namsos'.

Memories are mixed about those five days of continuous fighting, but the order in which things happened is really unimportant. The main thing to remember is that they did happen —and somehow Stannard survived.

He took *Arab* into the harbour amid a hail of gunfire from field guns and aircraft. Through his glasses he picked out the fleeting forms of British uniforms ashore.

Even as *Arab* steamed in, enemy bombers pounded the wharf area with high explosive and set off many tons of hand grenades which were stored there. Stannard could see that this wharf was the only suitable landing-stage, so he ran *Arab*'s bows right in against it.

There being no water-supply from the shore, he sent all but two of his crew aft in the *Arab* for safety from the leaping flames. With two volunteers, Stannard streamed the ship's hoses on the blaze from the forecastle. For two hours they fought the flames, but the task was too much for them.

Then he ordered the ship astern, and navigated her round to the far side of the wharf, which still burned. From this point just below the pier, *Arab* could take on troops. The incessant air attacks were telling on them. Just as the first few got on board, the pier began to creak, give way, and cave in. For the second time, Stannard ordered steam —to ram the collapsing underframe and so support the pier with the trawler's bows. In this way he got more of the men away.

Next Stannard turned his attention to the other ships. He fired on enemy planes which were trying to pinion them in one place in the harbour and sink them. *Arab* received a direct hit, but sailed on unperturbed.

Dive bombers took up the attack. One screeched down, and a line of livid bullets tore towards the ship. Stannard had his hands on the bridge. The bullets rattled against the metal bulwarks and one ripped into his right hand. He wrapped a handkerchief round it and kept up the fight.

Realizing that he must get some sort of base, as soon as an attack abated, he swung *Arab* away as fast as her damaged state would allow. He put her under a cliff-face for shelter and landed the crew and those of two other trawlers whose task was the same as *Arab*'s. Here he established an armed camp, more secure than a ship floating around in mid-harbour, a sitting target from the air. The cliff gave them some protection from the bombers, who dared not fly too near it, and yet they could direct their own guns at the planes —and perhaps shoot some down. This plan was imperative, for it looked as if the affair would last several days, and men could not go on fighting and manning guns without sleep. Here, those off-duty could actually sleep while the rest went on with the job. They attacked every enemy aircraft which was seen during the day, and kept a careful watch for submarines by night.

A day or two later, with their work still unfinished, the lookout saw some British soldiers beyond the cliffs. The planes would be due in to attack any time, and all the while the enemy's ground forces were firing at the retreating troops. So Stannard had the ship's anti-aircraft guns dismantled and installed in positions along the cliff to cover the soldiers as they withdrew to the comparative safety of the ship.

The armed camp ashore, under the lee of the cliff, and the Lewis gun position were repeatedly machine-gunned during the days they spent there. Bombers, too, did their best to drop their loads on them, but the position had been so well sited that only one man was wounded all the time the *Arab*'s crew and those of the other trawlers remained ashore.

The post survived thirty-one individual bombing attacks. They came with sickening regularity. While the ship was there, Stannard saw a batch of Sherwood Foresters —he could tell them by their distinctive uniforms —completely wiped out before his eyes, as he scanned the far shore through binoculars; but there was nothing he could do.

Then as another little group of men staggered from the cliff toward the armed post, dragging their wounded with them, the German planes dived once more and strafed the scene with machine guns.

At last no more troops came, and *Arab* sailed into the harbour again. Stannard has frostbite in his feet by now, through exposure during the five days' ordeal: for this was Norway, near the Arctic Circle. As *Arab* moved out, one of the other vessels received a hit from a bomb and caught fire. She blazed fiercely, and Stannard knew it could not be long before she exploded. But he took *Arab* alongside, called for a couple of volunteers to go aboard the burning ship, and leapt across. They did what they could to rescue the crew still aboard, and when they could manage no more, they returned to *Arab*. The flames were jumping across, too, and it would be only a matter of moments before the explosion occurred. Stannard could guess this by the state of the fire. He cut *Arab* free. The burning ship drifted less than 100 yards, then a huge explosion heralded the end of her.

He set course for home, with many precious lives in his charge. But the fight was not yet finished. As he left the fjord a German bomber veered on to the scene and signalled him to steer east or be sunk. An ironic moment, if he were to have lived through the last five days only to go down now as he was so near to escape.

Stannard ignored the order. He kept to his course.

'Hold your fire,' he told the gunnery officer.

A tense few seconds followed. The crew and soldiers all peered cautiously out as the plane swooped down towards *Arab*. It was still a mile off. Three-quarters. A thousand yards. Eight hundred.

'Fire.'

The first burst brought it spinning down into the sea near the course Stannard had set. Thereafter nothing stopped him. He put on full steam. *Arab* responded wonderfully and reached Engand so that the tale could be told.

CHAPTER FOUR

Two Bridge-busters

DONALD GARLAND AND THOMAS GRAY

Only one man came back from a formation of five bombers that attacked a vital bridge over the river Meuse on 12 May 1940. But two of the men who failed to survive this suicide raid had the unique honour of being the first VCs of the Royal Air Force in the Second World War.

May 1940 meant that the German juggernaut was thundering through the Low Countries. The enemy had invaded both the Netherlands and Belgium. The futility of the Maginot Line was exposed once and for all. Its whole strategy and safety relied on the Germans respecting the neutrality of the Low Countries. The Allies should have known better than to depend on this. Now they were paying the price. To try to stop the Nazis the Allies quickly continued the Maginot Line beyond the borders of France, right through Belgium to the North Sea. It was not nearly as strong as the original French defences, but it would have to do.

The Allies used the natural defence of the river Meuse as a portion of this emergency line, but at once the Germans threw their forces at this particular part of the makeshift Allied perimeter, forcing a rapid retreat. The German prongs penetrated still farther, actually piercing the river at a number of points by pontoon bridges. As they swarmed across the vital bridges the Allied air forces attempted to retaliate and prevent the advance, while the ground forces gave way to fresh defensive positions farther back towards the coast. Some success was achieved, but reconnaissance soon showed that the large-scale crossing of the Meuse was not by the temporary pontoon bridges but over the strong permanent one near Maastricht, by the Dutch-Belgian border.

So sudden and dramatically desperate had been the British and French withdrawal from the prepared positions along the Meuse that they had not had time to explode this Maastricht bridge, as they had done all the others on this reach of the river. Needless to say, the enemy lost not an hour in exploiting their luck, and the vanguard of two German armoured divisions began to pour over this, the one permanent bridge in the whole region. With the armoured vehicles went lorries by the dozen and accompanying ammunition. Then a lone reconnaissance plane reported a powerful force massing threateningly in this bridge area; while all the time the tanks and armoured units added to its strength. Stores, petrol, more ammunition —they all came over that one bridge. And they all added up to an immediate threat to cut the already retreating Allied front clearly in two.

The order went out to RAF bomber squadrons stationed in France to attack the bridge with all their power, but the methodical Germans had heavily defended their gain. Not only could anti-aircraft guns keep up a continuous barrage of fire on any attacking aircraft, but enemy fighters maintained constant patrols over the precious link between the two sides of the Meuse. Despite these defences, the RAF hurtled into the assault. Eight separate attacks were, in fact, made by the bombers. Pinpoint bombing at that stage of the war and in these conditions was clearly out of the question, however. The riverbank shuddered and was shattered by the exploding bombs; enemy fighters went spinning down in flames into the Low Countries' cornfields, and the bombers blasted ack-ack batteries out of action. But still there were always more guns and more fighters, And they could not get a direct hit on the bridge – the crossing over which the square-helmeted Huns continued to trudge or run – according to whether a raid was in progress or not.

So the eight sorties failed. The whole operation in Europe was now imperilled and, one might even say, to some extent it depended on that one bridge, so securely planted on the bed of the Meuse. Yet the German umbrella of fighter cover, coupled with the many remaining guns on both banks of the river, made any further attacks not only equally difficult but almost impossible.

On 12 May the Commanding Officer of No. 12 Squadron, Royal Air Force, stationed at Amifontaine, assembled his pilots. Without wasting more words than it took to sketch in the position at Maastricht, he at once launched into their aspect of it.

'That bridge has got to be destroyed at all costs,' he said. 'I'd like volunteers.'

Every pilot stepped forward.

But as only five planes were wanted, they scribbled their names on slips of paper, folded the scraps, and put them in someone's cap. An appointed person drew five out of the cap. So the five crews were chosen and briefed for their desperate raid. Then they took off from Amifontaine without waiting, or wasting even a minute –five Battle bombers, escorted by a fighter force of Hurricanes.

The leading aircraft of the five obviously had the most responsibility and ran the worst risks. In that aircraft, with the rest of the crew, were the two men destined to die –and win the Victoria Cross.

Piloting this leading light bomber, the single-engined Fairey Battle, was Flying Officer Donald Edward Garland. Still a few weeks off his twenty-second birthday, Garland was born in Eire, but his home was at Hovingham, Yorkshire. The flat landscape below him seemed very different from the moors, within reach of his home, he had known on leave. Only three months earlier he had been promoted Flying Officer from Pilot Officer. With him flew Sergeant Thomas Gray, a sergeant observer with over ten years' service in the RAF since his enlistment in 1929, as an apprentice. Gray wore a moustache and the familiar one-wing with the letter 'O' over the left breast-pocket of his tunic. Strange that Gray was born in 1914, the year the First World War broke out, and Garland in 1918, the year it ended. Gray was a West Country man, born at Devizes, and then living at Bath.

The pitifully small force of Battle bombers flew straight for Maastricht. There was no alternative, no elaborate detour they could make. Garland gripped the controls of his plane, gritted his teeth, and led his quintet in the direction of the bridge. The Hurricanes hovered in the vicinity, sweeping the skies to draw or ward off any opposition. Despite their help, Garland and Gray knew that in the broad spring daylight they could not hope to effect any surprise.

The run was bound to be through a pulverizing, peppering ack-ack barrage. The way back —if there was one —must be through the fast fighter formations of the Luftwaffe, which would fly in broadside at the Battle bombers.

Now the bridge —actually spanning a section of the Meuse known as the Albert Canal —swept into distant sight through a haze of early ack-ack bursts. It was at this stage that the enemy fighters put in their first appearance, but the Hurricanes kept them clear of the five bombers. The famous rounded-wingtip fighters could not prevent the anti-aircraft fire from getting an accurate range on the five planes, however, as they flew through a blasting blizzard of shrapnel towards Maastricht.

'. . . destroyed at all costs . . .' The CO's words seemed to echo in the minds of all five pilots, but particularly in Gray's, as he edged the nose of his Battle bomber down lower. Now German machine-gun posts joined the heavier fire, forming an appalling concentration of mixed explosions. Everything started to happen suddenly from that second onward.

The staccato bursts of the machine guns mingled with the deeper bursts all round the five planes. The Hurricanes were away above, engaging the fighters in a series of dramatic dogfights. The time for thought was past, but one remained in Garland's mind, to bomb that bridge. Somehow they were going to do it. They had to. The CO said so. It was as simple as that.

His hand again moved to the controls. Lashed by flak, the leading Battle bomber flew on, nose down, into the devastating, deadly focus of fire. Then came the stutter of more machine-gun bullets. Several ripped the fuselage, and embedded deep into it. The whole plane rocked to the blast of a too-near miss from the enemy ack-ack. German lorries were actually on the bridge now. Garland glimpsed them through the smoke.

Raked and rocked, he pushed the stick far forward —for the last time —and led the little group directly down to the bridge. The enemy fire rose to a climax. It was a poignant, pitiful position for the RAF men —some of the Few. Five light day bombers against a heavily fortified bridge: somehow it seemed to sum up and signify the whole war at that stage —the enemy poised for victory, the Allies at their lowest ebb. Yet the Few remained. Garland and Gray were two of them. The camouflaged planes divided now. But it would need more than camouflage to conceal or protect them. They must have known how slim the chances were, but, like all of their squadron, they had volunteered. The war was not over yet.

Garland dived straight through two brutal bursts of ack-ack over the bridge. The bomb load went. In spite of opposition he delivered his dive-bombing attack from the lowest possible altitude. The other four followed. The fighters could not see exactly what was happening, because of the smoke from the bombs bursting all around the bridge. A plume of water beside one of the supports signalled a very close thing. A lorry belched black oil-fumes about a third of the way across the bridge, halting the following traffic. Not that they could have continued, anyway, for one of the bombs scored a wonderful, blinding, bursting hit, bang in the centre of the road, on the bridge. The surface crumbled away, as if melted by magic, and the struts collapsed. The whole bridge area became a mass of flames obscuring the vision of the pilots in the Hurricanes high above; yet, as it cleared a little, they could be sure of one thing –the bridge was blown. No more enemy armoured units would penetrate into the Low Countries via that particular route. Later reconnaissance confirmed the victory.

But all this was happening in seconds. Garland and the others pushed their sticks up again. It was 'Bombs gone' all right; but they were still over Maastricht, with the whole artillery might of the Wehrmacht –or so it seemed –loosing a motley of murderous fire from the ground.

Garland had flown them there; Gray had navigated. The mission succeeded, due to Garland's leadership of the formation, and the 'coolness and resource,' to quote the official phrase, of Sergeant Gray, who had navigated the Battle in these chronic conditions so that the whole formation was able to attack the target successfully. No mean achievement.

But then, on the way out, it had to happen. The enemy fighters broke through the screen of Hurricanes, to spit a series of vicious bursts across at the already scarred light bombers. Exactly what did occur no one will ever know, but either by fire from the ground or the Luftwaffe, four of the five Battle bombers crashed to the earth. Garland and Gray attracted the majority of the Germans' attention, so it was inevitable that they would be hit. (The miracle was that they had remained airborne long enough to deliver the attack.) One of the Battle bombers plunged into the river itself, others ploughed final furrows somewhere amid the fields.

Back at the airfield, the commanding officer and others counted the fighters as they came in to land. Then they paced the operations-room, watching the brass wall clock, as the minutes ticked away.

'Surely they can't be any longer?' someone asked. No one answered. Losses were expected. One or two had been witnessed by the fighters. But surely some of the five would get back?

Then the faint throb of an aircraft engine heralded one much-damaged Battle. In fact, from this operation only one man came back out of the bomber force of five planes. The lone survivor taxied to a halt. The pilot was not Garland. Both Garland and Gray, of No. 12 Squadron, RAF Advanced Air Striking Force, France, died on that day.

But the bridge had been blown. And as a tribute to the amazing accuracy of the attack in the face of such overpowering opposition, a French general actually paused in the confusion of May 1940 on the Continent to write a letter to No. 12 Squadron. It was a typical French gesture. The man was General Georges, Chief of Staff to the Allied Generalissimo, Weygand. His message was received, understood, and appreciated. It said, 'Messieurs, je vous remercie.' The Squadron replied characteristically, 'The operation was successfully carried out.'

The announcement of the double Victoria Cross came only thirty days later, when Britain and France had really reached the lowest point. And the news of the sacrifice of Garland and Gray helped to lift the countries from their nadir, and steel them for the next round –the Battle of Britain.

CHAPTER FIVE

The Fight for France

RICHARD ANNAND, HARRY NICHOLLS, GEORGE GRISTOCK, CHRISTOPHER FURNESS, HAROLD ERVINE-ANDREWS

One hundred and twenty-seven VCs were awarded to Army men in the Second World War, and their individual stories make an amazing chronicle of courage from Normandy to New Guinea. They also give a good cross-section of the whole war on land, reflecting all our changing fortunes from near-defeat in 1940 to total victory in 1945. And Britain could hardly have been nearer defeat than in May 1940.

Five VCs were won in the bitter battle for France, summing up the desperation of the British Forces during those weeks leading to the final evacuation of Dunkirk. First came Second Lieutenant Richard Wallace Annand, who rescued his wounded batman in a wheelbarrow.

After serving in France and Belgium during those first months of the war, Annand found himself in Belgium on 15 May 1940, when the platoon under his command was on the south side of the river Dyle, astride a blown bridge.

During the night they beat off a bitter enemy attack, but at about 11.00 hours next morning the Germans renewed the attack with a violent thrust. They also pushed forward a bridging-party on to the riverbank below the bridge.

Annand knew he had to try to stop this and so opened up an attack. When ammunition ran out he went forward himself over open ground with total disregard for the enemy's fire. Reaching the top of the blown bridge, and not a little surprised to have survived, Annand proceeded to drive out the German bridging-party below, inflicting over twenty casualties with hand grenades lobbed from his elevated position. He could hardly have avoided being wounded in this exposed spot, and he was. Yet he managed to totter back to rejoin his platoon, have his wound dressed rapidly, and then carry on commanding the men.

During the evening of 16 May the determined Huns started a second attack, and again Annand went forward with his hand grenades. Again he hit the enemy hard, doing all one man could to hold up the advance. Eventually the order to withdraw came through to Annand, but while in the process of implementing this order he learned that his batman had been wounded and left behind. By now Annand's wound was starting to tell on him, but he nevertheless left the platoon to continue the withdrawal while he returned to search for his batman. Groping his way back to his former position, Annand discovered the batman and managed to find a wheelbarrow as well. Without this, he could never have got the man back. He tumbled the wounded batman into the wheelbarrow and wheeled him towards the new rear line. Soon afterwards the exertion in his own wounded state took effect, and Annand lost consciousness through loss of blood. The wound was not serious, however, and he survived the war.

But the first Army VC actually to be announced in the Second World War went to Lance Corporal Harry Nicholls, of the Grenadier Guards.

On 21 May 1940, just five days after Annand's action, the river Escaut presented a critical situation in the battle for France. The Germans had already wedged themselves firmly between those two famous Guards —the Coldstreamers and the Grenadiers.

Soon after midday Captain L. S. Starkey, with his headquarters and a remaining platoon, realized that a group of survivors in the centre of a certain cornfield could not hope to escape unless enemy machine guns on a place they had named Poplar Ridge were wiped out. Nicholls was commanding a section in this platoon when the order came to counter-attack. At the very start of the advance, even as they were moving up, he was wounded in the arm by shrapnel, but continued to lead his section forward.

The little group edged nearer to Poplar Ridge, and they knew they could expect drastic opposition as soon as they came over it. Nicholls was in front with his friend Guardsman Nash, who stayed at his side to supply him with ammunition from his pouches. As they appeared over the small ridge the enemy, as expected, opened heavy machine-gun fire from close range.

Nicholls, realizing the danger to himself and the rest of the party —not to mention the men still alive in the middle of the cornfield —dashed forward towards the machine guns, firing his Bren gun from the hip. He succeeded in silencing first one machine gun and then two others, in spite of being severely wounded in the head. Even this second wound did not stop him from tackling the enemy massed behind. He crawled forward on to a higher piece of ground above the poplars, and opened fire on the German infantry, causing many casualties, and continued firing until he had no more ammunition left.

Nicholls was wounded at least four times altogether, but refused to give in until he became unconscious. When he was last seen he was lying desperately wounded, in German hands. Nicholls's gallant action affected the whole course of events in this struggle for survival. He saved his comrades in the cornfield from almost certain death, and he alone inflicted such losses on the Germans that they withdrew across the river, no longer having the strength to press on or the morale to remain.

Nicholls was officially posted as 'Missing, believed killed.' His wife received his VC from HM King George VI, but this particular story had a happy ending, for in September 1940, at the height of the Battle of Britain, he was reported to be alive and well in a German hospital, and he survived the rest of the war.

x x x

On the same day and in the same area a member of the Royal Norfolk Regiment was also winning the VC. The citation adequately tells the story of how he did it:

> The award was for most conspicuous gallantry on May 21, 1940, when his company was holding a position on the line of the river Escaut, south of Tournai; after a prolonged attack the enemy had succeeded in breaking through beyond the company's right flank, which was consequently threatened.
>
> Company Sergeant-Major George Gristock, having organized a party of eight riflemen from company headquarters, went forward to cover the right flank. Realizing that an enemy machine-gun had moved forward to a position from which it was inflicting heavy casualties on his company, Company Sergeant-Major Gristock went on with one man as connecting file to try to put it out of action.
>
> While advancing he came under heavy machine-gun fire from the opposite bank, and was severely wounded in both legs, his right knee being badly smashed. He nevertheless gained his fire position some 20 yards from the enemy machine-gun post undetected, and by a well-aimed rapid fire killed the machine-gun crew of four, and put their gun out of action. He then dragged himself back to the right-flank position, from which he refused to be evacuated until contact with the battalion on the right had been established and the line once more made good.
>
> By this gallant action the position of the company was secured and many casualties prevented. Company Sergeant-Major Gristock has since died of his wounds.

The fourth VC of that fateful month of May 1940 went to Lieutenant the Honourable Christopher Furness for his action at Arras. During the period of 17–24 May, Furness was in command of a Bren gun carrier platoon, Welsh Guards, and his battalion formed part of the garrison of Arras. Throughout those seven days his platoon was almost constantly patrolling ahead of, or between, the widely dispersed parts of the perimeter, and they fought a lot of local actions with the Germans. Displaying dash and fine leadership, Furness fired his platoon with enthusiasm at this vital time.

While they were on patrol during the evening of 23 May, Furness was wounded, but refused to be evacuated and carried on with his duty. At this stage of the campaign in France the enemy were strongly reinforced near Arras and had actually encircled the town on three sides. The withdrawal of the Arras garrison to Douai was ordered during the night of 23–24 May. So short of men and materials were the Allies that Furness's platoon, together with a small force of light tanks, covered the withdrawal of the transport, consisting of over forty vehicles.

The enemy attacked at 02.30 hours on both sides of the town. At one point they reached the road along which the transport columns were withdrawing, bringing the British vehicles under anti-tank fire. The whole column looked like being stopped and annihilated.

The man to meet this situation was Furness. In spite of his wounds, he at once decided to attack the enemy, who had strongly entrenched themselves behind barbed wire.

21

Furness advanced with three Bren gun carriers, supported by the small force of light tanks. The light tanks were put out of action within seconds, but Furness went on until he reached the enemy strong position, which he circled several times, firing at close range.

The enemy reeled, but all three carriers were hit too, and most of their crews killed or injured. Furness's own carrier was disabled, and the driver and Bren gunner killed, leaving him on his own.

Fearlessly Furness jumped out and fought the Germans in hand-to-hand combat, although under the awful handicap of his wounds.

He was killed.

This act of self-sacrifice against odds, however, forced the enemy to withdraw temporarily, and so enabled the long column of vehicles to get clear unmolested. It also covered the evacuation of some of the wounded of Furness's own carrier platoon and light tanks.

Already the spirit of Dunkirk was being displayed. One week later it would be needed to the utmost if Britain were to survive.

The Dunkirk VC symbolized the spirit of every man at that immortal stand. Captain Harold Marcus Ervine-Andrews of the East Lancashire Regiment won it for his courage on the night of 31 May–1 June 1940

He took over about 1,000 yards of the defence in front of Dunkirk, his line reaching along a canal.

The enemy attacked with fury at dawn on 31 May. Every conceivable kind of weapon had its muzzle pointing towards the port that day: the fire power was terrific. For over ten hours Ervine-Andrews and his company held their sector. Half a mile and more to hold with a handful of men against the weight of such an attack was hopeless, but every hour was vital to Britain, and the evacuation of the forces.

The Germans could not be prevented from crossing the canal on both flanks. A company of Ervine-Andrews's own battalion, sent to protect his flanks, could not get through to him. At one stage it looked likely that one of his platoons would be driven in. He called for volunteers to fill the gap. Then, going forward, he climbed to the top of a straw-roofed barn, from which he attacked the advancing Germans with whatever fire he could muster, which was not much. Throughout this spell the enemy were sending a continuous volley of mortar bombs and armour-piercing bullets through the frail roof. With cool precision, Ervine-Andrews stuck to his job of dealing with as many enemy as he could, killing seventeen with his rifle and many more with a Bren gun. So the minutes were gained, giving precious, life-giving time for the Allied army struggling to survive, to escape to fight another day.

When a house he held had been shattered and set alight, and the enemy were closing nearer all the time, Ervine-Andrews, whose ammunition was expended, had to think quickly.

He sent his wounded back in the one remaining Bren gun carrier. When nearly surrounded he collected from this forward position the eight men left of his company, and led them back under the cover created by the company in the rear, nearer to the sea.

22

Now they were in the water, their backs to the sea. The great gloom of smoke and fire hung over Dunkirk. Somehow swimming or wading up to their chins for over a mile, they at last found boats. Ervine-Andrews had brought all that remained of his men safely back, their duty done. Like a captain leaving his sinking ship, Ervine-Andrews turned his back on the devastation and death of Dunkirk. His was certainly conspicuous courage that saved many lives that day.

CHAPTER SIX

Wounded in a Dozen Places

JACK MANTLE

I ndependence Day, the Fourth of July, was a fitting date for a VC to be won –
especially in 1940, the year when Britain struggled singlehanded.

Warburton-Lee's epic was twelve weeks old, immortalizing once more the proud name of Hardy, Nelson's captain colleague. Roope had died in April. Stannard survived. Now summer scorched in the sky over HMS *Foylebank*. And out of that summer sky, out of the sun itself, enemy planes suddenly swooped on *Foylebank*.

There was the staccato sound of 'Action Stations,' then feet running up metal steps, and the deck echoing with ordered urgency. Seconds passed and a plane screamed down to dive-bomb the boat. The crew heard the whine of the bomb, the plop in the water, and the sound of spray spurting over the bows.

A second plane, and a third, took up the attack, flying towards *Foylebank*. Jack Mantle, acting leading seaman, swung his pom-pom on to the targets. It shook a series of small fire towards the plane.

Then the next plane screeched down at the ship. Mantle gripped his gun tighter. The repeated pom-pom bursts broke all round the plane.

A bomb dropped straight at the ship, hit the port side at deck level, and burst in a thousand pieces. Mantle was only a few feet off. His left leg was shattered, yet he dragged it back to the gun-post. Another plane dived and he fired the pom-pom again. His hair flapped down over his eyes; no longer was it brushed straight back from his forehead. He sweated with the heat, the pain, and the fight.

The aircraft veered, banking steeply, but only to regroup for a second assault. The leader throbbed down again, out of the sun. The ship's guns fired, hit and exploded the plane. A second followed. Mantle was still shooting.

Then another bomb burst by his pom-pom. He was wounded in a dozen places, but still kept on firing. As the third wave withdrew, his hands slipped to his side, and he fell by the gun.

The award was announced on 3 September, the first anniversary of the outbreak of war. 'For valiantly standing by his gun after his left leg had been shattered' the Victoria Cross was conferred posthumously on Jack Foreman Mantle, acting leading seaman, P/JX 139070. P stands for a Portsmouth rating. Britain's premier naval port is proud of him.

CHAPTER SEVEN

Raid on the Dortmund-Ems Canal

RODERICK LEAROYD

B efore the Battle of Britain really got under way, another Victoria Cross was won over Europe. And, surprising as it seems, with Britain facing her darkest hour, it was awarded for an offensive action. In those far-off days, when the war was not yet a year old, the twin-engined Hampden bomber was one of the few heavy aircraft of the Allies. And in these planes Acting Flight Lieutenant Roderick Alastair Brook Learoyd had already repeatedly shown 'the highest conception of his duty and complete indifference to personal danger in making attacks at the lowest altitudes regardless of opposition.'

Twenty-seven-year-old Learoyd, a man of Kent, was attached to No. 49 Squadron, stationed at Scampton, Lincolnshire, in August 1940. His story splits into two. First, there is the overall outline of the mission. Second, his own part in it.

The operation consisted of eleven Hampdens, six of No. 49 Squadron and five of No. 83 Squadron, attacking the old aqueduct on the Dortmund-Ems Canal. The purpose: to upset water-traffic on this vital canal and play a part in paralysing transport of raw materials for the enemy's heavy industrial area.

Learoyd had attacked the Dortmund-Ems Canal on a previous occasion, and was well aware of the risks entailed. For a successful raid to be made, the aircraft had to approach from a direction well-known to the enemy —through a lane of specially sited anti-aircraft defences —and in the face of the most intense point-blank fire from guns of all calibres. Learoyd and the pilots and crews of the other ten Hampdens had, in the forefront of their memories, the knowledge that the very night before this, all the attacking force were hit, and two failed to get back to Britain. The odds in favour of surviving many nights like these seemed slender.

Nevertheless, equipped with special bombs for the old aqueduct, plus a mixed bomb load for diversionary operations, the Hampdens roared up from Scampton from 20.00 hours onward. All eleven got over Germany safely, but a couple of them failed to locate the aqueduct. They did the next best thing and attacked Texel Island instead.

Eight of the remaining nine made high- and low-level bombing attacks on targets in the vicinity of the aqueduct, and also on the aqueduct itself, between 23.00 hours and midnight. One of the bombs specially prepared to tackle the aqueduct fell just north-east of it, the remainder being unobserved because of intense ack-ack fire. Other bombs were dropped on some of the offending anti-aircraft batteries, and also on the searchlights, whose brilliant beams were crisscrossing the night sky over the canal with a fantastic and frightening geometric pattern. The lock gates at Münster and a variety of rivercraft elsewhere received the bombers' diversionary attacks.

Through all these assaults, and especially the main one on the aqueduct, Learoyd led his team of nine Hampdens. The ack-ack reception grew steadily fiercer as flak flailed the air at the exact altitude they were flying. But worse was to come. Learoyd then dropped to the aqueduct-altitude of 150 feet —a mere fifty yards off enemy soil —as his Hampden battered its way in the lead of the group. Flak fingered away large chunks of the plane, and they blew to earth like so many bits of silver foil. But still Learoyd went in.

The example of Garland and Gray was just three months old that day.

Now his Hampden was hit over and over again. It tottered across the sky, lurching as large pieces continued to come off it. Virtually blinded by the glare of the tracery of searchlights, Learoyd flew the twin-engined slowcoach over the aqueduct. Pressing home the attack at the closest range humanly possible, he bombed the target and directed the others in that shell-studded sky of flashes, lights, and intervening dark.

Learoyd's was the last of five Hampdens to bomb the main target, the other three reaching the area concentrated on the diversions. But these diversions did not do much to lighten the enemy opposition, and among further damage which Learoyd's Hampden received were hits on his landing-flaps, so that they became useless; his undercarriage indicators were also out of action by this time, so it was only to be expected that the return journey proved eventful.

After the attack eight of the eleven planes got back to Scampton, looking the worse for the experience, between 01.30 and 03.40 hours. Two more failed to survive the searing intensity of the ack-ack fire. That left one —Learoyd's. Flying a wrecked aircraft with great skill, he managed to coax it through the lane of flak, free of the fatal searchlights, and out over the North Sea. Soon after 02.00 hours they were over home ground, but the middle of the night could not be considered a suitable time to try to land a damaged Hampden with inoperative landing-flaps and useless undercarriage indicators. So Learoyd had to fly around till 04.53 hours and wait for the pellucid light of dawn before he made an emergency landing.

Learoyd trod the dewy airfield at Scampton in a fine August dawn. The air was wonderful; the world was too. Just to be alive was enough. But they were all damned tired.

In a subsequent speech Learoyd was persuaded to tell his story of the operation during which he won the Victoria Cross. He talked to factory workers about the raid that caused devastating dislocation of enemy canal-traffic. His account was vivid, yet characteristically failed to mention his own part in the plan —the core of the whole night.

This is his story:

It was towards 8 pm on the night: of 12 August, 1940, when I and my crew of three –Navigator Bomb-aimer (Pilot Officer John Lewis later killed on active service), Wireless Officer (Sergeant J. Ellis) and Rear Gunner (Leading Aircraftman Rich) – climbed aboard our Hampden bomber on an airfield somewhere in Britain.

Our target was an aqueduct situated half-way along the Dortmund-Ems Canal.

We became airborne at 8 pm. It was a good flying night –cloudy and with a half-moon. The journey out was uneventful except for the usual flak from the German anti-aircraft batteries along the route.

The cloud continued right up to the edge of the target, where we emerged into a clear, moonlit sky.

There were five aircraft, including my own, engaged in the attack. We were to go in one by one over the target, and I had been detailed to go in last.

As the bombs were fitted with a ten-minute delay, we were timed to attack at two-minute intervals from zero, which meant that the last bomb should be dropped at zero + 8 and the first bomb was due to explode at zero + 10. As can be seen, the timing of all the aircraft had to be very accurate because, in the case of the last aircraft, if he was too early he got mixed up with the others and if he was too late he got blown up by the bombs of the earlier aircraft.

Zero hour was 11.10 pm.

Owing to the splendid work of my navigator we were over the target at 11.00. I could see it quite clearly in the light of the moon as I circled at 4,000 feet, waiting for the other four machines to go in one after the other.

Fully alive to the importance of the target, Jerry had concentrated scores of search-lights and anti-aircraft batteries along both banks of the canal.

The resultant flak was intense and, as we stooged around, waiting for our turn to go in, I saw one of our bombers hit and catch fire. It climbed to about 1,000 feet, then its nose dropped before finally spinning to the ground in flames.

From reports which came through later, we learned that the crew had been taken prisoner.

It was now my turn to come in over the aqueduct and let our bombs go. By this time another of our bombers had been hit and was burning furiously on the ground.

In order to obtain the best possible view of the aqueduct, it was necessary to get it as directly as possible between us and the moon.

So, coming down to 300 feet at a distance of four to five miles north of the target, I commenced my run in, the aqueduct being clearly silhouetted against the light of the moon.

Within a mile of the target I came down to 150 feet. By this time, however, Jerry had got our range to a nicety, and was blazing away with everything he'd got.

The machine was repeatedly hit and large pieces of the mainplanes torn away. I was completely blinded by the glare of the searchlights and had to ask my navigator to guide me in over the target.

This he did with the utmost coolness and praiseworthy precision. Then, suddenly, I heard him shout:

27

'Bomb gone.'

The delayed-action bomb was fitted with a parachute which, provided the altitude was sufficiently low, gave us a chance of seeing just where it fell.

This is what happened on this occasion. For I heard a sudden triumphant shout from the Wireless Officer:

'Got it!'

The bomb had fallen on the aqueduct, which, as a result of the combined attack, was destroyed, and our object successfully accomplished.

Then for home!

Our Hampden was in bad shape. Amongst other damage, the hits she had received had put the hydraulic system out of action so that neither landing-gear nor flaps would function normally, but if the system had not been completely destroyed the emergency compressed-air bottle would operate the undercarriage. This it would not be possible to find out until the lever was pulled just prior to landing.

Homeward bound, I called up my base in England and told them how I was fixed. Not wishing to risk crashing the machine in the darkness, I said that I would stooge around until dawn, when I should have a better chance of making a decent landing.

So, for two-and-a-half hours, we flew around England. With the dawn I was back over my station, where I was fortunate enough to land safely without injury to any of my crew or further damage to the aircraft.

Roderick Learoyd was one of the seven VCs of the Royal Air Force to survive the Second World War.

CHAPTER EIGHT

The Battle of Britain

JAMES NICOLSON

So to the few. Just four days after the attack on the Dortmund–Ems Canal a Victoria Cross was won in the trail-torn air over Southern England: symbolic of the Battle of Britain raging in those cloud-flecked summer skies from Dorset and Hampshire to Kent and beyond. And it was in Kent that this next VC went to school, and over Hampshire where he gained his glory.

Nicolson was one of the Few. Flight Lieutenant James Brindley Nicolson, of No. 249 Squadron, was educated at Tonbridge School, and became a pupil-pilot in the RAF in 1936, when he was nineteen. He trained in his home county of Yorkshire. By 1940 he had married.

As France fell he was moved to the south of England, and August 1940 found him a fully trained fighter pilot eager for action. It was not long in coming, for every day Hurricanes from No. 249 Squadron hurled themselves into the air against the hordes of Hun bombers and fighters flying remorselessly against England and her southern ports.

The Battle of Britain was on —with a vengeance. Nicolson's particular chance came on 16 August. Answering a scramble signal, he eagerly thrust his Hurricane forward along the runway and into the warm air. He had always shown terrific enthusiasm for air fighting, and now, in his first engagement, his skill would at last be tested. He was impatient to get at the enemy.

Wild white trails streaked the sky over Southampton and the Isle of Wight as he engaged the enemy. With the wave of daylight bombers flew fighters as well. Nicolson was told to intercept the fighters. With other Hurricanes of his squadron, he made contact. Scrapping at 300 mph, the planes wove their weird exhaust fleece four miles over the port.

Nicolson took on a particular Messerschmitt, but as he was still trying to get into position to attack, the German fired at the Hurricane. Four cannon-shells screeched into it. One pierced the cockpit, injuring one of Nicolson's eyes; another hurt his foot badly; the remaining two damaged the engine and set fire to the gravity tank.

Petrol poured out of the tank, over the cylinders, and seeped into the cockpit below the control-panel. Flames started to spread and scorch the whole cockpit. The airscrew fanned them, until Nicolson could scarcely see the Messerschmitt's movements —hurt as he was in one eye. Now burns began to affect him too, and he could only control the fighter with the greatest strain.

By now the lower part of the control-panel and the floor of the cockpit were burning, and the entire plane would soon be an inferno. Nicolson reached for the hood-release and struggled out of the searing cockpit, his limbs already badly scorched. But just as he forced himself up to jump he saw the Messerschmitt in front of him.

Without stopping a second, he slid back into the flaming cockpit, took hold of the stick again, and his feet groped for the rudder bar. By now he hardly knew what he was doing or how he was doing it. The whole of the lower part of the plane flared into fierce flames. Somehow Nicolson kept the stuttering engine going, and sighted himself on the enemy plane. His wounded eye was worse each moment. Up to his waist in flames, his hands blistering on the controls, he battled on until his range was close enough to be entirely accurate. Nicolson pressed the firing-button.

A stream of bullets bore straight down at the enemy. The Messerschmitt reeled away, mortally hit, and careered to the ground; but Nicolson was still in a blazing furnace of a fighter. Summoning strength from somewhere deep within him, he struggled to raise himself a second time out of that candle of a cockpit. He operated the hood-release —and baled out. He pulled his ripcord, and then passed out, landing unconscious just outside Southampton, with bad burns on his hands, face, neck, and legs. They rushed him to the nearest hospital, where he hung between life and death for two days and two nights; a charred, charcoal colour.

Then followed recovery, recuperation, and a fierce fight with authority to fly again. Finally, he did fly, despite two illnesses and a car crash, becoming Officer in Charge of Training, South-East Asia.

But that was not the end of the story, although it should surely have been. Wing Commander Nicolson —known to all his friends as 'Nick' —lived until 1945; the year of victory. Yet he never saw that final day, for he died in a Liberator crash, in the Bay of Bengal, before the war was over.

So ended the life of James Nicolson, spirit of the Battle of Britain, and the only fighter pilot to win the Victoria Cross.

CHAPTER NINE

Firefighting in the air

JOHN HANNAH

The youngest VC of them all was Sergeant John Hannah, only eighteen years old when he won his award. It happened on 15 September 1940, at the very climax of the Battle of Britain, yet the action did not occur over England but in a Hampden engaged in a successful attack on enemy barge concentrations at the port of Antwerp.

A Scot, Hannah was born at Paisley, and his home was in Glasgow. Before he joined the RAF, in 1939, he worked as a salesman for a boot company. After training as a wireless operator he was later promoted sergeant, in 1940, and was the wireless operator and air gunner in the Hampden on the night of 15 September. Hannah was stationed at the same Hampden bomber airfield as Flight Lieutenant Learoyd, but his squadron was No. 83 and Learoyd's No. 49.

Before Hannah's particular act No. 83 Squadron had distinguished itself considerably, earning one DSO, thirteen DFCs, and five DFMs. The squadron took part in many of those all-too-frequent reconnaissance flights over the North Sea and Germany in the early days of the 'phoney' war. They also shared the nightly security patrols over German seaplane bases. And during the first few months of this fateful year, 1940, specially trained crews laid mines in enemy-occupied waters. So the offensive spirit survived even Dunkirk and the furore of the Battle of Britain, now at its height.

15 September: Hannah's Hampden, flown by a Canadian, Pilot Officer Connor, left the barges burning and reflecting their flames in the dark, mysterious waters of Antwerp. But then a holocaust hit the Hampden, as intensified ack-ack fire poured into the sky towards the small formation of twin-engined bombers, whose only aim now was to get back to base by the shortest possible route. Not all of them would. At the zenith of the opposition one of the Hampdens went down, down, to the Belgian waterline. Connor and Hannah looked away as it burst.

Then the next second their own Hampden had a direct hit from a projectile of an explosive and incendiary kind. It actually seemed to burst inside their bomb compartment. It at once started a fire which quickly enveloped the wireless operator's and rear gunner's cockpits. If ever there were grounds for panic, or at least alarm, here they were. A fire in an aircraft can be a terrible experience, and as if this were not enough, both the port and starboard petrol-tanks were pierced by the explosion or the shrapnel, and it seemed certain that the fire must soon spread throughout the whole bomber.

Hannah forced and fought his way through to get two extinguishers, to try to cope with the fire. He found that the rear gunner had already had to bale out of the plane. Hannah could have done likewise, through the bottom escape-hatch or forward through the navigator's hatch. He did not. Instead he stayed and fought the fire for ten minutes that must have seemed like eternity. Hell would have been a more apt description of that fire. He sprayed the flames with both the extinguishers until they were empty, and then he beat them with his log-book.

Hannah had every justification for leaving the blazing plane. In that rear cockpit things rapidly became an inferno. The very large projectile had set various parts of the interior alight by now, with the result that the whole of the bomb compartment –with the forced draught coming through the hole caused by the hit –was turned into a sort of blow-lamp.

All the aluminium sheet metal on the floor of Hannah's cockpit was melted away after those ten minutes, leaving only a grid formed by the cross bearers. The blinding draught, thousands of feet up, blew the molten metal backward, causing it to plate in great smears on the rear bulkhead.

The electrical leads and all other inflammable equipment inside the cockpit were firmly alight. Drums of ammunition were blown open, and thousands of rounds went off in all directions in this chaotically confined space. The outer layer of the sheet metal on the door and the bulkhead of the rear compartment had also melted. Almost blinded by the choking heat and fearful fumes, Hannah had the amazing presence of mind, not only to stay aboard, but to turn on his oxygen supply. This was the only way in which he could conceivably have carried on staying there. But stay he did. Wearing his oxygen mask, he went on tackling the flames, which were literally licking all around him now.

Luckily the flying-suit he was wearing was to some extent fireproof, but when exposed to prolonged heat it had been known to burn. If that had happened Hannah knew he would have been burned to death in a very few moments, even if he had managed to get out with his parachute. But by now, however, he was in a desperate plight, for his parachute became hopelessly burned, with the rest of the equipment, as he struggled to control the conflagration. The cords of the parachute lay, a charred and shrivelled maze, as he continued to combat the fire in the bomb bay. Subconsciously noting the charred cords, he realized that he had delayed too long if he wanted to escape. Gone was his last chance of getting away from this burning coffin.

But couldn't it be controlled? Must they perish? Hannah decided not. Burned and blackened on his face, eyes, and hands, he fought on with his pitiful little log-book, beating back the yellow heat. And all the time Connor continued to fly the Hampden home towards Scampton. Would they ever see the airfield again?

Yes –somehow Hannah got those flames under control, and the fires were actually extinguished completely. Through his action he probably saved Connor's life. And he certainly saved the aircraft. Connor, in his turn, rose to the occasion and piloted the badly hit Hampden home to a bumpy landing on the airstrip at Scampton.

As the commanding officer of the Hampden bomber group said, 'I can only add that no one who has seen the condition of the aircraft can be otherwise than amazed at the extraordinary presence of mind and extreme courage which Sergeant Hannah displayed in remaining in it.'

Hannah received the Victoria Cross, and Connor got the Distinguished Flying Cross, for a piece of very outstanding piloting.

Once more, however, the story does not have a happy ending. For after leaving the RAF, Hannah died.

CHAPTER TEN

Saga of the *Jervis Bay*

EDWARD FOGARTY FEGEN

To the life and death of Acting Captain Edward Stephen Fogarty Fegen the name of the ship *Jervis Bay* is sufficient testimony. Her story deserves to be retold as long as men sail the seas.

Fegen's naval life started at Osborne, where he joined as a cadet in September 1904.

In March 1940 Fegen became a captain and was given command of the *Jervis Bay*.

Out in the Atlantic, Convoy HX84 sailed from the New World to the Old, with vital supplies for the war —petrol and food. Thirty-eight ships comprised the convoy. They sailed in nine columns, with HMS *Jervis Bay* in the centre, and the commodore's ship, *Cornish City*, leading the fifth column. The *Jervis Bay* was an eighteen-year-old converted merchant liner. In her charge lay the protection of the thirty-eight ships. In fact, one was straggling as 5 November dawned. The day was fair and the sea calm for the time of year. Fegen was in his element as he shepherded the ships slowly, certainly, towards Britain. As he paced the bridge of the *Jervis Bay* he realized how inadequate were the armaments at his disposal, should the ship ever have to call on them. But the convoy came first: he never forgot that.

On 23 October the German pocket battleship *Admiral Scheer* left the port of Gdynia. As Fegen glanced at his calendar on the morning of 5 November and thought of the firework displays in his youth, the *Admiral Scheer* was at large in the Atlantic. And during that very morning she attacked the British ship *Mopan* about 52° N and 31° W in the North Atlantic —and quickly sank her. No distress message could be signalled, so sudden came the end. So other shipping sailed on oblivious. Morning turned to afternoon aboard the *Jervis Bay*. Midshipman Ronnie Butler scanned the seas, his young face lit fleetingly by a setting sun. Nothing disturbed the scene. A hawser groaned as the *Jervis Bay* rolled slightly. But before evening the sea calmed down completely. And the sun shone. Some of the crew had just finished tea: others were waiting for it.

The time, 16.50.

'Ship to port, sir, on the horizon,' said the midshipman.

A simple statement, followed by its bearings. But in a flash Fegen realized the possible situation. He got his glasses on it.

'Sound "Action Stations." Enemy raider. Tell convoy to scatter and make smoke. Report position to Admiralty and repeat to *Cornish City*. Raider at bearing 328°, twelve miles distance; her course 208°, position 53°N and 32°W.'

The continuous clang of the 'action stations' alarm shattered the silence.

Scheer was veering round ready for the attack, but did not get any nearer. A few precious minutes passed. The ships in the convoy put on full steam, and laid smoke screens. *Cornish City* was shelled, but not hit.

The first salvo came from a range of 17,000 yards —nine and a half miles. The convoy scattered rapidly, changing three dozen different directions. The *Scheer* could not catch all of them, nor did she even have the chance to try. Before she had time to fire again, Fegen too changed course —but straight in the direction of the *Scheer*, not away from her. The *Jervis Bay* of 14,164 tons steamed fast ahead.

Her seven 6-inch guns were completely outclassed by *Scheer*'s six 11-inch guns and eight 59-inch. But the convoy could escape. *Scheer* could not chase it while she was being attacked.

Jervis Bay closed in to the attack, getting between the *Scheer* and the convoy. A shell burst in the water near *Jervis Bay*. She returned the fire —but was still out of range, for *Scheer* had manoeuvred to stay on the fringe of the merchantman's range. It was a one-sided fight.

The second salvo came nearer. One shell hit *Jervis Bay*, raking the bridge and hitting the height-finder; the whole bridge burned, and the forward steering gear went out of action. Fegen was hit, too —terribly wounded, with one arm almost off.

But his ship's guns kept firing, and they made one hit. He staggered aft to the second bridge, his arm drenched with blood. Able Seaman Lane, at one of the guns, saw him groping his way along. Then Lane's gun got a direct hit. An ear-splitting crash and the whole gun and its crew were lifted bodily and hurled into the sea. Lane was the only one to escape.

Jervis Bay was holed below her waterline, and she blazed from bow to stern. Yet somehow men managed to keep going and her guns continued to fire. *Jervis Bay*'s engine room was the next to be hit, so no water could be got to tackle the fires. She began to list, slightly, then a little more.

Fegen was on the after-bridge now, trying to control the ship from there, but a shell struck this one, too, and it was shot away. The ship could only steam in a straight line. Then a second hit in the engine room stopped her once and for ever. Her guns could not be swung round towards the *Scheer*. The forward guns were out of action, and as the ship headed for the *Scheer* her aft guns could not bear on to the enemy. An hour had passed, the convoy sailed on. Danger came now from *Jervis Bay*'s own shells, likely to explode in the fire encircling her.

Ropes, cordite cases, and cordite itself lay about the deck, directly in the path of the flames. Fresh fires broke out among the debris, and the crew did their best to put them out by stamping on them. They threw burning wood and boxes overboard with their bare hands.

Jervis Bay listed more. The decks were awash now and the ship's flag had been shot away. Some one ran up the rigging amid the showers of shells and nailed a new white ensign to the mast.

Fegen somehow clutched a way to the main bridge. He was dying now.

'Abandon ship,' he choked.

Another officer called out: 'Aye, aye, sir,' and then hurried over to look at the lifeboats. Only one was left. *Jervis Bay* was settling by the stern.

Captain Sven Olander, skipper of a Swedish ship in the convoy which stayed behind the rest to watch the battle, trained his glasses towards the bridge of the *Jervis Bay*. He saw the ship slowly going down —and he saw Fegen standing on the shredded remnants of his ship, both arms limp at his sides.

Still the shells came from the *Scheer*, pouring at *Jervis Bay*. In clusters they came, five at a time. Only the ribs of the ship remained.

The crew piled into the lifeboat, but before it reached the water it was holed.

Middy Butler raced round to a man on the foecastle who had not heard the order to abandon ship. He was standing there alone, with earphones over his head, continuing his duty. He laid the phones down calmly and walked to the life-rafts.

The whole superstructure of the ship was burning. Four life-rafts were still usable. The crew —nearly seventy of them —leapt on to the rafts. Though the ship was sinking fast now, the Germans gave them no mercy. The *Scheer* poured shrapnel at the survivors as they struggled on to the rafts. Practically every one of them was wounded.

Still it was Guy Fawkes Day, and still the shells rose like fireworks. The rafts floated clear of the ship. A few of the crew manned the lifeboat, but it would not take many.

So sank *Jervis Bay*, Fegen aboard her. Five minutes later the *Scheer* went after the convoy.

Sven Olander aboard his Swedish ship mustered all his hands on deck.

'Well? Is it to be full speed ahead and escape —or stay to pick up survivors?' All voted to stay.

'Good,' the skipper said. 'They did so well to save us, I wouldn't have liked to leave without trying to save them.'

Back on the rectangular rafts, the numbing night was upon the men, the winter wind searing their skin and freezing their faces. The midshipman, Ronnie Butler, ripped off part of his clothes to bandage the injured. Two of the crew died on the rafts, but the Swedish ship returned to the scene on the still-rising sea and took off the men in the lifeboat.

It was 5 p.m. when the *Scheer* was first sighted; *Jervis Bay* had lasted till nearly eight. The Swedes manned the lifeboat and rowed over to two of the rafts, from which survivors were transferred, and then brought to the ship. When the Swedish sailors could not work the oars any longer, Olander brought his ship alongside the last two rafts and saved the rest.

Sixty-five of the *Jervis Bay*'s crew survived. Two-thirds of them were, in peacetime, members of the Merchant Service and had never been in battle before. Yet they had all stuck to their guns till the barrels no longer fired and the deck was at water level.

Even aboard the Swedish ship the wounded had to await attention, for she carried no doctor of her own, and the *Jervis Bay* surgeon was himself one of the wounded. Some one tended him, then he set about the job of attending to their wounds.

Although *Jervis Bay* and Fegen went down, their sacrifice could be translated into terms of ships and men saved from the *Scheer*. Of the thirty-seven ships in convoy HX84 thirty-one reached port. Three of these actually returned to Canada, where, incidentally, the *Jervis Bay* survivors were landed.

Nevertheless, five precious vessels perished: *Beaverford, Fresno City, Kenbane Head, Maidan*, and *Trewellard*. The Swedish ship *Vingaland* weathered the *Scheer*'s storm, only to be sunk by enemy aircraft three days later. Thus the toll was six ships out of the convoy lost –plus the *Jervis Bay*. Without her heroic fight, few would have made port.

Still the story is incomplete. For one of the thirty-one to get across the Atlantic, with a lethal load of petrol, was the tanker *San Demetrio*. She was set on fire and abandoned. Thirty-six hours after the *Jervis Bay*'s battle, on the morning of 7 November, one of her boat's crew rowed back, boarded her, put out the fire – within inches all the time of the 11,200 tons of petrol.

Then, steering only by wind and wake, the *San Demetrio* sighted the Irish coast six days later. A destroyer escorted her to the Clyde, where she delivered safely 11,000 tons of her cargo. It was an amazing adventure, second only to the *Jervis Bay*'s in its glory.

The *Scheer*'s attack disorganized all Atlantic convoys for twelve days, till the cycle was regained with HX89 on the 17th. The very next day Captain Fegen was posthumously awarded the VC.

Edward Stephen Fogarty Fegen was one of three brothers, who all became naval commanders. One of them summed up his last action: 'It was the end he would have wished.'

CHAPTER ELEVEN

Ship-busters against
Gneisenau

KENNETH CAMPBELL

Four Beaufort torpedo bombers took off from St Eval airfield in Cornwall before dawn on 6 April 1941. Their destination was Brest; their target –the 32,000 ton German battlecruiser *Gneisenau*. Three of the planes carried torpedoes; one carried bombs.

The captains of the three torpedo planes were Flying Officer Kenneth Campbell, from Ayrshire; Flying Officer Jimmy Hyde, an Australian and Sergeant Pilot Camp, a red-headed Irishman.

The four aircraft took off at various times between 04.30 and 05.15 hours. But the weather had now upset the navigation. The only pilot carrying bombs lost his way, and eventually dropped his bombs on a ship in convoy near the Île de Batz.

Camp also got a long way off course, and did not arrive at Brest until 07.00 hours. He approached the harbour from the south-west, as briefed, crossing the Île de Longue at 800 feet. It had been daylight for over half an hour, and he knew he had missed his rendezvous, but he was still prepared to go in.

The weather was atrocious, thick with early morning haze and mist. He came right down to sea-level and, almost before he realized it he found he was flying between the two arms of land encircling the outer harbour. But he could not get a definite pinpoint.

Suddenly his aircraft was boxed in by flak as he came under heavy fire from the flak-ships and shore batteries. He had little idea of his precise direction, and it was pointless to go on. He pulled up in a climbing turn to the east, and almost immediately found himself in cloud.

Camp was unaware that every gun in the harbour had been alerted half an hour earlier by the arrival of Campbell and Hyde.

These two pilots had reached Brest independently soon after dawn. Both had loitered outside the harbour, waiting for the bomb explosions in their unawareness that two of the bomb-carrying Beauforts had failed to take off, and that the third had lost its way.

Campbell, a few minutes ahead of Hyde, began a wide circuit, watching for some sign of the other aircraft. The light was seeping in under the horizon, like a chink in a curtain. It was going to be virtually a daylight attack, and that would surely multiply the already mammoth odds tenfold. Campbell had seen no explosions, but perhaps he was the last to arrive. He had better go straight in.

As Campbell set his compass to steer for the inner harbour, as yet invisible in the mist ahead, Hyde was making his landfall. Suddenly Hyde saw an aircraft flash by beneath him. He just had time to pick out an 'X' on the fuselage –the aircraft letter. He called his navigator.

'Who's in 'X'?'

'Campbell.'

'It looks as though he's going in. Has anyone seen anything? Any explosions, I mean?'

'Not a thing.'

'He's going in all right. I can't think why.'

Hyde continued to circle outside the harbour, waiting for Campbell to come out. He had been a long time on No. 22 Squadron –longer than anyone. Throughout he had been that rarity –a pilot who coupled dash with steadiness and a strict regard for orders.

There had been no explosions, so there could have been no bombs. The orders were to wait for the explosions.

Meanwhile Campbell had brought his aircraft down to 300 feet and was aiming for the right-hand end of the mole. In the outer harbour the cloud-base was low and he streaked along beneath it, intermittently in cloud. Ahead of him out of the mist he picked out the flak- ships.

There was the mole –a thin line on the water. If the *Gneisenau* was still anchored to the same buoy he was perfectly placed for a stern attack.

Campbell began his dive down towards the east end of the mole. He could see the flak-ships clearly now. Beyond the mole a massive shadow was resolving itself into the stern of the *Gneisenau*. He swung away to starboard, and then back to port, making an angle of forty-five degrees with the *Gneisenau*. He flattened out his dive, fifty feet above the water. The flak-ships were upon him.

He raced between them at mast height, unchallenged, squinting down the barrels of their guns. The mole was only 200 yards away. He looked steadfastly ahead, every nerve alert, steadied the aircraft, and aimed the nose deliberately. When the mole disappeared under the windscreen he released the torpedo.

Aircraft and torpedo crossed the mole independently, the nose of the torpedo tilted downward towards the water. The defences of Brest were taken by surprise. Still the Beaufort was unchallenged by anti-aircraft fire.

The *Gneisenau* towered above them like a mammoth warehouse, and there was no sign of any protective net. Campbell began to pull away to port to clear the hills behind the harbour, making for the sanctuary of cloud. In perhaps another fifteen seconds they would be safe.

But the peaceful harbour of Brest had been aroused from its lethargy. The

Beaufort now had to fly through the fiercest, heaviest, and most concentrated barrage that any single aircraft had ever faced or would ever face again. Nothing could live in such a wall of steel.

There was the blinding, withering fire which they had awaited and which they knew must come. Their last sight was of the flashing guns of the *Gneisenau*, lighting the hills behind the harbour, the hills over which they had watched the last dawn they would ever see.

The Beaufort, out of control, crashed into the harbour. What happened in those last moments will never be known. Stabbed by a hundred points of steel, the Beaufort kept flying when almost any other type of aircraft must have been brought down.

Campbell may have been killed some seconds before the crash came. Sergeant Scott, the Canadian navigator, may have tried to drag Campbell off the stick and take over. When they lifted the aircraft out of the harbour, it was said by the French Resistance that a blond Canadian was found in the pilot's seat. Campbell and his gallant crew took the secrets of those last despairing seconds with them.

A few months earlier Scott, as one of the first Canadian aircrew to arrive in England, had been invited to a British home to tea. That home was Buckingham Palace; the hosts the Queen and the two Princesses.

Although Campbell and his crew did not live to see their torpedo run true to its mark, there is no doubt that they knew that severe damage would be done to the *Gneisenau*.

What did the strike achieve? The damage was such that had the battlecruiser been at sea it would have sunk rapidly. The Germans had to put nearly every ship in the harbour alongside to support it and pump out the water, and it was only with the greatest difficulty that they were able towards the end of the day to get the *Gneisenau* back into drydock. Eight months later the starboard propeller shaft was still under repair.

Hitler's dream of joining the battlecruiser up with the *Bismarck*, in the North Atlantic, and ending the war in sixty days, or even in 160 days, was shattered. When the *Bismarck* came out it had to face the Royal Navy and Fleet Air Arm alone.

Although photographic reconnaissance suggested that the *Gneisenau* (we thought it was the *Scharnhorst* at the time) had been hit, we did not know for many months how serious the damage was. We could take nothing for granted in the war at sea, and we had to go on hitting at this ship for the next ten months. No one, anyway, could easily believe that the million-to-one chance had come off.

Campbell and his crew were buried by the Germans in the grove of honour, in the cemetery at Brest.

When the news of the strike eventually filtered through to London in March 1942 Campbell was awarded the Victoria Cross. There is a memorial to him at Sedbergh.

Only the bravest flew with the brave. Campbell's crew were Scott, Sergeant Mullins, and Sergeant Hillman.

These men were not automatons. Fear could not be drilled or disciplined out of them. They were human beings, with all the imperfections of their fellows.

Hillman, the wireless operator, had once been human enough to be late for take-off. This has how, three months earlier, he had lost his place in another crew —and thus found himself on the million-to-one chance.

CHAPTER TWELVE

Mainly Mediterranean

ERIC WILSON, NIGEL LEAKEY, JOHN HINTON, ALFRED HULME, CHARLES UPHAM, JOHN EDMONDSON, ARTHUR CUTLER, JAMES GORDON

The active war now moved to the Mediterranean: to North Africa, Greece, and Crete. The VCs won in Greece and Crete reflected the grim rearguard retreats from those two places. But before these operations, came two incidents farther down the continent of Africa, in Somaliland and Abyssinia. Captain Eric Charles Twelves Wilson, of the East Surrey Regiment attached to the Somaliland Camel Corps, won his award posthumously. This was how it happened:

Captain Wilson was in command of machine-gun posts manned by Somali soldiers in the key position of Observation Hill, a defended post in the defensive organization of the Tug Argan Gap in British Somaliland.

The enemy attacked Observation Hill on 11 August 1940. Captain Wilson and Somali gunners under his command beat off the attack and opened fire on the enemy troops attacking Mill Hill, another post within his range. He inflicted such heavy casualties that the enemy, determined to put his guns out of action, brought up a pack battery to within 700 yards, and scored two direct hits through the loop-holes of his defences, which, bursting within the post, wounded Captain Wilson severely in the right shoulder and in the left eye, several of his team also being wounded. His guns were blown off their stands, but he repaired and replaced them, and, regardless of his wounds, carried on, while his Somali sergeant was killed beside him.

On 12 August and 14th the enemy again concentrated field artillery fire on Captain Wilson's guns, but he continued, with his wounds untended, to man them.

On 15 August two of his machine-gun posts were blown to pieces, yet Captain Wilson, now suffering from malaria in addition to wounds, still kept his own post in action.

The enemy finally overran the post at 5 p.m. on 15 August when Captain Wilson, fighting to the last, was killed.

Fighting Mussolini's war the following spring, Sergeant Nigel Grey Leakey alone broke up an attack of Italian tanks. Abyssinia was the unusual scene of

42

this VC, posthumously awarded to a member of the King's African Rifles.

On 19 May 1941 at Colito in Abyssinia, two companies successfully crossed the Billate River, despite gruelling Italian opposition, and they set up a precarious bridgehead without any hope of immediate reinforcement.

Throughout the crossing Sergeant Leakey had been supporting the operation with 3-inch mortar-fire and, having expended all his ammunition, he went forward to see what he could do.

Out of the blue the enemy produced a shattering stroke : an attack with medium and light tanks, which thundered out of the tropical bush, threatening to overrun the two companies of the King's African Rifles. Advancing from the rear, one of these tanks was bearing down on the troops, who had no anti-tank weapons for their defence. For Leakey, this was a moment of decision, destiny.

Grinding machine-gun fire from the enemy's ground forces saturated the scene. As fire spat from tanks approaching him from the front, Leakey leapt on top of the tank coming in from behind his position, and wrenched open the turret.

With his revolver, he shot the commander of the tank and all its crew except the driver, whom he forced to drive in to cover.

Leakey tried to get the cannon of the tank to work, but he could not operate it, so called out:

'I'll get them on foot.'

He charged across the ground hot with the sun, swept with machine-gun bullets and bursting shells. These came from the other tanks, which continued rolling inexorably towards the troops. More men fell dead in the face of this grim inferno.

But Leakey was still alive. With an African company sergeant major, and two other Askari, he proceeded to stalk these tanks, calmly, amid the dust and death. The first two tanks passed before Leakey could take action against them, but he managed to jump up on the third tank. Forcing open the turret, he killed one of its crew before the fourth tank following directly behind levelled its machine gun at Leakey's form on the turret —and shot him off it.

Leakey's valour was entirely responsible for breaking up the Italian tank attack. By his own actions, he saved what must have been a most critical situation, for if the tanks had succeeded in their aim the bridgehead would have been lost and subsequent operations adversely affected. Leakey did what he did knowing that he faced certain death. Yet he was not defeated.

So to the two linked episodes of Greece and Crete, which yielded three VCs — all to New Zealanders.

Sergeant John Daniel Hinton won the only VC to be awarded for fighting in Greece.

On the night of 28-29 April 1941, a column of German armoured forces entered Kalamai. As they did so a large assembly of British and New Zealand troops were awaiting embarkation on a beach on the Greek coast. That was the setting for the VC action.

The German column contained several armoured vehicles carrying 2-inch guns, 3-inch mortars, and two 6-inch guns, and they were all rapidly converging on the Allied soldiers exposed on the beach.

When the order to retreat to cover was given, echoing weirdly on the spring night air, Sergeant Hinton shouted:

'To hell with this; who'll come with me?'

He ran to within a few yards of the nearest enemy gun. It fired but missed him. He hurled grenades which completely obliterated the gun crew. Then he came on with the bayonet, followed by a crowd of New Zealanders. German troops abandoned their first 6-inch gun and retreated into two houses.

Hinton followed them. He smashed the window and then the door of the first house, and dealt with the garrison inside by bayonet. He repeated the performance in the second house, and, as a result, until overwhelming German numbers arrived, the New Zealanders held the guns. Hinton then fell with a bullet wound through the lower abdomen and was taken prisoner.

A month after Hinton won the VC in the evacuation from Greece, two more fellow New Zealanders showed such courage in Crete that they too were rewarded by the same decoration.

Sergeant Alfred Clive Hulme revealed great courage from the moment he set foot on that wild island and was launched into the clash of conflict there.

On ground overlooking Maleme aerodrome, on 20 and 22 May 1941, he led men from the area held by the forward position and destroyed enemy groups out in front of the New Zealand line, from which they had been firing. Hulme handled numerous snipers himself. The number of dead counted here amounted to 130 enemy.

Between 22 and 24 May Hulme was continually launching lonely sorties, or taking one or two men with him, to neutralize German snipers.

Hulme rejoined his battalion on 25 May when they counter-attacked Galatos village. The attack was partially held up by a group of Germans in the local school, from which they had begun to cripple the New Zealanders. Hulme went into the attack alone, throwing grenades into the school so successfully that he disorganized the defences and he and his men were able to continue their operations.

So the heroic Hulme went on through these epic eight days. On Tuesday 27 May, when he and his troops were desperately holding a defensive line at Suda Bay during the final retirement there, five snipers had stealthily worked into position on the hillside overlooking the flank of the battalion line. Hulme again volunteered to tackle things, stalking and killing each one of the five in turn. He continued similar work successfully all through that decisive day.

Twenty-eighth May now, at Stylos, with an enemy heavy mortar severely bombing a vital ridge held by the battalion rearguard troops. The mortar started to play havoc with the New Zealanders, many of whom were blown up, suffering severe injuries.

Hulme again solved the problem; he penetrated the enemy lines, killed the German mortar crew of four, put the mortar out of commission in case anyone else should try to use it, and then went on with his normal duties. This materially helped the withdrawal of the main force through Stylos.

From the enemy mortar position, in fact, he worked round to the left flank, and killed three snipers who had been causing concern to the rearguard. This raised his total to an amazing figure of thirty-three enemy snipers stalked and shot.

Shortly after, Hulme received a severe wound in the shoulder while stalking yet another sniper. When ordered to the rear, in spite of his wound he directed traffic under fire and organized stragglers of various units into groups —so making the movement of troops easier. Hulme recovered from his wound to survive the rest of the war.

The only double VC awarded in the Second World War was to Captain Charles Hazlitt Upham, who won the awards in Crete and the Western Desert. He survived both actions —and the Colditz Castle prison camp.

During the operations in Crete, Upham performed a series of extraordinary exploits over a period of eight days, from 22–30 May 1941.

While commanding a forward platoon in the attack on Maleme, on 22 May, he fought his way forward for over 3,000 yards unsupported by any other arms. The platoon succeeded in destroying numerous enemy posts, during this onslaught, but on three occasions they were held up temporarily, until Upham, by courageous personal action, overcame the opposition.

The first occasion, the trouble came from a machine-gun nest, the fire from which made further advance too hazardous. Upham found the only method was to crawl so close under the muzzle of the guns that he was able to demoralize the occupants with hand grenades and revolver fire until his section could mop up the post and clear the way for a further advance. Upham went into the attack again, and from close quarters lobbed a grenade through the very window from which a gun was firing. The well-aimed grenade killed the crew and several other Germans inside. Fire from the section silenced the second nest in the house.

The next hold-up happened when they ran into yet another machine-gun post. Upham crawled to within fifteen yards of this post, until he reckoned he was within grenade-throwing range. That, of course, applied both ways and, had he been detected, he might have been at the wrong end of one from the enemy. But he got into position safely, withdrew the pin, and killed all the gunners with a well-lobbed grenade.

When the time came for his company to withdraw from Maleme he helped to carry out a wounded man under remorseless fire, and then, together with another officer, rallied more men to carry out other wounded. As a second lieutenant at this period, he was then sent to guide a company which had become isolated. With a corporal, he penetrated through enemy territory over 600 yards, killing two Germans on the way, found the company, and led them back to the battalion's new position. But for Upham and the corporal, the company would have been completely cut off.

During the following two days his platoon occupied an exposed position on forward slopes of the Cretan hills, and was continuously under fire. The blast of a mortar shell bowled Upham over, while a piece of shrapnel from another hit him behind the left shoulder. He ignored the existence of this wound, and remained on duty. He also received a bullet in the foot, which remained embedded until he later had it removed when in Egypt. Upham should, by this time, have been far from fully operational, but he carried on.

At Galatos, on 25 May, his platoon was being butchered by mortars and machine guns. While they stopped under cover of a ridge, Upham went forward alone to observe the enemy, and brought the platoon forward when the Germans advanced. They killed over forty with fire and grenades, and forced the rest to fall back again.

When his platoon did receive orders to retire he sent the men back under the platoon sergeant while he went to warn other troops that they were being cut off. When Upham finally came out of the engagement he was fired on by two stray Germans.

Acting instantly, he fell and shammed dead. Then, as the Germans moved in, he crawled into a convenient position from where there was some protection. Though he only had the use of one arm by now, he rested his rifle in the fork of a tree, and as the two men neared him he leapt up and killed them both. The second to fall actually hit the muzzle of Upham's rifle, propped in the tree-fork.

Those eight days had dragged by, and on 30 May, at Sphakia, Upham's platoon was ordered to deal with a party of Germans that had advanced down a ravine towards force headquarters. His wounds and efforts of the past week had exhausted him almost to the point of collapse, yet he climbed the steep hill to the west of the ravine, and placed his men in positions on the slope overlooking the ravine. Upham then took a Bren gun and two riflemen to the top of the hill, and cleverly deceived the Germans into exposing themselves. Then, at a range of 500 yards, he shot twenty-two of them, and forced the rest to scatter panic-stricken.

During the whole of these Crete operations Upham was not only wounded and badly bruised, but he suffered from dysentery, and could eat very little.

So ended the eight days for which Upham was awarded his first VC. It was a strange campaign, conducted in the brightness of a Mediterranean May, and in the rocks, olive-groves, and mountains of Crete. Strange too, for, although the New Zealanders had to quit the island, the Allied air and land forces hit Hitler's airborne troops so hard that it was as much a defeat for them as for the Allies.

Just over a year later Upham —now a captain —was commanding a company of New Zealanders in the Western Desert during the operations culminating in the attack on El Ruweisat Ridge, on the night of 14–15 July 1942.

Upham crossed open fire-swept ground to inspect his forward sections guarding their minefields, when he was wounded. He was hit again, while destroying an entire truckload of German soldiers with hand grenades, heaved from close to the vehicle. There was no question of his missing the final assault on the ridge, however, and, ignoring his wounds, he insisted on staying with his Anzacs to take part in it.

During the opening stages of the attack under darkness on El Ruweisat, Upham's company formed part of the reserve battalion, but when communications with the vanguard broke down he was instructed to send up an officer to report on the progress of the attack. Night fighting was bound to be confusing, so Upham set out himself, armed with a Spandau, and after several brushes with the enemy, during which brisk fire was exchanged, he succeeded in bringing back the required information.

Just before dawn the reserve battalion was ordered forward, but before the specified position could be reached the enemy launched an attack with machine guns and tanks. Although twice wounded in this action, Upham at once led the

New Zealanders straight for the two nearest strongpoints on the left flank of the sector. His rich voice rose over the din of battle, cheering on the Anzacs and after sustaining heavy losses, they succeeded in eliminating the enemy.

At the height of this queer pre-dawn devastation in the desert, Upham annihilated an enemy tank, and it was soon a sheet of orange-red flame against the eastern sky and, with more hand grenades, he stopped other vehicles of various kinds.

Again he was wounded by a bullet from a machine gun, which ripped right through his elbow and broke his arm; but he still went forward to bring back some of his men who had became isolated by the ebb and flow of the fight.

He continued to dominate the scene until his men had beaten back a violent counter-attack and had consolidated the position. Exhausted far beyond the point of normal endurance by the pain from his wound, and terribly weak from loss of blood, Upham was then removed to the regimental aid post to have his wounds dressed. But they could not keep him there, for he had only one thing in his mind : to get back to his men. And return he did, remaining all day long, on 15 July, under a blistering barrage of artillery- and mortar-fire.

The situation had now become desperate, and Upham was again severely wounded and unable to move. His gallant company had been reduced to six survivors when the enemy overran their position and took them prisoner.

Upham survived the ordeal of 14-15 July but had to endure prisoner of war camps for the next two-and-three-quarter years. The last of these was Colditz Castle, famous for the illustrious persons who were imprisoned there. The happy ending came on 15 April, 1945, when Upham was among the Allied officers and men of Oflag 4C (Schloss Colditz), twenty-five miles south-east of Leipzig, who were liberated by the American Army. Upham arrived in England five days later, after an adventurous four years since landing in Crete.

After Greece and Crete, the scene switched to North Africa for a considerable length of time, with a consequent crop of VCs.

With bayonet fixed, and in the nadir of night, Australian Corporal John Hurst Edmondson was wounded by bullets in the neck and stomach —but continued to advance. Bayonets must be about the most savage and frightening form of warfare, and that was why they were chosen on the night of 13-14 April 1941, when a party of German infantry had burst through the wire defences of the Australians of Tobruk, in North Africa, and established themselves with at least half a dozen machine guns, mortars, and two small field pieces. To dislodge them clearly called for desperate action.

The Australian sortie comprised one officer, Corporal John Hurst Edmondson, and five privates. Into the spring night this small force charged with bayonets fixed and with a short expectation of life.

The enemy opened fire furiously as the Australians advanced through the darkness towards them. Edmondson was wounded in the neck and stomach, but he went on just the same, killing one of the enemy with his bayonet.

At this moment Edmondson's officer, who had just bayoneted another of the enemy, had his legs pinned by the desperate man —and while in this position he was attacked from behind. The officer called for help, and Edmondson, some yards away, staggered over to the three of them, and killed both of the Germans, although himself mortally wounded and in a state of collapse. This action saved his officer's life, but, soon after he returned to their headquarters, Edmondson died of his wounds.

Second of three Australian VCs in this phase was Lieutenant Arthur Roden Cutler of the Royal Australian Artillery. Cutler lost a leg and won the VC. The Syrian campaign was proceeding bitterly in 1941, and at Merj Ayoun, on 19 June, an Allied infantry attack had been checked after suffering heavily from enemy tanks.

Enemy machine guns were sweeping the ground, when, with another artillery officer and a few other men, Cutler pushed on ahead of the infantry, and set up an observation post in a house. As the telephone-line was cut, he went out and mended it under machine-gun fire. Cutler returned to the house, and from there they managed to capture an enemy post and a battery.

That was quiet compared with what came next. The enemy attacked the house with infantry and tanks, killing the Bren gunner and mortally wounding Cutler's fellow officer. But Cutler fought back and, with another soldier, manned an anti-tank rifle and Bren gun, driving the enemy away again.

The German tanks returned to the attack, but the two men's fire forced them off for a second time. In the breathing space that followed, Cutler devoted himself to supervising the evacuation of the wounded in his party. After this he returned to thoughts of an advance, for he had been ordered to establish an outpost right in the town, which was occupied by the Foreign Legion.

Cutler knew all the while that the enemy must be massing on his left for a further counter-attack, and that he was in danger of being cut off. Nevertheless, he carried out his task of 'registering' the battery on the road and engaging the enemy's posts. The expected occurred. The enemy struck back, and he was cut off. Cutler was forced to go to ground, but after dark he managed to make his way back through the enemy lines. His work in 'registering' the only road by which enemy transport could enter the town was vital to the Australians, and subsequent artillery fire forced the Germans to retreat.

Four nights later, on 23-24 June, Cutler was in charge of a 25-pounder, sent forward into new defended localities to silence an enemy anti-tank gun and post, which had held up the attack. This he did, and next morning the recapture of Merj Ayoun was complete.

Already Cutler could have done enough to earn him the VC. But the actual action for which he really received it came nearly two weeks later. On 6 July, at Damur, the Allied forward infantry was being pinned to the ground quite literally by heavy hostile machine-gun fire kicking up the Syrian sand. Cutler disregarded the danger utterly and went out to bring a line through to his outpost. In so doing, he was badly wounded in his leg.

Unable to return, he lay out there in no man's land with a shattered leg. The enemy fire was so intense that no one could possibly reach him alive. Twenty-six hours dragged by as he lay there, the wound growing more septic each hour, until

48

at last on the following day they did get to him, and so saved his life. But he lost the leg.

On another summer night in Syria, Private James Heather Gordon killed four machine-gunners with his bayonet, and was awarded the VC for his bravery. It was the night of 10 July 1941, during an attack on 'Greenhill', north of Djezzine, that Gordon's company came under devastating machine-gun fire. Their advance was held up, and so severe was this fire that movement even by individual soldiers became virtually impossible. There they were, pinned; paralysed. Some did try to advance, but one officer and two men were at once hit and killed. Two others were wounded.

The enemy machine-gun position that had brought the two forward Australian platoons to a standstill was fortified and its firepower completely covered the area occupied by the Aussies. This did not deter Gordon. On his own initiative, he crept forward over ground mown by machine-gun bullets to within range of enemy grenades. Creeping, crawling, inch by inch, he managed to sneak up close to the post.

Then, out of the darkness, he charged it from the front, right into the face of a gun. He slew the four machine-gunners with the bayonet. This single action so demoralized the enemy in the sector, that Gordon's company was able to continue their advance to take the position.

During the rest of the night, and again next day, he showed equal courage.

Next followed a famous raid on General Rommel's headquarters in Africa: an audacious stroke, conceived to try to paralyse the enemy body by putting its brain out of action.

CHAPTER THIRTEEN

Killed by dive-bombers

ALFRED SEPHTON

The Mediterranean was the scene of many battles, of which perhaps the worst began on 18 May 1941. While Lieutenant Commander Wanklyn was slipping his submarine *Upholder* quietly out of Malta towards Sicily —where he won the VC the following week —a tremendous fight suddenly began in the seas off Crete.

The British Hospital ship *Aba* suddenly sent an SOS over her radio. Without waiting for further news, the cruisers *Coventry* and *Phoebe* steamed straight for the position given. En route, Nazi dive-bombers loomed out of nowhere, just as they had done over *Foylebank*.

The cruisers' anti-aircraft drill went into action. There was an exchange of bullets and bombs through thick, blackened air. Up in one of the gun-director towers, Petty Officer Sephton kept the *Coventry*'s fire on targets. He clenched his teeth as he thought of the *Aba*. The Nazis had attacked a hospital ship. Nothing was sacred. Sephton knew that the cruisers had to get through, and he was determined that the planes, which kept on coming, should be beaten off.

The tower was totally destroyed as two bullets spat into Sephton's body. Yet he kept standing at his post, his straight, thin face pale, his clothes dripping with blood.

The cruisers were winning, but he carried on with the routine in a dream. Though he was losing a lot of blood he had to hold on.

Sephton stayed at his post until he died.

CHAPTER FOURTEEN

Malta Submariner Supreme

MALCOLM WANKLYN

The setting for this saga was Malta in 1941 –defended at first by just three old aircraft nicknamed Faith, Hope and Charity. It was from this vulnerable and isolated island that our pitifully few submarines struck out to stop enemy supplies from reaching North Africa. The whole desert war depended on their success.

By the time the submarines were operating at full strength, half of all Axis shipping bound for the African coast was failing to arrive. The submarines sank no fewer than seventy-five enemy vessels. But half of the Royal Navy's submarines failed to return. Ten out of twenty –lost with all hands. Their exploits were enacted against the blitzed backdrop of Malta where, by the end of 1941, it was just as hazardous for submarines to be in harbour as at sea.

So to the submarine *Upholder* and her commander Malcolm David Wanklyn. He was a tall and lean man with a soft Scottish voice, a dark, submariner's beard and large powerful hands. His electric eyes could blaze with an intensity of purpose; or they could crinkle softly. For he was a gentle soul, too –one who hated to think of the consequences of his actions after a ship had been hit. Returning from patrol, his eyes would be red-rimmed with too little sleep and too much responsibility.

On her twenty-four successful patrols, *Upholder* sank more than twenty ships, including a destroyer and a cruiser. Wanklyn's seventh patrol took them to the northern approaches of the Strait of Messina. After four days, they attacked a tanker and registered a hit. Then their listening gear went out of action, so the submarine was deaf to the outside world. Then they saw a small enemy convoy. Wanklyn hit a tanker, which sank by the stern. *This was total war.* Twenty-six depth-charges cracked and crashed all around them. The submarine shuddered –and so did the crew.

By that time, *Upholder* had been on patrol for about a week. The next evening, Wanklyn took a last look around this enemy route starting from Sicily to the Libyan coast. The sun set on 24 May. Wanklyn's watch showed 20.20 hours when the VC action suddenly started.

In the stormy twilight gloom, Wanklyn sighted an aircraft patrolling to the north: nothing else. He held on for a few minutes more. The surface swell took *Upholder* with it –to and fro. Depth-keeping was difficult. The sub 'pumped' up and down. The horizon seemed shadowy, indistinct, to the east –but blood-red, clear-cut to the west. And one moment the horizon would be startlingly close; the next the swell raced by the top window of the periscope, blotting out everything except the darkening water.

Ten minutes passed. 20.30.

Then, strongly silhouetted against the afterglow of sunset, Wanklyn sighted three large two-funnel transports tearing at top speed on a south-westerly course.

'Ships, three of them.'

Wanklyn thought in a flash: light failing so periscope practically useless; listening gear out of order; only two torpedoes left. For some reason, these did not deter him. He may also have seen the top-masts of destroyers, but the swell made sighting more and more difficult each minute. He did not stop to see if the enemy were escorted or not. He was intent to close, as fast as he could. But he knew that ships such as these would not be proceeding alone. Light bad, sea bad, time short –and getting worse and shorter.

'They're getting on for 20,000 tons. One's bigger than the rest.' In fact they were troop transports, converted liners, sailing in a line at twenty knots for Africa. After four minutes of following them, they altered course.

'Here they are. Four or five destroyers. Didn't see them before. They're screening the convoy. Only two torpedoes left and a target like this! Have to shorten the range. Don't know their speed sufficiently to go ahead yet.'

He shortened the attack and brought the sub round towards the oncoming ships, looming in the last light of the day. He screwed up his eyes to make sure where they were and read off bearings on all of them. He estimated speeds again; checked direction; compared them to *Upholder*'s: and then he changed course. This marked the start of the assault. He had to hit first time with one of the two torpedoes. An audacious attack by one 'deaf and blind' sub on seven or eight big ships, four or five armed to their topmast.

It was 20.32 and dusk, with the periscope eye all but blind. He manoeuvred *Upholder* into the precise position planned. The mile-off attack was no good and surfacing would be suicide. So Wanklyn got the sub right in among the enemy. He peered through the periscope, swivelled it slightly, and saw the first of the transports, then the second. He had no idea where the enemy escorts were. Yet five destroyers roamed at large, and the danger of being rammed remained in his mind.

At 20.33, he said 'Fire.' The torpedoes slid out of the tubes, their back-lash shivering through the sub.

And then it happened. As the torpedoes left, Wanklyn saw a huge black V heading straight for the sub –the bows of a destroyer, thirty seconds off.

'Crash dive.' Then as an afterthought –'Deep.'

Down, down, went *Upholder*, while Wanklyn counted off the seconds from the time the torpedoes left. Fifteen, thirty, forty-five seconds. One minute. Seventy-seven seconds –then two mild and inoffensive explosions. But the same short interval separated them as the firing of the torpedoes from the tubes. Wanklyn had hit the middle transport twice. They heard the bangs without the aid of their 'ears.'

About 150 seconds passed. Then came the first of the battering bursts of the depth charges. The lights flickered; shades splintered across the deck; men were caught off balance. *Upholder* twisted and turned. Wanklyn could only guess where the destroyers were; which way they headed. It was a lethal game of blind man's bluff on either side, except that the ships knew roughly where *Upholder* was wriggling, through their asdic sets. Down the depth charges came, nearly two a minute. And all the while Wanklyn cocked his ears in the direction of the charges, estimated the positions of the attackers, and steered his sub as far from them as he could. Even so, some exploded close enough to break the bulbs. The whole area seemed as if it were being subjected to systematic depth charging. But, miraculously almost, Wanklyn dodged them all —by split-second navigation and course-changing of a high order. *Upholder* traced a crazy zig-zag at different depths.

Thirty-three charges came in nineteen minutes. Then they heard —without their 'ears' —the ominous, thunderous beat of propellers as the hunter hurried overhead. Nerve-shattering seconds passed that got worse and worse as the throb of the props grew louder, louder, till they were racing directly above the submarine. Every man in *Upholder* was sweating now. But the sound passed its climax. Then they heard the plop of the charges as they hit the water, down into the depths. How near to *Upholder*? On the answer to this depended thirty-three lives. For if you hear propellers by ear, it is too late to try and escape —you are right below them.

Four final charges cracked the water. 'Thirty-seven charges in twenty minutes' was what the log entry read. The last quartet would have caused broken blood-vessels to anyone not steeled to such an ordeal. But it passed, and then there was silence.

The next decision for Wanklyn was to choose between escape and the danger of using his motors at any speed. The engines gave away their position when the attackers came too close. So he stopped engines completely for an hour. Not a sound broke the stillness.

Wanklyn looked tired but happy having outwitted five destroyers. 'Serve some tea,' he whispered, and Cookie pressed his messmates to mugs of hot tea and slices of cake —and the last of the fresh-fruit salad.

By the time the meal was over, the enemy had evidently given up the hunt. It was 22.00. Nothing could be heard. If ever anyone felt cut off from the rest of the world, *Upholder*'s company did on that day. They were in a static submarine with no listening gear, and it was nighttime above. The world might just as well not have existed.

'Periscope depth,' Wanklyn decided. He grabbed its handles eagerly. He scanned the horizon round 360 degrees, but the periscope was practically useless at night.

'Stand by to surface' was the sign for a stifled cheer from the crew. They came up where the transport had gone down. There was nothing to be heard in the darkness as Wanklyn clambered on to the bridge, but the breeze blowing across the heaving waters wafted a strong smell of fuel oil. The moon came out from behind a cloud and lit fragments of wood, broken boats, and flotsam —all that remained above water of the 17,800-ton transport *Conte Rosso*.

They set sail for Malta, ninety-nine per cent sure of having sunk the ship. Their certainty was confirmed a few days later by a lifeboat of a large ship being washed up bearing the name *Conte Rosso*.

The official communiqué described the action in superlative terms. 'With the greatest courage, coolness and skill he brought *Upholder* clear of the enemy and back to harbour.'

The amount of tonnage sunk by *Upholder* gradually grew and with it the legend. Then Wanklyn received his reward for the *Conte Rosso* episode. On 11 December 1941, seven months after the action, the Victoria Cross was bestowed upon him.

So to the epic attack on the *Neptunia* and *Oceania*.

In the middle of September 1941 reconnaissance aircraft spotted three large liners at Taranto. *Upholder*, *Unbeaten*, *Upright* and *Ursula* sailed as soon as they could to a preconceived plan. They knew the rough route that these troop transports would take, so three of them took up a position at an angle across the enemy's expected line.

Early on, *Upholder* suffered a severe setback, which would have knocked off balance an officer less gifted than Wanklyn. The sub's gyro compass ceased to function altogether, leaving him to rely on the much less accurate magnetic compass. This put precise steering out of the question and increased the difficulties of any attack.

Unbeaten sighted the convoy at 03.20, in the middle of the night, but they were steaming too fast for her to attack in time. *Unbeaten* made an immediate report to *Upholder* and chased off after the enemy.

Wanklyn received the report and had little to do but wait till they came in sight. The night still stayed dark, ideal for an attack on the surface. What was he waiting for? The *Neptunia*, *Oceania* and *Vulcania*, escorted by six destroyers.

Upholder's First Lieutenant was on watch when they were sighted. In a flash, Wanklyn was on the bridge. He saw dimly the dark shapes against a dark horizon –an eerie, exciting moment. The sea was choppy. Wanklyn realized that the sub was some way off the enemy's track. He closed at full throttle.

With torpedo tubes at the ready and his glasses glued to the murky masses on the starboard bow, Wanklyn raced in to try and intercept the three monsters. After penetrating the ring of escorting detroyers with consummate skill, he realized he would have to carry out the attack at a far longer range than he would wish and more serious still, the submarine was still swaying wildly from side to side. It would have been a waste to fire a salvo of four under these conditions, for if he were wrong once through no fault of his own, the vital chance would be gone.

He drove on and on, and when he knew he could not get nearer than 5,000 yards, decided finally to fire. *Upholder* still swung from side to side, as the helmsman had to correct the course each moment almost.

'Never get on the line of fire,' Wanklyn shouted above the elements.

So as the sub swung across the target he made split-second assessments. Through the glasses he saw *Oceania* in the lead with *Neptunia* overlapping along the line from the sub.

Upholder swung across the line and Wanklyn fired. She swung back again, and he fired again. And a few seconds later, as she came on course for the third time, he fired once more. He was judging entirely by eye.

Through three miles of sea they had to travel, on a dark choppy night with aiming almost impossible. . . .

'Ready to dive, sir?' Number One called up to Wanklyn.

'Not quite, I want to see them hit first!'

In the end the First Lieutenant had to go aloft and persuade him it was high time they were diving! So she dived quickly and moved south.

The three torpedoes took over three minutes to reach the target area, so long was the range. Then, as *Upholder* gained depth, Wanklyn's watch became the focus. At the precise second planned, they heard three explosions. One hit on the *Oceania* and two on *Neptunia.*

Three out of three! It was a truly amazing achievement in the adverse circumstances.

The first torpedo tore into *Oceania*'s propellers. She was in no danger of sinking, so two destroyers dashed in to try to get her in tow. But exactly as they did so, the other torpedoes dug deep into *Neptunia* amidships, crippling her. Soon it was certain that she would sink, although she could crawl along at five knots. The third transport fled for Tripoli.

Obviously it was only a matter of minutes for *Neptunia.* Finally she limped and listed to a stop —and sank. The destroyers around her collected the survivors, and swung back to *Oceania.*

But Wanklyn knew nothing of all this. The unaccustomed absence of any counter-attack satisfied him that the destroyers were too busy searching for survivors to worry about *Upholder.* Wanklyn tried to get in touch with *Unbeaten* for help in completing the conquest. But he could raise no reply. So at 04.45 he said, 'Stand by to surface. I'm going up to survey the situation.'

Slowly, splashing as little as he could, Wanklyn brought the sub up, among the enemy destroyers. It was still dark, yet a ghostly glimmer from the east lit enough for him to see one ship stopped, with a destroyer standing by, and another vessel making to westward. Wanklyn concentrated on the stationary *Oceania.*

He took *Upholder* down again and made off to the eastward while reloading his tubes, to get a good position up-sun from which to attack after sunrise. At half past six, the sun blazed just above the horizon. The submarine came up to periscope depth, and approached the *Oceania* with her attendant destroyer. Both boats lay stopped but drifting slowly.

Wanklyn got *Oceania* in his sights, and the periscope slowly picked its way nearer, nearer to the transport. He was just going to fire when he shouted:

'Good God, forty-five feet.'

He had suddenly sighted a second destroyer bows on only 100 yards away. Undeterred, Wanklyn took *Upholder* along at forty-five feet —and ducked directly underneath the escort!

Then he realized that this delay, and the drift of the target, would bring *Upholder* much too close to fire so he altered depth again.

'Eighty feet.'

Upholder went on under the transport, too, so as to come up to windward. Wanklyn looked through his periscope next at an ideal range of 2,000 yards from *Oceania*. Two torpedoes hit her, and the ship sank in eight minutes. So Wanklyn, alone and unaided, had sunk two-thirds of this concentrated convoy.

While Wanklyn was making the final kill of *Oceania* the Commanding Officer of *Unbeaten*, an amazed man, was peering through his periscope not very far away. *Unbeaten* too had manoeuvred into a good position up-sun to attack the enemy transport, and was only a matter of seconds from firing at her when the Commander saw two columns of water gush up from the other side of the ship and heard two obvious torpedo explosions. He could hardly believe his eyes as *Oceania* began to sink before he could attack her!

Upholder sailed from Malta on 6 April 1942, for patrol in the Gulf of Tripoli. On 11 April, she was met by HM Submarine *Unbeaten*. After that rendezvous, nothing more was ever heard of *Upholder*. On 14 April, *Urge*, which was patrolling in an area near *Upholder* heard prolonged depth-charging. On 18 April, the Italians claimed that one of their torpedo boats had sunk a submarine. The assumption is that this boat located *Upholder* on 14 April while she was stalking an enemy convoy, and sank her. So the submarine was lost with all hands – including Malcolm Wanklyn.

CHAPTER FIFTEEN

Australian against Bremen

HUGHIE EDWARDS

T he fourth of July 1941. A good day for a VC. An Australian was the recipient this time: Acting Wing Commander Hughie Idwal Edwards, DFC, of No. 105 Squadron. Edwards was a month off his twenty-seventh birthday on this Independence Day. He had been living for flying since 1935, when he joined the Royal Australian Air Force as a cadet. He was a mixture of a fierce disciplinarian who abided by the regulations and a shy, unassuming man. The two aspects thrived side by side.

During the same week as the VC operation Edwards heard that he had won the DFC for a flight in June. Leading a formation in an operational sweep against enemy shipping off the Dutch coast, he encountered a convoy of eight merchant vessels at anchor off the coast opposite The Hague. In the face of intense and accurate pom-pom and machine-gun fire, they attacked at a height of only fifty feet. When we come to the VC operation it will be seen that this was a favourite attacking altitude for Edwards.

On this day in June he flew straight through the flak fire and set his sights on a 4,000-ton ship. On the run-in he raked bombs at literally mast level. An explosion shook the plane as it gained height. Debris shot up into the air, to be blacked out by columns of suffocating smoke. The vessel was either sunk or severely damaged. This award of the DFC marked the latest of numerous missions over enemy and occupied country, and against shipping such as that off The Hague. At all times Edwards led his formation skilfully and gallantly. This in spite of the fact that he was handicapped by a physical disability resulting from a flying accident.

So back to the Fourth of July —and an attack on Bremen: a raid which will go down in the records as the high-tension attack. In daylight early that morning, only a few hours after the last of the RAF night bombers had left the port of Bremen, the formation led by Edwards was over it again. Although Britain still stood more or less alone, she was showing real signs of offence now —a welcome change from a year before.

Bremen was one of the most heavily defended towns in Germany, but Edwards and his Blenheims had to go in again, with all the defences alerted, and bomb a specific factory and other targets. The nature of these targets made a night attack out of the question, so it had to be made at early morning, and no clouds floated in the sky to offer concealment.

Even on the approach to the enemy coast – 'Enemy coast ahead, sir' – several hostile ships were sighted, so that Edwards knew that he and his force would be reported, and the ground and air defences be in a state of even greater readiness – straining for a sight of them. Despite this bad luck, Edwards piloted his plane and led the rest fifty miles overland towards the target. Taking his courage in both hands, he flew at the rooftop altitude of a mere fifty feet, passing through a formidable balloon barrage en route!

They could hardly miss Bremen. Ahead of them lay the port, and from all around it rose a ring of fire, as from some sacrificial altar; but there was nothing to be done except fly into it, still at zero height.

This is how a sergeant pilot of another aircraft in the squadron saw the scene:

The first we saw of Bremen was the balloon barrage, and in a few moments we were flying just above the grey slate roofs of houses. By this time the Germans were fully awake to us, and we had to fly in formation through a solid wall of flak. I suddenly saw a high-tension cable straight ahead of me, but I managed to lift over just in time.

I thought the wing commander was going to hit it, but he ducked down below it at the last moment while his starboard wing missed a pylon by a couple of yards.

We had noted the position of the balloons and were avoiding the cables, but at the level we were flying we could not avoid things like telephone-wires, and the wing commander must have interrupted one or two early morning German telephone conversations when he cut through some wires without damaging his aircraft. A Scottish sergeant pilot, a friend of mine in the same formation, was more souvenir-minded, and brought back a fair strip of German telephone-wire wrapped round his tail wheel!

Flying through a barrage of criss-cross flak, we could see the Bremeners taking cover behind cars as our bombs burst on timber yards, factories, buildings, a railway junction, and on docks. There was one terrific impact on a factory, and flames and smoke shot out. I should think that the morale effect of a daylight raid of this type must be tremendous. As we lifted over the chimney-tops, the streets must have been filled with the noise of British aircraft flying across the town.

So, sweeping low over the rooftops, they all dropped their deadly loads of high-explosives and incendiaries on the targets. Even the HEs were released from fifty feet; a desperately dangerous height for the crews of the bombers. In fact, Edwards released his load from this less-than-a-cricket-pitch altitude, and the debris leapt to 700 feet. The Blenheim lurched. The gigantic explosions shook its tail as it made double-quick time out of the area.

The opposition at this level was naturally intense, and Edwards saw four of his precious machines destroyed in the maelstrom of fire from all sides. This had to be expected. No wonder the RAF crews were fatalists. Edwards did all he could to muster the surviving planes, and so successfully did he navigate them out of the target area that no more were lost and all got home. Taking a last look at Bremen from his limping Blenheim, Edwards saw large buildings tottering and black smoke rolling over the town. Finally, when the bombs had gone, they machine-gunned gun emplacements and raked barracks and railway depots –from only a few feet.

Then, with coolness and resource, Edwards took them home. All except the four lost.

When they landed they discovered that every single aircraft had been hit by either flak or machine-gun fire, which was not a pleasant thought. But they were home – to fight another day.

And fight many another day Edwards did. After receiving his Victoria Cross Edwards later led a special raid on the Belgian coast, and then later still was promoted Group Captain, commanding a station where there was an Australian squadron.

With this Aussie outfit, Edwards himself flew on one of the many memorable mass raids on Berlin. The date of this one was 23 August 1943. Seven hundred four-engined aircraft of Bomber Command attacked the enemy capital at a loss of fifty-eight bombers. They dropped 1,700 tons of HEs in less than an hour, and left smoke rising four miles high, visible 200 miles away. Next day no railway traffic could be seen by a recce aircraft either entering or leaving the capital.

Just as one of the Halifaxes was levelling out on its bombing run, a Messerschmitt Me 110 came swooping in from starboard, firing its cannon and machine guns. Within six minutes this bomber was attacked three times, probably by the same fighter.

Cannon shells smashed the tail turret of the bomber, blasting away all the glass and wounding the rear gunner in the leg and arm, but despite his wounds the gunner stayed at his post and kept on firing.

A bullet hit the flight engineer in the ribs, but he too remained where he was until the bombing run was over. The intercom system was shot away with the first burst from the fighter, but the mid-upper and rear gunners told the pilot where the fighter was by signalling to him with their emergency lights.

The last attack was made when the fighter was immediately over the Halifax. The mid-upper gunner had it full in his sight when he fired and hit it.

While all this was going on the bomb aimer was calmly waiting to pick out his target. As the fighter disappeared he released his bombs. The wireless operator, meanwhile, had gone to the help of the flight engineer, whose clothes had caught fire.

Sparks were coming from his flying suit, and the wireless operator had to turn an extinguisher on him before he could put out the flames.

Now for a Stirling's eyewitness version of one of the most dramatic incidents from a thousand that night:

They were five miles from Berlin when they saw a big bomber held in a cone of search-lights. Flak flew up the beams of light, and inevitably the bomber caught fire. But the pilot managed to get out of the lights, went on across the target, levelled out, and then down went the bombs.

The pilot of another Stirling, Flight Sergeant S. Mason, celebrated his twenty-first birthday over Berlin. The crew made their bombing run just before midnight, and as soon as the bomb aimer gave the signal, 'Bombs gone,' the crew all wished him a Happy Birthday over the intercom. They drank his health in orange juice on the way home.

Edwards was with these planes that night, and said that the raid had been an outstanding success.

> We had every reason to believe that the Germans would put a very heavy barrage around Berlin. We know that they have hundreds of light and heavy anti-aircraft guns there. But last night the Berlin ground gunners took second place.
>
> The first place was taken by what seemed to be as many fighters as the Germans could muster. They were obviously sent up to stop a concentrated attack, and they failed.
>
> I saw many other bombers fighting their way through the searchlights and past the fighters to the target. I myself was not engaged by a fighter. The Australian squadron at my station certainly put up an excellent show, and I am proud of them.

The feeling was doubtless mutual, since the Aussies knew Edwards was flying with them on that memorable night.

CHAPTER SIXTEEN

Wing-walking to Fight Fire

JAMES WARD

Now a New Zealander takes up the chronicle of courage, his Victoria Cross coming just three days after Edwards's exploit. His name: Sergeant James Allen Ward, No. 75 (NZ) Squadron.

Europe was just about as far as he could get from his birthplace of Wanganui. After starting his operational career in the air he did 'two Kiels, one Düsseldorf, one Cologne, one Brest, one Münster, and a Mannheim'. He was clearly at home in the air, and since the age of twelve; his main hobby had been building model aircraft.

So to 7 July 1941, and an attack on Münster. Ward was second pilot to Squadron Leader Reuben Pears Widdowson, of a Wellington engaged in this attack. They had rather a mixed crew aboard. Ward, the navigator, and the rear gunner were all New Zealanders. The front gunner and wireless operator were English, and the first pilot, Widdowson, was a Canadian from Winnipeg: a real Empire crew.

It was a beautiful moonlit night, and for a change they had had a comparatively pleasant time over the target. After they dropped their bombs; they did another circuit around the town just to watch what was going on, and then they set their course for base.

'Piece of cake. We'll soon be home now', thought Widdowson, as he glanced down from 13,000 feet to the surface of the Zuider Zee, lying far away beneath them. But nothing was ever sure while a bomber was in the air.

Suddenly a Messerschmitt Me110 zoomed up from below them, just where the captain had been looking, and raked the Wellington from end to end with fire. The damage was dramatic. In a second the starboard engine spluttered with severe damage, the whole hydraulic system was put out of action, the bomb doors simply fell open, the wireless and intercom sets went unserviceable, the front gunner gripped an injured foot, and the cockpit filled with smoke and fumes.

Widdowson kept his wits about him as he saw the tracer bullets whizzing past, just outside his windscreen. The plane took on a whining, protesting tone, but still throbbed on.

Then a fire broke out in the starboard wing. From Widdowson's position he had to get practically out of his seat to see it, but even sitting at his controls he could still see the glow of it.

He shouted to someone back in the cabin –he didn't really know who it was – to tell the rest of the crew to get their parachutes on and stand by ready to abandon the aircraft. One of them came and asked the captain if they were over land or sea.

'We're heading for land,' the skipper shouted. He had a blazing plane on his hands, and the responsibility for the lives of the men from three countries. 'Get hold of the extinguishers, and see if you can put the fire out,' he added above the din. But they found that it was too far away from the fuselage for the extinguishers to have any effect. They even tried pouring coffee from their flasks over the burning wing!

The Wellington was going down the coast of the Zuider Zee, still at the same altitude of 13,000 feet, for a few minutes when Widdowson yelled for Ward, to ask him how the fire was getting on. Ward told him that it was still burning but had not gained anything after that first flare up, so the skipper decided to try to make the sea-crossing to the English coast. Thoughts of abandoning the aircraft were now forgotten. It would be better than parachuting down, probably to be taken prisoner and spend interminable years in some prisoner of war camp. 'Yes', thought Widdowson, 'better to be in a dinghy in the sea than in a camp.' And they might well actually experience this if the bomber did not hold up for the crossing. The sea looked very calm in the moonlight, yet here, high above it, all was far from calm. The engine and the wing both had intermittent spurts of searing flame gushing from them: a torrid trail in their wake.

Widdowson suggested that someone might get the axe working and attempt to cut a hole in the side of the fuselage, so that he could lean out and at least see what might be done with the fire.

While Widdowson was grappling with the full-time task of trying to keep a heavy bomber under complete control with a fire raging in one wing, he did not know what Ward was doing to combat this danger to their return. By the time Ward decided to act, the fire had been fed by petrol from a split pipe and still seemed likely to get an overwhelming grip on the whole aircraft.

Ward began his amazing attempt to overcome the fire. He had in mind trying to smother it with a cockpit-cover which happened to be in use as a cushion. At first he proposed to discard his parachute to reduce wind resistance, but the rest of the crew finally persuaded him not to do so. Widdowson was flying at a reduced speed, but could not know exactly what Ward was proposing –to get out on the wing itself.

A rope from the dinghy was tied securely around him, though this seemed scant help and might actually become a danger if he were blown off the wing. With the help of the navigator, he climbed through the narrow astro-hatch, and put on his parachute. Despite the slower speed of the bomber, wind-pressure must still have made the operation intensely awkward.

Now let Ward take up the story in his own words:

First I had to hang on to the astro-hatch while I worked out how I was going to do it, then I hopped out on to the wing. I kicked holes down the side of the fuselage which exposed the geodetics and gave me my foothold. I held on with one hand until

I had got two foot-holds on the wing. Fire and blast from the Messerschmitt's cannon-shells had stripped part of the wing-covering, and that helped.

Then I caught hold of some of the sections of the wing with the other hand and managed to get down flat on to the wing with my feet well dug in and hanging on with both hands. Once I could not get enough hold and the wind lifted me partly off the wing and sent me against the fuselage again. But I still had my feet twisted in, and I managed to get hold of the edge of the astro-hatch and worked myself back on to the wing again.

It was just a matter of getting somewhere to hang on to. It was like being in a terrific gale, only much worse than any gale I've ever known.

As I got along the wing I was behind the airscrew, so I was in the slipstream as well. Once or twice I thought I was going. I had the cockpit-cover tucked underneath me, and as I lay flat on the wing I tried to push the cover down through the hole in the wing on to the leaking pipe, where the fire was coming from. But the parachute on my chest prevented me from getting down close enough to the wing, and the wind kept on lifting me up.

The cover nearly dragged me off. I stuffed it down through the hole, but as soon as I took my hand away the terrific wind blew it out again. My arms were getting tired and I had to try a new hold. I was hanging on with my left arm when, as soon as I moved my right hand, the cover blew out of the hole again and was gone before I could grab it. The rear gunner told me afterwards he saw it go past his turret.

After that there was nothing to do but to get back again. The navigator kept a strain on the rope and I pulled myself back along the wing and up the side of the fuselage to the astro-hatch, holding on as tight as I could. Getting back was worse than going out, and by this time I was pretty well all in. The hardest of the lot was getting my right leg in. In the end, the navigator reached out and pulled it in.

Although Ward could not keep the cover in the hole, he did what he set out to do: stop the fire from spreading. There was now no danger of it encroaching beyond the area of the petrol pipe, since no fabric remained near by, and in due course it burned itself out.

So the Wellington went on its way across the North Sea, while Ward recovered from his superhuman efforts; all in darkness, remember. When the plane had nearly reached home some of the petrol that had collected in the wing suddenly surprised them all by blazing up alarmingly —but it died down as quickly as it had begun.

All that was left now was for Widdowson to be able to bring the damaged aircraft down to ground again. There would be no dinghies in the North Sea if he could help it! He pumped the undercart down, and got it locked by means of the emergency system. Then the problem was to land without flaps or wheel brakes. But after all they had survived so far, these seemed almost trivial difficulties. Widdowson veered the Wellington round over the airfield, lost height, and came in pretty fast —though as slow as he could. The ground rushed up to meet them; then came the bump —but only a slight one. In the circumstances the landing was a fairly decent one. The bomber lost speed, but still plodded on too fast for the airfield. Ground staff saw that it would overshoot, but there was nothing they could do. Down to about twenty or thirty mph, its wheels ground and ripped through a barbed-wire fence surrounding the field. Then it stopped suddenly. They were all safe and sound.

'Sergeant Ward seemed to take what he had done as a matter of course,' said Widdowson afterwards, 'but in my opinion it was a most wonderful show.' Wing-walking at ninety mph, two-and-a-half miles up, in the middle of the night! It certainly was a wonderful show, and it won the Victoria Cross for Ward. Widdowson, too, won the DFC, and the rear gunner, Sergeant Allen Robert James Box, received the DFM.

Once again, however, this was not to be the end of the story. The award of the Victoria Cross was announced on 5 August 1941. Meanwhile, Ward went out on three more operational flights. Then, in recognition of his exploit, he was made captain of a Wellington, with a crew of sergeants –an experienced crew, some with as many as twenty-two flights. They were, in fact, the crew with whom Sergeant Ward had come to his squadron from their operational training unit. While Ward was serving as second pilot under Widdowson they worked under another captain.

On the night of 13 September they took part in an attack against the German battlecruisers at Brest. Then only a few nights later they were over Germany again. The next day the Air Ministry issued the following bulletin:

Sergeant James Allen Ward, who recently won the VC, is reported missing. His Wellington bomber, from 75 (New Zealand) Bomber Squadron, did not return from a recent attack on Germany.

The bomber took off a few minutes after eight o'clock, and nothing was heard from it after a signal at a time when it was almost certain that the target had been reached.

CHAPTER SEVENTEEN

Six Desert VCs in Ten Days

Geoffrey Keyes, George Gunn, John Beeley, John Campbell, Philip Gardner, James Jackman

The desert war was hotting up, and six VCs were won in a short spell of ten days. The first of these went to Lieutenant Colonel Geoffrey Charles Tasker Keyes, of the Royal Scots Greys, Royal Armoured Corps, for his part in the raid on General Rommel's German headquarters.

Early in October 1941 six officers and fifty-three other ranks of the Scottish Commando were placed under the operational command of the Eighth Army. It was decided to use them in a bold attempt at striking at the core of the enemy by landing far behind his lines and attacking his headquarters. Four detachments were formed for this purpose: the first to raid General Rommel's house at Beda Littoria; the second to assault the Italian headquarters at Cyrene; the third, the Italian Intelligence centre at Apollonia; while a fourth detachment was to cut telephone and telegraph communications.

The first problem was how to get the force to its destination. It was not possible to use destroyers, for the risk of air attack was too great, and it was therefore decided to take them in two submarines, HMS *Torbay* and HMS *Talisman*. On reaching their immediate destination they would paddle themselves ashore in rubber boats.

On the evening of 10 November the *Torbay* and the *Talisman* slipped and sailed from Alexandria, moving westward in fair weather, without incident. The Scottish Commando was in the highest spirits.

'All ranks were greatly interested,' runs the official report, 'in what was to us a novel method of approaching an objective, and the soldiers were high in their praise of the way in which they were fed and accommodated.'

The first landing was made from HMS *Torbay*, which closed the chosen beach at dusk on 14 November. That the submarine reached her exact destination without undue difficulty was due, not only to sound navigation, but also to the calculated daring of a British officer, Captain J. E. Haselden who, dressed as an Arab, had been moving behind the enemy's lines, and had established friendly relations with some of the local inhabitants. His signals from the beach were seen, and preparations to land the Scottish Commando began. The weather was deteriorating; the wind had freshened, and the swell was now considerable. Four of the rubber boats were washed away, and much time was lost retrieving them. Eventually the landing was successfully made; but, instead of the estimated one hour, it took five hours to accomplish.

Meanwhile HMS *Talisman* was lying some distance off, awaiting the signal that the landing from HMS *Torbay* had been completed. The weather got worse and worse, and Colonel Laycock had just decided to postpone the operation until the following night when the expected signal from the *Torbay* was received. The landing from the *Talisman* took place in a heavy sea which capsized most of the boats, throwing the men into the water. All of them, with the exception of Colonel Laycock and seven other ranks who reached the shore, swam back to the submarine.

Once ashore, Colonel Laycock and his small party, which had now joined those who had landed from HMS *Torbay*, took cover in a convenient wadi for the remainder of that night and for the following day. The bad weather continued with a heavy sea still running, and it did not seem possible that the *Talisman* would be able to land troops when darkness came. On the other hand, General Auchinleck's offensive against Rommel was about to open, and Colonel Laycock was well aware that any immediate action he could take against the enemy would be of great and immediate value to the Eighth Army, who were now getting ready to advance.

He decided not to wait, but had therefore to modify his plan, and divide the party into two detachments. Lieutenant Colonel Keyes, in command of the first detachment, was to attack the German headquarters and the house of General Rommel. He had with him Captain Campbell and seventeen other ranks.

The second detachment, Lieutenant Cook and six other ranks, was ordered to cut the telephone- and telegraph-wires at the crossroads south of Cyrene. Colonel Laycock decided to remain at the rendezvous with a sergeant and two men, to form a beachhead and keep the reserve ammunition and rations. They would also be ready to receive the remainder of the commandos who, it was hoped, would be put ashore on the following night.

Thus did Colonel Laycock and his officers plan through that long day hidden in the wadi. The weather was at no time good, and became very bad as the hours went by. A gale of wind, accompanied at times by torrential rain, howled through their place of concealment, and everyone was once more wet to the skin.

The detachments moved off at seven o'clock in the evening, accompanied by Arab guides who, however, abandoned them after a few miles. They therefore lay up in another suitable wadi and slept for four hours. The next day they again hid and in the evening, meeting with a party of Arabs who were friendly, were guided to a spot some ten miles from Beda Littoria, where they dumped their surplus clothing and rations. On both these nights Colonel Laycock visited the beach, but there was still a heavy surf, and conditions for landing were impossible.

At seven in the evening of 17 November the detachments made ready to move to their objectives. Torrential rain had fallen all day; they were cold and soaked to the skin, but their spirit was high. No. 1 detachment, under Lieutenant Colonel Keyes, were led to within a few hundred yards of General Rommel's headquarters by friendly Arabs. Here they lay up awaiting zero hour, which was to be at *one minute to midnight*, but while there they were apprehended by a party of Arabs in uniform.

Captain Campbell, however, allayed their suspicions by explaining in German that the force belonged to a German unit.

The plan was for Lieutenant Colonel Keyes, with Captain Campbell and Sergeant Terry, to enter the house of the German commander-in-chief and search it. Outside three men were to destroy the electric-light plant, five to keep an eye on the garden and the car park, two to stand outside a nearby hotel and prevent anyone from leaving it, and two more to watch the road on each side of the house. The two remaining men were to guard whichever way Lieutenant Colonel Keyes chose for entering the house.

Every one was in position a little before midnight. Then the house was reconnoitred, but no way in could be found either through the back or through any of the windows. Lieutenant Colonel Keyes and his companions therefore went up to the front door and beat upon it, Captain Campbell demanding in German that it should be opened. Inside was a sentry. Hearing a peremptory order shouted at him from outside, he pulled open the door, and was at once set upon. He showed fight but was overpowered, unfortunately not silently, and Captain Campbell was compelled to shoot him, and the shot roused the house. Two men began to run downstairs from the first floor, but a burst of tommy-gun fire from Sergeant Terry sent them scampering back again. The lights in the rooms of the ground floor were extinguished, but no one attempted to move.

Lieutenant Colonel Keyes and Captain Campbell began a search of the ground floor. There was no one in the first room, but in the second the Germans were awaiting them, and on throwing open the door Lieutenant Colonel Keyes was met by a burst of fire, and fell back into the passage, mortally wounded.

Sergeant Terry emptied three magazines from his tommy-gun into the darkened room, then Captain Campbell threw in a grenade and slammed the door. He and Sergeant Terry picked up Lieutenant Colonel Keyes and carried him outside, where he died. He received the posthumous award of the Victoria Cross. While bending over him, Captain Campbell had his leg broken by a stray bullet.

The enemy had been taken by surprise, but most unfortunately General Rommel himself was absent. He was apparently attending a party in Rome. Three German lieutenant colonels on his staff were killed and a number of soldiers were killed and wounded. Captain Campbell ordered Sergeant Terry to collect the detachment, and to throw all their remaining grenades through the windows. Captain Campbell then ordered the party to withdraw and to leave him behind, since in his wounded condition they could not hope to carry him over eighteen miles of difficult country to the beach. He was taken prisoner.

The party moved off, being joined by the three men detailed to destroy the electric-lighting plant. In this they had been partially successful, though some of the charges soaked by the torrential rain had not exploded. A grenade placed in the armature had, however, done considerable damage. Sergeant Terry led his party back, and eventually reached Colonel Laycock at the rendezvous on the evening of 18 November.

Meanwhile the other detachment had reached the crossroads of Cyrene and blown up a petrol distribution post. But they never returned to the rendezvous.

This was not the end of the story of the raid on Rommel. That night the sea was too rough for the submarine *Torbay* to pick up the party from the beach, though she did float ashore a rubber boat containing food and water.

At first light a defensive position was adopted, the main detachment near the caves they had occupied, while two smaller detachments protected the eastern and western flanks of the position. The morning wore on; all was quiet; the wind and sea were abating; the hopes of the party were rising. But at noon shots were heard. They came from the westernmost sentry group, who were in action against some Italian native levies, known to be in the neighbourhood. Colonel Laycock was not unduly worried. He felt confident that he and his men would be able to keep off the Arabs until darkness, and then retire to the beach. Two small parties were sent out to outflank the enemy, but did not succeed in doing so, for by now German troops had appeared, while beyond them was a considerable party of Italians. These remained on the skyline about a mile to the north, and took no part in the fighting.

One of the small parties returned, having been able to advance about a quarter of a mile and come into action. After their tommy-gun jammed, the officer with them, Lieutenant Prior, continued to advance alone until wounded. With great difficulty, he crawled back to the main position.

The Germans were by now maintaining a sustained fire, and it became evident about two o'clock in the afternoon that it would be impossible to hold the beach against such superior forces. The only alternative was to abandon the position, hide in the Jebel, the broken hills in the interior, and await the advance of the Eighth Army.

When the enemy were no more than 200 yards from the caves Colonel Laycock ordered the detachment to split up into small parties, dash across the open, and seek the cover of the hills inland. There they could either try to get in touch with HMS *Talisman*, which they knew would be lying off an alternative beach that night, or they could hide in the wadis which abounded, and await our forces. Lieutenant Prior, who was grievously wounded, was left behind with a medical orderly and ordered to surrender. The party then scattered.

Colonel Laycock found himself with Sergeant Terry. They crossed half a mile of open country, being continually sniped at, but neither of them was hit. Once in the shelter of the Jebel, which offered excellent cover, they set out together to join the Eighth Army.

Eventually the colonel and the sergeant joined the British forces at Cyrene, forty-one days after they had originally set out. They were the only members of the party to do so. It was Christmas Day, 1941, and when he had eaten his Christmas dinner Colonel Laycock flew to Cairo to make his report, which resulted in Lieutenant Colonel Keyes receiving the VC.

Now came one of the decisive encounters of the desert war. Three VCs were won on the same day in the battle of Sidi Rezegh, in the Libyan desert, one by a subaltern, another by a rifleman, the third by a major general. The date was 21 November 1941.

Second Lieutenant George Ward Gunn, Royal Horse Artillery, had command of a troop of four anti-tank guns, part of a battery of a dozen guns attached to the Rifle Brigade column. At 10 a.m. they engaged and drove off a covering force of enemy tanks, but by mid morning the main attack developed by fully sixty enemy tanks. Twelve guns were not much in the face of this force, much less Gunn's own four weapons. Despite the overwhelming weight of armour rolling towards them, Gunn drove from gun to gun during the attack in an unarmed vehicle, encouraging his men.

Soon it became a case of reorganizing his dispositions, as first one gun and then another was knocked out by fire from the apparently irresistible advance. At last, only two guns could still operate and these were the focus of converging fire from the tanks. Immediately after this, the enemy destroyed one of these remaining pair. The portee of the other was set on fire, and all its crew blown up or wounded, with the exception of the sergeant. The gun itself, by some fluke, was still undamaged.

The battery commander began to battle with the flames, and as soon as Gunn spotted this he ran through intense fire to help him. Gunn got the one remaining anti-tank gun into action on the burning portee, sighting it himself while the sergeant acted as loader.

The enemy fire concentrated increasingly on this sole surviving weapon, and any second the flames from the portee might reach the ammunition with which it was loaded. A hopeless plight, most people would say. Gunn got the weapon going, and, with this hell all around, he managed to loose off between forty and fifty rounds at the advancing tanks. So accurate was his aim in these chronic conditions that he hit at least two enemy tanks still about 800 yards away. The two tanks blazed away under the sun as Gunn damaged several others. But for his example of extreme courage, the enemy tanks would certainly have overrun the Eighth Army's position at Sidi Rezegh.

Suddenly Gunn fell dead, shot through the forehead. So to the MC, which he won for his deeds while one of the Tobruk garrison, there was added the VC.

Not far away, on that same day at Sidi Rezegh, a battalion of the King's Royal Rifle Corps were attacking a strong position.

Rifleman John Beeley's company was pinned down by fire at point-blank range, both from the front and the flank. The terrain was actually an aerodrome, so two of its main characteristics were flatness, and openness, which made the position very vulnerable. Things had gone badly in Beeley's company, and all the officers except one —as well as many of the NCOs —had been killed or wounded. It was a time to act.

Beeley knew there could be no sort of cover, yet on his own initiative he got on his feet, carrying a Bren gun, and ran right forward towards an enemy post. In this strongpoint there were three powerful weapons: an anti-tank gun, a heavy machine gun, and a light one.

The rifleman —one of twin brothers —covered thirty interminable yards over the empty expanse of airfield, discharging a complete magazine from his Bren at the post, from a range of just twenty yards, as if bowling a ball to a batsman. He killed or wounded the whole crew of the anti-tank gun, silenced the post altogether, and enabled his platoon to advance across the flat, lethal landscape. Lethal because by this time Beeley had been hit in at least four places, and fell dead across his gun, as he must have known would happen sooner or later. Yet, by his inspiration, his comrades went on to take their objective, and took 700 prisoners.

Gunn and Beeley were just two of the men who died in the battle of Sidi Rezegh.

The third Victoria Cross won in this battle went to Major General John Charles Campbell, who survived his VC action at Sidi Rezegh, only to die in a tragic way not long afterwards.

'Jock' Campbell was serving in the ranks of a territorial regiment at the outbreak of the First World War, and received a commission six months later. He fought in France and Belgium until a month before the Armistice, was wounded twice, mentioned in dispatches, and won the Military Cross. But he had another war ahead of him.

It was no accident that he was in the Royal Horse Artillery, for he was a famous horseman, and for four years between the wars had been an instructor at the Weedon Equitation School. He played polo, rode at point-to-point meetings, and hunted with the Pytchley.

For his leadership in Libya., in August and September, 1940, he had been awarded the DSO. On five occasions he commanded harassing sorties of tanks and guns, inflicting loss on the enemy, and showing great energy and endurance.

In December of the same year, in the first stage of General Sir Archibald Wavell's advance, he gained a bar to his DSO by coolly commanding his men to beat off air attacks over the desert. One day while performing his duties in an open truck he encountered seventeen bomber and twenty-four fighter attacks.

By November 1941 he had been made a brigadier, and commanded troops including a regiment of tanks in the area of Sidi Rezegh Ridge and the aerodrome where Beeley was to win his VC.

Campbell's small force holding this important ground was repeatedly attacked by hosts of enemy tanks and infantry on 21 November. The brigadier made it his duty to be wherever the situation seemed most dangerous, and his troops saw him all the time either moving about vulnerably on his feet or in his open car.

In this car he carried out several reconnaissances for counter-attacks by his tanks, whose senior officers had all become casualties early in the day. Standing in his car with a blue flag, oblivious to the danger, Campbell personally formed up tanks under close and concentrated fire from all nature of enemy weapons. By some providence, neither he nor his crew was hit.

On the following day enemy attacks intensified, and once more Campbell kept in the forefront of the fighting, staging counter-strikes with what tanks remained at his disposal, and personally controlling the fire of his guns. Twice he leapt to man guns and to replace casualties who had fallen from them.

During the final enemy attack on 22 November, Campbell was wounded, yet insisted on staying in the thick of the fight. In severe pain, he controlled the fire of batteries that blasted enemy tanks to molten metal from point-blank range. He even acted as loader to one of the guns himself. All the while he was yelling, shouting.

Like a man possessed, he ran from tank to tank, banging on the steel doors, encouraging, helping, ordering. It was while he was out in the open like this that something struck him in the side, but 'Jock' Campbell refused to stop, refused to be evacuated.

As his citation states prosaically, Campbell caused heavy casualties to be inflicted on the enemy.

On 26 February 1942, Campbell was a passenger in a car which overturned, and he was killed.

But back in the desert battles, on the morning of 23 November 1941, two armoured cars of the King's Dragoon Guards had been put out of action. Captain Philip John Gardner, Royal Tank Regiment, received orders to take two tanks to help these vehicles, which he found still under the guns of the enemy, and very close to them. The two cars were, in fact, 200 yards apart, and just standing there helplessly, being fired on from close range, and being systematically smashed to pieces. War in the desert was like war anywhere else now, with no mercy given.

Gardner told the second tank to give him covering fire, and then he manoeuvred his own tank close up to the foremost of the unfortunate armoured cars. He got out of the tank, and, with his head down, he ploughed towards the pulverized target on foot, and tied a tow-rope to the car.

An officer lay beside it with both his legs blown off. Gardner lifted him into the car, then gave the signal to start towing. But the tow-rope broke. Gardner had to return to the armoured car from the tank, and on his way bullets hit his arm and leg. Despite these wounds, he summoned up the strength to lift the other officer out of the crippled car and carry him back to the tank, placing him on the back engine louvers, and climbing alongside to hold him on. While the tank was being driven back to relative safety, heavy shellfire caught it, killing the tank crew loader. The legless officer lived, however, due to Gardner's gallantry.

Two days later, not far from the place where Gardner saved the officer's life, Captain James Joseph Bernard Jackman was in command of a machine-gun company of the Royal Northumberland Fusiliers in the tank attack on the Duda ridge.

As the British tanks reached the crest of the rise, they made clear targets for every sort of enemy gun, which hit them like some sudden storm blowing up in the desert. So overwhelming was this fire that a wave of doubt inevitably rippled through the brigade whether they could hold on to the position they occupied so vulnerably.

The tanks slowed to 'hull-down' positions, and settled to try and beat down the enemy fire before proceeding farther. As they did this, Jackman rushed up the ridge, leading his machine-gun trucks. Near the crest he spotted that anti-tank guns were concentrating on the flank of the tanks, in addition to the rows of batteries which the tanks were engaging in front of them.

At once he started to get his guns into action as calmly as though he were on manoeuvres somewhere near Salisbury Plain, and so secured the right flank. Then he turned to the left flank. Standing up in the front of his own vehicle, Jackman led the other trucks actually across, the front between the British tanks and enemy guns —there was no other way —to get them into action on the left of the Duda ridge.

Most of the tank commanders could scarcely help seeing this amazing action, and it did a lot to inspire the tank crews not to relinquish the position they had gained.

Throughout the attack on the ridge Jackman coolly directed his guns to their positions, and indicated targets for them. At that stage he seemed to be bearing a charmed life, standing exposed in his truck, but later on the inevitable happened, and he was killed.

Six desert VC in ten days.

CHAPTER EIGHTEEN

Japan Enters the War

ARTHUR SCARF

So Britain battled on in Europe, with the aid of the Empire troops and the free forces from occupied countries. When 1941 was nearly over, another aspect of the war began —with the attack on Pearl Harbor, on 7 December. Eyes suddenly swung to the Far East, although operations had been proceeding in the Pacific and elsewhere for over two years. Now America was in the struggle as well. And it was in the East —Malaya, to be more precise —that the next Victoria Cross was won. This happened only two days after Pearl Harbor, but the award was not made until 21 June 1946, when the full facts came to light from prisoners of war.

The man: Squadron Leader Arthur Stewart King Scarf.

Scarf was born at Wimbledon, where he later attended King's College School. When the award was announced the headmaster told the school of this latest addition to their record of six DSOs and Bars, seven DSCs, twenty-three MCs, seventeen DFCs and one George Medal. Mr W. H. Nicholas, one of the masters who taught Scarf remembered him then as 'a fellow with a very restless nature, whose main ambition was to join the RAF. A pleasant boy, maybe not frightfully brainy, but a fine, ordinary chap.'

It was this ordinary chap who would later earn the Victoria Cross in Malaya. Scarf fulfilled his ambition to join the RAF by entering as a pupil-pilot in 1936. Then came war, and in April 1940 Scarf met Sister Elizabeth ('Sally') Lunn at a dinner in Singapore. A week later they were engaged, and married before the end of the year. To be near her husband, she joined the Malayan Government nursing service, and it was at the hospital at Alor Star, Malay States, that she was serving when December 1941 dawned. By now Scarf had five years' service behind him — and a squadron. He had never reached the first fifteen at rugger, but this was much more important, both to him and his country.

On 9 December 1941, all available aircraft from the RAF Station, Butterworth, Malaya, were ordered to make a daylight attack on the advanced operational base of the Japanese Air Force at Singora, Thailand. From this base enemy fighter squadrons were supporting landing operations by the Japs.

The aircraft detailed for this sortie were literally on the point of taking off when the Japs struck. Out of the Malayan sky came a host of planes painted with the hated Rising Sun. Certainly this was now in the ascendant. How long before this whole new war would be over in the East? Screeching fiendishly as they came, the Japs dive-bombed Butterworth field, and coupled with it a low-level machine-gun onslaught for extra measure. The surprise was complete. Every British aircraft was either destroyed or damaged —except the Blenheim piloted by Squadron Leader Scarf. Somehow, and by some strange fortune, he had got his plane airborne just a few seconds before the sudden strike of the enemy. As the leader of the proposed sortie, he was the first in the air.

But just then all he could do was to circle the airfield in his unwieldy Blenheim bomber, and watch the Jap attack come and go. And then, just as suddenly, they had, in fact, gone. The smoke cleared, and the dry dust settled over Butterworth to reveal to Scarf the whole disastrous panorama. Planes lay gutted or burning. Men caught without protection lay dead, shot up by the machine-gun fire which had so thoroughly raked the field.

He thought quickly. It would have been more than reasonable for him to abandon the projected offensive operation in view of this devastation. In any case, it had been intended definitely as a formation sortie. The whole plan assumed different and infinitely more dangerous proportions when converted into terms of one lone aircraft attempting to attack a Jap airbase in daylight.

Scarf decided to press on to Singora in his single aircraft. Stung by the sight of what he had just seen, he was prepared to face anything to try and inflict some retaliatory damage on the enemy. He knew, of course, that this individual action of his could not really inflict much material damage on the enemy, but he did appreciate the moral effect which it would have on the rest of the squadron, who were helplessly watching their aircraft crackling with fire on the ground.

Scarf completed his attack quite successfully. That sounds simple, but it was far from so. The ring of ack-ack around the advanced airbase at Singora flared into furious activity at the appearance of his poor, lone Blenheim. Somehow he got through the flak safely. Then the Jap fighters swarmed and buzzed around the bomber, doubtless wondering what kind of man the pilot was, who would dare to launch a lone assault on a whole airfield. Scarf's luck was too good to last. The inevitable came. Whether by flak or fire from a fighter's spitting guns, he was terribly wounded. Despite the agony, Scarf flew on, out of the airfield area, back towards the Malayan border. He was losing blood in large amounts. The enemy engaged him in a running fight all that weary way back to the border. He fought a brilliant evasive action in a valiant attempt to return to his base, but although he hung on to consciousness as if it were life, he just could not humanly make it. The Blenheim began to lose height, and through a horrible haze of pounding pain that no one should have to endure, he somehow made a successful forced-landing at Alor Star, without causing any injury to his crew.

Scarf was rushed to Alor Star hospital as soon as possible. The bomber had come down quite close to this hospital, where his wife was serving as a nursing sister.

They brought him in on a stretcher. He was still conscious, even then. Elizabeth hurried out to meet him. His left arm was badly damaged and bullet holes had torn into his back, but he was cheerful and spoke to her. She hoped they would be in time.

A blood transfusion was necessary, and she volunteered. The two were put in adjoining beds, and Elizabeth gave two pints of her blood, but the transfusion was never completed.

They could not wait before operating on him. Scarf was taken to the operating theatre, while his wife waited. It was all like some nightmare. The wounds, the transfusion, and now the operation. But as a nurse she was used to such things. Meanwhile all she could do was wait. Wait –for two long hours. No news reached her, so she could not stand it any longer. She got up and went to see what had happened. Scarf had just died from secondary shock. Elizabeth walked away.

Bayonets out East

John Osborn, Arthur Cumming, Charles Anderson, Bruce Kingsbury, John French

Now America and Japan were in the war and eyes turned to the East.

Hong Kong, that out-post of the British Empire which was being defended by Canadians, among other troops, would soon be falling to the Japanese.

Company Sergeant Major John Robert Osborn belonged to a company of the Winnipeg Grenadiers, Canadian Infantry Corps. On the morning of 19 December, 1941, his company became divided during an attack by them on Mount Butler, a hill rising steeply above sea-level and overlooking the famous harbour of Hong Kong, with its quaint collection of trading and native craft.

But the Canadians were not admiring the view on that day. A part of the company led by Osborn captured the hill at the point of the bayonet, and held it for three hours, until superior forces of Japanese and fire at an unprotected flank made the position untenable.

Osborn and a small group covered the withdrawal, and when their turn came to fall back he took on the enemy single-handed while the other Canadians joined the company. Osborn had to run the gauntlet of heavy rifle and machine-gun fire. With no consideration at all for his own danger he helped and directed stragglers to the new company position, exposing himself to heavier than ever enemy gun fire to cover their passage.

Afternoon now. Things were deteriorating again. The company had been cut off from the battalion and completely surrounded by the Japs, who were able to approach to within grenade-throwing distance of the slight depression which the company fought to preserve.

The enemy threw a grenade, followed by a second one, then several more. Each time Osborn rushed to pick it up and hurl it back before it had time to burst. Any moment he might have been killed. But each time he saved more Canadian lives.

Then the Japs got a grenade into a position where it was impossible for Osborn or anyone to pick it up and return it. Osborn at once realized this. It must have taken him a single second to decide what to do.

Shouting a sudden warning to his comrades, he threw himself down on top of the grenade, which went off, killing him instantly. His ultimate self-sacrifice certainly saved the lives of many other men.

> Company Sergeant-Major Osborn was an inspiring example to all throughout the defence which he assisted so magnificently in maintaining against an overwhelming enemy force for over eight-and-a-half hours, and in his death he displayed the highest qualities of heroism and self-sacrifice.

But Hong Kong fell, and it was not until after the war, when the prisoners of war returned to tell their story of Osborn's death, that he was awarded the VC, on 2 April, 1946.

The Japs swarmed south through Malaya. And with two bayonet wounds in the stomach, Brigadier Arthur Edward Cumming, 12th Frontier Force Regiment, carried on fighting, to try and stop them.

The events leading up to his actions are described well by Lieutenant General A. E. Percival in his book *The War in Malaya.*

> Events on the west coast had an immediate effect on our whole strategy in the east, for it was no longer certain that we should be able to hold the enemy north of the Kuala Kubu road junction for the specified time. Rapid decisions had to be taken but, before dealing with them, let us see what had been happening in the Kuantan area.
>
> We have seen that, after the fall of Kelantan, the Kuantan defences had been re-orientated so as to strengthen the northern flank facing the State of Trengganu and that the bulk of the force and its transport had been withdrawn west of the Kuantan River. After patrol encounters on the Trengganu coast, a Japanese column, which had been brought down in M.T., attacked our forward posts on the morning of the thirtieth (December, 1941) and confused fighting over a wide area took place in the rubber plantations throughout the day. At the same time, the Japanese Air Force made repeated attacks on targets in the Kuantan area, including the ferry across the Kuantan River, which had been split into two working halves. One half only remained in action. By the morning of the thirty-first, the Japanese were attacking the ferry and here some desperate fighting took place. They were held off, however, and during the following night our rearguards were withdrawn across the river and the ferry was destroyed. The effect of this, unfortunately, was not as great as had been hoped because, as a result of the dry season, the river higher up was in places quite fordable.
>
> During the next two days, no major action took place, but there were patrol encounters north of the aerodrome indicating that the enemy intended to attack from that direction. Reports were also received of a large enemy concentration in Kuantan Town itself and on this our artillery was turned —apparently with excellent results. Throughout the campaign, the Japanese troops showed an extraordinary lack of appreciation of the effect of artillery fire and frequently failed to take the most elementary precautions. There is no doubt that an artillery, when it got an

opportunity, did great damage. The pity was that the close country and lack of observation made opportunities so scarce.

Heath was now faced with the choice of relinquishing the Kuantan aerodrome or risking the loss of the 22nd Indian Brigade Group as a result of its communications being cut. The decisive battle was likely to come in the west, and we couldn't afford to lose this brigade with all its equipment. So early on the morning of the third (January, 1942) Painter received orders from Barstow to withdraw to Jerantut forthwith. By dusk the Kuantan force, except for the rearguard of the 2nd Frontier Force Regiment with some attached troops, was already on the way. At 7.30 P.M., the enemy delivered a furious attack against the rearguard as it was about to leave the aerodrome. There was fierce and bloody fighting at close quarters in which the darkness, added to the noise of shots and bursting shells, caused great confusion. Attack after attack was repelled as the rearguard gradually withdrew. Throughout Lt.-Col. Cumming, commanding the 2nd Frontier Force Regiment, was a tower of strength . . .

When the enemy penetrated into the positions Cumming took a small party of men and immediately counter-attacked until all his men had been killed or injured, and he himself had received two brutal bayonet wounds in the stomach.

In spite of great pain and weakness, Cumming drove in a carrier for more than an hour, under the heaviest fire, collecting isolated detachments. The dark made the whole scene unimaginably macabre, with friend and foe hard to distinguish. Cumming continued, however, and then got two further wounds, and fell unconscious.

The driver of the carrier tried to evacuate him, but he regained his senses and insisted on staying until he had ensured that the two of them were the sole survivors in the locality. Only then did he decide to withdraw. He lived to be decorated with the VC.

The Australians were in Malaya too. During the operations in Malaya from 18-22 January, 1942, Lieutenant Colonel Charles Groves Wright Anderson, in command of a small force, was sent to restore a vital position and to assist a brigade. His force destroyed ten enemy tanks. When later cut off he defeated persistent attacks on his position from air and ground forces, and forced his way through the enemy lines to a depth of fifteen miles. He was surrounded and subjected to very heavy and frequent attacks resulting in severe casualties to his force. He personally led an attack on the enemy with great gallantry. The Japs were now holding a bridge, and had succeeded in destroying four guns. Lieutenant Colonel Anderson, throughout all this fighting, protected his wounded and refused to leave them.

He obtained news by wireless of the enemy position, and so attempted to fight his way back through eight miles of occupied country. This proved to be impossible, and the enemy were holding too strong a position for any attempt to be made to relieve him.

On 19 January Lieutenant Colonel Anderson was ordered to destroy his equipment and make his way back as best he could round the enemy position.

Throughout the fighting, which lasted four days, he set a magnificent example of brave leadership, determination, and outstanding courage. He not only showed fighting qualities of a very high order, but throughout exposed himself to danger without any regard to his own personal safety.

The enemy had spread south to the very islands next to Australia, so it was appropriate that Aussies should win the VC defending their country and New Guinea.

Can one soldier save a battalion ? Yes —because this is what happened here. Firing his Bren gun in the face of most murderous automatic fire, Private Bruce Steel Kingsbury forced a path through Japanese lines in New Guinea, enabled vital ground to be taken, and saved his battalion from a deadly end.

His battalion had been holding a position in the Isurava area of the Kokoda Trail, on Papua, for two days against attacks that seemed never to stop.

On 29 August 1942, the enemy massed for an attack which broke the battalion's right flank. This created a desperate threat to the rest of the battalion and to its headquarters.

The only thing to do was regain the lost ground, but that would be easier said than done. Kingsbury was one of the few survivors of a platoon of the Anzacs who had been overrun and chaotically cut about. He at once volunteered to join a different platoon for the counter-attack.

It was then that Kingsbury rushed forward into terrific machine-gun fire and cleared a path right through the enemy. A human wedge, forcing himself through with the hammering of his Bren. Continuing to sweep and rake the Japs, he managed to kill a considerable number of them. But he could not spot a sniper hiding high in a tree above the battle zone. The sniper shot him dead at his moment of triumph. But he saved the battalion, and made possible the recapture of the position.

A week later at Milne Bay, on the afternoon of 4 September 1942, a company of an Australian infantry battalion attacked the Japanese position east of the Buna Mission, where it encountered terrific rifle and machine-gun fire.

The advance of the section of which Corporal John Alexander French was in command was held up by the fire from three enemy machine-gun posts, whereupon Corporal French, ordering his section to take cover, advanced and silenced one of the posts with grenades. He returned to his section for more grenades and again advanced and silenced the second post.

Armed with a Thompson sub-machine gun, he then attacked the third post, holding the gun low, and firing as he went forward. He was seen to be badly hit by the fire from this post, but he continued to advance. The enemy gun was silenced and his section pushed on to find that all members of the three enemy gun crews had been killed and that Corporal French had died in front of the third gun-pit.

By his cool courage and disregard of his own personal safety, this non-commissioned officer saved the members of his section from heavy casualties and was responsible for the successful conclusion of the attack. As long as there were men like French, the Japanese would never get to Australia.

CHAPTER TWENTY

Biplanes against Battleships

EUGENE ESMONDE

N ow a naval officer takes his place among the VCs of the air —one of the two Fleet Air Arm men to be considered worthy of the bronze cross of courage. And since he was in the Navy, it is only proper that his action be concerned with ships; in fact, with that redoubtable trio, the *Scharnhorst, Gneisenau,* and *Prinz Eugen.* Just ten months had passed since Campbell's attack on Brest, and now this operation would go down in history alongside its predecessor: two amazing attacks on the pride of the German Navy.

In the spring of 1939, the Royal Navy invited Eugene Esmonde to join the Fleet Air Arm with the rank of lieutenant commander. Esmonde had been a pilot with Imperial Airways, but now he threw his energies and experience into service with the wings of the Navy.

He was commissiooned to HMS *Courageous.* She was torpedoed only days after war broke out; Eugene escaped. Next came a period at Lee-on-Solent, and at another air station in the south, where he trained pilots.

1940 passed. In the spring of 1941 Eugene and his twin brother, James, motored from Dublin to Drominagh. James was on leave from the Gold Coast. Eugene knew that he would soon be off once more aboard HMS *Victorious.* At this time, April 1941, he was leading a squadron of Swordfish aircraft on the carrier.

May now. A precious convoy sailed well to the south of Esmonde's beloved Ireland. Many miles away the German battleship *Bismarck,* with the *Prinz Eugen* as her scout, steamed in their direction; but throughout May twenty-four British cruisers and the *Prince of Wales* shadowed the two ships. Admiral Tovey, in the *King George V,* was also closing on the enemy. Admiralty threw in all they had got to try to catch them. *Rodney* was summoned to the scene: *Ramillies* and *Revenge* too. Cruisers were guarding a breakout on another side, and a force under Admiral Somerville steamed at speed north from Gibraltar. The Germans sensed a net. *Bismarck* turned in her tracks to tackle her pursuers. But the brief encounter was made only to enable the *Prinz Eugen* to escape to Brest.

Eugene Esmonde came into the action. Tovey sent the *Victorious* on ahead to launch an air attack, with the aim of cutting the enemy's speed.

The *Victorious* had been commissioned only a short while. Some of the aircrew had hardly any battle experience. She released her nine torpedo-carrying Swordfish into a biting head wind, raging rain, and low cloud, on a 120-mile flight. For two hours they struggled. Then late in the evening they found the *Bismarck*. Going in under ferocious fire, they somehow scored a direct hit with a torpedo under the bridge.

Now it was night. An Atlantic night, void-black, and still lashed with rain. The squadron had scant experience of deck-landing in daylight. The captain of *Victorious* was very worried about their safe return —even assuming they located her. The homing beacon aboard had failed. Signal-lamps were lit instead, and, just as they had recorded that direct hit against all the odds, so somehow all nine of the Swordfish staggered back to their base.

Eugene peered into the gloom, and saw the pinpricks of light flickering, winking, through the rain: white specks in a black ocean. Surely he could never land there? He lost height. Still no sign of the carrier; just the lamps, closer now. How far off? It was hard to tell. They could be bigger lights farther off, or smaller ones nearer to him. Life was all hit or miss in these chronic conditions. He guided the Swordfish down to the deck. It bumped; the nose lifted, dropped —and he was down. And so were all of them very soon. They went into the wardroom —lights, drinks, another world. Lights, yes —but never could they be as friendly as the lamps burning up aloft along the flight deck, which had brought the nine aircraft back to the carrier.

The final chase, capture, and sinking of the *Bismarck* are history now. But the other naval Esmonde, John, played a part too. He was in the *Zulu*, one of Captain Vian's destroyers which was called in to help seal the *Bismarck*'s fate.

Eugene received the Distinguished Service Order.

First, the *Courageous*, then the *Victorious*, next the *Ark Royal*; the first and third —fated ships. Eugene joined the *Ark Royal* in August 1941.

Then came that day during November, and the voice over the BBC: 'The Admiralty regrets to announce the loss of HMS *Ark Royal*.' The news went on: 'Of the large ship's company, only one man lost his life.'

Gradually the story pieced itself together. Mortally hit a few miles from Gibraltar, the famous aircraft-carrier limped along in tow for nearly twelve hours. A torpedo had done its work well, though, and the vessel began to list badly. But by this time her Swordfish squadron had flown several sorties, carrying members of the crew to the safety of the Rock. A destroyer took off the rest of the 1,600 ship's company, and before the flight deck tilted too much, the last Swordfish ever to take off from the carrier winged its way towards Gibraltar. Eugene took a last look down at her as he circled round and headed for safety. The *Courageous* and *Ark Royal* — what next? he wondered.

He returned to England in late November for a review and march past of the Swordfish squadron at Lee-on-Solent, the Fleet Air Arm's base, where before the war people were often halted on the cliff-top road between Lee and Hillhead as a seaplane slid down the slipway, right across the road, and splashed and rocked into the summer sea opposite the Isle of Wight. Planes were still a novelty in those days —the mid-thirties. Now it was 1941, and a different story. On 2 December 1941, the Admiralty released pictures of the last hours of *Ark Royal*, and another chapter in Eugene's crowded life was concluded.

It was all recent history then. Only a few weeks earlier, before the Battle of the Channel, Eugene spent nearly a month's leave with his mother. Throughout December he relived part of his youth at Drominagh, and saw again, at an age of thirty-two, some of the scenes which were engraven on his memory through the intervening years, while the world's images had moved across his windscreen. Yes, it had been a long, long way back to Tipperary, from the pioneering peace days, and the whirl of war. The lough lay still. The leafless trees traced stark shapes across the skyline. But indoors the haven of home gave Eugene a peace he had not known for more than two years.

Soon the December days fell from the calendar till Christmas had come and gone; and with it went Eugene, back into battle. He wrote home to his mother regularly; personal letters, with no news of war. She could only wait. His letters told her he was well. That was all that mattered; as long as he kept well and did his duty. She hoped both would be possible.

Mrs Esmonde was not to know that the German battleships docked in Brest Harbour had to find a safer port soon. The battlecruisers *Scharnhorst* and *Gneisenau*, with the cruiser *Prinz Eugen*, all still needed repairs after the regular hammerings from the RAF bombers over the months. Now the need became increasingly urgent. The Allies knew this was so, and Esmonde's squadron, based on the Kent coast, at its own request, stood by at the beginning of February for immediate action if any or all of the big three decided to make their run up the coast for home. The squadron had been formed by Esmonde from his colleagues of the *Ark Royal*.

So to Thursday, 12 February 942, and the Battle of the Channel, or what has been recorded in naval annals as The Gallant Sortie.

11.00 hours. RAF HQ reported that the three ships had at last broken cover with an escort of destroyers, torpedo-boats, E-boats, minesweepers, and a fighter escort described as 'the biggest ever seen over a naval force'.

The Fleet Air Arm did not waste time. Already the enemy ships would be well along the French coast and nearing the Strait of Dover. The aim was to try and intercept this massive force of more than a couple of dozen surface craft, and attack before they could reach the sandbanks north-east of Calais; much more than a couple of dozen craft; some thirty-three in all, focused on the big three.

So six slow torpedo-carrying Swordfish biplanes battled towards their formidable target. Only a few MTBs, the Dover shore batteries, and a handful of fighters were able to support them in their desperate mission. The fighters zig-zagged across the course to keep their speed down to the trundling Swordfish, which looked like something out of the First World War, not the Second —and about to take on three of the greatest vessels in the world. Although the Swordfish had served the Royal Navy faithfully, they were, by 1942, regarded as definitely out of date, with their Pegasus III engines and single-gun turrets.

The enemy force had been sailing since fairly early morning. Now it was nearing noon, four hours later. They were through the Strait of Dover and in a position some ten miles north of Calais when Esmonde first spotted them. The other five crews of his depleted No. 825 Squadron had heard his orders earlier, and were intent on carrying them out. 'The *Scharnhorst, Gneisenau,* and *Prinz Eugen* have had the cheek to put their noses into the Channel. We're going to deal with them. Fly at fifty feet; close line astern. Individual attacks. Find your own way home.'

So the Swordfish sighted the enemy —first, the white wake of the destroyer-screen all around. The planes were six sitting targets for a hundred and more guns. Into the Channel of death . . .

They flew in arranged as two sub-flights of three aircraft each, flying in echelon. The first sub-flight, headed by Esmonde in his plane No. 5984/825, met a brutal barrage of fire as it covered the air only fifty feet above the wintry water. This came only from the smaller ships yet. A shell actually ricocheted off the water and hit the belly of Esmonde's plane, scarring those numbers. At the same time the gunner of the following plane was killed. But both aircraft, and the third one in this first half of the assault, struggled on towards their target.

Then the accompanying fighters came into action as Messerschmitt Me109s and Focke-Wulf 190s swooped down towards the trio of Swordfish. Some of the Luftwaffe managed to rip through the RAF fighter screen, and attacked Esmonde and his pair of following Swordfish. The Messerschmitts and Focke-Wulfs lowered their flaps and undercarriages to keep them down to the speed of the slug-gishly slow, torpedo-laden Swordfish. Esmonde lost contact with all his fighters.

Then almost at once a Focke-Wulf picked out Esmonde's plane, loosed a stream of fire down from its guns and completely destroyed the upper main plane of the Swordfish. Esmonde and his crew spun into the sea, never to be seen again.

Now it became merely a matter of time before all, or practically all, of the others were hit too. Carrying on at house-top, or mast height, the next two received a raking from sea and air so devastating that it seemed superhuman to expect them to stay in the air another moment. Hit after hit crashed into the cumbersome biplanes, but still they flew on, and managed to deliver their attacks before plunging into the sea close to the enemy vessels. Five men of the two crews were later rescued.

These wet and wounded survivors said that they had seen one of their torpedoes travelling well, and believed it had scored a hit. These men all received either the DSO or CGM.

So much for the fate of the first sub-flight. The second one followed, and flew in behind the ill-fated first three aircraft. Shattering salvoes spat across the inter-vening air towards them. An inferno of fire now focused on this last little flight. Shells, fragments, tracer —all converged around them as they went into the attack close line astern. The last that any of the survivors saw of these three planes was when they had to take violent evasive action over the thickest part of the German destroyer-screen. None were ever seen again. So the price exacted was all six Swordfish and thirteen men. All of these were mentioned in dispatches, and Esmonde, of course, became the first member of the Fleet Air Arm to win the Victoria Cross. His aim was to do what the fortunes of war had assigned to him to the full extent of his ability. It was not his fault that half a dozen Swordfish could not hope to sink what seemed to be half the German Navy. He had done his duty. For the Germans, it was all too easy.

One of the many tributes to Eugene Esmonde came from one of those five survivors:

'I know that if "Winkle" Esmonde were alive, and the same call came again, he would not hesitate to form another striking force —and we would follow him.'

Eugene Esmonde's body floated back to Britain, to the mouth of the River Medway. He is buried in the Catholic part of Gillingham cemetery.

The Little *Li Wo*

THOMAS WILKINSON

Few have heard of HM ship *Li Wo*, a patrol vessel of about 1,000 tons commanded by Temporary Lieutenant Thomas Wilkinson, Royal Naval Reserve.

Like Fegen of the *Jervis Bay*, Wilkinson came of seafaring stock. And like him, too, he was to serve in the Merchant Navy. He was born on 1 August 1898, and when he was just a boy of fourteen he joined his father's sailing sloop. During the War of 1914 he served in the ss *Alicinious*, a Blue Funnel Line vessel converted into a troopship. Four years after the armistice, he joined the Indo-China Steam Navigation Company. In 1936 he became a Master.

The *Li Wo* was launched at Hong Kong in 1938. She was designed for the company as a river boat to sail the upper reaches of the Yangtze, but because of the Far Eastern war, it was decided that she should be confined to the Yangtze Delta, working from Shanghai. With her tall and sedate sides and fairly flat bottom, she was clearly a river boat first and last.

Thomas Wilkinson was appointed her skipper and under his command she sailed the waters at the mouth of the Yangtze for a year or so. When war broke out the Royal Navy took her over, and she became a ship of war –though all that this meant was the addition of a single four-inch gun far forward, a couple of machine guns mounted on the high sun deck, and a depth charge thrower fixed at the stern. Her three-deck structure stayed; decks that reached right to the rudder, where they curved one over the other, and she still looked more like a ferry boat, a river boat, a peaceful transport, than a man-of-war. Those decks rose sheer, with no streamlining for extra speed. She was never intended to need speed. High up on the top sun deck hung two lifeboats, one to port, the other starboard. The White Ensign fluttered now above this deck. And *Li Wo* went to war.

Wilkinson became a temporary lieutenant, RNR. He took her out of the sheltered waters of the Yangtze, into the China Seas, and south to Singapore. On 12 February 1942, Singapore was a seething city. The harbour was dive-bombed repeatedly by Japanese aircraft; shrapnel and other scars marked the decks of the *Li Wo* as she lay there at anchor. Then Wilkinson received the order to make for Batavia. In the early hours of 13 February, two days before Singapore finally fell,

Wilkinson took her quietly out of harbour, with HMS *Fuk Wo*, another converted river boat, commanded by Lieutenant N. Cooke, RNR.

The ship's company of *Li Wo* was eighty-four officers and men, including one civilian. Mostly they were survivors from ships which had been sunk, but a few of them came from army and air force units. Her armoury was even less adequate, there being only a few dozen shells for her 4-inch gun.

The *Li Wo* and *Fuk Wo* moved silently through the before-dawn darkness of the Singapore Straits and anchored near the Raffles Light about 05.00. They waited for the first streaks of daylight before negotiating the Durian Strait minefield to the south-west of the Straits.

In the afternoon Japanese bombers attacked, and their relentless, high-level bombing scarred the ship. She beat all the attacks off, not without sustaining damage, and by teatime the assault finished.

After a conference, with the two ships anchored near a small island, Wilkinson and Cooke decided to steam full ahead through the night which was nearly upon them, and then anchor during the following day off Singkep till darkness dropped once more. That way they hoped to elude the enemy planes. Wilkinson put the plan into effect, knowing the odds against them were already heavy, but not yet overwhelming.

On 14 February 1942, two bombers discovered the hideout, but the ships managed to drive them off again. Clearly it was no good trying to hide any longer. The two river boats –now far from the Yangtze and plying a peaceful trade –separated. Still before noon, they parted. Soon afterwards, about 11.50, the *Li Wo* was sighted by a seaplane. Between 12.00 and 15.00 her hull and decks were damaged by very near misses from further air attacks. Still there was a chance, though.

Suddenly, at 16.00 to the north-east a convoy of small ships loomed out of the sea haze. This was bad enough with only the 4-inch gun as protection. But then came a second convoy of fifteen ships, some of which were as large as 6,000 tons, escorted by Japanese naval units, including a cruiser and several destroyers.

The moment of decision had arrived. Thomas Wilkinson called his First Lieutenant, Temporary Sub Lieutenant Ronald George Gladstone Stanton, RNR.

'What about it?' Wilkinson asked. 'Shall we go ahead?'

'I'm with you, sir,' Stanton said quickly.

They called the scratch ship's company together and Wilkinson told them that rather than try to escape he had decided to engage the convoy and fight to the last in the hope of inflicting some damage. Wilkinson knew, they all knew, that destruction of the ship was certain and their lives liable to be forfeited within hours.

He took the decision to fight in the knowledge that, after all the attacks they had sustained so far, the total number of shells left for the 4-inch gun was –thirteen. The figure could hardly have been more symbolic.

About 16.30 Wilkinson swung the ship round towards the enemy convoy. *Li Wo* hoisted her battle ensign and steamed straight for a transport some three times her size, which was four and a half miles off. The range of the nearest Jap destroyer was rather more, some seven miles.

Sub Lieutenant Stanton volunteered to man the 4-inch gun, totally exposed as it was on the fore deck.

'I want some help with this,' he called to the crew nearest him.

'Count rne in, sir,' The voice of Acting Petty Officer Arthur William Thompson came clear over the late afternoon air as the wake of the ship became wider and whiter with her increased speed. Thompson served as gun-layer coolly, effectively. Two officers besides Stanton, an Aussie stoker, and two able seamen completed the scratch gun crew.

Heading heedless of opposition right at the transport, *Li Wo* opened fire on the enemy. With the third shell from the little gun, a direct hit was scored, and the transport caught fire.

Still the *Li Wo* steamed in. The transport and three others of the convoy veered off abruptly, but the river boat was not to be defeated. Running the gauntlet of a hail of heavy calibre shells and machine-gun bullets, she pressed home her attack. Wilkinson meant to sink at least one of the enemy before his own flags were lowered. *Li Wo*'s two machine guns, firing from near the funnel, on the sun deck, returned all the fire they got.

The transport blazed badly. Wilkinson glanced down at his wristwatch. Time was running out fast for the genial skipper. He was not smiling now. It was 17.45. Minutes mattered. Before anything final happened to *Li Wo*, he had to make sure of the transport. For already the river boat was critically damaged.

'I'm going to ram her,' he told the coxswain. No other way could he be sure. The bows of the *Li Wo* turned towards the midships of the transport. Stanton and his men still stood by the gun only a few feet from the bows. Nearer, nearer, loomed the larger ship. Fifty yards, forty, twenty, ten, five.

They met, metal grinding against metal,. The transport was mortally hit. The crew abandoned her, and the next day she sank. But before that, long before, the end came to *Li Wo*. Wilkinson got the bows clear of the transport, leaving a gaping hole and dent, but by this time, nearly 18.00, the cruiser had closed in. *Li Wo* had no ammunition left. A short salvo finished the fight. Her main steam pipe and steering gear were both shattered, corpses of the crew lay grotesquely across the decks. The ship drifted helplessly.

'Pipe abandon ship,' Wilkinson ordered.

Rafts and wreckage supported those of the crew who still lived. One of the Japanese ships swung her machine guns round to the men struggling in the waters around the sinking ship. Bullets skimmed the surface, sending up tiny spurts, like stones thrown to skid over the water. The numbers of survivors dwindled: of a ship's company of eighty-four only ten got free from the ship.

At 18.07 Wilkinson was still standing on the bridge. At 18.08 the *Li Wo* sank silently from sight. The ten survivors reached land twenty miles from the point of the attack, but they were caught and made prisoners of war. Three of them died during the remaining years of the war. Only seven of the original eighty-four lived to tell the tale. Stanton was one of them. He received the Distinguished Service Order for fighting 'with steadfast courage in the face of overwhelming odds'. After the war he served the Indo-China Steam Navigation Company as a master.

Nine awards were announced as well as Wilkinson's Victoria Cross, including two posthumous mentions in dispatches.

The little ship *Li Wo*, of only 1,000 tons, lies at the bottom of an eastern ocean. But in the Imperial War Museum in London her scale model stands proud –as she was before she lived her last forty-eight hours out of Singapore; with broad streaks of camouflage down her sides and up to both the upper-deck bulwarks, with her anchor raised right at the bows, with her little companionway starting just above the waterline, with the Union Jack fluttering at her bows and the white ensign at the masthead. This is how she shall be remembered, as a little ship of peace which went to war and won the highest honour of all.

CHAPTER TWENTY-TWO

Bomb-disposal on Submarine

PETER ROBERTS, THOMAS GOULD

Mid-February, 1942, proved to be a vintage period for valour. Esmonde's gallantry on the 12th and Wilkinson's final heroism of the 14th were followed forty-eight hours later by another action which won not one VC but two. As with Wanklyn of the *Upholder*, a submarine was the setting. In fact, at one stage of his service, Lieutenant Peter Scawen Watkinson Roberts spent a short while under Wanklyn's command.

In February 1942, Peter Roberts was serving as First Lieutenant aboard HM Submarine *Thrasher*. He was also second in command.

Off the North African coast they got some remarkable intelligence information about the strength and sailing times of enemy convoys in the area. About this time, Lieutenant H. S. Mackenzie took over the *Thrasher*'s command. One of *Thrasher*'s assignments was to try to find the limits of a minefield off the coast. By a bit of intricate steering and the 'ping' of the Asdic they were supposed to trace its perimeter, but somehow *Thrasher* got in the middle of the mines, an acutely dangerous position. However, by still more intricate steering, they extricated themselves.

Then came a cloak-and-dagger interlude before 16 February dawned. *Thrasher* picked up an agent, who had once been an official of Imperial Airways and looked on the Mediterranean as Londoners do the Thames. They took him to Crete, dropped him offshore, and departed. The battle of Crete went badly just now. Several weeks later *Thrasher* received a signal to rendezvous at a certain beach at the south-west end of the island. Mackenzie and Roberts conferred. 'Signal says our agent friend may have got hold of some Aussies who'll have to pull out of the island. We've got to be ready to take an indefinite number aboard.'

'Sounds as if it's going to get a bit cramped,' said Roberts, 'not to mention stuffy.'

The submarine steamed at periscope depth towards Crete. When darkness fell she surfaced. Roberts went aloft to look at the shore. From the dim outline of a monastery at the top of a towering cliff a light flickered. On, off, on. Then a break. On, off, on. Roberts made an answering flash with his torch —only twice: there were German gun-posts on both sides of the bay. All seemed still, as water brushed lightly against the side of the sub.

'Have answered signal, sir,' he said quietly down to Mackenzie.

'Right. Then we'll go in. Trim for'ard,' the captain called. The vessel slid towards the shore. Her bows dipped and touched bottom. Engines stopped. For a moment nothing happened.

'What's happening up there, Peter?'

'As far as I can see, there are dozens of Aussies —and they all seem to have their girl friends with them!'

'Well, for God's sake let's get them aboard. This isn't the place for fond farewells.'

A rope was hurled ashore. And slowly the soldiers were coaxed towards the sub, wading out with the aid of the rope. Seventy Aussies clambered through the conning tower, dripping, practically naked, before the *Thrasher* removed to safety.

Then she went back to the waters off Crete, and on 16 February followed several ships into Suda Bay. She fired torpedoes at a heavily escorted supply ship, which was almost certainly sunk. She spotted an enemy aircraft when she was at periscope depth and just diving. About forty feet down the crew heard two loud 'clonks,' but they forgot them as the first of thirty-three depth charges fizzed down in the surrounding waters and rocked the sub to its very bolts. At length the counter-attack ended. *Thrasher* remained submerged till night, then surfaced, still close to the enemy coast and in waters where anti-submarine patrols were active day and night. The crew always knew that the sub might have to crash dive at any second while she was taking in fresh air and recharging batteries. As she came up to the surface, *Thrasher* began to roll.

'What do you think it is?' Roberts asked Mackenzie. But before an answer could be given the two senior officers heard a loud 'clang' and a grating noise as of metal rubbing against metal.

'Sounds as if there's something up on deck causing it.'

The conning tower was opened, and a rating reported a dark object rolling about on the casing (deck).

'Someone will have to go and take a look. The only thing it can be, I suppose, is a bomb from that blessed aircraft,' Mackenzie said tautly.

The inevitable surge forward followed. All the crew within range rushed to volunteer.

'Now wait a minute.'

'I'm the obvious one for this,' Roberts got in. 'You can't go,' he added to Mackenzie.

'And I'll go with you, sir,' Petty Officer Gould said quickly.

'Very well, you two,' Mackenzie decided. 'See what you can do, will you? But be careful.'

Gould was second coxwain in charge of the seamen on the upper deck, so he knew the shape of the sub outside better than most of the others. He would have to soon, too, because the night was fairly black and they could not risk torches. He was also quite an old hand in submarines, having joined them five years previously.

Mackenzie tapped his fingers on the periscope below. He knew that apart from the hazards to the crew of a bomb exploding, the effect on Roberts and Gould would be fatal. More than this, if he had to crash-dive due to an enemy attack, he would have no alternative but to slam the conning tower shut and leave the two men on top –to drown: for every single second counted in a crash-dive. They would be between the casing and the hull –trapped as the sub dived, buried beneath an ever-growing volume of water pouring in through the perforations of the casing.

Roberts got up on deck first. Gould followed. It was cold. They got their eyes used to the dark, but they could not waste too much time. Every minute was a danger not only to themselves, but the rest of the crew.

Peter Roberts saw the bomb. Then he saw a second . . .

'Two of them to tackle, PO. Better get a couple of empty sacks and a rope.'

Gould reappeared with them.

The first bomb lay fairly accessible on the perforated metal platform which is the casing. They crouched low over it. Just then the sub gave a lurch under the extra weight of the weapons and the bomb rolled from the port side of the casing over to starboard, where a rail stopped it. Between them they slipped the sacks underneath the bomb, and girdled it with the rope. Roberts eased past the bomb, then motioned the PO to do likewise. Roberts held the rope and handed a length of it to Gould. Together they dragged the bomb along the casing. Even on the sacks, it still seemed to grate and rub.

'How are you getting on?' Mackenzie called. 'Tell me when you've got it to the stern and I'll send her full speed ahead.'

Two hundred pounds of high explosive they pulled to the stern.

'Steady now. I'll shout *Now* when we're about to ditch it.'

'Now.'

Mackenzie sounded full speed ahead. The engines roared to life. A final heave and the bomb plopped into the water. No report. The sub had steamed clear just in case, though.

The second bomb was a different proposition.

'Not going to be so easy, Gould,' Roberts summed up after peering down at it.

The danger in dealing with it was going to be greater. It had penetrated the perforated casing and lay among the maze of pipes and torpedo tubes between the pressure hull and the casing. To reach it, Roberts and Gould had to wriggle a way through the hole the bomb had made in the metal grating. The torn metal edges scratched their clothes as they eased themselves through on their stomachs. Now they were really in cramped quarters –trapped beneath the mesh of metal that is the platform, with a live bomb for company.

Roberts did not recognize the type of bomb, so slipped his hand in his pocket and managed to get out a notebook and pencil. Gould shone a dimmed-out torch on the fuses of the bomb while Roberts wrote their details down shakily.

'Right. Now let's get on with shifting it.' He stuffed the book back in his pocket. His elbow hit the deck.

Still on their stomachs, they set about removing the bomb. Gould worked his way round to the after side and pushed at it. Roberts pulled it from the forward side.

The gap it had torn through the casing was not really enough to let them get it out that way. The nearest exit was a grating some twenty feet from its present position. Between this spot and the grating lay various projections which could not have been better designed as obstacles. Very slowly Roberts pulled it.

Suddenly it emitted a loud twang. They both gasped. A sound like a broken spring trying to make a contact. This could be the reason why the bomb had not gone off, and why any moment it might.

Gould pushed it gently, Roberts pulled. Over a pipe it bumped. Again the twang, sounding loud on the middle-of-the-night air. Up top a seaman peered anxiously down and reported progress back to the Commanding Officer.

Another effort and the bomb moved another foot. For half an hour now they had been working, yet there was still seventeen feet to go to the grating, and still the bomb twanged. It was a bomb with big tail-fins, and it measured some three feet six inches, and like its companion weighed about a couple of hundred pounds.

They could not use a rope on this one: just their bare hands, which slipped every so often round the smooth sides of the black metal bomb.

Roberts gripped the hull with his knees as he pulled it along. Gould got it almost lovingly in his hands. And all the while the wintry waters washed against the side of the ship. Still no moon shone; only the faintest glimmer of ghost light –and that broken by the casing above them.

'Not much further,' Roberts whispered.

Three-quarters of an hour had passed since *Thrasher* surfaced. They got past the last obstacle.

'Right. Let's lift it now.'

The seaman lent a hand from aloft, and in a minute they appeared through the grating, groping with the bomb. Soon it was up on the casing.

Roberts lifted himself up by his arms. Gould followed. The rest was easy. They rolled the bomb gently along the same way that the first one had gone. At the stern they gave the signal. The engines turned, the sub shot ahead, the bomb dropped astern. They were safe. Roberts and Gould clanged a way back amidships; down the conningtower; into control. A slap on the back from Mackenzie for both of them.

'Come and have a drink, you two. You deserve a double, and you're going to get it.'

Thrasher eventually got back to base. Peter Roberts went on a commanding officer's qualifying course, and on 9 June 1942, he heard that he had been awarded the VC.

But the course did not go well. He had had only two and a half years in submarines, scarcely sufficient for a commanding officer. The day after the news of the VC came the anti-climax: he had failed his course and was out of submarines –a bitter blow at the time, especially to a man who had thought that what he did off Crete 'wasn't very difficult.'

But the war was being waged and there was no time for second chances.

CHAPTER TWENTY-THREE

Submarine attack in Corfu Harbour

ANTHONY MIERS

Along with Wanklyn, Tomkinson, and Linton (whose story will be told later), Anthony Miers ranks as one of the four greatest submariners of the war: and he was a Commander, RN, at the age of only thirty-five when he won the VC.

In command of HM Submarine *Torbay*, Miers won the DSO and then a bar to it for his part in sinking eleven enemy ships in Mediterranean waters. On the very last day of 1941 he got his other half ring to become a full Commander.

The familiar pattern of patrols in the Mediterranean and attack on supply ships went on and on.

Patrolling at periscope depth on the third day of the third month of 1942, Miers suddenly spotted a large convoy on the horizon escorted by three Italian destroyers.

'All out of range,' he announced curtly to Lieutenant Hugh Kidd, who wore the ribbon of the DSO for gallant submarine service.

'I'm going to trail 'em,' Miers decided. 'May take some time, but it should be worth while.'

The Mediterranean day drew on. Miers took *Torbay* along well behind the enemy convoy. Hours dragged by.

'Land ahead,' he said, after one of his periodic peeps through the sub's 'eyes'.

'Looks like a harbour. Must be Corfu.'

The convoy changed course slightly as the leading ship in the line reached the approach to the harbour.

'They're going in. We'll follow later. Can't catch them otherwise, and we're not coming all this way for nothing —don't you agree, Kidd?'

The two-ringer nodded from the depths of the electrical equipment.

The long convoy wound its way into port, the destroyers bringing up the rear, tucking the supply ships in safely, as it were.

Miers took *Torbay* towards the harbour entrance. He saw further warships at anchor inside the harbour. 'Not going to be easy,' he decided.

He observed the route the ships took, noticing that the only way in was through a single narrow channel. If he went off course he risked grounding the sub or else striking a mine.

With infinite care Miers guided his craft in slowly, slowly, along the channel. Through his periscope he could see the enemy ships getting slightly nearer. They were still a long way off, however, much too far to chance a torpedo with any high hope of recording a hit. No one spoke much in the sub when she crept gradually into the heart of the harbour.

They were in, surrounded on three and a half sides by enemy territory —and enemy vessels. There were probably as many more again warships as the three escorting the convoy: half a dozen destroyers all within gun-range.

Delicately, so as not to disturb the surface of the water more than necessary, he glided the periscope up above sea level and scanned the scene. The sun had set, and the outlines of the ships were already becoming hazy in the March evening air. He would have to wait for next morning to make an attack, for the trip up-harbour had taken most of the afternoon and conditions were against a sucessful sub assault.

Miers pulled the periscope down again and then took a walk beyond the control room along to the messes. He ran into Engine Room Artificer Pinch.

'Hello, Pinch. Bit of an awkward spot to spend the night, eh, under the water in some strange port? How long is it since you joined *Torbay?* You've got about the longest service in her, haven't you?'

'Two years ago this week, sir. March 1940, I first saw her, and we've been a few miles in her since, sir.'

'We certainly have. Well, there's many a patrol to be done after this, so don't worry —we'll get back to base.'

Miers wandered as far as he could, watching the ratings at rest and on watch. One read a book. Another wrote a letter home. (Miers wondered where he would post it.) A third sailor smiled at him as Miers passed his bunk.

The night wore on in quietness; the engines, which had never turned above slow once the sub was in the harbour, had been stopped for hours.

Kidd came up to Miers.

'Some bad news, sir. We'll have to re-charge batteries. Never make it tomorrow out of here unless we do.'

'Hmm.' Miers said no more. He could try to take the sub out of harbour now, of course, and surface in safety clear of the coast; but he preferred to stay.

'Right. Nothing for it, I suppose, but to take her up. I'll just take a look aloft first.'

Miers screwed up his eyes to get them used to the darkness he expected to see through the periscope. What he saw gave him a shock. It was almost as light as day. A brilliant full moon shone over the water, streaking the harbour with quicksilver shafts.

'It's as bright as broad daylight,' he said, then added, 'Stand by to surface.'

Unbelievably slowly, the sub broke surface, the bows and the conning tower parting the wavelets in two places. She slid to a stop, and a duty rating eased the two hatches open to take in some fresh air. There on the surface, well within the foreign harbour, the sub lay silhouetted for all to see; black as jet against the silver-grey sea.

'No talking. Nothing above a whisper,' went the order.

Minutes ticked by. The batteries gained new life. The men sat around, still. The brass clock turned one revolution, then a second. Two hours *Torbay* had to stay surfaced. If just one look-out had spotted her she could not have escaped destruction; but no one did. The moon moved behind a cloud after the first hour, then came out again a minute or two later and the light seemed brighter than ever. They heard in the distance some sailors changing watch at the dead of night.

'How much longer?' Miers asked.

'Batteries charged,' came back the welcome assurance.

'Well, let's get below again as quick as we can.'

The hatches were closed carefully, quietly. The engines turned over scarcely above a murmur, the men breathed more freely, and the long metal craft vanished underwater as quietly and mysteriously as she had risen a couple of hours earlier.

Morning came.

'Periscope depth.'

Miers grabbed the periscope eagerly and swung it round to get a look at the shipping in full daylight.

'Convoy all gone,' he told the First Lieutenant, 'but there are a couple of supply ships left over there, about 5,000 tons each, I'd say, and one of the destroyers. The others seem to have flitted. Must have been after we submerged. Right. Stand by to attack.'

The engines moved faster. The sub swung forward now, full speed ahead. He pressed her home fairly close to the anchorages and on a swinging turn smacked a torpedo at each of the three ships in ultra-rapid succession. Her periscope traced an arc of white in the glassy-calm water. As the sub completed her turn, or even earlier, both supply ships exploded amidships with a shattering sound.

Miers took the sub down deep the moment the tubes had fired, and almost touched bottom. She lay there for half an hour. At that stage he did not know that he had sunk the two supply vessels and missed the destroyer.

He brought *Torbay* up to periscope depth —still right in the harbour —and ran right among some small boats all searching frantically for his sub. He crash-dived deep again as depth charges volleyed down after the sub. The crew kept count. Ten; twenty; forty. Miers made for the nearest exit from the harbour, in a very straight line. He was at periscope depth now to guide them through.

'Nearly at the end of the channel now,' he reported. Then: 'My God. Crash dive.'

Into the periscope at the shortest possible range headed a patrol vessel, only yards from the sub's bow. For the second time the crash dive came off. He had thwarted the anti-submarine craft who were hovering all along the long exit channel —and also the continuous air patrols overhead.

It was mid-morning when Miers reached open water —seventeen hours after he had led the *Torbay* into the enemy enclosure.

A few months later, on 28 July 1942, a unique occasion occurred at Buckingham Palace. Commander Anthony Miers was invested with the VC; Lieutenants Kidd,

Chapman, and Verschoyle-Campbell received a DSO and two bars to the DSC; and twenty-four ratings received DSMs or bars to the DSM.

It was the first time that officers and men of one of HM ships had been awarded their decorations at the same investiture.

The story goes that the four officers were to have been invested at one ceremony and the ratings at another. Miers is quoted as having said that if they could not all attend together, then he did not want his VC. And so the ship's company were not separated, but stayed united —as they had been those long hours, and months, beneath the Mediterranean.

CHAPTER TWENTY-FOUR

The Raid on St Nazaire

ROBERT RYDER, STEPHEN BEATTIE, WILLIAM SAVAGE, AUGUSTUS NEWMAN, FRANK DURRANT

The French ports of Brest and St Nazaire were causing concern to Allied naval command early in 1942, for they were being used by the trio of German battleships *Scharnhorst, Gneisenau,* and *Prinz Eugen.* Brest was a high priority on Bomber Command's list of objectives, but a target such as the Normandie Dock at St Nazaire could hardly be bombed sufficiently to render it useless.

By February 1942 Brest was no place for the three battleships, so on 12 February, under cover of low visibility and a strong fighter support, they slipped out of the harbour, round the north coast of France, and through the English Channel home to Germany.

But St Nazaire remained a dangerously efficient port, capable of catering for the new German battleship *Tirpitz.* At present she was confined to Norwegian waters, where she sailed restlessly during the months of January and February 1942. She had been completed only that winter, and with her were the pocket battleships *Scheer* and *Lützow* and heavy cruisers of the Hipper class.

The possibility now existed of a powerful force erupting from Norwegian waters, and causing chaos to Allied convoys by operating in the Atlantic. But to do this the *Tirpitz* would need a port in the Bay of Biscay, where repairs or maintenance could be done. St Nazaire was the one port possible to take the *Tirpitz.* It could be berthed only in the Normandie Dock, built before the war for the famous French liner.

A fortnight after the three German warships had eluded us in the Channel, Operation Chariot was submitted to the commander-in-chief, Plymouth. By 3 March it had been approved, and on 26 March a great combined operation was launched. The Navy were to land a military foce on enemy-occupied territory, and destroy the dock installations of the German-controlled naval base at St Nazaire. Commanding the Naval force was Captain Robert Ryder. The military force was under Lieutenant Colonel Augustus Charles Newman, of the Essex Regiment attached Commandos.

The force headed for position Z. Ten o'clock at night, forty miles off an enemy port, and a secret rendezvous at a position Z. An exciting prospect. The meeting was still more thrilling —with a British submarine, *Sturgeon*, which was waiting submerged until the approach of the convoy and then surfaced to show a screened light to seaward as a beacon.

At this point the escort destroyers broke away leaving the strange force to complete the last lap alone. The lights of a large number of fishing vessels away to port northward indicated that the raiders were still undetected. Detection by radar would also prove more difficult with so many ships in the vicinity.

The Commandos and sailors began to hold their breath almost by now, as they glided through the water on a still, silent night.

By midnight they were seventeen or so miles out. Gunflashes began to be seen in the distance to the north-east. At 00.30 they were ten miles offshore, and it became clear that heavy air activity was in progress. Gun-flashes and flak burst over a wide area. But the air attack was not going according to plan. With an overcast sky and light drizzle, the bombers could not see their targets. As attacks were not allowed unless the targets could be distinctly identified, owing to the risk of killing civilians, most of the bombers brought their loads back again —a devastating blow to the overall assault. The planes had alerted all the defences in the area without causing the chaos for which they had been specifically included in the attack. Whether or not the results would prove serious remained to be seen. Fortunately, as the ships sailed in, they were oblivious to this alarming development.

At 00.45 land was sighted, five miles off. *MGB 314* echo-sounded the bottom for shoals. They were crossing the mud-flats now. The time was 01.00. Beattie on the bridge of the *Campbeltown* kept her to ten knots for quiet. Suddenly the speed slackened to seven to eight knots. She had touched the bottom, but without increasing engine revolutions she shoved clear. Again the same thing happened, and again she got off and caught up the few lost yards.

Into the mouth of the estuary they went, their excitement turning to cheerfulness. They were nearer the northern shore now; less than two miles out, and running parallel to it. It was a mile and a half away.

A mile and a half out, the bright beam of a searchlight swept astern of the ships. Then it went off. Both banks had hidden danger —coastal defences or anti-aircraft batteries. Lieutenant Commander Stephen Beattie's eyes narrowed as he peered through the slits in the protective plating of *Campbeltown*. Ryder and Newman crouched under cover in *MGB 314* —the first in the line: a dangerous place to be.

So far so good. No minefields or obstructions had been met; nor had there been any casualties on the mud-flats. At 01.22, when they were a mile and a quarter out, searchlights suddenly skimmed the water from both banks, blazing beams of light which blinded Beattie as he took *Campbeltown* towards her position for the final ramming. Every craft must have been silhouetted in this intense concentration, but they were painted dark and flew tattered ensigns, and *Campbeltown* looked like a German torpedo-boat.

They sailed in. They were challenged from shore: a coast battery first, then one from the dockyard. A minute had passed, but each second was precious if they were to reach their objective.

01.23. It was for this very moment that Leading Signalman Pike had been attached to Ryder. He could send and receive German morse, so made a succession of K's which was the sign of a friendly ship. This delayed the onslaught from the shore. Then he launched into a long message about having been 'damaged by enemy action' and 'requested permission to proceed up harbour without delay'. An amazing deception only a mile from shore. The challenging firing stopped for a second.

Fire from the north bank broke out: still restrained fire, as if the Germans were not sure what to think or do. *MGB 314* made the 'friendly forces' signal with its brightest Aldis lamp, and the firing ceased!

In six more minutes *Campbeltown* would be home and ready to ram the lock. Already she was past most of the heavy batteries.

Three of those minutes passed; then at 01.27 the force was fired on in earnest from all sides. There was no point now in not replying. The *Campbeltown* opened up first, followed by all the others.

Fire screamed in a four-way exchange —from both shores to ships, and ships to both shores. Almost horizontal tracer tore across the harbour only a few feet above water level. *MGB 314* came up to the flak ship on guard duty. The ship lay less than half a mile from the dock gate. At 200 yards from her, the MGB saw the vessel floodlit in the full glare of a searchlight —and three bursts of pom-pom fire silenced her in a second.

'Well done, Savage,' called Ryder to the Able Seaman gun-layer lying in an exposed position near the bows of the MGB. The poor flak ship got hits from each of the convoy on passing, and also intercepted fire from its own shore-guns aiming at the British ships. Finally she scuttled herself to escape the holocaust.

The gun-layers of all the coastal craft were doing a wonderful job, for after a further three minutes the shore fire slackened considerably. The momentary respite enabled Beattie to swing *Campbeltown* round and head her for the lock. She was hard to handle, with a large turning circle, and still he was being blinded partially by searchlights. The responsibility for running in on course was great. There would be no second chance. Once ashore, the ship could not be ' backed' for another try at the target.

Yet still the firing came. Beattie stepped up the speed to twenty knots. The coxswain was shot away from the wheel. Beattie controlled her from the after-wheelhouse. She raced past the Old Mole promontory on her port side, only 200 yards off.

Now a quarter of a mile remained between her and the lock. She completed her change of course to port. Beattie checked direction. There was less than a minute to go. Thirty seconds, 200 yards. She felt a slight drag as she cut the torpedo net.

At 01.34, four minutes after the intended time, she struck the lock caisson squarely, with a crash. The MLs heard the impact clearly, but Beattie did not feel it as strongly as he had expected. The engine room men did not even know they had rammed.

Beattie went down below to see that the troops were getting ashore satisfactorily, then he looked out and saw the forecastle deck high and dry over the top of the lock gate. Down below the waterline of the ship, the bows had buckled back to a distance of some thirty-five feet —exactly the amount calculated and wanted.

Eighty or so Commandos scrambled ashore over the forecastle down their scaling ladders, and on to their tasks. The eight Oerlikons of the destroyer kept up a covering fire during this landing, which was being bitterly opposed. Scuttling charges were fused and the explosive charge near the bows, which was now right up against the lock, a perfect position to wreck it when the charge went off, finally fixed. The ship began to sink slowly, settling by the stern. She had suffered badly and an ML came alongside to take off the injured.

In the hail of fire during those few mad minutes of the approach into the harbour, much of the plan so meticulously worked out on paper had to be drastically revised —even abandoned. As the *Campbeltown* sped towards the lock gates, the MLs were in twin columns astern, one port and one starboard. The port column was to land its Commandos near the Old Mole, it will be remembered, and the starboard column continue on and swing in nearer the harbour, on each side of its Old Entrance.

Under the bombardment, *ML 192* leading the starboard six was hit early. She was carrying the senior officer of the MLs and troops detailed for the Old Entrance assault. She caught fire, crossed to the port column, and turned in to beach herself in the shallow water south of the Old Mole. *ML 262* and *267* following missed their landing-place in the great glare and proceeded too far up-river. *ML 268*, fourth in the column, turned in correctly but was hit while approaching the Old Entrance and enveloped in flames. *ML 156* came next, but she had been hit hard very early in the action. Her steering-gear shattered and most of her military and naval personnel injured or killed, she turned out of line somehow and withdrew on one remaining engine.

Last in the line to starboard came *ML 177*, undeterred and undaunted. She swung round successfully into the Old Entrance and landed her troops on the south side. Leader of the whole nineteen ships, *MGB 314* who had been giving valuable covering fire for *Campbeltown*, followed the ML in, and Colonel Newman and his staff were landed. Ryder told *ML 177* by hailer to hurry to *Campbeltown* and take off survivors, as already mentioned.

MGB 314, the headquarters ship still, then turned and lay up against the steps of the north side of the Old Entrance —bows pointing out.

The two MLs who had missed their mark turned and landed their troops, but these parties were repulsed severely and forced to re-embark almost at once. Cascades of fire forced the MLs to cast off —back to the fire and fury of the harbour. Thus the only ML of the starboard column to get its Commandos ashore according to plan was *ML 177*.

The Old Entrance adjoined the lock gate end of the dock where the *Campbeltown* lay, so it can be seen that the destroyer and her crew were uncomfortably close to the strong enemy guns around the Old Entrance.

As *Campbeltown* rammed the lock and the six starboard MLs struggled against superior gunfire further up-harbour, the column of seven MLs to port turned sharply in to the Old Mole, situated on the Île de St Nazaire. The Commandos aboard knew that their task was to capture the island, isolate it by demolishing bridges and lock gates connecting it to the mainland, and hold the Old Mole as the point to re-embark all the forces landed.

Fire and flames flashed across the waters as before.

ML 447 led the column round, was hit by flak, and burst into flames. *ML 457* got her troops through the barrage defending the Old Mole, but circling round afterwards was attacked and hit while backing into the slightly calmer waters midstream. *ML 307* passed *447* on fire, closed into the Old Mole, was struck by flak and grenades, and suffered heavy casualties. They could not get in, so withdrew and engaged batteries and searchlights on the opposite bank of the river.

ML 443 overshot the mark in the midst of searing searchlights, returned to the Old Mole, but could not land her troops. *ML 306* found *ML 192* burning to the south and *447* to the north, so circled round under heavy fire in an attempt to get alongside. She could not –so withdrew. *ML 446* did the same. Series of splitting shells and bullets wounded most of the troops, including the officers and sergeant. The only course was to withdraw.

As at the Old Entrance, only one ML – *457* this time –got through the overwhelming defences. That accounted for most of the MLs, but the pair right in the spearhead of the assault, just behind the MGB, had been placed there to torpedo or shoot up any craft challenging the raiders' approach. They met none, so proceeded to their next task –providing covering fire for *Campbeltown* as she went into the attack. *ML 270* was hit in her stern off the Old Entrance and had to withdraw, resorting to hand steering. *ML 160* on the port side of the St Nazaire bank of the estuary, bombarded a specific flak emplacement north of the landing positions, then fired her torpedoes at an enemy vessel by the south jetties.

Looking round for ways in which he could help other craft in distress, the commanding officer of *ML 160* saw *447* still ablaze, went alongside with the flames fanned across the gap in a threatening manner, and rescued most of the personnel on board. And all the while, *ML 160* came under devastating point-blank fire from pillboxes on the Old Mole.

Last of the MLs was *298*, which passed through petrol burning on the water caught fire, becoming a mark for enemy gunners, and eventually blew up.

Aboard *Motor Gun Boat 314* Ryder watched the crazy geometric patterns made by the 'perforations' of tracer as it sped low through the night sky. A burst early on had broken the wireless aerial, so the boat became isolated from other W/T contact among the raiders.

Ryder directed the MGB to be berthed on the north –Normandie Dock –side of the Old Entrance. Already many of the ship's company of the *Campbeltown* had been taken off by *ML 177*. The rest came running down the steps towards the MGB some of them seriously wounded. Ryder checked that *Campbeltown* was completely evacuated. Guarded by Leading Signalman Pike, he dashed over to the destroyer. Four scuttling charges exploded as they watched her, sending them hurrying back again. The MGB was coming under very heavy fire now, but Ryder kept it on this exposed point between the Old Entrance and the Dock until all the wounded were aboard. Looking over his shoulder as they returned to the MGB he saw the *Campbeltown*'s stern already awash.

Meanwhile, above all the roar, the sound of demolition coming from the pumping-house regions reassured them all that the Commandos from the *Campbeltown* were well away on their disruptive duties.

MGB 314 moved on from the lock to the Old Mole to see what the situation looked like there. Before leaving, Ryder told *MTB 74* to shoot her torpedoes at the Old Entrance. The tubes hit the lock gates of the Entrance. Then she hastened back to the gunboat, took off nine survivors from the crowded decks (which were living targets) and set course for home at forty knots.

It was half past two in the morning when the MGB came round towards the Old Mole, and Ryder could see that this 'embarkation point' was still stoutly defended by the enemy. The dark waters of the Loire leaped alight with spilt petrol bursting into flames –an amazing middle-of-the-night scene. The pillbox on the mole still spat out fire: the MGB engaged it. Able Seaman Savage –the pom-pom gun-layer –sent a burst towards the pillbox, then a second which entered the embrasure and silenced it.

Savage then took on skyline gun positions on surrounding buildings, but a Bofors battery on the opposite bank began to get the range of the gunboat. Then the pillbox leaped to life again.

The gunboat was thus being attacked from three sides –each flank of the Old Entrance and from the Bofors –and was fighting for her life. Savage silenced the pillbox a second time, but the boat was being hit almost continuously. By a miracle only it still floated. The sole gun remaining in action was the pom-pom, to which Savage stuck throughout this three-sided battle. The Bofors received a direct hit, and Savage was killed –heroically.

Ryder told Curtis, in charge of the MGB, to go into the entrance again, but the fight grew fiercer and they could not tell friend from foe. Someone had boarded *Campbeltown* and fired one of the Oerlikons across the Old Entrance.

The position was becoming desperate. The maximum time for the operation had been fixed for two hours, and already one hour and sixteen minutes had passed. Both possible places of embarkation were in enemy hands. Looking round the river, Ryder saw no other craft –only eight blazing wrecks, sunk or on fire. The MGB had forty or more survivors, many critically injured. A decision had to be taken urgently. They dropped a smoke float, had a hurried conference in the midst of the action, and decided that the time had come to go. Miraculous as it seemed, neither the steering-gear nor the engines had been damaged. Curtis gave the order 'full speed downstream' and the boat moved out at twenty-four knots.

Coolly Colonel Newman stood on the bridge of the leading craft, as the small force steamed up the estuary of the river Loire on that night of 27–28 March. Coolly, although the ships had been caught in enemy searchlights and consequent cross-fire from both banks. Many men were lost even before landing.

Although Newman need not have gone ashore himself, he was one of the first to land, and during the next five hours of frenzied fighting in that wild night, he personally entered several houses used as enemy strongholds, and shot up the occupants. At the same time he somehow managed to supervise operations in the town, and never wavered at any time.

An enemy gun position on the roof of a U-boat pen had been causing casualties to the landing-craft, so Newman directed the fire of a mortar against it so effectively that the gun went suddenly silent.

Still fully exposed, he then brought machine-gun fire to bear on an armed trawler in the harbour, forcing it to withdraw, and so preventing further casualties in the main demolition area.

Vastly superior enemy forces struck through the gloom of the night at this audacious assault, but under Newman's leadership they were repulsed until the demolition parties had completed their work of destruction.

By this stage, however, most of the landing-craft had been sunk or set on fire, throwing a ghostly light over the beaching-zone. Evacuation by sea seemed out of the question. Although the main object of the operation had been achieved, Newman was now nevertheless determined to try and fight his way out into open country, and so give all survivors a chance to escape capture.

The only way out of the harbour area lay across a narrow iron bridge, completely covered by a wide group of German machine guns. Just about this moment a hand grenade burst right at Newman's feet, severely shaking him. Yet he personally led the charge that stormed the position, and under his leadership the pitifully small force fought its way through street after street to a point near the open French countryside. But by then all the ammunition was gone, and they were finally overpowered by the enemy, and made prisoners of war.

Only after the war was over did the London Gazette announce the award of Lieutenant Colonel Newman's VC, on 19 June 1945.

The position was a difficult one. The main objective —ramming the dock gate —had been accomplished, but whether the explosive would detonate correctly remained to be seen. Some of the subsidiary targets had been dealt with, others, not. Casualties had been heavier than hoped.

Still the withdrawal of the rest had to be effected, *MGB 314* moved over to the south bank of the river, and kept up her twenty-four knots. Searchlights soon spotted her flight, but luckily the smoke floats she was dropping engaged their attention more than the gunboat itself. The shore batteries were firing astern of her, hitting the smoke!

She overtook a limping ML and made smoke with the chloro-sulphonic acid equipment in the hope of protecting the craft. The flak began to fade a little, when suddenly a salvo from a heavy coast battery fell a few yards ahead of the boat, spraying her as she ploughed out of the estuary.

By now, Newman had won his VC; Savage, a second one; Ryder, a third; and Beattie of the *Campbeltown*, a fourth.

Beattie and other officers of the *Campbeltown* had been taken on *ML 177*, which set off downstream at a brisk fifteen knots, making her leaving signal about 02.20. The chances for her escape seemed good. Then after ten minutes, two hits set her afire. She drifted downriver blazing. The crew and *Campbeltown* officers clambered overboard. Beattie got an arm over the side of a raft, clung on —and dozed off to sleep! For four hours *ML 177* burned. For longer than this the survivors held on to hope and life.

Meanwhile the searchlights had lost *MGB 314*, which had altered course southward. The gunfire was radar controlled, however, and not until four miles offshore did they give up the fight. Ryder and the rest watched the flash of guns along the coast heralding heavy salvos landing in the water around them several seconds later.

Ahead, they seemed to be gaining ground —or water —on another ML. They closed towards her and found out too late it was an enemy patrol vessel. She opened fire on the MGB at short range. A stream of tracer ripped into one of the petrol tanks. They waited for the boat to burst into flames, but it did not. The only gun still working was the pom-pom, but as the MGB swerved away this could not be brought to bear on the enemy. Further afield, she swung back again, and a few accurate shots with the pom-pom stopped the enemy's firing and started a fire.

Next on the scene was *ML 270*, steering by hand. The MGB cut her speed to twelve knots and stayed with the ML. As an added hazard, the sea seemed to be exceptionally phosphorescent that night, so that the bow waves and the wakes were lit up as brightly as in daylight.

By 04.50 the MGB reached the rendezvous point Y but did not stop, in view of the radically altered plans of the entire little fleet. About two hours later, the gunboat and *ML 270* observed heavy action to eastward, which later proved to be the destroyer *Tynedale* in a running action with five German torpedo-boats. Both *Tynedale* and *Atherstone* altered course south to lead the enemy away from the smaller craft. In the fight that followed *Tynedale* came under the five vessel's concentrated fire for nine minutes and was hit twice. She saw hits on the third enemy ship. Then she made smoke and broke off the action at 06.45.

The MGB and *ML 270* were cheered to see *ML 156* coming up astern and *ML 446* a mile away to the north. In addition to these four, a further four had managed to get away from the Loire: *MLs 443, 307, 160* and *306*.

Others had been less lucky. *ML 267* was abandoned on fire in the night. *ML 298* got only one mile before being set on fire. *MTB 74* the forty-knot craft, which could have been well on her way home, had gallantly gone to the rescue of one of the burning MLs and was set on fire herself.

Now in the early dawning, *Atherstone* stopped and took off the crew of *ML 156*. Then the escort destroyer came on to the MGB. After its heroic hours, the shabby gun-boat presented a picture both poignant and proud. As the commander of the *Atherstone* surveyed the scene he saw the little boat holed in many places, particularly forward, and he bit his lip as his eyes looked down on many, many men wounded and suffering on the deck —which was slippery with their blood. The sea was flat, yet even so, getting the wounded aboard *Atherstone* proved no easy affair.

While *Atherstone* took on the crew of *ML 156* and the wounded of the gallant gunboat, *Tynedale* was embarking the injured men from *MLs 270* and *446*. The vessels had to stop for a full half an hour, from 07.20 to 07.50, a sitting target. A Heinkel 115 actually appeared on the scene, circled the collection of ships, and then bombed and sank an abandoned ML astern!

By 08.00 the force had formed up and was making knots westward and away from the St Nazaire nightmare.

A Beaufighter greeted them: then a Junkers 88. The German was at once attacked by the Beaufighter. As if sensing the ordeal of the forces at sea level, and determined to protect them from further suffering, the pilot of the Beaufighter rammed the enemy plane in mid-air over the vessels and was killed.

Back in the estuary of the Loire, the sun had come up and those of the *ML 177* who had not been drowned were picked up by a German trawler and made prisoners of war, among them Lieutenant Commander Beattie. The rest of the war, three years and more, he spent in a prison camp in Germany.

Besides the HQ force, *MLs 160, 307,* and *443* also failed to make contact at the rendezvous point. So they made up for a pre-arranged position 46°N and 7°W, thence to sail up the meridian. On their way, however, enemy bombers struck them several times. A Heinkel III was the first unwise enough to try to sink the intrepid trio, but their concentrated fire sent it crashing into the sea. Next a large Blohm and Voss seaplane withdrew diffidently after being hit. Detouring many miles out into the Atlantic to avoid further unwelcome visitors, these three eventually reached Falmouth quite alone, and with no more than a gallon or two of petrol between them.

ML 341 whose engine had broken down before the attack, also reached a home port after a long voyage without any escort —another amazing achievement in waters infested with U-boats and enemy patrol vessels. All her troops had been transferred to another ML as soon as her engine trouble was first noticed.

The operation was still far from finished, however. Not until the morning of the 28th, about 09.00, did Ryder hear of the end of *ML 306*. Her memory may be dimmed, but the last minutes deserve to go down in the annals of valour; for it was to recognize such spirit as this that the VCs were awarded to the St Nazaire men.

ML 306 had made repeated attempts to land her troops at the Old Mole, according to orders; but at 02.00, with only one Oerlikon still serviceable, she left St Nazaire, speeding at eighteen knots and making smoke as she sailed. She succeeded in getting clear of the coast. Just before first flush of light, though, she sighted five large ships on the port bow coming close past. The Captain did not know if they were friend or foe, so stopped engines hoping to pass unobserved. It was still dark and the ships passed only 100 yards off without seeing her.

When they were clear, the captain started up engines —whereupon a single searchlight swung round from the last ship of the line. The unidentified craft were the five enemy torpedo-boats. They circled the poor lone ML considering the kill. They opened fire with small arms. The boat's guns manned by the Commandos responded valiantly. Then the enemy decided to ram. But the ML swung sharply round, escaping with a glancing blow, yet enough to fling several men into the water. As the enemy ship drew away she raked the ML with short-range weapons. At fifty yards she crashed 4-inch shells into the British boat. The bridge was hit; the captain, Lieutenant I. B. Henderson, RNVR, was killed, and the rest of the officers were wounded. The enemy closed to come alongside and hailed the ML in broken English. Nearly everyone aboard was injured, so the little ship had to surrender. The men were taken prisoner. The story of Frank Durrant, VC, summed up the saga of *ML 306*. Sergeant Durrant, Royal Engineers attached Commandos, had charge of a Lewis gun on *ML 306*.

The exchange of fire grew fiercer, more frequent. Durrant was severely wounded in the arm. Above the din, some one tried to drag him below for attention, but he replied:

'No —I'm staying here.'

Durrant continued to fire the gun, though in increasing pain, and as the motor launch proceeded she was attacked at the ridiculous range of fifty-sixty yards; in fact, at times closer than that. All through this phase Durrant went on handling the Lewis gun coolly, aiming for the enemy's bridge.

By now an enemy searchlight stabbing through the night air had illuminated the unlucky launch, and Durrant drew on himself the individual attention of all the enemy guns.

He was wounded. And wounded again. Despite these further terrible injuries, he stayed where he was, still firing away. A little later he had to support himself by holding on to the gun-mounting.

The vessels were sailing parallel, with the enemy pumping heavier calibres into the little craft. After a running fight the commander hailed across to the motor launch, calling on her to surrender. His answer came from Durrant: a further *tap-tap* of fire. Durrant was extremely weak, continuing by sheer willpower, yet using drums of ammunition as fast as they could be replaced.

A renewed attack by the enemy destroyer eventually finished the firing from his gun, but Durrant refused to give up until the ship actually came alongside, grappled the motor launch, and took prisoner those who remained alive after the death struggle downriver.

After boarding HM *Motor Launch 306*, the German officers commended Durrant's gallantry, and took measures to have his wounds treated, but, sadly, he died later of the many injuries he had received.

As soon as C.-in-C., Plymouth, heard of the five torpedo-boats in the Bay, the two escort destroyers were doubled in number by the dispatch to the scene of a further pair, *Cleveland* and *Brocklesby*. They joined the remnants of the raiders at 09.06.

The situation still seemed dangerous and difficult, for since the loss of the Beaufighter, the enemy had the air to themselves, and the cloudy sky looked just right for bombing attacks.

A breeze blew up from the north-west, and the damaged MLs became slower and slower, and began to ship water. This was tantalizing, for the destroyers wanted to sail at full speed with the wounded, many of whom might not live unless treated promptly.

A couple of air attacks on the craft —now reduced to ten knots —were repulsed without damage, and *Brocklesby* shot down a Junkers 88, which spiralled into the sea. The speed continued intolerably slow. Commander G. B. Sayer, RN, of the *Cleveland,* had taken over charge of the journey home, allowing Ryder and the others to sleep. He made a careful survey of the situation and decided to transfer all personnel to the destroyers and scuttle the three limping MLs. By 13.50 this was done, enabling the four fast destroyers to step-up their speed to twenty-five knots.

Back at St Nazaire the morning moved on. At daybreak a strong cordon of

German troops were thrown around both sides of the lock. About the same time that Beattie was being picked out of the sea, an inspection party of forty or more German officers threaded their way over the approaches to the lock gate and clambered up on board *Campbeltown*, to see how she could best be moved. The destroyer had settled by the stern now, of course. Her bows were still wedged over the top of the gate. With the inspection party walked the German Admiral in charge of the whole port.

French dock workers were barred from the lock, but the assembly had been swollen by German soldier sightseers. The officers poked about here and there near the bows, uttering guttural oaths about the awkward predicament.

The Admiral returned the salute of port naval officers and stepped ashore. His chauffeur opened the car door, and he vanished back to his offices. The officers continued their tour of exploration. Soldiers huddled round the lock gate.

Far out in the Bay of Biscay, Sayer had just decided to scuttle the MLs.

Suddenly a thunderous explosion shook the city. Every window in St Nazaire within a mile of the dock shattered, splintered. The *Campbeltown* had gone up. The lock gate was smashed. Sixty enemy officers and 320 men lay dead or dying.

The twenty-four depth charges, each of 200lb, were within a yard or so of the caisson. Five tons of high explosive had done its worst. As the smoke cleared, the forward half of the ship was seen to have disintegrated —as far aft as the foremost funnel. The water surged into the dock; the after half of *Campbeltown* was swept down the dock; two merchantmen surged forward, too, with thousands of gallons of water. A chaotic cauldron bubbling, foaming, frothing, roaring, rushing.

The main mission was accomplished.

The British destroyers drew level with Brest by evening. At 18.50, *Cleveland* contacted the other three MLs, *160*, *443*, and *307*, and she took *Brocklesby* out as far as the 7°W meridian to try to find them. Meanwhile, *Atherstone* and *Tynedale* put on all possible speed with the wounded and made Plymouth in the very early hours of the following morning. By a coincidence, they docked at 01.45 on 29 March – exactly twenty-four hours after the attack, when the battle was at its height.

'A lot can happen in a day,' Ryder observed to Sayer.

At last Ryder had time to think, to compare the blueprint for the raid with the event itself. He realized what a tragedy it was that Bomber Command could drop scarcely a single bomb because of bad weather. As things turned out, all the air raid really accomplished was to raise the alarm. Guns were already manned; duty and fire patrols had fallen in or were standing by; the look out system had been alerted. All that the gun crews had to do when they finally realized that an enemy force was sailing up the estuary was lower their weapons, all of which were dual-purpose and sited to defend the waterfront. Wooden MLs could hardly have been easier targets.

As Ryder received reports from the individual commanders of craft he gradually began to see the whole operation in a clearer perspective. He appreciated more, too, the way in which the navigator for the force, Lieutenant A. R. Green, RN, had piloted the force unerringly up the Loire Estuary without the aid of lights or buoys.

This he did after a voyage of 450 miles —and yet *Campbeltown* hit the dock only four minutes after the calculated time!

Still the story remains unfinished. Not for several days were the full effects to be observed. Meanwhile, the German radio lost no time at all in representing the raid as a defeat for the Allies, even the repulse of a second front in Europe. They took advantage of the British delay in announcing the results to produce for inspection by neutral nations photographs they had taken of *Campbeltown* during the morning following the raid, but *before* she had exploded with such shattering effect.

As Ryder and the Admiralty awaited reconnaissance photos —which were obtained ultimately on 1 April —the rest of the story of St Nazaire was being written. About half-past four in the afternoon of the raid, just as the city was beginning to recover from the impact of the destroyer's explosion, one of *MTB 74*'s torpedoes blew up, its firing delay having run off. This shook the whole port area near the Old Entrance and blew one man into the Loire.

An hour later a second explosion shattered what was left of the Old Entrance. All the French workers anticipated trouble from the Germans and rushed towards the one remaining bridge to the town. But it was barred by enemy sentries. The Frenchmen overpowered them and rushed the bridge, but the sentries opened fire on them. Panic broke out all over the port. Most German officers were dead near the *Campbeltown*. The sentries turned their machine guns on the throng of Frenchmen, killing many, for the Germans, of course, still imagined that Commandos were round every corner.

The air pictures duly arrived. They confirmed the complete success of *Campbeltown*'s first-time ramming. The outer caisson was destroyed. The inner caisson the Commandos had put out of action by hand-placed charges. The machinery for opening both outer and inner caissons was all destroyed, in one case the building housing it collapsing. The pumping machinery, also, could be written off, together with culverts and conduits deep down; heavy charges had been dropped into these. Indeed, so thorough did the destruction of the dock prove that four and a half years later it was still out of action —far beyond the end of the war.

Part of the secondary objectives failed. The attempt to obstruct the operation of U-boats by rendering the basins tidal was one example of these. Another was the neutralization of the concealed fuel depot adjacent to the Normandie Dock. But these were outweighed a pound to an ounce by the triumph of the *Campbeltown*.

Under the circumstances, the cost of it all in terms of life and injury was not more than might have been expected.

Excluding the supporting forces the total naval and military men amounted to 630. Of these, 144 were killed: twenty-three per cent.

The analysis of the fate of the 630 is as follows:

Killed or missing	144
Prisoners of war	215
Returned to England	271
Total	630

Campbeltown had eighteen coastal craft with her in the attack. The enemy sunk ten, four were scuttled and four reached England, including the immortal *MGB 314*, from which Ryder and Newman had directed the operations, and in the bows of which Able Seaman Savage had died winning his Victoria Cross, awarded also 'in recognition of the valour shown by many others in motor launches, the motor gunboat, and motor torpedo boat in this action'.

CHAPTER TWENTY-FIVE

Rooftop Raid on Augsburg

JOHN NETTLETON

The war was beginning to turn at last, as progressively more frequent forces of RAF bombers penetrated into the depths of Germany to destroy vital factories and other targets. The day raid aimed at Augsburg on 17 April 1942, was a case in point, and it also happened to be the occasion when the first South African Victoria Cross of the war was won. Acting Squadron Leader John Dering Nettleton, No. 44 (Rhodesia) Squadron, was already used to large-scale raids before the great day.

Nettleton might have been a naval man if he had not changed his mind before the war. The sea called him after leaving school, and he joined the merchant service for eighteen months. Even then flying had not exercised its effect on him, for he decided that civil engineering was what he really wanted. He worked in various parts of the Union for three years, while remaining in the South African Division of the RNVR. Then, soon after the Munich crisis, he entered the RAF.

By 1942, needless to say, any pilot of such long standing must have had considerable experience of operations. Nettleton's included the great daylight attack on Brest, on 24 July 1941, and night raids on Essen, Berlin, and other targets.

Then came the RAF's biggest week of the war to date. Sunday marked the fiercest day fighting since the Battle of Britain, followed by night raids on the Ruhr, Turin, Genoa, and Le Havre docks. Monday meant big-scale daylight sweeps. The Tuesday day offensive lasted from 10.00 to 19.30 hours; then the Ruhr at night. Wednesday —day sweeps; and night the Ruhr, St Nazaire, Le Havre, and aerodromes. On Thursday 400 Spitfires, Hurricanes, and Boston bombers were out during the day. Even bigger fighter forces went out on Friday, with night raids as well by bombers. Finally, targets in northern France were attacked on Saturday.

The list leaves out only one attack: the VC story of the twelve Lancasters against Augsburg. This daring daylight onslaught, fully 500 miles inside the Reich, marked the farthest point penetrated by RAF bombers, and meant a two-way ordeal of 1,000 miles over enemy territory, at any stage of which the Lancasters would be liable to ground or air opposition —those that managed to survive the actual raid.

The target was the MAN (Maschinenfabrik Augsburg Nürnberg AG) factory, famous, or notorious, for making a variety of war materials. With the U-boat war still at its height, the most important product emanating from MAN was half of the engines used by the enemy's total underwater fleet. If the output of these diesel engines could be interrupted, then a blow would have been struck in the remorseless Battle of the Atlantic. In addition, the MAN factories at Augsburg also turned out heavy tanks and engines for other armoured fighting vehicles. If a raid could really succeed it would seriously dislocate the flow of these vital war weapons. The diesel engine workshops sprawled over numerous extensive sheds, which were difficult for the enemy to camouflage or conceal. The main problem was clearly going to be to get in a position over these tempting targets to drop the special delayed action bombs.

The twelve Lancasters consisted of four sections led by Squadron Leader J. S. Sherwood, DFC, Squadron Leader J. D. Nettleton, Flight Lieutenant D. J. Penman, DFC, and Flight Lieutenant R. R. Sandford. They took off in broad daylight for Augsburg, which was to be the target –one of the most important raids of the war. A long time had passed since Chamberlain and Hitler had met at Munich. This was what had to happen all the time. Nothing could have stopped it; just as nothing could prevent some of these dozen Lancasters from finding the MAN factories. Half of the outward 500 miles over enemy ground had to be covered before darkness dropped on them; the attack itself was timed for 20.00 hours.

Twelve Lancasters, the latest and best bombers, took off, and crossed the Channel safely. But that is where any semblance of safety finished for the whole operation. Ack-ack guns took advantage of the spring sunshine to shoot down four of the dozen south of Paris, long before they were anywhere near Bavaria.

Now Nettleton takes up the story of this famous flight to Augsburg and back:

As soon as the French coast came into sight I took my formation down to 25-30 feet and we flew the whole of the rest of the way to Augsburg at that height. Soon after we crossed the enemy coast, fighters appeared in fairly big numbers.

A fierce running fight developed. It was our job to pierce straight through to our target, so we kept the tightest possible formation, wing tip to wing tip, so as to support each other by combined fire.

Fighter after fighter attacked us from astern. Their cannon-shells were bursting ahead of us. We were continually firing at them from our power-operated turrets.

We rushed over the roofs of a village, and I saw the cannon-shells which had missed us crashing into the houses, blowing holes into the walls and smashing the gables of the roofs.

The fight lasted 15 minutes or so, and aircraft were lost by ourselves and the Germans. Then their fighters gave up –probably they were running out of ammunition.

After that we had no more trouble until we reached the target. We swept across France, and skirted the border of Switzerland into Germany.

I pulled the nose of my aircraft up a trifle to clear a hill; pushed it down on the other side; and saw the town of Augsburg.

We charged straight at it. Our target was not simply the works, but certain vital shops in the works. We had studied their exact appearance from photographs, and we saw them just where they should be.

Low-angle flak began to come up at us thick and fast. We were so low that the Germans were even shooting into their own buildings. They had quantities of quick-firing guns. All our aircraft had holes in them.

The big sheds which were our target rose up exactly ahead of me. My bomb-aimer let go. Our bombs, of course, had delayed action fuses, or they would have blown us all up.

We roared on past the town. Then I saw one of my formation catching fire. The aircraft was ablaze, hit all over by flak. It turned out of the formation, and I was thankful to see it make a perfect forced-landing. I feel sure that the crew should be all right.

At that moment all our bombs went up. I had turned, and so could see the target well. Debris and dust were flying up in the air.

Then I set course for home.

There were a few details that Nettleton overlooked, or omitted to mention.

In the thick of the skirmish with the fighters over France, his rear guns went out of action. And so savage did the dogfight become that only one other of his particular formation survived besides his own Lancaster.

Then towards Augsburg, with great spirit, and almost defenceless, Nettleton held his two remaining aircraft on their arduous flight. Most of the 500 miles were covered at an altitude of under fifty feet. Over the town itself, intense, and almost fanatical, fire greeted them. The two Lancasters in his group came lower still —if that was possible —diving from an already-minimum height of 200 feet down to factory-top level. And their long shadows, cast by a softening sun, shot across the target. Despite the point-blank fire from the ring of guns covering the precious collection of sheds, they stayed the course to drop their bombs true on the target. It was this other aircraft that Nettleton described as being hit by flak, bursting into flames, and crash-landing safely. Nettleton's Lancaster was by now a mass of round and jagged holes held together by his determination to 'bring it back alive'. This he did; the only one of the flight of six to survive.

So Nettleton hedge-hopped all the way back from Augsburg, manoeuvring a Lancaster riddled with fire. The only two lighter notes were these: first, a lot of German civilians waved gaily at them as they sped house-high over them, mistaking the new and unfamiliar Lancasters for their own bombers about to begin a night attack; for now it was dusk at last. Secondly, they raised a smile as the low-flying Lancaster stampeded a German horse battery, so that both horses and guns careered along at a fire-engine rate.

For nine hours Nettleton stayed at his controls, munched bars of chocolate occasionally, and generally held the whole attack together. Finally, they were home soon after midnight; not a jolly crew, but glad to be back. For out of the twelve Lancasters, seven were lost. There was not much to laugh about as they thought of the others. Over half of them had gone.

The raid was revealed next day as having been by the RAF's latest four-engined Lancaster bombers, details of which were still being kept secret. The Air Ministry did disclose that they were the four-engined version of the two-motor Manchester, and it was the first time that they had been used in a daylight raid, for that is what the Augsburg attack was; in daylight at fifty feet.

Winston Churchill sent a characteristically couched message to Air Marshal A. T. Harris, C.-in-C. Bomber Command, on 19 April:

> We must plainly regard the attack of the Lancasters on the U-boat-engine factory at Augsburg as an outstanding achievement by the Royal Air Force. Undeterred by heavy losses at the outset, the bombers pierced in broad daylight into the heart of Germany and struck a vital point with deadly precision.
>
> Pray convey the thanks of His Majesty's Government to the officers and men who accomplished this memorable feat of arms, in which no life was lost in vain.

Nettleton confirmed this view. 'The families of those who did not come back may ask, Was it worth the loss involved? My answer to that is, "Absolutely". We have now a report that shows that the factory was heavily damaged.'

Only eleven days later Nettleton was awarded his Victoria Cross —and at once he was dubbed by the Press the 'Roof-top VC.'

Examination of the MAN factory from reconnaissance photographs revealed that the whole of the roof of the assembly shop was wrecked by high explosive and fire. The roof covered an area of 626 feet by 293 feet. Most of the machinery must have been either destroyed or damaged. Other shops received similarly severe damage.

On 1 June 1942, Nettleton became engaged to Assistant Section Officer Betty Havelock, WAAF, just before leaving for an American tour with other British and US heroes. They were fêted in New York at Madison Square Garden before starting a tour of twenty-one cities.

Returning in July, Nettleton married his WAAF fiancée in Lincoln, and was soon back on operations after the unreality of America, even in wartime.

Then a year later, towards the end of July 1943, after a heavy RAF attack on Turin, Wing Commander Nettleton and his crew were posted missing. His death was presumed on the same date, 23 February 1944, as an announcement was made of the birth of a son to his wife. The boy was christened the same as his father: John Dering Nettleton.

CHAPTER TWENTY-SIX

Self-sacrifice in 1,000-plane Raid

LESLIE MANSER

Courage has many countenances, and none finer than the kind shown by Flying Officer Leslie Thomas Manser, RAFVR, No. 50 Squadron. At the age of twenty he was captain and first pilot of a Manchester bomber, taking part in the mass raid on Cologne during the night of 30 May 1942. This was the very first 1,000-plane raid in history. What a sound that had! A thousand aircraft, whereas a couple of years earlier Britain had only a handful of fighters and bombers for defence and attack. And this historic raid would be destined to go down also as one in which Manser won his Victoria Cross.

Most of No. 50 Squadron were out that night. The squadron was nicknamed 'Bull's Eye', for its reputation of hitting the target often and hitting it hard. Now would be a good chance for them to show what they could do.

As Manser's Manchester was approaching its objective, the insistent, peering glare of the enemy searchlights found the plane. Caught in them, it naturally soon became the target of some accurate anti-aircraft fire –enough to make many a pilot divert course. But Manser knew that Cologne could not be far off by then, and refused to be budged. The bursts got nearer now, and began to jolt the cockpit. He was rewarded by finding the target through this dangerous course, and he bombed it successfully according to plan from a height of 7,000 feet.

The Manchester was damaged from the furore of the flak, but set about the equally awkward job of getting back to base. The flak continued its persevering pounding as Manser tried to evade it. Under really heavy fire, he took violent evasive action in an effort to shake it off, descending to as low as 1,000 feet; but nothing was any use. Both flak and searchlights followed him beyond the outskirts of Cologne.

Hits hammered on the plane as regularly as some one knocking on a door. The rear gunner fell wounded by one of the hits. Now things began to get worse steadily. Smoke started to seep all over the area of the front cabin. The port engine was over-heating seriously. At this stage Manser knew that they could all escape safely by parachute –which would mean being taken prisoner.

He was flying the aircraft, however, and while he knew that the others could still get out, he decided it was worth disregarding the obvious hazards, and to go on trying to save both the aircraft and crew from falling into enemy hands. Coaxing everything left in the machine, Manser almost literally lifted the Manchester up to 2,000 feet again.

It was at that height the port engine burst into flames. It had been growing steadily hotter for some time.

Ten more minutes passed before the fire was mastered, but by then the engine, as well as the fire, was out too. Manser made a quick recap of the situation. Part of one wing was burnt, the port engine had packed up for good, the air-speed of the plane had become dangerously slow, and still the smoke continued to fill the front cockpit. And the rear gunner was wounded.

The plane started to lose height.

This was the beginning of the end.

Despite all their efforts, it went on losing altitude. The needle fell remorselessly round the dial. Any second now he would have to decide: whether or not he was going to bale out with his crew. But his answer was simply to set a new course for the nearest base, and resolve to try and keep the plane flying as long as humanly – or superhumanly –possible. Then things started happening in seconds.

The Manchester became harder to handle all the time, so that he knew once and for all that he could not avoid a crash.

He thought of his crew of six. He was the only single among them, so they must get out safely. A sergeant handed him a parachute. Manser waved it away from him.

'I can only keep her steady for a few seconds more. Jump now. Go on –jump!'

There was no time to argue; not an instant; it was now or never.

Each man in turn went to their escape hatch. The three sergeants jumped first. And then, as each of them vanished into safety, Manser gave them the thumbs-up sign and a 'Cheerio'. The two pilot officers protested to Manser at leaving him. His second pilot pleaded with him to be allowed to stay and help –or at least wait till Manser had put on his parachute. But the captain would not have it. He waved the second pilot away too, just as he had done the others.

The parachutes of the crew mushroomed out and they dangled, intent on the plane as they fell. It too was falling. They saw it plunge and plough into the German earth, burst into flames, and take with it Flying Officer Leslie Manser.

His station commander said, 'He was the epitome of what a pilot should be. To him flying was not merely an adventure, but also a duty to be performed to the very best of his ability. He disregarded all danger in achieving his aim, not from reck-lessness, but from a firm conviction that he must play his part in righting a wrong.

'His end was fitting, because he died as a direct result of pressing on to his target, and at the same time gave his life to save his crew. He died with as little thought of self as there had been in his life. His talent for friendship endeared him to all.'

And as one more tribute to add to this, from Air Chief Marshal Harris, who knew only too well the heartache that must be caused by the offensive he had to sustain till the war was won. It was a letter in his own handwriting to Manser's father:

Accept from me personally, and on behalf of my comrades and my Service, salutations upon the signal honour so well merited, which the King has seen fit to confer upon your gallant son. No VC was more gallantly earned.

I cannot offer you and yours condolences on your personal loss in circumstances wherein your son's death, and the manner of his passing, must so far surmount, by reason of the great services he rendered to his country and the last service to his crew, all considerations of personal grief.

His shining example of unsurpassed courage and staunchness to death will remain an inspiration to his Service, and an imperishable memorial to all.

CHAPTER TWENTY-SEVEN

Tanks in the Desert

HENRY FOOTE, QUENTIN SMYTHE, ADAM WAKENSHAW, KEITH ELLIOTT, ARTHUR GURNEY

Tanks were the weapons that would win the war in the desert, but they were also very vulnerable. They called for courage, which was not lacking.

For twenty days in Cyrenaica, Lieutenant Colonel Henry Robert Bowreman Foote, Royal Tank Regiment, displayed dramatic gallantry, from 27 May to 15 June 1942. Already the holder of the Distinguished Service Order, Foote added the VC to it.

Ten of the twenty days had passed when 6 June dawned. Foote and his battalion had been the target of very heavy artillery barrages in their vulnerable tanks, and now they found themselves pounding in pursuit of much larger forces of the enemy. A stray shell aimed at the advancing tanks of the Royal Armoured Corps exploded by Foote's own vehicle, forcing him and the crew to transfer to another tank. While Foote was dashing from the knocked-out tank to the other one, a bullet from an enemy gun hit him, wounding him in the neck. Despite this, Foote reached the tank. He scorned the comparative safety of its interior, however, and continued to lead the battalion from an exposed position on the outside of the armoured vehicle.

The enemy were holding a strongly entrenched situation with anti-tank guns, and soon after this they attacked his flank. As another tank Foote was using had also been disabled in the swirling exchange of fire-flaying vehicles, he decided to turn infantryman. Under a scorching sun, and still more scorching fire, Foote lived up to his name and strode about encouraging his men. Throughout the afternoon the enemy choked and churned in desperate measures to try and encircle two of the British armoured divisions, but by Foote's supreme skill in deploying his surviving tanks, the encirclement was never achieved. By dusk they had given up the attempt altogether.

The struggle in Cyrenaica continued, and exactly a week later, on 13 June, Foote and his tanks were ordered to delay enemy tanks so that the Guards Brigade could be withdrawn from the famous Knightsbridge encampment. The enemy destroyed the first wave of British tanks in a fog of fire and flame. Foote remained calm, and reorganized the remaining tanks. As before, he forsook the shelter of a tank and walked from one vehicle to the next, offering advice and encouragement, while artillery and anti-tank guns growled and spat at him.

To try and delay the enemy tanks, it was vital that the battalion should not give ground. Every minute was valuable in the withdrawal operation of the Guards Brigade. So Foote returned to his tank, entered it, and placed it in front of the others in order that he should be plainly visible in the turret as an encouragement to the other crews.

He did this, moreover, despite the tank having been badly damaged already by shellfire and with all its guns out of action. The men of the Royal Tank Regiment rose nobly to this example, and they succeeded in keeping open the narrow corridor so that the Guards Brigade could march to temporary safety. Foote managed to be at the crucial point at the right moment, a remarkable feat, considering that he covered ground on foot often, and the distances involved were quite substantial. During those critical days the name of Foote was a byword for bravery.

For bravery, too, it would be hard to imagine a more extreme case than Sergeant Quentin George Murray Smythe. Sergeant Smythe led a platoon, though suffering severely from shrapnel that had pierced his forehead. Here is the citation of this courageous South African:

> For conspicuous gallantry in action in the Alem Hamza area on June 5, 1942. During the attack on an enemy strong-point in which his officer was severely wounded, Sergeant Smythe took command of the platoon although suffering from a shrapnel wound in the forehead.
>
> The strong-point having been overrun, our troops came under enfilade fire from an enemy machine-gun nest. Realizing the threat to his position, Sergeant Smythe stalked and destroyed the nest with hand grenades, capturing the crew. Though weak from loss of blood, he continued to lead the advance, and on encountering an anti-tank gun position again attacked it single-handed and captured the crew. He was directly responsible for killing several of the enemy, shooting some and bayoneting others as they withdrew.
>
> After consolidation he received orders for a withdrawal, which he successfully executed, skilfully defeating an enemy attempt at encirclement. Throughout the engagement Sergeant Smythe displayed remarkable disregard for danger, and his leadership and courage were an inspiration to his men.

By now, it was midsummer in the Western Desert, and on 27 June 1942, south of Mersa Matruh, Private Adam Herbert Wakenshaw was one of the crew of a 2-pounder anti-tank gun that was sited on a forward slope in front of the infantry position.

Just after dawn the enemy launched an attack, and one of their track vehicles towing a light gun was brought to within a short range of the Durham's position. The crew of the 2-pounder at once opened fire on the enemy, and was able to put a round successfully through the engine of the enemy vehicle, completely immobilizing it. But another mobile gun then burst into life.

The aim was good, and a shot exploded fatally close to the British gun. All the crew manning the 2-pounder were killed or badly wounded in an instant, and the weapon itself put out of action. In the respite they thus gained the enemy moved forward towards their damaged tractor in order to try and get their light gun into action against the Durham Light Infantry.

The explosion had blown off Wakenshaw's arm above the elbow, and he was lying there in agony near the gun. But through the pounding pain he realized the danger to his infantry comrades if the enemy did get their gun going.

Swept by bullets, bombs, and flak, the British gun-site was a death spot. But nevertheless, Wakenshaw crawled on his legs and one arm back to the gun. He left a line of blood as he went. With his remaining arm, he loaded the anti-tank gun, and fired a round at the enemy. Then a second, and a third. Pain nearly prevented him from seeing, yet, with a gun-aimer, he fired five rounds altogether, set the tractor on fire, and damaged the light gun. It was amazing that he could still move.

Then an enemy near-miss killed the gun-aimer, and blew Wakenshaw bodily away from the gun, inflicting more severe wounds.

His responses were now beyond the normal call of duty. Somehow he slowly dragged himself back to the gun, which was the centre of his ebbing life. He forced a round into the breech, and was actually preparing to fire when a direct hit on the adjoining ammunition killed him, and destroyed the gun. In the evening, after the action, his body was found stretched out at the back of the breechblock beside the ammunition box.

This act of conspicuous gallantry prevented the enemy from using their light gun on the infantry company which was only two hundred yards away. It was through the self-sacrifice and courageous devotion to duty of this infantry anti-tank gunner that the company was enabled to withdraw and embus in safety.

And now a New Zealander and an Australian are reminders that the desert war was very much a cooperative Commonwealth effort. Dawn in the Western Desert, 15 July 1942. This was the strange setting for a New Zealand VC.

The battalion to which Sergeant Keith Elliott belonged was attacked on three flanks by enemy tanks at Ruweisat. Men versus machines. Under heavy tank fire, plus some shell and machine-gun fire for greater strength, Elliott led the platoon he was commanding to the cover of a ridge. That 300-yard trek seemed like a lifetime of normal living, a million miles of space. Their legs felt leaden. Bullets, shells, sand, dust, and death. During that 300-yard dash Elliott sustained a severe chest wound.

Behind the ridge Elliott reformed his men, and led them to a dominating ridge a further 500 yards away. Yet even here they were no safer, still under a paralysing, pounding barrage. He located enemy machine-gun posts on his right and front flank, and, while one section attacked to the right, Elliott led seven men in a bayonet charge across 500 yards of open ground, in the teeth of terrific fire from the enemy.

They captured four machine-gun posts and an anti-tank gun, killing a number of the enemy, and taking fifty prisoners. Seven men capturing fifty.

But then his section suddenly came under fire from a machine gun over on the left. Elliott immediately charged this post alone. He killed some of the enemy, captured fifteen others, and took the post itself. During these last two assaults he sustained three more wounds in the back and the legs.

Although wounded so appallingly, Elliott would not leave his men till he had again re-formed them, handed over his prisoners, and arranged for his men to rejoin their battalion. The prisoners had reached the remarkable total of 130.

Entirely due to Elliott's lightning grasp of the situation, his great courage, amd his leadership, nineteen men, who were the only survivors of B Company of his battalion, captured and destroyed a total of five machine guns and the anti-tank gun, as well as killing a large number of men and capturing those already mentioned.

Elliott sustained only one casualty among his own men, and this man he brought back personally to the nearest advanced dressing-station.

The happy ending on this occasion was that Elliott did not die of his wounds, but recovered to receive his VC in person.

The Australian's action, unfortunately, did not have a similar outcome. Private Arthur Stanley Gurney put enemy machine-gun posts out of action by a bayonet assault at Tel El Elisa, on 22 July 1942, thus allowing his company to continue their advance.

During an attack on strong German positions in the early morning the company was held up by intense machine-gun fire from posts less than 100 yards ahead. Heavy casualties were inflicted on the Australian troops, and all their officers were killed or wounded.

Grasping the seriousness of the situation, Private Gurney charged the nearest machine-gun post, bayoneted three men, and silenced the post. Then he continued on to a second post, bayoneted two men, and sent out a third as prisoner.

At this stage a stick-grenade was thrown at Gurney, knocking him to the ground. He got to his feet, picked up his rifle, and charged a third post, using the bayonet with great vigour. Then he disappeared from view, and later his body was found in an enemy post.

By this singlehanded act of gallantry in the face of the enemy, Gurney enabled his company to press forward to their objective, inflicting heavy losses as they went. The success of the action was due entirely to Gurney's heroism at the moment it was needed.

CHAPTER TWENTY-EIGHT

The Dieppe Raid

PATRICK PORTEOUS, CHARLES MERRITT, JOHN FOOTE

The second of the two Commando raids on French ports in 1942 was made against Dieppe on 19 August. Three VCs were won in this inspiring, tragic raid. Inspiring, for the courage of the Allied assault force. Tragic, for the losses they endured.

They landed in the face of brutal bullets, searing shells. Major Patrick Anthony Porteous, Royal Regiment of Artillery, had been detailed to act as liaison officer between two detachments whose job was to assault the heavy coast defence guns.

In the initial assault Porteous was working with the smaller of the two groups. A German shot him at close range through his hand, the bullet passing right through his palm, and entering his upper arm. Porteous proceeded to attack his assailant, who had already turned his aim on a British sergeant. Before the German could fire, though, Porteous managed to disarm him and kill him with his own bayonet. This was kill or be killed. So Porteous killed. Though his hand was bleeding profusely, he managed to save the sergeant's life.

Meanwhile the larger of the two detachments assaulting the guns had been held up. The officer leading the group lay dead, and the troop sergeant major fell seriously wounded. At the second Porteous saw this situation the only other officer of the detachment was also killed.

Between the two groups the open ground was being systematically sprayed with withering coverage of fire. Yet Porteous dashed straight through it to take command of this second detachment. It is an amazing fact how much fire a man can run through without being hit –if he is lucky. Porteous was.

Rallying the officer-less group, he led them in a charge that carried the German defensive position literally at the point of the bayonet. For the second time Porteous was wounded severely. This time he was shot through the thigh, but, trying to forget the agony of it, and his hand and arm, he went on to their objective, and commanded the destruction of the guns. Only when the last one had been put out of service did he collapse from loss of blood. But he did not die.

'Tenacious devotion to duty' was the official phrase used to describe what he did. And his VC citation pointed out that this duty was supplementary to the role really assigned to him. So Porteous goes down as the one British VC won at Dieppe. The other two, quite rightly, were Canadian.

While Porteous and his men were struggling to assault the heavy guns, Lieutenant Colonel Charles Cecil Ingersoll Merritt had led in and landed his Canadian battalion of the South Saskatchewan Regiment in the teeth of terrific fire.

From the very point of touching down, his unit's advance looked like being deadly. Their headway had to be made across a bridge in Pourville, which was swept by fire focused from machine-guns, mortars, and artillery. The first to try to cross the bridge were mostly destroyed, and the bridge itself covered thickly by their bodies. Here was one of the crucial moments in an operation. Someone had to lead the rest across. They knew what the prospects were.

Merritt rushed forward, took off his helmet, and waved it, shouting:

'Come on over. There's nothing to worry about here.'

He thus personally led the survivors of at least four parties in turn across the bridge. Thereby, of course, multiplying his own chances of being killed. Once over, he quickly organized the Canadians, leading them, forward all the time.

When they were next held up, by enemy pillboxes barring their way, Merritt again led head-on rushes that succeeded in clearing them. Once he, himself, destroyed all the German occupants of a post by aiming a grenade accurately. After several of his runners became casualties, Merritt personally kept contact with his different positions: the true commander in action.

Although he was wounded twice during the raid, Merritt ignored these injuries, and kept on directing operations vigorously, perhaps stung to extreme determination by the very pain of his wounds. While organizing the withdrawal he stalked a sniper with a Bren gun, and silenced the enemy.

Then he coolly gave orders to prepare for the departure, and announced his intention to hold off and get even with the enemy. When the men who got away last saw him he was collecting Bren guns and tommy guns and preparing a defensive position which successfully covered their withdrawal from the beach. Their safe re-embarkation was largely due to Merritt's magnificent daring.

Soon after the action Merritt was reported to be a prisoner of war, and within six weeks of the Dieppe raid the awards of the VC were announced to Merritt and Porteous.

The third Dieppe VC was won rather differently.

He had no gun, yet he won the VC. He was Honorary Captain John Weir Foote, regimental chaplain with the Royal Hamilton Light Infantry. Foote represented religion in action, the kind of faith that the Canadians could understand, the kind that went with them all the time, and was not just a comfort for Sundays. He had been with many of the men for three years. He was with them in this moment of trial.

Bullets could kill chaplains just as easily as other soldiers. And bullets were whining their way towards the shore as Foote landed. Bullets parallel to the beach and just a few feet above it.

Coming in under heavy fire, Foote attached himself to the regimental aid post. This was where he would be most needed, he thought. It had been set up as an emergency in a slight depression on the beach, a dip just enough to give cover to men lying down but not standing.

The blast of the battle went on over his head in that cramped aid post, but for the following eight hours Foote forgot it as he helped the regimental medical officer in ministering to the wounded. He choked back his feelings as he saw each fresh torn body brought into the post.

Foote did much more than just purvey comfort, though heaven knows they needed this badly. Time and again on that dramatic day he left the shelter of the aid post regardless of the danger this involved. Countless times he crawled or somehow got across the beach to inject morphine into injured soldiers where they lay, and to give general first-aid, and help carry the wounded from the fatal slopes of that beach to the little haven of the aid post.

Every time he did this he exposed himself to an inferno of enemy gunfire, but certainly saved many lives.

At one stage of the day, as the tide went out, the regimental aid post was shifted to the shelter of a stranded landing-craft; one which had never completed its mission. From then on Foote continued to carry the wounded from the beach to the landing-craft. The enemy eventually got the range of this stranded craft, and one of their shells struck and set fire to some ammunition still stored inside it. This meant moving the wounded away. But the question was —where? Fortunately, other landing-craft came to the rescue, and Foote did his share in carrying the wounded Canadians from the aid post to the newly-arrived craft. Even as he and the others staggered over towards them, the German guns emptied shell after shell, round after round, in an effort to finish them off.

Now the time to withdraw was near. Merritt was leading his own rearguard action to give his men a good chance to get away. And down by the aid post, too, they were beginning to board. Several times officers asked Foote if he was ready to leave, but each time he returned to the beach to care for the wounded, and see that they all got away safely. Time was running out now. He had seen a lot of them off. It was now or never, as the German counter-attacks made final evacuation imperative at that instant. The last chance came and went.

Foote refused the chance, choosing to stay and suffer the fate of the men of his Royal Hamilton Light Infantry. So, still on the fire-swept stretches, Foote helped lessen the pain. The last landing-craft chugged away through the afternoon, followed by fire from the shore. Then Foote and those left were taken prisoner.

The announcement of his VC was made years later, on 14 February 1946 —the Cross of Courage and the Cross of God.

CHAPTER TWENTY-NINE

El Alamein and Tebourba

WILLIAM KIBBY, PERCIVAL GRATWICK, VICTOR TURNER, HERBERT LE PATOUREL

I n the Western Desert, they were sweltering and slogging on. And in October 1942, on Miteiriya Ridge, two Australians died winning the VC. They were Sergeant William Henry Kibby and Private Percival Eric Gratwick.

During the initial attack at Miteiriya Ridge on 23 October the commander of No. 17 Platoon was killed. Kibby assumed command of the platoon, and no sooner had he done so than they were ordered to attack strong situations holding up the company's advance.

Kibby realized the need for quick, decisive actions. He dashed forward firing his tommy gun at the enemy post. This courageous individual action completely silenced it, three of the enemy being killed and a dozen captured. The company could then carry on as planned. What was more, Kibby had risked only one life — his own.

After the capture of a position designated Trig 29 three days later, on 26 October, the enemy artillery swung round on the battalion area, followed by a series of tank and infantry thrusts. Throughout the attack that culminated in the capture of the position Trig 29, and also in the reorganization period that followed, Kibby was in the thickest of the fray, cheering his men on though they were continually suffering casualties. The toil and the terror did not seem to touch him.

Several times he went out right into the machine-gun bullets to mend the platoon line communications, thus allowing mortars to be aimed more effectively against the enemy attacks.

But battles seldom stop suddenly, and this campaign was dragging on day after day, night upon night. On the night of 30–31 October, when the battalion launched a lunge behind the enemy lines, No. 17 Platoon had to move through the most powerful machine-gun output imaginable. It could not be helped; there was no other way to reach their goal.

Once again Kibby almost seemed to enjoy these conditions that called forth all a man had in him.

The platoon was mown, riddled, shot up by the fire from point-blank range, but Kibby and the survivors pressed, forced their way forward to the goal. They had got to get there. And they did. But one pocket of resistance remained. Kibby advanced alone into the night, throwing his grenades as he went. Now the enemy were mere yards away. Just as it seemed certain that he would succeed and survive, a burst of bullets kicked out of a nearby gun and killed him.

'He left behind him an example and the memory of a soldier who fearlessly and unselfishly fought to the end to carry out his duty.'

Five nights earlier, on 25-26 October during the attack on the position Trig 29, Private Gratwick was also winning a VC. A serious situation had developed, and Gratwick's platoon was directed at enemy strong-points delaying the Australian advance.

As they set out for these posts ruthless fire cut into them. The platoon commander was killed. The sergeant and many others too, all lay there dead in the Western Desert night. The total strength was now no more than seven men, one of them Gratwick.

Rushing out on his own, he charged the nearest post, scattering hand grenades before him as he ran. Among others, he killed a complete mortar crew. Still under the sights of the enemy weapons, Gratwick stormed the second post with rifle and bayonet. It was from this post that the heaviest fire had been coming. He inflicted further casualties, and was within striking-distance of his goal when he too fell in the face of a burst of bullets.

But by his action, which unnerved the enemy troops, the rest of the company was able to move forward and mop up its goal. So Kibby and Gratwick both paid the supreme penalty.

It was still October in the desert, and the El Alamein VC knocked out eight enemy tanks in a twenty-hour fight.

Lieutenant Colonel Victor Buller Turner joined the Rifle Brigade in 1918 straight from school, and when the first battalion was re-formed after Dunkirk he took over a company. Then he sailed for the Middle East with his battalion, of which he was then second-in-command, in October 1941. The next thing that was heard of him was how he had been taken prisoner, but had turned on his captors and had taken them prisoner ! He arrived back in his own lines with a convoy of enemy trucks full of a surprised enemy!

Then came 27 October 1942 and El Alamein.

In the six-round battle that began at 23.00 hours and continued until 19.00 hours the next day, a group of the Rifle Brigade destroyed or disabled fifty-eight enemy tanks and self-propelled guns —an average of three to each of the nineteen 6-pounder guns in position.

The group successfully attacked a saucer-shaped depression called Snipe, but because of shellfire and soft going only nineteen of their twenty-seven guns arrived. Two enemy Lagers were broken up by machine-gun fire from carriers, a Mark IV tank and a self-propelled gun were destroyed, and seventy prisoners were captured.

In the next round of the battle, at dawn, eight tanks were knocked out. At 07.30 hours twenty-five to thirty enemy tanks and guns formed up in the morning light about 1.000 yards away. The Rifle Brigade 6-pounders set many of these on fire, and a tank, hit at a range of exactly a mile, was towed away by the enemy.

09.00 hours. Thirteen Mark III tanks counter-attacked. One was at once annihilated and three hit. Simultaneously, thirty tanks were engaged on the southern flank. When half of them swung in to attack, eight were set afire with accurate aim from the little 6-pounders.

All this time the Rifle Brigade were coming under disturbingly heavy shellfire. Only thirteen of the nineteen guns were still in action, and ammunition was running short, especially in the west and south-west sectors. This was turning into a long, bitter battle.

The enemy attacked with eight tanks and several self-propelled guns just after midday. Only one gun was able to engage them. At this gun, Turner acted as loader, while another officer and a sergeant manned it.

As every round was precious, they refrained from firing until the enemy were 600 yards away. Then, with a series of spectacularly accurate shots, the 6-pounders set five tanks and one self-propelled gun blazing.

But they had only four rounds remaining now. Steeling themselves for the task, Turner and the others waited until the oncoming three tanks were at a 200-yard range. With three rounds, the sergeant hit and set on fire the last three tanks.

While he was still acting as loader for these remarkable rounds of firing, Turner was wounded in the head, but he absolutely refused all aid until that last tank had been destroyed.

Finally came a sixth and last tank attack. Thirty tanks advanced against another sector. The 6-pounders there engaged them at 500 yards, and, in a cacophony of shattering sound at the receiving-end, nine tanks were seen to be set on fire. Five minutes later another group of fifteen Mark III tanks drove towards the defenders. Only three guns, with ten rounds each, were fit for action. They hit six tanks, and the rest retired at speed.

So the total score was fifty-eight wrecked out of a total of nearly 100 hurled against the British. And Turner's citation ends:

> His personal gallantry and complete disregard of danger as he moved about encouraging his battalion to resist to the last resulted in the infliction of a severe defeat on the enemy tanks. He set an example of leadership and bravery which inspired his whole battalion and which will remain an inspiration to the brigade.

The story of the next desert VC is the story of the Battle of Tebourba. The VC was won by Major Herbert Wallace Le Patourel, the Royal Hampshire Regiment.

This battle in Tunisia was to last four days. It was a desperate and an heroic fight, essentially a junior leaders' battle, and a most severe test for men who had landed only a week before. The Germans outnumbered the 2nd Battalion by four to one; they had modern tanks and complete air supremacy. Before the battle the battalion strength was 689 all ranks; afterwards it was 194. The positions the battalion took up were bequeathed to them, and they were ill-suited to defence, being overlooked by high ground to the right and to the front. Yet the battalion denied passage to the enemy to Tebourba for four days, a feat of the utmost importance to the division, and the news of this dogged and resolute fighting came as a most valuable tonic to every one at home at a time when such a tonic was of the greatest value.

Colonel Lee had made a reconnaissance of the position and at once saw the danger of the situation. He asked to be allowed either to attack Djedeida immediately, and take up positions based there, or else to form a strong defensive position with his right on the Medjerda River and his left in contact with the East Surreys, where he would be able to present a formidable front; but neither plan was permitted. Ironically enough, on the fourth morning the battalion fell back, and took up the precise position Colonel Lee had advocated, but with a greatly depleted battalion.

On the first day of the battle, Monday, 30 November 1942, the battalion was subjected to heavy shelling by infantry guns and mortars, and there was considerable air activity. The brigade commander came up and said that the battalion must hold the ground it stood on. During the day Captain Page, commanding the carrier platoon, established a standing patrol on the high ground behind Y Company, with one of his sectors, to observe any enemy movement to the rear and north of the position. The mortar detachment with X Company scored a direct hit on a lorry-load of enemy infantry approaching the railway on the right of the company's position. Fighting patrols probing the vicinity of the positions after dark made no contact with the enemy, except one which went forward to the outskirts of Djedeida, where contact was made with enemy machine guns on fixed lines. So the first day was passed.

During the morning of Tuesday, 1 December considerable enemy activity was observed on the battalion front, and in the early afternoon the enemy attacked along the fronts of both forward companies, using infantry supported by mortars and machine guns. In front of X Company, they advanced into the wood, but they were resolutely driven back, so that the company commander was able to report the situation under control and casualties slight. The attack on the left of the battalion was also held off by the fire of Y Company.

Towards the evening the enemy made an attempt to get some men and machine guns established in a small farm in front of the right-hand platoon of Y Company. Z Company was accordingly ordered to counter-attack the farm with a platoon, and Lieutenant Griffith, attached to the battalion from the Welsh Guards, led his platoon in a spirited attack, supported by artillery and mortars. It happened that the approach to the farm was down an exposed forward slope, and the platoon suffered severe casualties, among them the platoon commander himself. The attack was then pressed home, however, and some men reached the farm, which was set alight by enemy fire. Later the platoon was ordered to withdraw to the company as the position was considered to be untenable with so few men. The withdrawal was completed at dusk, with the exception of some badly wounded, and seven men who were missing. After dark Lieutenant Wright, second-in-command of Z Company, although himself wounded in the ankle, went out with stretcher bearers. The wounded platoon commander, eight badly wounded soldiers, and the seven men previously reported missing were brought in. For this action Lieutenant Wright was awarded the MC.

The second night, 1 December, was again fairly quiet, and patrols reported no enemy on the battalion's immediate front, but soon after daylight on 2 December the enemy got snipers and machine guns on the high ground on the battalion's right, across the river. These machine guns opened fire on the whole front, and the enemy advanced in strength, supported by tanks. There were also tanks advancing on the right of Y Company's position, one of which was able to fire direct into the right-hand platoon, commanded by Lieutenant Seth-Smith, from a range of only twenty yards, and nothing more was seen or heard of this platoon.

Meanwhile both 6-pounders and 2-pounder anti-tank guns were actively engaging the enemy, and two tanks and an infantry gun towed by a lorry were set on fire, while one other was stopped and put out of action. One tank got into a position where it was able to fire into battalion headquarters, causing many casualties, which included Lieutenant Pritchard, the signal officer, and five signallers. Headquarters was then heavily mortared, and withdrew to a position behind W Company, leaving the anti-aircraft platoon and the pioneers to strengthen the W Company position.

At the same time very heavy fighting had been going on in X Company positions. The company had been attacked heavily all morning, but time after time Captain Thomas, the company commander, and Lieutenant Hart, drove the enemy back with bayonet charges. At one stage the western end of the wood was defended only by Captain Thomas and five men; he gathered his few men together, and, firing a Bren gun from the hip, led a most gallant bayonet charge clean through the enemy tanks to the infantry beyond and drove them back. But at last the enemy's recurrent attacks with tanks and infantry overran the positions. The anti-tank guns were put out of action, and all who remained of X Company were one officer, one sergeant, and five men. For this very gallant fighting, Captain Thomas was awarded the DSO.

W Company, with three anti-aircraft detachments and some pioneers, were moved up to the position previously held by battalion headquarters, and became the right forward company. The second-in-command, Major Chamberlain, was killed endeavouring to locate enemy mortar and machine-gun positions. An enemy tank, approaching over a ridge about 300 yards to the left front of battalion head-quarters, was stopped and set on fire by a 25-pounder gun. W Company then reported by wireless that enemy infantry were advancing in strength down the wood and were close to his position. Colonel Lee ordered Z Company to send a platoon down the wood to drive the enemy off with the bayonet, and Lieutenant Freemantle, leading his own platoon, carried this order out most successfully; he drove the enemy off, killed or wounded some forty of them, and took six prisoners. Lieutenant Freemantle himself, his platoon sergeant, and four men were wounded. The platoon went back to its original position in very high spirits.

The situation on Y Company's front was obscure, and enemy infantry and machine guns could be plainly seen on the hills to their left and rear. As Colonel Lee had not been able to get in touch with them since midday, he feared that they had been overrun. At about 16.00 hours, however, two runners, one the company clerk, the other the NCO in charge of transport, got into battalion headquarters with a report on the situation. To get back, they had crossed very open ground swept by machine-gun fire, after they had already seen one runner seriously wounded in attempting to get across.

The message from Y Company commander, Captain Brehaut, showed that the situation was indeed desperate. Casualties had been very heavy, they were out of ammunition and water, and they were cut off from the rest of the battalion; they were, however, still holding on to their position. Captain Wingfield and a few men at once set off with a carrier loaded with ammunition and water, and succeeded in fighting their way through to the beleaguered company.

Shortly before dusk the liaison officer with brigade, Lieutenant Symes, got through to the battalion to get the situation, as communication between battalion and brigade had broken down before midday. Colonel Lee reported that he was still preventing the enemy from reaching Tebourba, but in view of the heavy casualties he had suffered he did not think he would be able to withstand another full-scale attack by infantry supported by tanks.

The enemy attacks died down after dark, and the battalion set about finding and bringing in its wounded. Just before midnight Lieutenant Symes returned from brigade with the order for the battalion to take up another position about a mile and a half to the rear, with its right on the river and its left holding a high feature, Point 186.

The battalion had been in violent battle for three days, harassed constantly by a most desperate enemy. Yet, when the troops passed Colonel Lee as he stood in the clearing between the two woods, discipline and morale were perfect. Every one was alert, silent, and most orderly; it was an exemplary retreat.

The battalion withdrew to its new position at 01.30 On the morning of 3 December. The depleted companies were disposed with W Company on the right, Z Company on the left (including Point 186), and Y Company astride the railway line, slightly to the rear of the other two, covering the gap between them. By dawn Colonel Lee had been round the new positions, and had arranged his artillery support. He ordered two sections of the carrier platoon to cover the right flank of W Company, which was very thin on the ground for the area it was holding. In these positions the battalion awaited the fourth day of the battle.

At first light on 3 December the enemy began a very heavy artillery and mortar attack along the whole front. This was maintained until ten o'clock, when they launched a general and very determined advance, paying most attention to the battalion's left flank, held by Z Company.

An hour later Major H. W. Le Patourel, commanding this company, reported that the enemy had gained possession of some high ground on his immediate left, which they had captured from a company of another unit after a furious battle. The Germans were establishing themselves there, and were bringing heavy machine-gun and mortar fire on his left hand section at Point 186. The fighting at this stage was extremely heavy and confused.

It was in a desperate attempt to clear the enemy from the high ground on the battalion's left that Major Le Patourel led a party of four volunteers in a most gallant action, for which he was awarded the Victoria Cross. To quote from the citation:

> On the afternoon of December 3, 1942, the enemy had occupied an important high feature on the left of the company commanded by Major Le Patourel . . . This officer then personally led four volunteers under very heavy fire to the top in a last attempt to dislodge several enemy machine-guns.
>
> The party was heavily engaged by the machine-gun fire, and Major Le Patourel rallied his men several times and engaged the enemy, silencing several machine-gun posts. Finally, when the remainder of his party were killed or wounded, he went forward alone with a pistol and some grenades to attack the enemy machine-guns at close quarters, and from this action he did not return . . . Major Le Patourel's most gallant conduct and self-sacrifice, his brilliant leadership and tenacious devotion to duty in the face of a determined enemy, were beyond praise.

It was believed that Major Le Patourel was killed, and, indeed, his Victoria Cross was awarded posthumously. But it was discovered later that he had been seriously wounded and taken prisoner.

For the rest of the day the Hampshires fought on, till by 17.00 only one gun remained in action. The battalion was reduced to ten officers and 200 men. These lined up and charged the enemy, battling back to the outskirts of Tebourba, when it was found that all troops had withdrawn to Medjez-el-Bab. The main road back from Tebourba was cut by the enemy, and the only solution was for all troops to make their own way back in small groups, getting through the enemy positions as best they could. Thus ended the Battle of Tebourba.

CHAPTER THIRTY

Cutter at Oran

FREDERICK PETERS

A big, burly man was Captain Peters: a man for the attack, the right man, in fact, to be taking part in special Allied landings on the North African coast at Oran in November 1942. But his naval life started some thirty-seven years earlier —in 1905, when he was sixteen.

A brother officer has described him as 'a typical Elizabethan gentleman adventurer. His entire soul was in the Navy. It was a fanaticism with him.' He won the DSO and DSC during the 1914–18 war, beginning it with the rank of lieutenant, ending it as a commander. In 1919, when he was just thirty, he was one of the 400 young officers who had to be ' axed' when the personnel of the Navy was reduced.

Instead of moping, he accepted his lot and took a civilian job out on the Gold Coast —starting at the bottom as a clerk. Needless to say, he made good. Later on, he journeyed to Canada, where his father was an advocate in Montreal. As soon as war was declared, Peters worked his passage back to Britain in a tramp steamer, and within a month he was in the Navy commanding an anti-submarine flotilla on convoy work. In 1940 he won a bar to his DSC.

He was a lieutenant again now. Aboard the *Meteor* in an action on the Dogger Bank, the ship was hit. The commander shouted to ask where Peters was. The reply came:

'He's gone down to the boiler-room to turn off the steam-cocks.'

The boiler-room is an uncomfortable place when a ship has been hit.

During 1942 Captain Peters was detailed for special service, which turned out to be to command an expedition in miniature to try to take Oran harbour. The two tiny ships comprising this 'fleet' were the ex-American coastguard cutters *Walney* and *Hartland*.

Together these little cutters sped into the harbour at dead of night, crashed into the defences, and broke the boom. Peters stood on the bridge of the *Walney* and saw an enemy motor-launch ploughing straight for her. He swerved to avoid it, and was immediately caught in the concentrated beam of a Vichy-French searchlight. But they were through the boom, and that was one hazard over. The dash was still suicidal. The second *Walney* had been lit, every shore battery swivelled round on her and the searchlight kept her in constant view. As a barrage of fire flew over the water of the harbour, *Walney* was hit again and again. Peters did not let it deflect him one degree, but took her half-way up the harbour. The French guns were firing at closer range every second, and of the seventeen officers and men standing on the bridge of the cutter every one fell. Only Peters survived, though a bullet blinded him in one eye, and managed to steer the ship inshore, towards the quay which was the objective ordered. The firing intensified as he approached. But he reached it.

He found a French cruiser lying there, which stopped *Walney*'s shock troops, United States Rangers, from going ashore; so he ordered the cutter to be laid alongside the enemy. By now three submarines were on the attack, too, and *Walney* was ablaze. Somehow they shot grapnels into the deck of the cruiser. Boarding parties with tommy guns at the ready stood by to carry the cruiser by storm. But the cutter had had enough. Her boilers burst, she leaned over exhausted, and sank.

Many of the men were drowned. Several, including Peters, got ashore on a Carley raft. Peters looked back from the raft as the ship went down, and the last part of her he saw was the flag flying to the end.

The other cutter, *Hartland*, had also reached the jetty by this time, but too few men remained alive for them to haul on the ropes and secure her. She drifted away again, blew up, and sank. So both small ships met the same fate.

Much later, the French picked up Peters and the others on the raft. He was taken before the French admiral in charge of the port and questioned closely. The Frenchman tried to make Peters admit having fired the first shot, which he would not do. So at length he was put in prison.

However, he spent only a short spell there, since Oran capitulated and the Free-French population broke in and bore Peters off literally shoulder-high through the streets, scattering flowers over him.

Peters was recommended for the American Distinguished Service Cross for this exploit carried out in company with the United States troops, but he never received this medal, for soon afterwards there came the sad announcement that a plane had crashed in North Africa. Among its occupants was Peters, already on another mission. Thus not one of the seventeen men on the bridge of the *Walney* that fateful night survived.

CHAPTER THIRTY-ONE

Wounded but brought Bomber Home

RAWDON MIDDLETON

nother Aussie this time: Flight Sergeant Rawdon Hume Middleton, No. 149 Squadron. A real New South Wales man, Middleton worked for his father, who was the manager of the Wee Wang sheep station at Brogari Gate, NSW. And the colourful name given to this occupation is jackaroo. So Rawdon Middleton was a jackaroo. What stopped him being one we will never know, except that on 14 October 1940, he decided it was time to start to think of the war. He joined up.

This lean, quiet, unassuming chap was also tough. In the RAAF he became an earnest, plodding pupil. All he did was thorough, though unspectacular. He is said to have brooded a lot on the German bombing of unprotected cities, and followed a common trait among outback Australians in being inclined to bouts of melancholy. But this was actually more apparent than real, as indicated by the entries in his diary.

Middleton's first chance came as a second pilot on the night of 6 April 1942, in No. 149 Squadron. They never reached the target of Essen, and their bombs had to be jettisoned live twenty-five miles north of Aachen. The main cause of this spot of trouble was an attack by a Messerschmitt Me110, which caused considerable damage to the starboard wing. The bomber, a Halifax, hobbled home from the Dutch coast on three engines, and literally gave up the ghost altogether on landing. According to Middleton's fellow squadron members, this operation seemed to have an astonishing effect on Middleton, shaking him out of his melancholy, and galvanizing him into a mood almost of buoyancy. The probable explanation for that phase is that he, like so many others, got sick of waiting for operations to start. Once they did, there was no time to brood —or certainly far less.

Middleton was in a series of big attacks on Rostock, Lübeck, Duisburg-Hamborn, the Ruhr, and Hamburg, all as second pilot.

On 31 July 1942, he walked into the mess with a broad Australian grin. He had been given the captaincy of a Stirling, and that same night he was airborne on a big one-hour raid on Düsseldorf. He had bad luck, however, because his rear turret went unserviceable, and he had to return early. In his crew were Mackie, Cameron, and Crough, who will also figure in Middleton's last flight.

Then came Osnabrück, Frankfurt, Wilhelmshaven, Munich, Genoa, and Turin, and some steady routine mine laying-trips around Europe's coast. The previous operation before his final mission also had Turin as its objective; more specifically, the target was the Royal Arsenal there and the date of this raid was 20 November.

Incidentally, in August Middleton was posted to No. 7 (PFF) Squadron with his crew to become a Pathfinder unit. On his return from a mission to Nuremberg, the CO told Middleton that he could continue as a Pathfinder pilot, but that his navigator was not up to standard, so that navigator and crew would be posted back to No. 149 Squadron. The authorities reckoned without the 'quiet, unassuming man'. Middleton refused to be parted from his crew, and returned to his old squadron with all of them.

His final mission was his twenty-ninth —one short of a complete operational tour. Seven aircraft were detailed for this operation on the Fiat works at Turin, near the Italian Alps. It was just after a week since their previous long-distance onslaught on Turin, on 20 November.

Now the night of 28 November 1942 arrived, and the seven Stirlings set out.

They got airborne from Lakenheath at 18.14 hours on that early winter night. Darkness was just falling. The single summer time kept it light till nearly 18.00. This was Middleton's crew:

Second Pilot: Flight Sergeant L. A. Hyder, a former Glasgow student.
Navigator B: Pilot Officer G. R. Royde.
Wireless Operator Air Gunner: Pilot Officer N. E. Skinner.
Mid Upper Air Gunner: Flight Sergeant D. Cameron —formerly a gamekeeper.
Front gunner: Sergeant S. J. Mackie.
Rear gunner: Sergeant H. W. Gough —a garage hand in peacetime.
Flight engineer: Sergeant J. E. Jeffery.

Middleton, of course, flew as captain and first pilot. Trouble started before Turin. They experienced great difficulty in climbing to the necessary 12,000 feet to cross the Alps. This led to excessive fuel consumptions, which was to make its effect felt later on. Added to this hazard, the night had grown so dark that the mountain peaks around and before them almost faded into invisibility. Only by screwing up their eyes could they distinguish these deadly Alps. It was no night to be trying for Turin. As things turned out, only four of the seven aircraft did get through. At this stage over the Alps Middleton had to decide whether or not to go on, since the drain of fuel through the great climb meant that they would have barely enough for the return. And there were few places to ditch a bomber between Italy and the English Channel.

They sighted flares ahead. These seemed to clinch it for Middleton. He could hardly turn back now, having come so far, and with the flares actually in sight. There would be time to worry about fuel later. Now the raid would take all his mind. He pressed on south, and even dived down to 2,000 feet to identify the target for certain, despite the difficulty of regaining height. Middleton made three lights over the Fiat works before he was satisfied he had identified it exactly, and more precious petrol burned away in the process.

Now it was 22.00 hours and the epic battle began in earnest. All that had gone before became child's play; all the fuss over the Alps in pitch-black. And there was no second from now on in which to think of fuel —or the lack of it.

Light anti-aircraft guns fired at Middleton's Stirling and another one close behind. The first hit came when a large hole appeared in the port mainplane, making it difficult to maintain lateral control, or —more simply —the aircraft would not stay balanced.

A shell struck the cockpit, burst inside it, shattered the windscreen, and wounded both pilots —Middleton and Hyder. Here was war at its worst.

A piece of shell splinter tore into the side of Middleton's face, destroying his right eye totally, and exposing the bone over the eye. He was also wounded in the body and legs.

Hyder was wounded in the head and both his legs, which bled profusely. The wireless operator was also hit in the leg by a splinter. The Stirling started to go down, far from England and Lakenheath. Middleton lost consciousness as the plane dipped down to 800 feet above Italian soil. Hyder snatched the controls just in time and jerked the plane up. They still had the bombs aboard. At 1,500 feet he gave the order, and the welcome phrase came back: 'Bombs gone.'

The flak poured up the short distance from ground to plane. It varied each moment from light to heavy. And the ground gunners could hardly help recording more hits. The three gunners in the plane fired continuously until the rear turret was put out of action. One more blow, and the four aircraft left the target area with good fires burning in the Fiat works.

Middleton drifted back to consciousness again. As soon as they were clear of the immediate target zone, he ordered Hyder back to get first aid. Middleton was in obvious agony. Before Hyder had been properly fixed up, he insisted on returning to the cockpit, as he knew that Middleton could only see slightly —and could only barely speak because of the loss of blood and surges of pain.

This magnificent crew set course for base from the other side of Europe. They faced an Alpine crossing, the homeward flight, most of them wounded, and in a badly damaged aircraft without enough fuel to reach the English coast. Here was heroism on the most massive scale imaginable.

They discussed abandoning the plane or landing it in Northern France, but Middleton was adamant.

'I'm going to try to make the English coast,' he insisted, so that the crew could leave by parachute. Mackie sat at Middleton's shoulder all those long, weary, agonizing hours homeward, giving the captain visual assistance. Mackie was on his thirty-third trip —three over the operational tour —having volunteered to continue with his captain. Middleton must have known by now that there could be little chance for him, but he kept going for the sake of the others. The war brought out this close friendship among aircrews. Men who faced death together had the biggest bond between them it was possible to find.

Middleton's wounds worsened, and as the hours passed strength ebbed too. Midnight came and went, then 01.00, 02.00, hours. Even now their ordeal was not yet over. Soon after 02.00 hours the Stirling shuddered over the French coast at 6,000 feet. It was asking too much of any man. More anti-aircraft fire attacked them. For eight hours Middleton had kept the plane up. Intense ack-ack hit it yet again.

How many more hits could they take? Yet Middleton mustered up enough strength from somewhere –the inner resources beyond the understanding –to take evasive action. The very thought of the crippled bomber being bounced over the sky, out of the way of ack-ack, by a mortally wounded pilot seems too wild to be true; yet it happened all right, about 02.30 hours on the morning of 29 November.

There was only the Channel now between them and the south coast of England. Could the fuel last out? If not, it would be a wet end. As these next twenty minutes ticked off, the fuel gauge read practically zero. 02.30, 02.40, 02.50. Middleton could not last as long as the petrol it seemed –just a matter of chance which drained out first. Somehow, no one will ever know how –not even the crew –Middleton managed to keep the Stirling airborne. Riddled with splinters of shells, it chugged on till the Kent coast loomed dimly into view below them. They gave him an accurate reading of the fuel.

'Five minutes more.'

Summoning up his reserves of strength, Middleton said that he would not take the risk of hitting houses by trying to land the big bomber. So he ordered them all to abandon aircraft while he flew parallel with the coast for a few miles. After that, he said, he was going to head out to sea. Middleton insisted, and this was not the time or place to argue about it. He might still make it, they thought. He had come this far, to the very cliffs of Dover.

Hyder, Royde, Skinner, Cameron, and Gough, all baled out safely and survived.

Mackie and Jeffery stayed to help Middleton till the last minute. Then they jumped. Their 'chutes opened all right, and they fell into the sea –but they fell too far out. Neither survived the night. The following afternoon, about 15.00 hours, a naval launch recovered their bodies with the parachutes open.

At 02.55 hours the Stirling ran out of fuel. Middleton might still have been conscious, or he might not. In any case, the Stirling crashed into the sea off Dymchurch.

As the citation ends:

> While all the crew displayed heroism of a high order, the urge to do so came from Flight Sergeant Middleton, whose fortitude and strength of will made possible the completion of the mission. His devotion to duty in the face of overwhelming odds is unsurpassed in the annals of the Royal Air Force.'

All the surviving crew were awarded either the DFC or DFM.

On 15 January 1943, Middleton was awarded the Victoria Cross.

On 1 February 1943, his body was washed up at Shakespeare Cliff, Dover.

CHAPTER THIRTY-TWO

Ten Out of Ten Planes Lost

HUGH MALCOLM

Do you know why the famous Malcolm Clubs for the RAF were so called? It was in memory of Acting Wing Commander Hugh Gordon Malcolm, of No. 18 Squadron, to perpetuate the name of one of the RAF's most gallant flyers.

Born at Broughty Ferry, Dundee, Scotland, in 1917, Malcolm went to Trinity College, Glenalmond, Perthshire, and then spent the whole of 1936 and 1937 at the RAF College, Cranwell. Before he joined he was a quiet, shy youth, yet with an engaging manner. He was good at games, especially golf, and later he became devoted to hunting.

Commissioned as a pilot officer, he was posted to a squadron for general flying duties early in 1938. It was while with this squadron that his courage and presence of mind both had a severe test which was to stand him in good stead for similar experiences when war broke out.

On an Empire flying display at Manchester, in his Westland Lysander, something went wrong with the aircraft, and it got out of Malcolm's control. He realized that it would be bound to crash, and there was nothing he could do but await it. The inevitable came closer and closer. Malcolm faced it —'with such fortitude as I could muster,' as he wrote to a friend afterwards. Now it was nearer. Then it happened. The Lysander, with Malcolm in it, lay spread all over the ground. He was rushed to hospital with a fractured skull, where his friend found him with a fearful gash in his head.

After the crash he was told he would never fly again, but despite his severe injuries he made an amazing recovery. He was determined to get back into the air again. It had become his life. And with this determination, he was well enough to return to his unit in September 1939, just after war was declared.

While in the hospital to which he had been taken, he met a VAD nurse, Helen Swan, and in 1940 they were married.

To many men, even recovered sufficiently to rejoin the RAF, the crash might have meant the end of flying. But not to Malcolm. A Flying Officer in 1939, it was not very long before he had persuaded the authorities he was well enough to fly and not just fit for ground duties. Flight Lieutenant was followed by promotion to Squadron Leader, as Malcolm made many operational trips from Britain, until in the autumn of 1942 he reached the rank of Acting Wing Commander, with the command of No. 18 Squadron, a light bomber formation based in Tunisia. He was a Scottish bomber ace at the age of twenty-five.

That autumn, therefore, found him many miles from Worth and his wife, flying in the sunshine and comparative warmth of the Mediterranean and North Africa. On 8 November the Allies landed in French North Africa. Just nine days later Malcolm was detailed to carry out the first of the three operations which would win him the Victoria Cross and cost him his life: three classic attacks in seventeen days.

On 17 November 1942, he received orders to carry out a low-level formation attack on Bizerta airfield, taking advantage of existing cloud-cover. The Met men were not quite right in their anticipation of cloud, for twenty miles from the target –formidable enough even with cover –the sky suddenly cleared. Malcolm peered anxiously out of his Blenheim, but there was no doubt. They were leaving the cloud behind with every mile they flew. So here they were, a small force of Blenheims without a fighter escort, proceeding towards an enemy-held airfield in the broad, brilliant daylight of the Mediterranean coastal belt. The German fighter opposition pounced on such a heaven-sent opportunity. Junkers Ju52s and Messerschmitt Me109s screamed into the air. The Blenheims braved the assault and pressed on right to Bizerta. The fighters scorched the air all around the RAF force with fire, but despite everything they could do, Malcolm and his men managed to drop all their bomb-loads within the airfield perimeter, as ordered by the operation..

Replying to the Luftwaffe fighters, the Blenheims actually shot one of each type down into the scorching sand around the North African port. Then they went on to rake many of the enemy aircraft dispersed on the airfield with machine-gun fire. Still the battle ebbed and flowed high in the sky over Bizerta, and the Germans shot down one of the precious Blenheims. With typical Mediterranean unreliability, the weather, which had cleared to expose the bombers to view of enemy ground and air defences, now had another nasty trick up its sleeve. The whole sky darkened with cloud. In the chaos caused by this sudden storm two of the Blenheims collided and crashed. Malcolm kept a firm leadership on the rest, however, and by his skill he extricated all of them from this doubly dangerous area, and shepherded them back to the comparative calm of their own airfield in Tunisia. So ended the first of Malcolm's three great raids.

The second was on 28 November, aimed at the same Bizerta airfield. Not surprisingly, after the earlier attack, the airfield was much more heavily defended from the ground. The Germans had evidently rushed in all the mobile and other guns they could to resist future attempts to neutralize this vital Bizerta airbase. Despite this reinforcement, which Malcolm knew would exist, he led his squadron in at low level, again in daylight. The barrage broke before they reached the airfield. Low-angle flak cut across the sky directly in front of the Blenheims. They flew on, right into the face of it. Just to do this called for courage of a high order. The ack-ack got fiercer and fiercer as they reached the target. But they bombed it just as effectively as before. And not content with the success of this aspect of the operation —which anyone could well have been —Malcolm veered his leading Blenheim back again and again to attack the field with machine-guns. This they continued to do till their ammunition was more or less exhausted. Only then did they decide to call it a day and put the noses back to Tunisia.

As the official citation states at this stage of Malcolm's three attacks: 'These were typical of every sortie undertaken by this gallant officer; each attack was pressed to an effective conclusion however difficult the task and however formidable the opposition.'

Malcolm did not know it then, but he had less than a week to live. And five times during that week he had led the squadron, and had gone in to attack from almost ground level.

On 4 December 1942, Acting Wing Commander Malcolm, having been detailed to give close support to the First Army, received an urgent request to attack an enemy fighter airfield near Cheuigui, Tunisia.

There was no time to arrange a fighter escort. Malcolm knew that to attack such an objective without an escort would be to invite almost certain disaster. But believing the attack to be necessary for the success of the First Army's operations, his duty, to him, was quite clear. He decided to attack.

Malcolm took ten Bristol Bisleys —the improved version of the original Blenheims —and set off on his audacious attack on an enemy forward fighter aerodrome at Cheuigui.

The ten planes reached the target area completely unmolested, as they had reasonably expected to do. But that did not mean anything. The danger would come as soon as their presence became known. And bombs were not the best way of concealing the presence of planes in the vicinity.

Malcolm and his men reached the target, delivered their attack from the phenomenally low level of only 200 feet, and then began to get out of that deathly dangerous area as soon as they could. It was not to be soon enough. The sky suddenly blackened with a force of fighters flying straight at the Bristol Bisleys. That was it. Malcolm fought back, and tried to control his hard-pressed squadron. Poignantly he attempted to maintain formation as the fighters lunged and lanced through the bombers. One by one his aircraft was shot down before his eyes. Ten had set out. Then there were nine, eight, seven, six. Could it go on? The massacre did go on in those December skies over Tunisia. Now half of them had gone, then another and another, till after only a few minutes the only aircraft left flying was Malcolm's. In the end he too was shot down in flames.

All ten planes were lost.

But there were a few survivors left to tell the story of this attack. Sub Lieutenant K. G. Wallace, RNVR, had been lent to the RAF for special observer duties, and was with the Bisleys that week. This is what he said after it was all over:

Our bombs were still going down when 50 to 60 Messerschmitt fighters came in at us. In the tightest possible formation we weaved as a single unit through the valleys of the hills. We could see the fighters' cannon-shells bursting all along the mountainsides on a level with our faces. Finally, we were forced out of formation, and with the starboard engine on fire, the fuselage on fire, and a large piece of wing missing, we went into a hillside at about 150 miles per hour.

Out of the blazing aircraft all three of us emerged more or less in one piece, and as we were in No Man's Land, we began to run like hell. Behind us were a party of men rushing down a hillside, and ahead was a second party of men —our own troops —coming to meet us. We were accelerated by cannon-shells from an enemy fighter who was trying to get us, but we made it. Then I passed out, and the party was over.

So the story of Hugh Malcolm was told: the story of a doomed squadron.

CHAPTER THIRTY-THREE

Russian Convoy

ROBERT SHERBROOKE

With the turn of the year from 1942 to 1943 the tide had really turned, too. The offensive spirit spread. After Oran came the thrilling triumph of Captain Sherbrooke. How appropriate that the action on this particular run to Russia should be marked by the VC, for of all convoy routes — indeed of all sea-lanes anywhere —during the war, this was the worst. 'The world's worst journey' it has often been described as, and that is no exaggeration. Why was it so bad? Because the combination of the enemy and the elements, coupled with the imperative need for supplies to reach Russia from Britain all conspired to produce conditions which made survival of ships —and men —hang in the balance each time they set sail. The only course was boldness. And it was just such brilliant bravado that Sherbrooke showed.

He commanded the destroyer HMS *Onslow* and served as senior officer of all the destroyers escorting an important convoy headed for Russia. On New Year's Eve, the convoy were off the North Cape, north of Norway.

All the ships were keeping their appointed station well, but it was midwinter and heavy seas swelled around them. Although the time approached noon, the day carried on in an almost continual darkness, for they were not far from the North Pole with its six-month, black out. Conditions were all against mere men. The intense cold created navigational hazards in the form of ice freezing on to vital parts of the ships. What slight sight there was from daylight was curtailed by cloud, reducing surface visibility to a minimum, and even this semi-darkness was reduced further by frequent snowstorms.

In this setting, the convoy suddenly made contact with an enemy squadron of vastly superior strength. Usually in such situations little hope exists for the smaller ships. All other things equal, it is a case of cold statistics; the number and range of the larger ships' guns can hardly fail to outstrip their adversary. But all other things were not equal. The British convoy had in command Captain Sherbrooke.

The strength of the forces opposed to him was believed to be as follows; one pocket battleship, one cruiser, and a number of destroyers. It was the battleship and cruiser that counted.

Unhesitatingly, Sherbrooke aboard *Onslow* led his destroyers into the attack and closed with the enemy. The wild seas swirled to the bow-wake of destroyers of both sides, plus the two enemy capital ships, jockeying for positions to pierce the defence of the merchantmen —or from the British viewpoint, prevent it being pierced.

Four times the enemy vessels swung into the attack in the murky midday, to try to force a gap and get at the convoy. Four times they had to withdraw hurriedly behind a smokescreen. Even a screen was needed for their safety despite the gloom! The threat of torpedoes became too great for them.

Not content with just keeping them at bay behind their own smokescreen, Sherbrooke pursued them with *Onslow* and his small destroyer force. He worried them out of gunshot of the convoy, mauled them, intimidated them.

So the first of the four attacks was beaten off, and brought home to the Germans' own ground —or sea. What was the precise power of the destroyers which were winning this scrap? The heaviest gun aboard *Onslow* had a calibre of 4·7-inch. Against this the *Lützow or Admiral Scheer,* whichever pocket battleship it was, mounted no less than half a dozen 11-inch guns and eight 5·9-inch guns. And the cruiser, of similar tonnage to the battleship —about 10,000 —had at her command eight 8-inch guns. She turned out to be *Hipper.* Even the German destroyers mounted modern armament of five 5-inch guns. Thus the odds were overwhelming.

Into the second assault the enemy swept. By brilliant navigation, Sherbrooke once more headed them off. After the action had been in progress for forty minutes *Onslow* received a hit, as was almost inevitable. Then a second shell screamed into her, exploding with a roar above the wind and the water. The bridge was rocked and rent, and shrapnel splintered into a thousand particles. Several struck Sherbrooke, one right in the eye, depriving him of all sight for a second or two, but he gripped the remnant of the rail. He could see nothing from one eye. Agonized, he blinked the other eye open. Blood streamed from another wound, but he insisted on continuing to direct operations. For the second time the destroyers ran circles round the Germans, and not until he saw the smoke screen filtering through his remaining eye would he hear of receiving attention. Further hits on *Onslow* forced Sherbrooke to disengage and leave the enemy for the moment behind their hideout. Even so, he refused the surgeon's plea to go below till he had made sure himself that the next senior officer had assumed control.

Sherbrooke staggered below, helped by the surgeon and a rating. The surgeon made him as comfortable as he could. The eye was worse, if anything.

'You must tell me how it's going,' Sherbrooke whispered and he meant it. The state of the battle was reported to him for the next hour. Two more attacks were repulsed in the second hour of the engagement. The credit for the first half of the battle went largely to him and his cool, prompt decisions. That the rest of it went as well as it did was also due considerably to his inspiration, for battles are often as much a matter of morale —and quick, calm thinking —as of armaments. The human element counts for more than might be imagined.

After the persistent pummelling they received, the Germans had no stomach for further fighting —or for lunch! The last straw came when the lookout aboard their battleship sighted through the mists the shadowy silhouettes of heavier British ships rushed to the scene by radio.

'Achtung!' he shouted, terror-stricken. If destroyers did this to them, what would warships of the same size as the Germans' manage? Not waiting to find out, they turned a complete circle and raced back for the sanctuary of their bases on the north Norwegian coast. They were only a few hours out, so they could scarcely fail to make port. Once there, they nursed their wounds and admitted that a destroyer of the *Maas*-class had been lost. Admiralty claimed damage to one of the two heavier enemy vessels —and also regretted to have to announce the loss of HM Destroyer *Achates*, under Lieutenant Commander A. H. Tyndall Jones. She was damaged in the defence of the convoy and then subsequently sunk.

The fantastic fact which will remain to Captain Sherbrooke's eternal credit is that the complete convoy got through to Russia with its vital military supplies for the Eastern front —unscathed by a bullet or a single shell. The First Lord of the Admiralty said of the achievement that there had 'never been anything finer in naval annals'.

Despite all the doctors' efforts, Captain Sherbrooke lost the sight of his eye. He returned to active service a year later —to his first 'shore' appointment for twenty-seven years! He took over the command of one of the largest naval air stations in Britain. So he was still serving, with a glass eye as memento of that Arctic morning which ended 1942.

This, however, is not the end of Sherbrooke's story. After the war, the other side of the struggle at North Cape came to light in the German Admiral Raeder's speech on his retirement. At a conference on 3 December 1942 —the day before the battle, notice —Goering was present when Hitler began talking of the superiority of the British Navy, and described the German one as 'but a copy of the British and a very poor one at that. He said that the German ships were not in operational readiness, and lying idle in the fiords of Norway, utterly useless like so much old iron.

At that very moment, Admiral Krancke read a tele-typed message from the Operations Division that a German surface force was in contact with a British convoy off the North Cape. At the evening conference no more news had come in, but Hitler was promised reports the second they arrived, for, as Krancke said, 'I know he cannot sleep a wink when ships are operating'.

Next day Hitler became impatient, despite Krancke explaining the exigencies of radio silence. Hitler suggested they ask the task force for a very brief report by wireless, but Raeder refused to order ships to break radio silence.

Noon next day brought no news. It seemed a bad start to the New Year, and the Fuehrer became restless and ranted about the failure of the German Navy. Then that evening they heard the result of Operation Rainbow, as the Germans had called it. The destroyer *Friedrich Eckoldt* sunk; *Hipper* damaged and her speed reduced; only one British destroyer sunk; and the convoy continued!

The Fuehrer was furious.

'This is typical of German ships,' he roared. 'Just the opposite of the British who, true to their tradition, fought to the bitter end. The whole thing spells the end of the German High Seas Fleet,' he went on.

Raeder was told of Hitler's decision to put most of the German surface navy out of commission, apart from a few ships for training. This was an amazing decision. As Raeder observed, the fleet was to all intents and purposes scuttled.

Raeder failed to get a reprieve for the surface ships —and resigned. Doenitz, the U-boat admiral, took his place.

From these highest German sources, therefore, comes the evidence that Sherbrooke's superb Arctic action resulted directly in the immobilization of the entire enemy surface fleet.

No one man could hope to do more than that.

CHAPTER THIRTY-FOUR

Fifty-two Far East Missions

WILLIAM NEWTON

Sometimes a story of courage needs the narrative of an eyewitness to do it full justice, to bring it to life from the page. Other deeds simply speak for themselves. The reader fills in the gaps between the facts from his own imagination, amplifies the personal feelings that must always exist behind any activity –particularly one involving a VC. It is thus in the case of Flight Lieutenant William Ellis Newton, Royal Australian Air Force, No. 22 Squadron. His award swung people's minds out east again, farther still than Scarf's area of operations in Malaya, to the prehistoric island of New Guinea, in fact. Newton was the first and only member of the Royal Australian Air Force to win the Victoria Cross. So here are the bare bones of his action, as announced by the Directorate of Public Relations, Air Ministry:

> Not for publication, broadcast or use on club tapes before 0030 hours on Wednesday, 20 October 1943. This embargo should be respected overseas by prefacing any message with this embargo.

> The King has been graciously pleased on the advice of Australian Ministers to confer the Victoria Cross on the undermentioned officer in recognition of most conspicuous bravery:
> Flight Lieutenant William Ellis Newton, RAAF (Missing) No. 22 RAAF Squadron.

Flight Lieutenant Newton was born at St Kilda, Victoria in 1919. He was educated at Melbourne Grammar School. He was vice-captain of Melbourne Grammar School Football Team, and played in their Cricket XI, also representing his school at swimming. He was at one time a member of the Victoria State 2nd Cricket XI. In civil life he was employed at a silk warehouse, in Melbourne.

On the outbreak of war, he was one of the first to apply for enlistment in the Royal Australian Air Force. Called for interviewing in October 1939, he was commissioned in 1940, and subsequently went into action against the Japanese in New Guinea.

This is the actual citation:

Flight Lieutenant Newton served with No. 22 Squadron, Royal Australian Air Force, in New Guinea, from May 1942, to March 1943, and completed 52 operation sorties.

Throughout he displayed great courage and an iron determination to inflict the utmost damage on the enemy. His splendid offensive flying and fighting were attended with brilliant success.

Disdaining evasive tactics when under the heaviest fire, he always went straight to his objectives. He carried out many daring machine-gun attacks on enemy positions involving low-flying over long distances in the face of continuous fire at point-blank range.

On three occasions, he dived through intense anti-aircraft fire to release his bombs on important targets on the Salamaua Isthmus. On one of these occasions, his starboard engine failed over the target, but he succeeded in flying back to an airfield 160 miles away.

When leading an attack on an objective on 16 March 1943, he dived through intense and accurate shell fire and his aircraft was hit repeatedly. Nevertheless, he held to his course and bombed his target from a low level. The attack resulted in the destruction of many buildings and dumps, including two 40,000-gallon fuel installations. Although his aircraft was crippled, with fuselage and wing sections torn, petrol-tanks pierced, main-planes and engines seriously damaged, and one of the main tyres flat, Flight Lieutenant Newton managed to fly it back to base and make a successful landing.

Despite this harassing experience, he returned next day to the same locality. His target, this time a single building, was even more difficult, but he again attacked with his usual courage and resolution, flying a steady course through a barrage of fire. He scored a hit on the building, but at the same moment his aircraft burst into flames.

Flight Lieutenant Newton maintained control and calmly turned his aircraft away, and flew along the shore. He saw it as his duty to keep the aircraft in the air as long as he could, so as to take his crew as far away as possible from the enemy's positions. With great skill, he brought his blazing aircraft down on the water. Two members of the crew were able to extricate themselves and were seen swimming to the shore, but the gallant pilot was missing. According to other aircrews who witnessed the occurrence, his escape-hatch was not opened and his dinghy was not inflated. Without regard for his own safety, he had done all that man could do to prevent his crew from falling into enemy hands.

Flight Lieutenant Newton's many examples of conspicuous bravery have rarely been equalled and will serve as a shining inspiration to all who follow him.

CHAPTER THIRTY-FIVE

Valour and Victory in Africa

DEREK SEAGRIM, MOANA-NUI-A-KIWA NGARIMU, LORNE CAMPBELL, ERIC ANDERSON, JOHN ANDERSON, WILLWARD CLARKE, LORD LYELL, JOHN KENNEALLY

Eight more desert VCs remained to be won in 1943 before the Allies finally beat the Axis in Africa —one of them being the first stretcher-bearer to win the highest award. But before this incident came the heroism of Seagrim of the Green Howards; the Maori VC; and an Argyll and Sutherland Highlander's valour.

He led his men up a scaling-ladder that attracted a cone of fire at the top. For this, and much more, Lieutenant Colonel Derek Anthony Seagrim was awarded the VC.

On the spring night of 20–21 March, 1943, in Tripolitania, a battalion of the Green Howards had to attack and take a vital feature on the left flank of the main British punch at the Mareth Line.

The defence of this feature was extremely strong, and protected by an anti-tank ditch fully twelve feet wide and eight feet deep. Minefields off both sides added to the perils of the post. This formed a new part of the main defences of the Mareth Line, and its successful capture was essential to the attack as a whole.

From the very minute the attack was mounted, the Green Howards were subjected to a shattering barrage from artillery and a closer-range battering by machine guns and mortars. It looked likely that the battalion would be delayed, endangering the timetable and actual achievement of the entire operation. So Seagrim at once stepped straight to the head of his battalion, being cut about cruelly at the time, and led it literally through a solid sheet of fire.

Then, he personally helped the team which was placing the scaling-ladder over the anti-tank ditch, and was himself the first to cross it. Seagrim started the assault by firing his pistol, hurling his hand grenades, and neutralizing two enemy machine-gun nests holding up the advance of one of his companies. He killed or took about a score or more Germans in this phase, and it resulted directly in the capture of the objective.

When dawn broke the battalion was securely established, though the enemy did all they could to dislodge the Green Howards. Quite undismayed, however, Seagrim held on.

Tragically, Seagrim subsequently died of wounds received in action.

From all ends of the earth men came to fight dictatorship, and the next two VCs could not be farther apart; a Maori and a Scotsman.

The magnificent Maori is how Second Lieutenant Moana-nui-a-Kiwa Ngarimu is remembered —the only one to win the VC.

During the action on the Tebaga Gap in Tunisia, on 26 March 1943, Ngarimu commanded a platoon in an attack on a vital hill-feature, Point 209. He had the task of taking an under-feature forward of Point 209 itself, held in considerable strength by the enemy.

He led his men straight up the face of the hill, undeterred by the mortars and machine guns screaming down. Men began to crumble, but enough of them were behind him as he himself was first on the hill crest. Ngarimu just annihilated two posts there. In face of such courage the rest of the enemy decided there was no answer, and fled. Ngarimu could not pursue them any farther, however, as the reverse slope was swept by machine-gun fire from Point 209 itself.

The tide of fighting turned for a while after that and, under cover of a tempestuous mortar-barrage, the enemy returned to the attack. Ngarimu told his men to stand up and engage the enemy man for man. This they did so literally that the attackers were mown down in their tracks. Ngarimu personally slew several.

About this time Ngarimu was wounded for the first time, by rifle fire in the shoulder. Later, for the second time, by shrapnel splinters in the leg. Though urged by his company and battalion commanders to leave, he refused, saying that he would stay a little while with his men.

As darkness fell it found Ngarimu and his depleted platoon lying on the rocky face of the forward slope of the hill-feature, with the enemy in an exactly similar spot on the reverse slope, only about twenty yards away.

So the long night started. The enemy tried to fling fierce onslaughts at the Maoris time after time, in an attempt to dislodge them, but each one was beaten off by Ngarimu. During one such attack the enemy resorted to hand grenades, and succeeded in piercing a certain part of the line. Without any hesitation, Ngarimu rushed to this threatened area, and those of the enemy he did not kill he drove back with stones or his tommy-gun.

Far into the Tunisian night the enemy made another frantic thrust, and part of Ngarimu's line broke before the weight of it. But, yelling orders and encouragement at the top of his voice, he rallied his men, and led them back to their old positions. His shoulder and leg wounds still troubled him, but he did not show it at all. All through that night of 26-27 March he and his men suffered either actual attacks or the continual harassment of machine-guns and mortars. Ngarimu watched his line vigilantly as the stars faded into dawn.

Morning came with them still holding on to their precious hill-feature as ordered, but only Ngarimu and two unwounded soldiers remained. Three men.

Reinforcements were sent up to them, to take the strain for a while, but the enemy soon counter-attacked again.

Ngarimu would not give in. Standing defiantly on his feet, he faced the enemy, firing his tommy gun. Finally, he was hit, and he fell, coming to rest almost on top of those of the enemy who had already died at his hands. So Ngarimu died too, leaving a memory of a Maori ready to fight for his country even on the other side of the world.

The Argylls would follow him anywhere. That is what they said about Lieutenant Colonel Lorne Maclaine Campbell in 1940, when he also earned the title of the man who saved 200. Just after the Battle of France, when much of the famous 51st (Highland) Division had been lost, Campbell led his unit in the retreat of St Valery, and Dunkirk. Ostensibly they were surrounded, cut off. But, after reconnoitring alone at night, Campbell came back, and led the 200 Highlanders right through the enemy lines to safety. He was awarded the DSO for that enterprise, and the VC in Tripolitania three years later.

On 6 April 1943 the battalion of the Argyll and Sutherland Highlanders commanded by Campbell was allotted the following task in the attack on the Wadi Akarit position: to break through the enemy minefield and anti-tank ditch to the east of the Rcumana-feature, and to form the initial bridgehead for a brigade of the 51st (Highland) Division.

The attack had to form up in complete darkness, and to traverse the main offshoot of the Wadi Akarit at an angle to the line of advance. The inevitable heavy fire met them in the early stages of the attack in that strange spell between night and day.

Campbell carried out this difficult job successfully, capturing 600 prisoners and leading his battalion to its objective. To do this, moreover, they had to cross an unswept portion of the enemy minefield.

When he actually got to the objective a little later he found that a gap that had been blown by the Royal Engineers in the anti-tank ditch did not correspond with the vehicle lane cleared in the minefield. At once appreciating the vital need of establishing a gap for anti-tank guns to pass, he took personal charge of the task.

It was now broad daylight. Across a bullet-swept stretch of desert he made a reconnaissance that in due course led to the establishment of the necessary vehicle gap.

Throughout the long, hot day Campbell held his bridgehead position in the face of frenzied shellfire, brought to bear by the enemy through direct observation and not mere estimation. About 16.30 hours the enemy counter-attacked with tanks.

Realizing that for the future success of the army plan they had to hold the bridge-head, Campbell inspired his men by sheer valour and utter disregard of danger. When his left forward company was forced to give ground he went forward alone into a furore of fire, and personally reorganized their position, staying with them until he felt quite sure that the attack at this point had been held.

At some stage Campbell was painfully wounded in the neck by shellfire. But after this, as reinforcements trickled into the battered bridgehead, he was seen standing in the open, directing the battle under close-range fire of enemy infantry. It was not till the fighting finally died down that he would let anyone dress his wounds, and even then, though in agony, he refused to be evacuated. Instead, he stayed with his battalion, to inspire them by his presence.

Darkness fell with the Argylls still holding their precious positions, though many of their officers and men had become casualties. With bayonets and hand grenades, they had held on. The bridgehead had been saved.

Campbell displayed unsurpassed leadership. And at a Rover Scouts conference, subsequently, he gave this advice on the qualities necessary for leadership.

> The whole secret of leadership is confidence, and the one essential requirement for a leader is to be able to win and to retain the confidence of the men he leads.
>
> To do this there are certain qualities which he must possess. By far the most important is sincerity. A leader must be sincere in all that he thinks, does, and says.
>
> Besides sincerity, a leader must have enthusiasm, and not just the enthusiasm of the follower who carries out keenly the suggestions of someone else, but the enthusiasm of the leader: the enthusiasm which looks ahead and sees great visions in the future, and can find the energy to work to realize them, and the courage to persevere when failure threatens.
>
> A leader must also have knowledge. He ought to know a little more than the men he is to lead, and he must have knowledge if he is to have that confidence in himself without which he cannot inspire confidence in others.
>
> Finally, a leader must show unselfishness and be ready to sink his own pride for the good of the community.

Private Eric Anderson was the first stretcher-bearer of the war to win the VC, making four treks across a bullet-swept slope of no man's land in the Wadi Akarit, on 6 April 1943; the same place and date as Campbell.

His battalion of the East Yorkshire Regiment launched a dawn attack on a strong enemy locality in the Wadi Akarit, Tunisia. Anderson's own group, A Company, led the assault, which made a measure of progress over an exposed forward slope. Suddenly it came under shatteringly accurate fire from machine guns and mortars, well concealed a couple of hundred yards away.

The fire from these weapons was so withering that any idea of further advance in the particular direction was out of the question. Indeed, it turned out to be all they could do to withdraw behind the crest of a hill. The company managed it, however, with the exception of a few men who had been wounded over no man's land, and lay in pain and pinned to the ground by strong, sustained small-arms fire.

Anderson saw them there. And saw it as his duty to do his best to save them. So singlehanded, while the crest of the hill shielded the rest of the company, he staggered forward alone through the fire to one of the wounded soldiers. Anderson got hold of him, and managed somehow to drag or carry him through the firing to a safe spot, where medical attention could be given.

This was not nearly enough for the stretcher-bearer. Knowing that more men

1. Captain B.A.W.
   Warburton-Lee, VC.

2. Lieutenant Commander
   G.B. Roope, VC.

3. Lieutenant R.B. Stannard,
   VC, DSO, RD.

4. HMS *Glowworm* rams the German *Admiral Hipper*.

5. Flying Officer D. Garland, VC.

6. Sergeant T. Gray, VC.

7. Squadron Leader R.A.B. Learoyd, VC.

8. Flight Lieutenant J.B. Nicolson, VC.

9. Flight Sergeant J. Hannah, VC.

10. Captain E.S. Fogarty Fegen, VC.

11. Flying Officer K. Campbell, VC.

12. Petty Officer A.E. Sephton, VC.

13. Lieutenant Commander M.D. Wanklyn, VC, DSO**, (with beard) and three of his officers stand in front of their submarine, *Upholder*.

14. Lieutenant Colonel G. Keyes, VC.

15. Squadron Leader A.S. Scarf, VC.

16. Lieutenant Commander E. Esmonde, VC, second from left, with his Swordfish crew.

17. Temporary Lieutenant T. Wilkinson, VC.

18. Commander A.C. Miers, VC, DSO★.

19. Roberts and Gould remove a live bomb from HM Submarine *Thrasher*.

20. Sergeant F. Durrant, VC.

21. Squadron Leader J.D. Nettleton, VC

22. Lieutenant Colonel C. Merrit, VC.

23. Hon. Captain J. Foote, VC.

24. A damaged German 88-mm gun following the breakthrough at El Alamein

25. Flight Sergeant R.H. Middleton, VC.

26. Wing Commander H.G. Malcolm, VC.

27. Captain R. Sherbrooke, VC, DSO.

28. Flight Lieutenant W.E. Newton, VC.

29. Squadron Leader L.H. Trent, VC.   30. Commander J.W. Linton, VC, DSO, DSC.

31. Wing Commander G.P. Gibson, VC, DSO★, DFC★ (at top of ladder) with his crew on the Dams raid.

32. Flying Officer L.A. Trigg, VC.

33. Flight Sergeant A.L. Aaron, VC, as an Air Crew Cadet.

34. Lieutenant D. Cameron, VC.

35. Lieutenant B.C.G. Place, VC, DSC.

36. Captain J. Randle, VC.

37. Company Sergeant Major P. Wright, VC.

38. Landing supplies in Anzio harbour.

39. Flight Lieutenant W. Reid, VC.

40. Rifleman Lachhiman Gurung, VC.

41. Warrant Officer N. Jackson, VC.

42. Pilot Officer C.J. Barton, VC.

43. Captain R. Wakeford, VC.

44. Company Sergeant Major S. Hollis, VC.

45. Landing on the Normandy beaches.

46. Pilot Officer A.C. Mynarski, VC.

47. Flight Lieutenant D.E. Hornell, VC.

48. Flying Officer, J.
Cruickshank, VC.

49. Group Captain G.L. Cheshire, VC, DSO*, DFC, (centre front) with his crew.

). Squadron Leader I.W. Bazalgette, VC, DFC.

51. Captain Lionel Queripel.

52. Flying Officer D.S.A. Lord, VC.

53. Lieutenant I.E. Fraser, VC, DSC.

54. Leading Seaman J.J. Magennis, VC.

55. Lieutenant R.H. Gray, VC, DSC.

were lying out there in the open, probably in agony, Anderson crawled across the bullet-swept slope for a second time, found another of the wounded, and carried him round the crest. Fire followed the two men all the way, but they were not hit.

For a third time Anderson went forward, and safely reached and evacuated another soldier. The whole area had become a focus of fire on his figure flitting across the ground. Yet, without stopping to hesitate or consider his safety for a second, he set out for a fourth time to try and get one more wounded man.

He was the enemy's sole and sitting target by this time, yet miraculously he stumbled through to a fourth injured man of A Company, East Yorkshire Regiment. Anderson actually started to administer what first-aid he could to prepare the soldier for the return across the slope, when he was hit and mortally wounded.

Completely ignoring his personal safety, and revealing courage and coolness under the assemblage of fire, Anderson probably saved the lives of the three comrades he managed to bring back from no man's land –the strip of slope from which he never returned alive.

So the pipe-smoking Yorkshireman from Fagley, near Bradford, became the first stretcher-bearer VC. A man dedicated to saving life, who lost his own in serving his cause.

The battle for Longstop Hill was one of the great hill fights of history. The hill marked the strongest German point barring the road to Tunis. Major John Thompson McKellar Anderson, the Argyll and Sutherland Highlanders, won his VC there on 23 April 1943.

Anderson had just taken a degree in history and modern languages at Cambridge when war broke out and on 3 September 1939, he dashed back to his university to join up there with the Territorials. At the time of Dunkirk he was one of the 200 men brought back to England from Cherbourg by Lieutenant Colonel Lorne Campbell, VC. He married the same year, and his wife described him as one of the most determined men she had ever met, always devoid of personal fear. As an example of this, they were in Liverpool that same year during one of the air raids on that port. His wife heard a bomb screaming down, and threw herself flat on the floor, but her husband looked up in surprise and said, 'Get up, Moira. Don't forget that you're an Anderson.'

Anderson hated inactivity, and tried to transfer to the RAF at one stage as things were too quiet for him. He was happy when he got out to North Africa, and proceeded to win the DSO by walking coolly through heavy machine-gun and mortar-fire, and leading his company up a rocky cliff at Hunt's Gap and forcing the enemy to withdraw. He even omitted to mention winning the DSO in his letters.

So to the VC action as a battalion commander in the First Army.

It was St George's Day when Anderson led the Longstop Hill attack; the barrier the British had to break, the hill they had to have. Anderson and his battalion battled on the steep, rocky hillside for five torrid hours, faced by mines, weapon-pits, and withering fire. Their casualties were heavy. One by one the officers were hit and killed, but Anderson fought on up that 1,000-foot hill.

Throughout those five hours of hell, Anderson led the attack upward, through machine-gun and mortar-fire that literally rained down on them. As leading company commander, Anderson was out in front for the assault on the battalion's first objective in daylight. This initial point involved advancing across a long expanse of open, sloping hillside, most of the time without benefit of cover from smoke.

Determined enemy infantry fire caused the casualties, which included all other rifle company commanders, before even this first objective had been gained. But at last the remnants of the assault across the long, lethal slope did reach the first point, still under non-stop fire. Anderson paused momentarily to reorganize and rally the battalion, especially the men whose commanders had been killed or wounded. This meant most of the force.

The commanding officer was one of the killed, so Anderson took over the battalion and led the assault on the next objective in that bitter battle for Longstop Hill. From then on the objectives merged into each other in a confused mêlée, yet the overall advance somehow went on steadily. Fire grew so intense and exact that the rest of the battalion were pinned down at the rear and unable to advance until Anderson could occupy the hill.

So he struggled on, despite receiving a leg wound. During the fierce final assault Anderson personally led attacks on at least three enemy machine-gun posts, and in every case he was the first man actually into the pits. The most amazing thing was that he had not yet been killed. Anderson also led a successful attack on an enemy position of four mortars, defended by over thirty Germans.

On and on Anderson went, until he and his force had captured some 200 prisoners and killed many more. He knew that without Longstop Hill there could be no blitzkrieg on Tunis, so with fewer and fewer men he plodded on uphill to cross the open and rush the Germans on top. They did this while being shot at from in front and behind. But when they reached the enemy there on top they found the Germans cowering back with arms over their eyes.

Five hours: 300 minutes without a second's respite. And when Anderson and the rest finally cleared the hill and counted the cost they found too few left. Only four officers and under forty other ranks. It was largely due to Jack Anderson that Longstop Hill was captured.

Anderson was subsequently killed in action that same year.

On the same day that Major Anderson was winning his VC on Longstop Hill, Lieutenant Willward Alexander Sandys Clarke, the Loyal Regiment, also of the First Army, was countering an alarming development at Guiriat-el-Atach. So two Tunisian VCs were won on St George's Day, 1943.

By dawn on that day, during the attack on the Guiriat-el-Atach feature, Clarke's battalion had been very fully committed. His own group, B Company, gained their goal, but were then at once counter-attacked, and almost obliterated in the process. Clarke was the sole surviving officer, and he had been wounded in the head. But, gathering together a composite and very shaken platoon, he volunteered to attack the goal again.

As this platoon closed on to their objective they were met by murderous fire. Clarke thought instantly, and manoeuvred them into a position to give covering fire, while he set out to tackle the post alone. He killed or captured all the crew, and knocked out the gun. His head wound was getting worse.

Almost at once the platoon came under the sights of two more machine-gun posts. Lethal lead whined towards them through the desert air. Clarke went forward once more alone, and somehow killed both crews or compelled them to surrender, dealing with their guns as well.

Clarke then led his platoon on to the ordered objective and consolidated. This was when they came under fire from two sniper posts. Yet again Clarke leapt from cover to clean them out, but was killed outright within a few feet of the enemy.

A week later a son was born to Clarke's wife at Egerton, Lancashire.

Concluding the desert VCs come representatives of the Scots Guards and the Irish Guards. First, Captain The Lord Lyell, Scots Guards, whose citation was as follows:

In Tunisia from April 22, 1943, to April 27, 1943, Captain The Lord Lyell commanded his company, which had been placed under the orders of a battalion of the Grenadier Guards, with great gallantry, ability, and cheerfulness.

He led it down a slope under heavy mortar-fire to repel a German counter-attack on April 22, led it again under heavy fire through the battalion's first objective on April 23 in order to capture and consolidate a high point, and held this point through a very trying period of shelling, heat, and shortage of water. During this period, through his energy and cheerfulness, he not only kept up the fighting spirit of his company, but also managed through radio telephony, which he worked himself from an exposed position, to bring most effective artillery fire to bear on enemy tanks, vehicles, and infantry positions.

At about 1800 hours on April 27, 1943, this officer's company was taking part in the battalion's attack on DJ Bon Arara. The company was held up in the foothills by heavy fire from an enemy post on the left: this post consisted of an 88-millimetre gun and a heavy machine-gun in separate pits. Realizing that until this post was destroyed, the advance could not proceed, Lord Lyell collected the only available men not pinned down by fire – a sergeant, a lance-corporal, and two guardsmen – and led them to attack it.

He was a long way in advance of the others, and lobbed a hand grenade into the machine-gun pit, destroying the crew. At this point his sergeant was killed, and both the guardsmen were wounded. The lance-corporal got down to give covering fire to Lord Lyell, who had run straight on towards the 88-millimetre gun-pit, and was working his way round to the left of it.

So quickly had this officer acted that he was in among the crew with the bayonet before they had time to fire more than one shot. He killed a number of them before being overwhelmed and killed himself. The few survivors of the gun crew then left the pit, some of them being killed while they were retiring, and both the heavy machine-gun and 88-millimetre gun were silenced.

The company was then able to advance and take its objective.

There is no doubt that Lord Lyell's outstanding leadership, gallantry, and self-sacrifice enabled his company to carry out its task, which had an important bearing on the success of the battalion and of the brigade.

After the Scots Guards, the Irish Guards, in an action beginning just as Lord Lyell was killed.

An Irishman with a Bren gun routed 200 Germans and influenced the whole course of the last assault on Tunis. The man: Lance Corporal John Patrick Kenneally.

The Bou-feature dominates all the ground east and west between Medjez-el-Bab and Tebourba. It was essential to the final thrust on Tunis that this feature should be captured and held.

A Guards brigade took part of the Bou on 27 April 1943. The Irish Guards held on to Points 212 and 214 on the western end of the feature. The enemy frequently counter-attacked, and, while a further assault to take the complete feature was being prepared, it was vital for the Irish Guards to hold on. They did so.

On 28 April the positions held by one company of the Irish Guards on the ridge between Points 212 and 214 were about to be attacked. Reconnaissance reported one company of the enemy forming up before they advanced.

Kenneally decided that this was the moment to launch a single-handed attack on them. So he charged down the bare forward slope of the feature straight at the main enemy body —firing his Bren as he ran. The dramatic dash of this one-man charge completely unbalanced the enemy company, which broke up in disorder before they had even begun their operation. Kenneally turned round and returned to the crest again, harassing their retreat from there too. One man had dispersed a force of 200 Germans. That was not the end of the affair.

On the morning of 30 April Kenneally actually repeated this most remarkable exploit. Accompanied this time by a sergeant of the Reconnaissance Corps, he again charged the enemy forming up for an assault on the precious position. He harassed them so much, and hit so many of them, that it looked likely that the projected attack would be abandoned. The strength of the enemy was once more equal to about one company. Two hundred to two, this time.

It was only when he was noticed hopping from one fire position to another farther on the left, in order to support another company there, that they realized he was wounded. He carried his gun in one hand and supported himself on a guardsman with the other, hopping along gamely.

But he would not give up his gun, maintaining that he was the only one who understood a Bren. Despite the wound, Kenneally continued to fight all through that hot desert day, not complaining.

And as his citation ends :

The magnificent gallantry of this N.C.O. on these two occasions, under heavy fire, his unfailing vigilance, and remarkable accuracy were responsible for saving many valuable lives during the days and nights in the forward positions. His actions also played a considerable part in holding these positions, and this influenced the whole course of the battle. His rapid appreciation of the situation, his initiative, and his extraordinary gallantry in attacking singlehanded a massed body of the enemy, and breaking up an attack on two occasions, was an achievement that can seldom have been equalled, His courage in fighting all day when wounded was an inspiration to all ranks.

CHAPTER THIRTY-SIX

One Out of Eleven
Bombers Survived

LEONARD TRENT

J ust two days after the self-sacrifice of Hugh Malcolm, on 6 December 1942, No. 487 (RNZAF) Squadron carried out its very first operation. It was to be five more months before one of their prominent pilots earned the distinction of becoming an Anzac VC, and three years, in fact, before the award was announced.

But back to 6 December, and a low-level attack on a radio works at Eindhoven, in Holland.

A little past 12.00 hours the squadron's sixteen Ventura medium bombers joined an Australian squadron of similar aircraft. So the two Allies from down under thundered across the English countryside, literally brushing the tree-tops, and leaving them quivering with the wind. On over the North Sea, still at about ten yards altitude, the Anzacs flew in two fairly tight squares of eight, one of these led by Wing Commander F. C. Seavill and the other by Flying Officer G. W. Brewer, DFC. In the first of these 'boxes' was Squadron Leader Leonard Henry Trent, who had already collected a DFC and the following year would carry out the mission which eventually won him the Victoria Cross. Not all the pilots were as experienced as Trent and Brewer, however, and, in fact, it was Seavill's first operational flight.

Over the sea they became just a part of a bigger assembly of aircraft, all of which had Eindhoven as their objective. The engines went on and on, emitting a hypnotic sort of sound, but they were broken by the crack of guns being tried out. Every one was getting keyed up now for this first 'op'. They had, it seemed, been training too long. The preparations continued, as navigators set their bomb-switches and plotted the course.

Still a mere thirty feet from the sea, the coast of Holland emerged into sight, its flat wastes scarcely distinguishable from the water. But then came the flak. Orange pricks marked the German gunfire, and black smoke the explosions around the aircraft. So this was what 'ops' were like. Here was the baptism of many: a hard initiation, flying at a few feet in daylight against such a target as a radio works.

On over the dunes they went. The Venturas rose fractionally, as if to be sure of clearing these obstacles. Then they hurtled on again at under 100 feet. The enemy gunners firing tracer up at them had to do a quick turn. One moment they fired ahead. Next second they had to swivel and swing right round, and try to hit the rear of the aircraft rapidly retreating farther inland and out of range.

Over the enemy airfield next —not the best place to be at 100 feet. Fire from all round the perimeter outlined the entire field and hit one of the Venturas. In a second the plane was bouncing and bounding on the aerodrome. One down. Two others all but collided and crashed. The whole outburst lasted only perhaps twenty seconds. Then they were on once more, still parallel to the ground, and much too near it.

Ten minutes over the sleepy Holland landscape, and they were jolted out of their brief lull by the sight of fires started by Mosquitoes who had hit the target earlier.

They were near, very near, the radio works now, and everything rushed at them at once: tracer, shells, all in a dramatic kaleidoscope with the Venturas bang in the middle of the picture. Guns fired from the tops of some buildings, and one of the Venturas exploded in the air, and just seemed to vanish: a terrible end.

The bomb-switches were all set long ago. Now the bombs were gone, followed by incendiaries. There was no point in hanging about over such an inferno. The chance always seemed conceivable that a plane would find itself blown up by its own, or someone else's, bombs, if the time-delay happened to fail. But there was enough to worry about without that. The hail of hell rose and fell as the flak continued. The Anzac squadron had the satisfaction, before they flew out, of seeing the fires from the previous raid stoked up well and truly and new ones lit. Low clouds helped the whole operation, including their return, but some never did get back from that first 'op'. Trent saw one Ventura erupt exactly ten yards away from him. Two others had touched wings without damaging either (by some sort of miracle that occasionally occurs). Those which did survive saw signs of their good fortune as they examined their Venturas afterwards. Some had already had evidence —like the plane hit by an explosive cannon-shell, which set a Very light blazing, which in turn filled the aircraft with smoke. But they put out the fire and got home.

On the credit side of that original operation was the smoke fuming and pluming 300 feet above the radio works. On the debit side was the loss of Wing Commander Seavill, who had been in the Ventura which had crashed in flames on the airfield near the Dutch coast. Seavill was not a young man by flying standards, and had joined up in 1930. He had even refused a posting as group captain so that he could have the honour of leading this New Zealand squadron. But that was how things went. For much of the time in bombers it was good luck or bad luck —sheer chance. Of course, good piloting came into it as well, but if you got a direct hit there was nothing you could do about it. And that was what happened to Seavill.

So the stage was nearly set for Trent's famous flight. This was to be another of those operations from which not a plane was to return. But it was one with a difference, as we will soon see.

Trent was born at Nelson, and married and made his home at Wakefield Quay, Nelson. He joined the RNZAF in 1937, and was transferred to the RAF the following year. If anyone could be said to have been in it from the start, he could, because the day before war was declared he flew to France with a Fairey Battle squadron. Trent spent some of his time during the next few months photographing the Siegfried Line and other such enemy defences and locations. There seemed no future in that, so about Christmas 1939 he returned to England to be transferred to Blenheim bombers. It was in one of these that Trent took part in the Garland-Gray operation against the Maastricht bridge during the German advance into Holland. So he was with the two men who each won the Victoria Cross first of all in the Second World War.

Following this, he later bombed Rotterdam airfield, and helped to cover the Dunkirk evacuation. The odds against survival in those days can be gauged from these typical statistics. Out of the original eighteen officers who had landed in France on that day, 2 September 1939, only four now remained alive. One of these was Trent. After his first tour of operations he became an instructor at an operational training unit, and from there he was posted to No. 487 Squadron.

So to 3 May 1943, and the VC operation. The squadron had got a lot of 'ops' behind them by now. It was Trent's twenty-fourth sortie altogether. Still in its faithful Venturas, the squadron was detailed to attack the power station at Amsterdam, in daylight. This operation had been intended to encourage the Dutch workmen in their resistance to enemy pressure. With the power station out of action, they could resist more easily.

The squadron knew that the vital target would be heavily defended. But the importance of bombing it, regardless of fighters or flak, was strongly impressed on the Anzac crews taking part.

'I'm going over the target whatever happens,' Trent told his deputy leader before they took off.

All went well until the eleven Venturas and their fighter escort were nearing the Dutch coast. Then one bomber was hit so severely that it would never be fit to make the two-way trip, so it turned back to base.

Suddenly swarms of German fighters loomed out of nowhere, near the coast, and hotly engaged the New Zealanders' fighter screen. This manoeuvre proved so successful that the Anzac fighters were forced into losing touch with their bombing force —already one short. Soon the Venturas were to be much shorter still. As Amsterdam hove into sight, with its quaint waterways, cobbled sidestreets, and characteristic Dutch architecture, the Venturas closed up for mutual protection. They had no eyes for anything in Amsterdam except the power station.

But at this stage the operation struck a serious snag. The Venturas commenced their run up to the target. Unfortunately, the fighters detailed to support them over the target had reached the area too early and had been recalled.

This left the remaining bombers utterly at the mercy of fifteen to twenty Messerschmitts, which dived on them incessantly throughout the approach to the target.

Six Venturas were destroyed in four minutes.

Squadron Leader Trent continued on his course with his own, and the other three aircraft left.

Four out of eleven still airborne. But in a very short time two more went down in flames on the outskirts of the city. So now there were only Trent and one other left —two out of the eleven that set out. Then the aircraft following him was pounced on by a Messerschmitt, actually over the target which sent it spiralling down into the environs of the power station.

Trent kept his word that he had given to his deputy leader —'I'm going over the target whatever happens'. And whatever happened turned out to be that every other aircraft was shot down. Only Trent and his crew were left in the sky over Amsterdam, surrounded by the menacing Messerschmitts, as they buzzed around, waiting for the final kill.

With his deputy leader dead, Trent felt more than ever impelled to carry out his word. Heedless of a mass of murderous attacks and ack-ack fire, he completed an accurate bombing run, and even shot down a Messerschmitt at point-blank range. But his luck could not hold much longer; not with fighters flying at all points of the compass at twice his speed.

The Ventura was hit, went into a devilish, deathly spin, and broke up. Two of the crew died. But Trent and his navigator were miraculously hurled clear of the crash, lived, and were taken prisoners of war. The citation called it 'cool, unflinching courage and devotion to duty in the face of overwhelming odds'.

Safely in Stalag Luft III, Trent was one of the officers who constructed a 100-yard escape tunnel. He drew ticket No. 79 in the order of escape, and was at the top of the tunnel when the Germans discovered the escape. The sentry fired two shots in the air as he lay flat on the ground, and he was more than surprised to find himself still alive.

CHAPTER THIRTY-SEVEN

HM Submarine *Turbulent*

JOHN LINTON

Commander Linton was the last of the three great submariners to be recognized with the VC. Following in the wake of Wanklyn and 'Tony' Miers — who was under his guidance, as we shall see later on —John Wallace Linton proved as great as either of them. A tremendous trio these men made. 'Tubby' Linton, as he was known to his friends, actually sank as large a tonnage of enemy shipping as Wanklyn, that is, about one-eighth of a million tons.

In the early years of the war he sailed his submarine *Pandora* to New Hampshire, USA, for a refit, and came back to Britain to build the *Turbulent*. From then on the name of the ship might be applied to Linton's life. When it was completed, at Barrow-in-Furness, in January 1942, he took it straight into the fray —after the initial proving trials, of course. He sailed her down to the Mediterranean: not to Gibraltar or Malta, but the Eastern Mediterranean around Alexandria and the Levant.

Only a month or so after the submarine's commissioning came news of her first success. On 27 February 1942, she sank a small 60-ton motor craft, rapidly following this on the 2 and 3 March during the same patrol with four schooners sunk and one damaged.

Now in his late 'thirties, Commander John Wallace Linton was much older than many of his fellow commanders of subs. Wanklyn, for instance, was seven or eight years younger. He proved fighting fit for the arduous life led submerged beneath the Mediterranean surface. Sailing the seabed, or prowling at periscope depth, Linton left a trail of enemy ships strewn across his course. His record began to look like the long list of successes which Wanklyn had chalked up.

One night in a mixture of mist and moonlight, Tubby Linton (his weight was down now from the seventeen stone region to about fourteen) took the *Turbulent* up to a strong convoy consisting of two merchantmen and two destroyers. He watched it from afar at periscope depth before diving with the intention of attacking as the ships crossed the splintered line of reflected moonlight on the water. He brought *Turbulent* up again to periscope depth, grabbed hold of the handgrips, swung the sights round, peered in —and saw one of the two destroyers almost on top of *Turbulent*. He smacked his lips, kept to his course, then called:

'Fire One.'

One, then another, torpedo streaked through the night sea. The first struck and sank the other destroyer. More torpedoes accounted for the two merchantmen. Linton dived deep as the destroyer overhead counter-attacked. By skilful handling he managed to bring the sub clear.

And so it went on: audacity and skill, hand in hand. An Italian destroyer, a U-boat, a German armed merchant cruiser were added to the list of ships he had sunk. Out of 365 days in the year since the start of the campaign, 254 days were spent at sea, nearly half that time submerged: thus he lived one-third of his life underwater! Coupling this to his previous service in the war, it is likely that by now he held the world's record for operational time in submarines.

Back at base he was always impatient to get into the battle, and passed his hours on depot ships talking over tactics with other submariners. On and on he went until the *Turbulent* could claim one armed cruiser, one destroyer, one U-boat, twenty-eight supply ships mostly bound for North Africa and Rommel's army. All these sunk by a man who was quiet, reserved, but determined. He had no time for small talk.

Now it was spring 1943. Linton wore the DSO and the DSC. At home in Gloucestershire his wife kept the decorations safely in their cases: the DSO with its white cross, green, red, and gold centrepiece, and red and blue ribbon –the DSC with its silver cross, and blue and white striped ribbon. The DSC he had received in person from HM George VI at an investiture.

Yet in addition to all these ships sunk, *Turbulent* claimed several other more unusual 'kills.' On the copy of the sub's Jolly Roger flag are the following insignia:

White bars for enemy ships sunk.

White U for the U-boat.

Red bar for the Italian destroyer.

Eight stars around crossed guns represent each successful gun action against enemy shipping.

And the unusual operations: a locomotive, a lorry, and a rail van with a streak across it are for gun actions against various forms of enemy shore transport. Three times *Turbulent* surfaced near enemy coasts and shot up a goods train, road convoy, and an electric train (represented by the streak of lightning).

She lay offshore in daylight once at periscope depth. Linton watched up-coast as the goods train chugged slowly along the seaside line. Waiting till it was only a mile or so off the point in the track perpendicular to the position of the sub, he surfaced. Visibility was moderate. The engine driver did not see the sub. Neither did any coast defences, the area was wild. Suddenly the sub's gun cracked out across the water and an exploding shell told of a train shot from the rails in its very own country.

More intriguing still are two daggers for operations which even now cannot be revealed.

Linton refused to be relieved of underwater duties, and it was with a heavy heart that he sailed from port on his last scheduled patrol. After it he was due to be sent home for a rest earned a dozen times over. But on 4 May 1943, the world heard that *Turbulent* had failed to return to base and must be presumed lost on patrol. The last known of her was when she was sailing close to a minefield between Corsica and Sardinia, and the rest can be imagined. Through no conceivable fault of his own, Linton was lost —on his last trip.

But before this, on 26 March the Admiralty had sent a most secret cypher to Commander-in-Chief, Mediterranean, repeated to Commander-in-Chief, Levant. It would be wrong to reproduce more —or less —than this signal:

> It is with the deepest regret that their Lordships have learnt of the loss of *Turbulent* with the presumption of the death of Commander J. W. Linton. In view of very special and distinguished services of this officer, who has been in command of S/Ms throughout the whole period of this war and whose outstanding characteristics and achievements were so well known throughout the Mediterranean commands, they wish to express their sympathy to you and to the Mediterranean S/M Flotillas.
>
> Their Lordships do so with assurance that Commander Linton's inspiring leadership will long be remembered by all those who are so worthily upholding the traditions of the Royal Navy and the submarine service in the Mediterranean at the present time.

On 25 May 1943, the Victoria Cross was awarded to the late Commander Linton. Nancy Linton later received it. And as she opened the case and saw the plain purple ribbon and simple bronze cross, she remembered many things. She and her mother then wrote personal letters to all the next of kin of those who were lost with Linton.

CHAPTER THIRTY-EIGHT

The Dam Busters

GUY GIBSON

Gibson was one of the two most brilliant bomber pilots of the war. Leonard Cheshire was, of course, the other. Wing Commander Gibson VC DSO DFC was born at Simla in India in 1918 and educated in England. He joined the RAF as a pupil pilot when he was only eighteen and at twenty-one he flew on his first operation, to the Kiel Canal, the very day that war was declared. The next day he attacked the battleship *Tirpitz*.

Once in 1940 flak cut his steering cables. Another time that year, a flak shell tore his rudder bar from under his very feet, but fortunately failed to explode. In November 1940, Gibson became a night fighter pilot and flew ninety-nine sorties in eight weeks. On one of these, his aircraft was badly shot up and his observer wounded. Another time, he had to crash-land into some trees.

Back in Bomber Command, he flew missions to Berlin, Cologne, Danzig, Nuremberg, Stuttgart, Genoa, Milan and many more. He carried out seventy-four missions before the Dam Busters raid.

His most awkward adventure was when flak hit a bank of accumulators beside the wireless operator. Potent sulphuric acid fumes wafted into the cockpit. Most of the crew began to feel faint, but Gibson kept conscious by sticking his nose out of the window. Thank goodness it was summer, he said later.

Boyishly handsome and with an engaging smile, Guy was always modest about his achievements, and he insisted 'I've only been shot up six times, you know.' He had a natural, easy manner which made him beloved by his crews. He knew all of them by their Christian names, although he could also be a strict disciplinarian. Off-duty he was everyone's friend. Add to all this, he was a born leader with a genius for finding the weak spot in enemy defences. Guy even had time for sidelines, too. He loved photography. And perhaps a surprising side was a love of Shakespeare, with Henry V as his favourite play. He also had a strong sense of humour.

By March 1943 he was famous for his many exploits. Then came the day when the Dam Busters were born –17 March 1943.

No. 5 Bomber Group Headquarters received a letter from Bomber Command telling of a new mine weapon which was intended to be used against 'a large dam in Germany'. The attack had to be during May, and a new squadron formed to carry out the attack.

Four days later this new squadron started to form at Scampton, while the twenty Lancasters it would later receive were being built. The whole project was top secret, top priority. Everyone picked for it had to be top grade, therefore, air and ground crews alike. The personnel had to be chosen first of all, before the modified Lancasters were ready. And the man chosen to command the new squadron was — Guy Gibson. All he knew about the project was that it would involve low-level flying across country, and training started along these lines at once on standard Lancasters. All twenty crews reached Scampton before the end of the month, within ten days of the squadron starting to form.

All they had yet learned, was that they would have to fly at 100 feet and at 240 mph. A mine had to be dropped from each bomber within forty yards of the precise point of release. They went into training in earnest, putting in many hours flying over reservoir lakes in Wales and the Midlands, for only six weeks were left to perfect this demanding technique. This ability to fly at 100–150 feet over water in the dark, and to navigate and drop mines accurately as well, was the first key factor in the operation. There were many more, not least of them being able to avoid enemy fighters and ack-ack in the target area.

But, amazing as it seems, Gibson did not yet know his target area. He was literally flying in the dark. Then he met the inventor of the mines, Barnes Wallis, who told him roughly how the mines would work. They would bounce along the water to their target. This whole thing became more fantastic daily.

Meanwhile Gibson and his crew practised flying over Derwentwater reservoir, in Yorkshire, which bore resemblances to the conditions to be expected over the ultimate targets —only he still did not know where they were! After some trial runs Gibson discovered he could estimate his altitude and direct a bomb at the specified speed of aircraft with reasonable accuracy by day. But by night he only barely escaped actually striking the gloomy, invisible water of the reservoir. And the attack was to be carried out at night. A lot had to be learned in the coming weeks.

Then, the following day, Gibson was let into the secret. They were to attack the great Ruhr dams of Germany —Möhne, Sorpe, and Eder. The main target was the Möhne Dam, 830 yards long, 150 feet high, and 140 feet thick at its base — 150 feet of concrete and masonry. If Gibson and his squadron could smash one or more of these, the havoc caused to enemy industries and communications might be tremendous. Apart from the difficulty of flying to the rigid requirements vital for the success of the idea, there was one other detail —the mine had not yet had its full-scale trials!

One of the many problems involved was solved when an accurate range-finder was devised which enabled the squadron to keep within an average twenty-five yards of their target, and so within the forty yards tolerance allowed.

The first full-size trial of the mine came in mid-April when an inert mine was dropped from one of the first modified Lancasters at the required height of 150 feet over the water. The outer casing of the mine disintegrated as soon as it struck the sea off the Dorset coast. No time was lost in strengthening this casing, but without success.

Gibson too had his worries, just as fundamental as Barnes Wallis's setbacks.

They found it impossible to fly at exactly 150 feet over the water, maintaining that height accurately. Then a backroom boffin found the answer: to train two spot-lights downward from the nose and belly of the plane so that their beams would meet 150 feet below the Lancaster –making a spot where they intersected. In this way, with the help of a couple of Aldis lamps, the plane was flown at a height whereby the spotlight remained at water-level. This simple solution allowed them to keep within a couple of feet of any required height.

The next panic: the inventor found that they could only expect effectiveness from the modified mine if it were dropped not from 150 feet but sixty. Without the spotlight device, this would have been more than frightening, just plain fatal. More practice sixty feet with the device, and before they knew it the month of May had opened.

Early in May an inert mine was dropped from the new height of sixty feet and operated successfully; then an active mine, which went off exactly as expected. While this went well just one more panic presented itself at the operational end. A complicated signalling system had to be worked out to control about twenty bombers over several tricky targets. The answer was very-high-frequency radio-telephone sets –twenty in number. These arrived on 7 May, but a lot of routine testing and procedure had to be accomplished before the attack. This was done by 9 May, except for minor adjustments.

Next, the nearness of the 'op' was suddenly brought home to them all by the dress rehearsals. Number One of these was timed for the night of 6 May –and a film company was actually called on to assist by building dummy structures in the Uppingham and Colchester reservoirs, so that the squadron had something to aim at as they roared in for their dress rehearsal raid.

This stage had not been reached without more hazards and headaches, for a few days earlier half of the dozen Lancasters in one trial received really bad damage, with rear turrets dented, elevators broken, and fins bent. The trouble occurred because the planes had been flying a few feet too low, and despite the fact that the mines they dropped were only inert, they caused gigantic splashes as they struck the water, which reacted on the bombers flying at 232 mph.

On 15 May Gibson got word at last: 'Be prepared to take off tomorrow.' He sat up late that evening committing the detailed operation to paper –in case none of them got back. They had been so busy training that the danger of the mission may, in fact, have partially escaped some of them, especially since it was only the following morning that the aircrews knew the complete plan.

16 May, 21.28 hours. The first of nineteen Lancasters took off. The main force of nine was to go to the Möhne dam and then on to the Eder, if it was destroyed before all their mines had gone.

The second force of five was to head for the Sorpe dam. A third force of five was to form a reserve to fill in at any necessary gap, according to how the plan progressed.

Over the sea they skimmed towards the Continent at a mere sixty feet or so, and went still lower after they crossed the Dutch coast. Moonlight helped them, but navigation at that altitude proved hard.

Gibson gave his own account of the whole operation in his book *Enemy Coast Ahead*, including the difficulty of flying at so low a level by night.

He and the other two Lancasters in his immediate section of three hurtled overland, rolling right and left to confuse the defences. No guns opened fire. But in a couple of minutes they found themselves over the sea again! They had flown over one of the several islands they had tried to avoid, and instead of being inland were only now crossing the real Dutch coast. By good chance none of the ack-ack guns on the island had opened fire on them. Thenceforth, on their fresh course, Gibson's bomb-aimer was shouting to him regularly over the intercom to lift the aircraft to avoid trees or high-tension wires. All three aircraft in the section kept formation right until the Rhine wound into view, when it was found to everyone's alarm that Gibson's plane, leading the whole flight, was no less than six miles too far to the south and heading for Duisburg – one of the most heavily defended towns in the whole Ruhr! He made a sharp turn to remedy the situation, and flew along the line of the Rhine, under heavy fire from barges on the river equipped with quick-firing weapons.

On to the Ruhr valley, with half an hour to go before the Möhne dam. Ceaseless anti-aircraft fire forced Gibson to take evasive action. The three were also continually caught by searchlights, some of which Gibson managed to avoid by 'dodging behind trees,' as he put it.

Then they flew over a new and heavily defended airfield near Dorsten, not marked on their maps, where all three were held by searchlights. Gibson's rear gunner fired at the beams, but stopped when some tall trees came between the lights and the aircraft. Suddenly the searchlights were extinguished by a long burst from the rear turret of one of the other two Lancasters.

It was about here that the only aircraft of the first wave of nine was lost. Gibson sent a radio warning of this new airfield to the following planes. Lancasters B, N, and Z formed the second section. Shortly before it was lost aircraft B broke formation, presumably for the pilot to check his position. The pilot of Lancaster N, then flying at 100 feet, reported that soon afterwards he saw a plane being shot at by anti-aircraft guns and returning their fire. Then he saw an explosion on the ground. The inference was that Lancaster B had crashed, its mine probably exploding at the same time. The other eight Lancasters flew on, past Dortmund and Hamm, avoiding more fire from the ground. Then hills rose ahead, and open country apparently without defences. Gibson gained height to get over a hill, and then saw the Möhne dam lake ahead, and in a moment the dam itself. From all along the dam, which looked, Gibson says, rather like a battleship, guns were firing, as well as from a power house below the dam, but there were no searchlights. Gibson estimated that tracer was coming from five positions, and probably a dozen guns in all. They all circled round getting their bearings, and each time one of them came in range of the ack-ack guns on the dam they received accurate fire. One of the eight planes was hit, but not fatally.

Although the attack on the Sorpe dam had been planned for this precise time, as an effective diversion to the efforts of the main force of Lancasters against the Möhne, only one of the five aircraft aiming for the Sorpe dam had, in fact, reached it. They met heavy opposition early on. Lancasters K and E were both shot down near the Dutch coast; H hit the sea and lost its mine in the process, so returned to base; W was hit by flak, which disrupted the intercom, so that the pilot had to return home. Only Lancaster T attacked the Sorpe dam at all of this five, a minute or two before 03.00 hours, on 17 May.

Back at the Möhne dam, the Lancasters had scattered ready for the attack. Gibson was due in first. He made a wide circle, and then came down over the hills at the eastern end of the Möhne lake. He dived towards the water. The dawn was visible through the haze. They flew at exactly sixty feet, with the spotlights meeting on the water below. With these lights on, the bomber made a still simpler target for the gunners on the dam, who could see it coming from more than two miles away. Tracer shells streamed towards it as Gibson flew straight and level towards the dam. The bomber's gunners replied. Gibson said that he expected to die at any moment. But the Lancaster was not hit anywhere. The mine was released, and Gibson flew in a circle. Looking back at the lake, the crew saw a fountain of water, white in the moonlight, and 1,000 feet high. The surface of the lake had been broken, and sheets of water were pouring over the dam. At first Gibson thought it had gone at the first attempt, but soon realized that it was only the water churned up by the explosion. The mine had gone off five yards from the dam, but Gibson had to signal home that there was no apparent breach. Back in England, 'Bomber' Harris, Barnes Wallis, and the rest, received the news breathlessly, and waited for the next report. They had to hang on for fully thirteen minutes.

Gibson waited for the water to subside, then signalled to Lancaster M to make its attack. The same thing happened all over again. The enemy guns focused on the lone bomber. A hundred yards from the dam a jet of flame sprang from the plane. Gibson inferred that the bomb-aimer had been wounded because the mine fell late on to the power house below the dam. The pilot was striving desperately to gain height for his crew to bale out of the blazing plane. He got up to 500 feet, then there was a flash in the sky, and one wing fell off. The whole aircraft came apart in the air, and fell to the ground in fragments. Almost immediately afterwards the mine that had fallen on the power house exploded. This made so much smoke that Gibson had to wait some minutes for this to clear before he could direct the next aircraft to attack.

For this third attempt Guy Gibson had a plan. As Lancaster P flew towards the dam Gibson went alongside, a little ahead of it, and then turned. His rear gunner fired at the flak positions on the dam, and at the same time helped to draw off their fire from the bomber about to attack the dam.

Lancaster P was hit several times despite Gibson's help, and all the petrol was drained from one of the wing tanks, but the mine was accurately released and exploded only yards from the dam. Again circling near the scene, Gibson thought he saw some movement on the wall, but although the same huge fountain of water was thrown up, it was clear that the dam was not yet breached.

Now it was Lancaster A's turn. Gibson developed his diversionary tactic still further this time, and as the bomber began its run in to the dam Gibson flew up and down on the farther side of the dam and ordered his gunners to fire on the enemy's positions. To make sure that they would concentrate on him rather than Lancaster A, Gibson had his identification lights switched on. The plan was successful and the enemy did, in fact, keep their guns trained on his Lancaster while the attacking one flew straight towards the dam. As the mine exploded, a huge wave went over the dam, but although it had gone off in contact with the wall, they could report no apparent breach. Back at headquarters the tension was becoming unbearable, as each attack failed to bring about the desired breach.

Gibson ordered Lancaster J to attack. The fifth mine went up almost exactly in the correct spot. Just before the moment of release, however, the pilot reported seeing a breach in the centre. The bomber's own mine flung up the usual fantastic fountain, and then the plane became badly harried by gunfire. Gibson himself could not see the dam at that moment so was in no position to confirm a breach. He knew that time was running out, however, so decided to send the next bomber to attack. Gibson judged that he had better order Lancaster L to start. He did so, and then turned, and came close to the wall of the dam.

But it had rolled over. They could not believe their eyes. Quickly he told Lancaster L to turn away. Gibson flew close and looked again. Then he saw plainly that there was a breach 150 yards wide in the dam. A huge cataract of water was rushing through the breach.

00.56 hours: Gibson signalled to Group Headquarters the prearranged codeword, 'Nigger,' meaning that the Möhne dam had been breached. Nigger, his dog, had been run over and killed the day before the attack.

The valley below the dam was filling with fog, evaporating from the water that was pouring down it. It was moving in an unimaginable wave, and in front of this Gibson could see the headlights of cars racing for safety. The headlights changed colour, first to green, and then eventually to dark purple, as the water overtook them. The water surged on towards the eastern end of the Ruhr valley. The powerhouse beside the dam was by now completely submerged. Gibson circled for three minutes, and then called up the rest of his force. He ordered J and P to make for home. Lancaster M had been shot down. The rest of the force Gibson ordered to set course for the Eder dam, Gibson's G and Lancaster A no longer had their mines, but they went as well: L, Z, and N still carried their mines intact.

It was getting late by the time they all reached the Eder dam, which lay in a deep valley among wooded hills, and at the far end of the lake was a hill about 1,000 feet high with a castle on top of it. They had to approach the dam by flying over this hill, and dive steeply, from above the castle, down to sixty feet over the water.

Lancaster L made three runs before the bomb-aimer released the mine. A great spurt of water was followed by a gap about nine feet wide towards the east side of the dam. Next Z followed, after two attempts. Gibson saw a vivid explosion on the parapet of the dam itself which lit up the whole valley. Then no more was seen of the Lancaster, which must have been blown up by its own mine on the parapet.

01.52 hours: Lancaster N attacked, successfully, this time. A spurt of water, then a thirty-foot breach below the top of the dam, leaving this top intact for the moment. A torrent of water cascaded downward and rushed in a tidal wave to the valley below.

Gibson's wireless operator signalled the code-word: 'Dinghy'.

The Eder dam too had been breached.

So the five aircraft set course for home, with the enemy's fighter force now fully aroused. Lancaster A failed to survive. K, E, and C, from the rest of the whole formation, were also lost.

Later Gibson's rear gunner warned him that there was an enemy aircraft behind. Gibson lost height, though he had already been flying very low, and made towards the west, where the sky was darkest; by this manoeuvre he evaded the enemy.

One of the reserve managed to get through to attack the Sorpe dam at 03.14 hours.

Eight of the Lancasters making this historic Dam Busters raid were lost: eight bombers, and more important, eight crews. But without Gibson's heroism in drawing enemy fire on his own plane, the losses would have been heavier.

There is no need to repeat the catastrophe and chaos caused by the result of the raid. The headlines have told the story before:

'Growing devastation in the Ruhr.'

'Flood waters sweep into Kassel.'

'Damage to German war industries.'

'Dam floods stretch for sixty miles.'

The dams may not have been hit quite as badly as believed, but it was still a heroic operation. After a tour of the United States on behalf of Britain, Gibson returned to flying duties. There is a school of thought that suggests he became over-confident and was not sufficiently experienced with the Mosquito he was flying on 19 September 1944. On this date, Guy Gibson, 'Master Bomber,' led one last raid on Rheydt, in the Rhineland, a strongly defended rail centre and traffic terminus for the Ruhr.

He was flying below the main force, guiding the bombers, talking to his fellow pilots, telling them where and when to strike.

Over the target, they heard his voice on the radio telephone, calm, unhurried. His instructions came clearly, and they followed his orders. The bombs hit an ammunition train and started a series of fires and explosions. The crews heard his final orders.

His plane crashed near Bergen-op-Zoom, on the East Scheldt estuary, where his body was found and buried.

But Guy Gibson, VC, can never die.

CHAPTER THIRTY-NINE

First VC Attack on U-boat

LLOYD TRIGG

Two unique 'firsts' made by a single VC. This was the remarkable record of Flying Officer Lloyd Allan Trigg, DFC, RNZAF, No. 200 Squadron. He was the first airman awarded the Victoria Cross while engaged on operations against a U-boat. And as if this were not enough, Trigg won his Victoria Cross as a result of evidence entirely originating from the enemy.

Trigg came from North Auckland, where he left his wife and two small sons in 1941 to join up. But he told his wife that he 'would not go looking for decorations'. They just seemed to come to him. After a period in Canada, completing his training under the Joint Air Training Plan, Trigg was commissioned in 1942. He lost no time in becoming operational.

He seemed to specialize in sea 'ops' from the first, and undertook a large number of shipping reconnaissances and convoy escorts during the following months. Then, in March 1943, he was detailed to provide anti-submarine escorts to a convoy that was being attacked by several U-boats. When in the vicinity of the convoy Trigg spotted an enemy submarine and, although flying in an unfavourable position, he delivered a vigorous and effective attack. Two days later he sighted another U-boat, and once again made a determined air attack, one of his depth charges exploding on the bow of the enemy vessel. Following these and other distinguished operations, the DFC went to Trigg in June 1943.

So the stage was nearly set for his Victoria Cross. But before the action occurred, Trigg's operations over the ocean off the north-west African coast served as a timely reminder of the continuing Battle of the Atlantic in all its phases.

Day after day men of Coastal Command such as Trigg faced all the possible consequences to hurl themselves and their aircraft at Hitler's U-boats in an all-out attempt to win the war at sea —and above it. As the men knew even at the time — for it was reported in the British Press —both their planes and their lives were 'expendable' in this grim Atlantic battle which would go on and on till the whole war was over.

Gradually Coastal Command seemed to be getting the upper hand in this joust with the submarines. But then the U-boats began hunting in packs, like the deadly wolves they were, and fitted new, heavier anti-aircraft guns. No longer did the U-boat commanders order an urgent dive when a Liberator or other bomber was sighted. Instead the underwater vessels stayed on the surface, and assembled a blanket of barrage so complete that the attacking aircraft must almost certainly be hit —if not shot down.

The success of this particular aspect of the Battle of the Atlantic now swung over on the Coastal Command crews themselves. Unless they showed a high order of heroism, all the scientific aids such as advanced depth charges and other anti-submarine projectiles would be useless. There was nothing for it but to 'fly down the barrels of the U-boat guns' —not a pleasant assignment, even in fast planes. And they had to handle heavy, cumbersome flying boats or bombers, designed to operate from high altitudes. To come down to virtually zero feet meant making a tragically tempting target to the U-boat's gunners.

More than this, these air attacks inevitably occurred several hundreds of miles out to sea, in the cruel, cold water where rescue was rare. It even came to accepting the exchange of a plane for a submarine, and yet the crews did not complain —they accepted the new strategy of the enemy and set about beating them at it. The results that started to come in soon after this 'pack hunting' started suggested that the aircraft were actually sinking more U-boats than ever, but with the danger of additional RAF and RNZAF losses. The submarines obstinately stayed on the surface, hoping to deter the pilots from actually making an attack. But the airmen were not to be put off at any price, even at the price of their lives. Time and again the U-boats remained visible on the rolling Atlantic, offering too good a target to overlook. The planes dived down, usually only one to a pack of the enemy, and thundered at a big angle right into the stream of shell-fire from the subs.

Often they scored successes. Just as often the Germans got the plane as well. The best that the crews could expect was to survive somehow. Some did, others didn't. It was as callous and calculated as that —like the whole war on so many fronts.

For instance, Wing Commander R. B. Thompson, captaining an RAF Fortress, was lucky, or had to consider himself so. They sank the U-boat but crashed into the sea, beside the wreckage of the vessel they had just destroyed. They managed to get themselves and a dinghy clear of the Fortress, and then set about staying afloat and alive. Thompson and his crew drifted in the dinghy for four days and nights, in the wild Atlantic.

Flying Officer A. A. Bishop, in a Royal Canadian Air Force Sunderland flying boat, forced his attack home on a U-boat, which he sank, But again, the almost suicidal assault met its expected end, as the flying boat's front turret was half shot away before the U-boat finally went down. And its wings, galley, and bomb bay all blazed badly in the air over the sullen watery wastes of the ocean. The U-boat vanished. The flying boat crash-landed on the sea, The end of this particular story was happy; the survivors of both the Sunderland and the U-boat were picked up sodden and shivering by a British destroyer churning to the rescue. By a curious chance, most of the aircrews making these suicidal attacks on the U-boats survived, even though their planes perished.

By this time Trigg had rendered outstanding service on convoy escort and anti-submarine duties. And already he had completed no less than forty-six sorties with skill and courage.

The date was 11 August 1943. Trigg undertook as captain and pilot a patrol in a Liberator bomber, although he had not previously made any operational sorties in this type of plane. No. 200 Squadron had only quite recently switched over from Hudsons to Liberators.

This was the patrol which would be reported only by the crew of an enemy U-boat. So the Liberator took off, with Trigg at the controls, and a crew of four fellow New Zealanders and two Englishmen. They left the airfield of Yundum, near Bathurst, West Africa, behind them, and set course westward – another routine patrol, if anything could be called routine with such a background of death and destruction around and below them. In those very seas several Coastal Command bombers and flying boats had recently found their final resting place. And now the Liberator reverberated out over the Atlantic in its patrol pattern; hour after hour in the air; back and forth, covering the sea where the U-boats were most expected.

After eight hours' flying they spotted one U-boat on the surface, fitted with the latest large-bore anti-aircraft guns. Trigg prepared to attack at once. He nosed the Liberator down to be sure of getting in a good position, but in doing so the plane met the full force of these new guns, especially the forward gun. Trigg made his first run right across the U-boat. Then he wheeled round and came in again. Bombs burst on each flank of the vessel, spuming water all over her. But the Liberator received many hits. The plane burst into flames, and a further hit as it flew from the U-boat after the second run caught its tail. Fire enveloped the tail rapidly.

Here was the critical moment. Trigg had to decide in a split second almost whether to break off the engagement and make a forced landing in the sea. All question of keeping the Liberator airborne to fly back to base was already past. If Trigg continued the attack, the Liberator would offer a 'no deflection' target to deadly anti-aircraft fire, while every second spent in the air would increase the extent and intensity of the flames now coursing inside and out of the plane. This would also, obviously, diminish the chances of survival for himself and his crew.

There could not have been a shred of hesitation in his mind. Trigg maintained his course in spite of the precarious condition of his aircraft, and carried out a masterly attack on the already smouldering U-boat. Skimming over the vessel at less than fifty feet, with anti-aircraft fire entering his opened bomb doors, he dropped his bombs on and around the U-boat, where they exploded with undoubted and devastating effect. The Liberator limped clear of the vessel, and a little way farther on it dived into the sea, taking Trigg and his crew with it.

But the U-boat was already doomed. Trigg's duty was done. In twenty minutes the submarine sank. Some of her crew struggled through the chilly Atlantic waters to swim clear of their ship, and towards the wreckage of the Liberator. For there they saw the bomber's rubber dinghy, which had broken loose. The Germans got hold of it and aboard it, to be rescued two days later by the corvette, HMS *Clarkia*.

This was the story they had to tell of the attack and their own subsequent ordeal.

On its third attack the Liberator had been hit full and square by a shell but, continuing on its course, had dropped its bombs near the hull of the submarine, damaging the submarine so severely that its batteries began to release deadly

172

chlorine gas. The aircraft roared on at over 200 mph, hit the sea, and sank in a few seconds.

The Germans who watched it disappear, however, had not time to celebrate their victory, for with at least half the crew overcome by gas, the U-boat circled helplessly for twenty minutes before taking its final plunge. Twenty-four survivors were left, swimming in the water.

One of the Germans saw an object floating in the sea about half a mile away, near the spot where the Liberator had crashed. He swam towards it in the hope that it was something to which he could cling. It was, in fact, the Liberator's dinghy, which had freed itself from the sunken aircraft. The German reached the dinghy about half an hour after the U-boat had disappeared; and he clambered into it gratefully. He then paddled in the direction of his companions.

Although there had been twenty-four survivors when he set out on his long swim, the number now was greatly reduced. Sharks, attracted by so many bodies in the water, had done deadly work. Only six men, including the captain, were able to reach the dinghy, and although the Germans paddled round the spot for a long time, they found no further trace of their companions.

The men in the dinghy spent a lonely, miserable night, but the following day, to their surprise and delight, an aircraft of the RAF circled them and dropped supplies. At that time they were thought to be the survivors of the Liberator, for which a search had been made as soon as it had been posted overdue. The location of the dinghy was reported and the corvette *Clarkia* was diverted from patrol to rescue the survivors.

A search was conducted through the night without success, but at last, just before dawn, the corvette's searchlights picked out the dinghy. When the survivors told their story they were generous in their praise of the captain and crew of the Liberator, for their daring and courage in the attack which had brought them victory at the cost of their lives. Trigg's crew was as follows: Flying Officer I. Marinovich, of Auckland; Flight Sergeants T. J. Soper, of Takaka, Nelson; A. G. Bennett, of Wellington and L. J. Frost, of Auckland; Flying Officer J. J. S. Townsend, of Stroud, Gloucester; and Pilot Officer A. R. Bonnick, of Hendon, Middlesex.

They were 'expendable' in the Battle of the Atlantic, but without them and other Coastal Command crews it could not have been won.

CHAPTER FORTY

Shot in Face; Brought Bomber Back

ARTHUR AARON

The Alps had their part in the life and death of Arthur Aaron, for he used to cover the walls of his bedroom at his Leeds home with pictures of mountains. Several times before the war he spent his holidays in Switzerland, climbing the Alps he loved; his mother was of Swiss extraction.

Then on the night of 12 August 1943, Acting Flight Sergeant Arthur Louis Aaron, DFM, No. 218 Squadron flew his Stirling bomber over those same Alps on the last journey of his life.

All his life Aaron had this love of mountains: the heights. And it was exemplified too in his profession as an architect —once more the love of seeing things rise before his eyes; creations of God or man, an image to aim at in life.

But his life at the Leeds School of Architecture was interrupted —and destined never to be resumed —when he enlisted as a pilot observer in 1941. After part of his training in Texas he returned to England and went to war. Nineteen operations, most of them against strongly defended targets in Germany, with ninety operational flying hours in his logbook. One of these 'ops' won him the Distinguished Flying Medal, when a fire was started in the rear of the bomb doors. The wireless operator and flight engineer managed to control this outbreak. Meanwhile Aaron remained outwardly unperturbed as he pressed home his attack on their target.

This 'Gold Coast' Squadron –No. 218 –was certainly an outstanding one. And Aaron was to add yet another act of bravery to its illustrious deeds.

The date of 12 August was the very next night after the Trigg operation in the Atlantic. And those Germans were actually still in the Liberator's dinghy, floundering about in the Atlantic, when Aaron took his Stirling on a raid on Turin. South they flew over his beloved Alpine terrain for the last time, till the outskirts of Turin rolled dimly into view below them. They soon had confirmation that they were near the target, for an enemy fighter suddenly swung at them out of the darkness, firing bursts at the Stirling from a few yards' range. The bomber got it properly – three engines hit, windscreen shattered, front and rear turrets put out of action, elevator control damaged; aircraft hard to handle.

The navigator was killed outright, and other members of the crew were wounded.

A bullet belted into Aaron's face, breaking his jaw and ripping away part of his face. He was also wounded in the lung, and his right arm was rendered useless. He fell forward over the control column, and the aircraft dived several thousand feet. The ghastly roar grew more grisly. Then at 3,000 feet the flight engineer regained control. Unable to speak, Aaron urged the bomb-aimer by signs to take over the controls. They set course southward in an endeavour to fly the three-engines-hit bomber, with one right out of action, to Sicily or North Africa.

They helped Aaron to the rear of the bomber, where he was treated with morphia. His strained eyes closed for a while as he rested. Face, lung, and arm wounded. Surely, he could do no more? But he rallied after a time, and his responsibilities as captain of the aircraft wafted into his mind.

He insisted on returning to the cockpit, where he was lifted in to his seat, and had his feet placed on the rudder bar. Twice Aaron made determined attempts to take control of the Stirling and hold it to its course, but his weakness was all too evident, and they persuaded him with difficulty not to try further. Aaron was in great pain now. His fractured face bled badly. His wounded lung impeded his breathing. His arm hurt. Though suffering from all this pain and its accompanying exhaustion, he went on helping by writing directions with his left hand, the only one he could use.

Five interminable hours from Turin the petrol began to run low, but thankfully they sighted the flare path of the Bone, North Africa, airfield. Aaron summoned strength to direct the bomb-aimer in the highly hazardous job of landing the crippled aircraft in the darkness with the undercarriage retracted, at night over a strange airfield, with 4,000-lb load of bombs in the racks, and a plane that hardly had the right still to be airborne.

The task was extremely tricky, even for a fit pilot. Four times they tried under his direction. At the fifth Aaron was now so close to collapse that he had to be physically restrained from further efforts by the crew.

'It was the greatest thing I have every known,' said the rear-gunner, Sergeant Thomas McCabe, of Manchester, later. 'His whole thought was for the "ship" and for his crew.'

The bomb-aimer brought the plane in for a safe landing, with all the landing mechanism jammed and the bombs still live.

Nine hours after landing Aaron died from exhaustion. As the official citation says: 'Had he been content, when grievously wounded, to lie still and conserve his failing strength, he would probably have recovered, but he saw it as his duty to exert himself to the utmost, if necessary with his last breath, to ensure that his aircraft and crew did not fall into enemy hands.'

So Arthur Aaron died: the man who wanted to be an architect, and specialized in designing interiors for churches.

This was not the end of his name or his deeds, however, for the year after his Victoria Cross was announced an insistent and growing demand for some suitable memorial reached really large proportions. To meet this demand, the governing boards of the Leeds College of Art and the Roundhay School, with the co-operation of the local education committee, created a fund for an Aaron Scholarship to be made available at the School of Architecture for Roundhay and other Leeds secondary schoolboys.

This chance for other boys to follow in the footsteps of the Leeds VC was warmly endorsed by his parents, and met with immediate response from the city. The necessary capital sum was soon subscribed for the annual award for each year of the five-year course of the School of Architecture. The fund was known as the Arthur Louis Aaron VC Memorial Fund, and its achievement called the Aaron VC Scholarship.

To set the seal on this civic memorial, and in gratitude for the way it was received, Aaron's parents later gave the actual Victoria Cross as an outright present for all time to Leeds City Museum.

CHAPTER FORTY-ONE

Midget Sub Versus *Tirpitz*

DONALD CAMERON, BASIL PLACE

Two VCs were won by British submariners in their midget subs, or X-craft, in their famous attack on the German battleship *Tirpitz* as she was moored in Kaafjord, northern Norway.

The date of the attack was 22 September 1943.

The overall plan included attacks on the 26,000-ton *Scharnhorst* and 12,000-ton *Lützow* as well as the main prize, the 40,000-ton *Tirpitz*. Eighteen months' training over, six steel X-craft set out on their mission. They were towed by submarines most of the way, and passage-crews in the midgets spent a tiring eight days seeing them safely across the North Sea and up towards northern Norway. Two men out of the three in each of the midgets had to remain on watch for most of the twenty-four hours. Four times each day the little craft surfaced for a quarter of an hour, while keeping submerged for the other twenty-three hours. The operational crews, including Donald Cameron and Godfrey Place, meanwhile, got more fresh air as the full-size subs steamed on the surface all night.

Final orders received on the fifth day out told X5, X6, and X7 to attack *Tirpitz*; X8 to go for *Lützow*; and X9 and X10 to aim at *Scharnhorst*. Until now all had been quiet, but the receipt of them seemed to step-up the suspense and to coincide with the first difficulties.

At the worst possible time, 04.00, the bows of X8 suddenly swung downward, showing that her tow had most probably parted from her big brother sub, *Seanymph*. Within five minutes Lieutenant J. E. Smart, in command, surfaced the midget raider, clambered on to her casing, and looked round. No sign of *Seanymph*. Smart decided to plod along the surface at three knots and hope to be found.

Seanymph did not discover the parted tow until a couple of hours later. The sub was swung round to retrace her course, but after a six-hours' search in rough sea, she found nothing.

Meanwhile, X8 had located and lost again the submarine *Stubborn*, towing X7. The cause this time was that a course had been wrongly heard in the fury of wind and sea. Although *Stubborn* lost contact with X8 she did see *Seanymph*, and thus was able to let her know the approximate position of the latter's small sister. At 17.00 hours, after a day and a half, *Seanymph* and her charge were reunited. Smart spent practically all those hours on his feet, and the operational crew took over.

Next morning at 09.00, *Syrtis* fired the usual underwater exploding signals to tell her small craft to surface. No response. At 09.20 they hauled in the tow, which was found to have parted. *Syrtis* carried out an exhaustive search for hour after hour, but none of the towing submarines ever saw X9 again. The midget *Syrtis* had been towing became the first X-craft lost on operations. What surely happened was that the tiny sub sailed trimmed heavy at the bow to offset the upward pull of the tow from the big sub. The tow suddenly snapped. The bow took the extra weight of the heavy rope –and the sub was swept down too deep before compensating action to balance her could be taken. Her sides would have caved in and the water pressure have proved fatal. The passage crews had a job just as dangerous as the operational crews.

The next craft to get into difficulties was X8, whose trim seemed to be all wrong, and who was hard to handle. At last the main ballast tanks were called in correct trim. The trouble was traced to an air-leak from the buoyancy chambers to starboard. With the trim still extremely difficult to maintain, Lieutenant B. M. McFarlane, RAN, decided to get rid of the starboard explosive charge. The depth of water here was 180 fathoms, and this side-cargo was set 'safe,' in other words not to explode. Fifteen minutes later, however, it went off with a very big bang only 1,000 yards astern of the midget. Neither X8 nor *Seanymph* suffered any harm, but X8 was certainly keeping up a reputation for unpredictability.

Despite jettisoning the starboard charge, trim remained hard to control, and eventually the port side-cargo had to go, too, much to the disappointment of the crew.

Distrusting the 'safe' setting of the first charge, the COs decided to fire this one after a two-hour delay. Although the two subs were nearly four miles away when it went off, the impact of the explosion inside the midget proved far worse than the first. The 'wet and dry' chamber was flooded, doors distorted, pipes fractured, and the craft altogether made useless for further operations. The crew were taken on board *Seanymph*, and X8 was scuttled so that she should not be on the surface and endanger the rest of the operation. The only change in the plan as a result was that the *Lützow* would not now be able to be attacked.

By dusk on 17 September the weather relented a little and Godfrey Place took Lieutenant 'Bill' Whittam and the rest of the operational crew aboard X7. The changeover occurred outside Altenfjord, and Place borrowed the passage-crew CO's best boots, fur-lined and leather.

The other three submarines waited until the next day before they transferred operational crews. *Thrasher* was towing X5; *Truculent*, X6; and *Sceptre*, X10.

The crews had been transferred a night ahead of schedule, but still the midgets were being towed. The plan was for them to make their attacks and return to the big brother subs.

Truculent, *Thrasher*, and *Sceptre* towed their X-craft. *Syrtis* had none. *Stubborn* would arrive soon with X7. *Syrtis* sighted a U-boat at less than a mile but could not attack it –by order. They did not want to attract any attention, however tempting a target came into view. All of them, moreover, managed to keep out of sight in this way.

Later that day, *Stubborn* sighted a mine with its mooring rope caught in the tow of X7. The deadly weapon came right along the line of the hawser until it reached the bows of X7. Place crawled along the casing of the midget and untangled it from the hawser and bows with his feet, while all the time it bobbed about on the Arctic waters. Sweat streamed down his face despite the cold. At last he managed to push it clear of the X-craft, by clever kicks on its shell between the lethal-looking horns.

Early evening on 20 September the four little craft slipped their tows and left their guardians, who withdrew out to sea. Thus the midgets made their way into the Soroy Sound just about the ordered time, after nine difficult, dangerous days.

From this point onward, the two X's bound for the *Tirpitz* —6 and 7 —kept pretty well together without ever encountering each other. The starboard charge of X6 had been flooded since the very first day of the tow, but by stowing the stores and spare equipment slightly differently, the craft kept a good enough trim.

Both craft crossed the minefield off Soroy during the night of 20-21 September. *Tirpitz* would be coming within striking distance soon. They proceeded up the Altenfjord during daylight on the 21st. Cameron's periscope on X6 developed a defect, but the danger of 'blindness' passed. As she crawled up the fjord at periscope depth, X7 saw several enemy vessels during the day. Fortunately visibility was fairly good, and Place could dive the sub in time to avoid being seen. Even the telltale periscope trail at that stage could still ruin the whole operation if it were noticed, but no one did notice anything so unusual as a pair of midget subs picking a steady course straight for the pride of the German Navy. En route, in the lee of Aaroy Island, about teatime, Place was tempted by the sight of the *Scharnhorst* close to X7. His orders were to attack *Tirpitz*, so all he could do was to swing his periscope away from so beckoning a target and remember the one a little further on, half as big again.

On the port side of the fjord lay the Brattholm group of islands, and here at 70° North X6 and X7 spent the night of the 21st-22nd. X10 arrived later. X6 had to dive during the night on more than one occasion as she lay very near to the shipping lane to Hammerfest. X7, too, had some narrow squeaks as she tried to charge batteries and small boats chugged to and fro only a mile or so off. It would be heartbreaking if anything went wrong so near *Tirpitz*. The only other excitement of the night was Engine Room Artificer Whitley's successful efforts to fit a spare exhaust pipe —which he finally managed with the assistance of sticky tape and chewing gum!

At last they reached the final fjord. They had negotiated all Altenfjord. Soon after midnight, X7 left the lee of the Brattholm's for Kaafjord, off the head of the longer waterway. X6 followed one hour afterwards.

The first —and a foremost —obstacle loomed upon them quickly: the anti-submarine net at the entrance of the fjord; a metal mesh, reaching almost to the bottom of this inland sea so far from the real sea. But they were ready for it. Place got X7 through the net, but Cameron had more difficulty. His periscope had begun to flood soon after leaving the islands, and time and time again it did this, so that Cameron could scarcely see anything up top. He made out the watery shape of a small coaster about to go through the net. This 'boom' had just been opened to let the vessel through, so he daringly surfaced and put on all possible speed. X6 actually swept through the anti-submarine net at early light of morning in the wake of the enemy coaster! The sub's size —or lack of it —was certainly an advantage.

Once through the net, Cameron dived to sixty feet and sailed by dead reckoning. He stripped the periscope but still it was imperfect. Hardly surprising was it, therefore, that X6 only barely avoided head-on collisions. Once she passed just beneath the bows of a stationary destroyer; another time up, Cameron found her heading straight for the mooring buoy of a tanker half a mile from *Tirpitz*. Not a sound nor a ripple must disturb the scene now. The waters of Kaafjord were glass-still. E. R. A. Goddard had to keep all his wits about him on the wheel of X6. By 07.05, X6 had reached the anti-torpedo shore-net defence of *Tirpitz* and was through the boat entrance.

Meanwhile, X7 had been forced deep by a patrolling launch and been caught in a square of anti-torpedo nets once used to protect the *Lützow*, but now no longer needed. For an hour or more before dawn Place pumped and blew until the craft at last shook herself free and shot up to the surface. Then a single strand of wire hooked itself across the periscope standard. By 06.00 this came clear, and Place set course up-fjord for the target.

By 07.10, X7 reached the anti-torpedo net defences. Place tried to negotiate these by diving to seventy-five feet —but was caught. While she began to try and extricate herself, X6 followed a picket boat through the boat gate. Breakfast was being prepared aboard the *Tirpitz* in blissful ignorance of the double danger so near at hand.

In calm, shallow water, X6 ran gently aground. She managed to free herself, but for the first time they started a stir in *Tirpitz* for in freeing the craft from the bottom they broke surface for a few seconds. A lookout aboard the battleship spotted them and reported 'a long submarine-like object'. His senior thought it might be a porpoise and delayed passing the report on for five vital minutes. X6 was now inside the range of *Tirpitz*'s main and secondary guns. Again, just as the message had been conveyed to an officer, X6 struck a rock and broke surface. She was identified, but before she could be fired on Lorimer swung her down again. She was a mere eighty yards abeam of the battleship, but the gyro was out of action and the periscope almost fully flooded. All Cameron could do was to try to fix their position by the shadow of the battleship.

Yet another five hectic minutes passed. X6 became tangled in an obstruction hanging down from the *Tirpitz* herself. To wriggle clear, she had to surface once more —to the accompaniment of strong small-arms fire and hand grenades tossed from the deck of *Tirpitz*. Cameron knew that escape was out of the question now. With the vast armament the battleship carried and all the other auxiliary vessels in the fjord, X6 could never get away.

'Smash all the secret equipment,' he ordered, in case the Germans salvaged the craft. 'I'm going to scuttle, her.'

Cameron took X6 astern till the hydroplane guard was touching *Tirpitz*'s hull, and released the two charges, set to fire one hour later. Then the time was 07.15. He scuttled the craft and they bailed out in turn through the wet and dry compartment.

In a matter of seconds they were struggling in the water near *Tirpitz*. The German ship put out a picket boat and picked them up, and also made a vain attempt to slip a tow around X6 as she sank.

'Action stations' had been sounded aboard *Tirpitz*, and from the state of unreadiness it was all too clear that complete surprise had been achieved. (This took twenty minutes; the slowness with which the Germans prepared to shift the ship was unbelievable.) All watertight doors were closed. Then steam for the boilers was ordered. While steam still was not up to pressure for sailing, divers went over the side to see if they could trace the charges laid on the bottom.

Cameron, Lorimer, Goddard, and Sub Lieutenant 'Dick' Kendall stood in a group to one side while orders went to and fro. No one interrogated them yet, but they had been given hot coffee and schnapps after their icy dip.

Cameron glanced down at his watch surreptitiously. It was eight o'clock. Only a quarter of an hour before the charges were due off. Things had not gone quite according to plan, of course, for they were not meant to be aboard *Tirpitz* on the receiving end of their own charges. They shifted a trifle restlessly from one foot to the other.

Meanwhile X7 had stuck in the net at seventy-five feet depth –no picnic place, as they knew that X6's charge would fire any time after 08.00. Place decided they must get clear as soon as humanly possible. He blew the tanks to full buoyancy and steamed full astern. She came out, but turned beam on to the net and broke surface. Then he dived quickly.

The boat stuck by the bow. The depth this time was ninety-five feet. After five minutes of wriggling and blowing, she started to rise. The compass had gone haywire. Place did not know how near the shore he was. He stopped the motor, and X7 came up to the surface. Amazingly, she must have passed underneath the nets or through the boat gate, for Place now saw *Tirpitz* straight ahead –thirty yards off.

'Forty feet . . . full speed ahead . . .'

She struck *Tirpitz* on her port side and slid quietly under the keel. Place released the starboard charge.

'Sixty feet . . . slow astern . . .'

The port charge was released 150–200 feet further aft.

It was 07.30 now and X6 had been scuttled. Place ordered 100 feet depth for X7 and guessed the position they had got through the net, for the compass still would not work. At sixty feet they were in the net again. Air was getting short now. Their charges would go off about 08.30, and X6's any time after 08.00. The situation became urgent.

X7 became entangled amongst first one net, and another, and another. At 07.40, her crew extricated her from one by sliding over the top of the net between the surface buoys. Luckily they were too close for heavy fire from *Tirpitz*, but they were peppered with machine-gun bullets which hammered against the casing.

After passing over the nets, they at once dived again –to 120 feet and the bottom. Once more they tried to surface or reach periscope to see where they were and so be able to get as far as possible from the forthcoming bangs, which could easily prove fatal to the midget. But in so doing, they ran into yet another net at sixty feet and, frantically frustrated, tried to get clear.

Back aboard *Tirpitz*, divers returned to the vessel, having examined the hull for limpet mines stuck to the ship.

Cameron slipped his sleeve up a fraction.

'It's 08.10,' he breathed to Lorimer.

Then they were summoned to questioning and asked what charges they had placed —and where.

Still the ship had not moved. All but an hour had passed. They stalled their answers, praying, too, that the ship would not sail clear of the explosions.

08.11: they prayed again that they were not directly over the charges.

08.12: a shattering explosion from the bowels of the fjord below the boat.

They were thrown off their feet by the force of it. Their own four tons of amatol had also sent up X7's four tons. Eight tons of explosive were tearing into the *Tirpitz*.

There was complete panic aboard. The German gun-crew shot up some of their own tankers and small boats, and obliterated a shore position. The chaos was unbelievable. About 100 men were lost, mainly through their own lack of self-control.

True, *Tirpitz* still floated, but with the force of the explosion the great ship heaved five or six feet upward and at once listed five degrees to port. A huge column of water streamed into the air on the port side and fell on to the decks. All the lights failed, and oil fuel started to leak out from midships. Much more damage was obviously done.

The surge of the explosion cracked through the water to X7, shaking her clear of the net. Place took her to the surface, saw *Tirpitz* still afloat, then dived deep again. Her crew gathered themselves together and took stock of the damage. Compasses and depth gauges out of order, but little wrong structurally. Nevertheless the craft could not be controlled, and broke surface several times. Each time she did so, *Tirpitz* fired on them, denting and damaging the hull more.

Place decided to abandon ship and brought the craft to the surface. They could not use the escape chambers from a submerged position as depth-charges were being dropped which might have killed them while ascending from the craft. She surfaced close to a gunnery target, but before the crew could get out of the control room, the gunfire sank her. Place was up on the casing, however, so stepped clear to the gunnery target —to be picked up and taken aboard *Tirpitz*.

At about that moment, at 08.43, X5 was sighted 500 yards outside the nets. *Tirpitz* opened fire and claimed to have sunk her. Depth-charges were dropped, too, and nothing was ever heard of the third X-craft to get within sight of *Tirpitz*.

Back in X7, it was a matter of life and death for the next two or three hours. After diving for the last time she struck the bottom within seconds. Luckily the hatch had been shut in time. Bill Whittam took over. The diving escape sets were cut down from the stowage spot. Whittam began to flood the ship. There was no panic. They decided to use both escape hatches. Lieutenant Whittam. and E. R. A. Whitley would use one each, and Sub Lieutenant Aitken whichever one was clear first. But they could not pass each other with their escape gear on, so Aitken was left by the 'wet and dry' hatch forward.

Flooding was frighteningly slow, nor could it be speeded up. The icy cold water rose gradually up their bodies, then fused an electric circuit —and the craft filled with fumes. They breathed their escape-oxygen. With the boat about fully flooded, Aitken tried the forward hatch, but it would not open.

He climbed back into the control room and found that Whitley had slipped. Aitken groped under the water to find that the breathing-bag was flat and the two emergency cylinders had been consumed. Whitley was dead.

In the darkness Aitken started to try and find Bill Whittam —but as he straightened up his own oxygen bottle gave out, too. In a flash, he broke open the two emergency-oxylets, which at that depth gave him only a breath or two each. He was very nearly dead, his last oxygen-reserves gone, in a flooded submarine at 120 feet with two men, both presumably dead, and the hatch still shut. All he had left in life was the breath he was still holding in his lungs. He scrambled somehow back into the escape compartment for a last lunge at the hatch. Then he blacked out — till he opened his eyes to see a stream of oxygen bubbles as he sped to the surface. He must have managed to open the hatch and done his escape drill in a dream.

At 11.15, Bob Aitken broke surface. A few minutes later he was drinking coffee and schnapps, wrapped in a German blanket. He sat shivering still, remembering Whittam and Whitley.

Later it was learned that all three main engines of the *Tirpitz* were put out of action; a generator room, all lighting and electrical equipment, wireless telegraphy rooms, hydrophone station, A and C turrets, anti-aircraft control positions, range-finding gear, and the port rudder. The German naval war staff announced that she had been put out of action for months. Not until the following April was she able to limp from her anchorage, still crippled, only to be damaged and finally destroyed by air attack.

The six survivors of the X-craft attack were made prisoners of war. All were decorated, Cameron and Place with the VC. Theirs had been 'A magnificent feat of arms,' as Sir Max Horton described it.

CHAPTER FORTY-TWO

The Immortal Chindits

RICHARD KELLIHER, THOMAS DERRICK, ALEC HORWOOD, CHARLES HOEY, GEORGE CAIRNS, JOHN HARMAN, JOHN RANDLE

Two Aussies opened the next phase of the Far East war. Their deeds were then followed by five of Wingate's immortal Chindits fighting the savage battle for Burma. The Australians were Private Richard Kelliher and Sergeant Thomas Currie Derrick. This is what Kelliher achieved against the Japanese.

Three times he defied death, and three times he came back alive. This Irish-Australian from County Kerry and Brisbane was fighting the Japanese in New Guinea on the morning of 13 September 1943.

During an attack by his platoon on an enemy position at a place called Nadzab, a concealed machine-gun post about fifty yards away got a deadly line on the men as they advanced. In a flash of firing, five of them had been killed and three wounded. To go any farther would have meant suicide for the rest of the platoon.

Private Kelliher had thick eyebrows and typically Irish eyes. They were not twinkling now. He felt furious at the tragedy that had hit his platoon. In the face of these casualties Kelliher dashed towards the machine-gun post which was responsible for the heavy losses, and pitched two grenades into it. The explosion killed some but not all of the Japanese inside.

Kelliher was aware of this as he ran back to his section. It was no good doing half the job. Seizing a Bren gun, he lunged out a second time to defy death, dashing to within thirty yards of the stricken post. Taking calm aim from a completely exposed point, Kelliher fired his Bren gun into the Japanese position, silencing it once and for all. These two deeds would probably have been enough to win him the VC.

When he got back again to his section he learned that his section leader was wounded and lying out in front.

'Permission to go and get him, sir?' Kelliher asked.

He received this, and so set out for the third time. There must be such a thing as tempting providence, but he did not stop to weigh up the odds. All he knew was that a man lay out there in need of rescuing or he might die.

Heavy rifle fire cracked across towards Kelliher from another position, but he avoided it to reach the wounded man and achieve what he wanted; to bring him back for treatment. Not only did Kelliher save his section leader's life, he also enabled the advance to continue.

His name is one of the select few belonging to Irishmen on the Irish Roll of Honour at the Shamrock Club, London.

The other Aussie in this phase of the Far East campaign was Sergeant Thomas Currie Derrick. Ten enemy posts were tackled by this one man in the south-west Pacific on 24 November 1943.

During the final assault on Satelberg, in the East Indies, a company of an Australian infantry battalion received orders to outflank a strong enemy position sited on a precipitous cliff face, and then to attack a feature 150 yards from the town.

Derrick commanded his platoon in the company. As the country was so difficult, the only possible approach to the town lay through an open Kunai patch directly beneath the top of the cliffs. Over a prolonged period of more than two hours, the Australians tried time and time again to clamber up the steep slopes to their goal; they were not only harassed by enemy machine-gun fire but also hand grenades were thrown at the advancing Aussies.

The last light would soon be leaving the western sky. It seemed that not only might they fail to reach their goal, but they could also easily have to yield the ground already occupied. In fact, the difficulty of holding on to it any longer resulted in an order for the company to retire. As soon as he heard the command, Derrick asked for one last chance to reach the top, and his request was granted.

Just about dusk Derrick moved ahead of his forward section, and personally annihilated, with his grenades, an enemy post that had been holding up his particular section. Next he ordered his second section around on the right flank. They came under fantastic fire from the light machine guns and grenades of no fewer than six enemy posts. Oblivious of his own safety, Derrick clambered forward well in front of the leading men of this second section and hurled a shattering series of grenade after grenade at the enemy, who became so demoralized that they fled there and then, leaving weapons and grenades in their store.

By this action alone the Australian company could gain its first foothold on the precipice-like ground they somehow had to win.

Not content with the work he had already done, Derrick hurried back to his first section and, together with the third section of his platoon, advanced to tackle the three posts remaining between them and their goal. Four separate sorties he made, dashing forward in the face of the fire to grab out the pins from the grenades and fling them at the posts from ranges of six to eight yards. So, from only the length of a room away, Derrick risked everything on this last series of assaults, and finally silenced every single one of them.

Altogether he had reduced ten enemy posts —an amazing achievement. And, by some star that sometimes shines, he survived the bullets and the blast of grenades to witness the result of his efforts.

From the vital ground he had captured, the cliff-face and feature on the outskirts of Satelberg soon fell, and the remainder of the battalion moved on to take the town itself next morning. Derrick's refusal to admit the possibility of defeat –even after the withdrawal order –resulted in the capture of the town despite the seemingly impossible situation. He inspired not only his own platoon and company, but the battalion as a whole.

The announcement of the award of the VC to Derrick came, as befitted his nationality, from Government House, Canberra.

The first of the five Burma VCs on the opening months of 1944 prompted the question, How long can a man avoid death once he has decided to ignore all risks? The three days of 18, 19 and 20 January provide one answer.

At Kyauchaw, in Burma, on 18 January, Lieutenant Alec George Horwood, of the Queen's Royal Regiment, went with the forward company of the Northamptonshire Regiment into action against a Japanese-defended locality. He used his forward mortar observation post.

Throughout that day he lay in an exposed position, which had been totally bared of cover by concentrated air bombing previously. Horwood effectively shot his own mortars and those of a half-troop of another unit while the company was manoeuvring to trace the exact location of the enemy bunkers and machine-gun nests. All day Horwood was under intense fire from three perennial weapons, rifle, machine gun and mortar. But at night he came back with most valuable information about the enemy dispositions.

19 January: he moved forward with another company, and established an observation post on a precipitous ridge, one of the many in that part of Burma. From here, while once more under steady, streaming fire, he directed accurate mortar barrage in support of two attacks which were put in during the day. Horwood also carried out a personal reconnaissance along and about the bare ridge, deliberately drawing the enemy fire. The reason was so that the fresh company which he had led into place might see the Japanese positions. This company was due to execute an attack very shortly.

19-20 January: all night he remained on the ridge in case of any enemy movement.

Next morning, 20 January, he shot off the mortars again, to support another attack by a different company put in from the rear of the enemy.

Horwood felt convinced that the enemy would soon crack, and volunteered to lead the attack planned for that afternoon. He led it with such calm resolution that they reached the enemy. This was well into the third day now that he had been in the van of the battle. He directed the men with no thought of his own extremely dangerous state. Standing up, he urged the men forward. The enemy fire by then had become point-blank. He was shot and killed.

Leadership under continual fire earned him the VC. He had reconnoitred, guided, brought up ammunition, all in addition to his duties at the inferno of the forward mortar observation post. For three days he kept going, almost without pause. The position was finally captured on 24 January, just a week after the company first went into action against it.

The next Burma award added a VC to an MC already won. From Vancouver to Burma was a long way for Major Charles Ferguson Hoey, the Lincolnshire Regiment, to have travelled. His home was the western seaboard of Canada, but on 16 February 1944, his company formed part of a force ordered to take a position in Burma at all costs. After a night march through enemy-held territory, the Lincolns under Hoey were met at the foot of their goal by penetrating machine-gun fire.

Hoey personally proceeded to lead them under this and rifle fire right up to the target. Although wounded at least twice in the leg and head, he seized a Bren gun from one of the men, and holding it low, he kept up a deadly fire and, though dizzy with pain, led them on to the objective. The company actually could scarcely keep up with him; but, despite his wounds, Hoey managed to reach the enemy post first.

He killed all its occupants before being mortally wounded himself. So to the MC he added the VC, awarded posthumously, as so many had to be.

Normally the VC is announced within a few months of the actual action, as soon as the facts have been fully verified. But here is the story of how a VC was awarded more than five years after the action. The date of the act: 13 March 1944. The date of the citation: 20 May 1949.

Wingate's raiders –the 'knife artists' who invaded Burma from the skies in 1944 –were nothing like the raw recruits assigned to him the previous year. Now they were a *corps d'élite* of jungle fighters probably unique in the world; even including the Americans in the Pacific.

On 5 March 1944, the 77th Independent Infantry Brigade, of which the 1st South Staffordshire Regiment formed a part, landed by glider at Broadway, in Burma.

Lieutenant George Albert Cairns was one of the troops landed by this method. As so often happened, the operation went far from well. Some gliders crashed on landing; others crashed into the wrecks. Twenty-three men were killed and many injured, but more than 400, complete with stores, landed safely. Engineering equipment did not, however, arrive.

Next night the operation continued with fifty-five Dakotas landing at Broadway, and between 5 and 10 March a total of 100 gliders and 600 Dakota sorties flew in 9,000 troops and 1,100 animals. With other land forces in the vicinity, Wingate could now claim to have almost 12,000 troops 'in the enemy's guts,' as he put it.

The broader picture of operations does not concern the story of Cairns, which is taken up now on 12 March, just a week after landing. On this day columns from the South Staffordshire Regiment and 3rd/6th Gurkha Rifles managed to establish a road-and-rail block across the Japanese lines of communication at Henu Block.

The enemy, as expected, counter-attacked this block in the misty early morning of 13 March 1944, and the South Staffordshire Regiment was ordered to attack a hill-top from which the Japanese attack on the block was based.

Cairns took a foremost part in this action attacking the hilltop, and the struggle became literally hand-to-hand. During the assaults a Japanese officer rushed at Cairns, and, with his long sword, slashed off the lieutenant's left arm. Cairns did not drop, but killed his attacker. Then, with his arm missing and losing blood, Cairns picked up the enemy sword and continued to lead his men into the attack, lunging left and right with the captured sword, and killing several of the enemy.

Eventually Cairns himself fell to the ground, and subsequently died from his wounds. Though the enemy was routed, it was still a rare occurrence at that stage.

But that was not the end of the epic of Cairns. After the usual evidence of three witnesses had been checked, a recommendation for the award of the VC to Cairns was submitted to General Wingate. Tragically, the aircraft carrying Wingate and the records crashed, the general being killed, and all the records destroyed. Later, when the proposal was revived, it was found that two of the three original witnesses had been killed themselves. This complication led to further delay and the eventual shelving of the whole concept of an award to Cairns.

His widow, Mrs Ena Cairns, however, never gave up hope of the case being reopened, though it did seem more and more unlikely as the years began to pass. Her determination to do something about it was revived in December 1948 by a broadcast describing her husband's action, so she obtained a copy of the BBC script, and sent it to her Member of Parliament. Early in April 1949 the case was officially reopened by Major Calvert, who commanded the brigade of which Cairns' regiment formed part, and the VC citation was announced in the London Gazette on 20 May 1949.

There was no such delay in the award to Lance Corporal John Pennington Harman, of the Queen's Own Royal West Kent Regiment. Lance Corporal Harman released the lever of a 4-second grenade, but did not throw it at once. To get instantaneous effect on his target, he held on to it for one or two seconds. Only then did he hurl it. This cool courage was just one of two incidents for which he was awarded the VC.

It was 8 April 1944, at Kohima, in Burma, and Harman was commanding a section of a forward platoon of the Queen's Own Royal West Kent Regiment. During the darkness of the jungle night the Japanese set up a machine-gun post within fifty yards of his own position. This gun naturally soon turned out to be a serious menace to the rest of his company, and, owing to the lie of the land, Harman was not able to aim the fire of his section on to this post.

Unhesitatingly, Harman went forward himself, fifty yards. Six seconds' running flat out. But much longer in this country. And liable to be shot any second. When he was nearing the post he got out his grenade, released the lever, and counted off those two interminable seconds. He dare not wait longer, or it might easily explode in the air and kill him. Yet he did not want it to reach the target too soon. He timed it just right, as things turned out, and annihilated the post, returning to his section with the prize of the enemy machine gun.

Early next morning Harman recovered a position on a forward slope 150 yards from the enemy, in order to strengthen another platoon that had been heavily attacked in the night. When he had occupied this spot on the forward slope its vantage-point enabled him to see a party of enemy digging in under cover of machine-gun fire and snipers. The snipers, as usual, were frequently covered with leaves and perched in the branches, and so invisible against the jungle backcloth.

Harman told his Bren gun crew to give him covering fire. As it throbbed out through the sloping land he fixed his bayonet, and charged the post alone. He shot four Japanese, and, bayoneting one, wiped out the post.

But when walking back to the forward slope once more a sudden stammer of machine-gun fire echoed around the site. Some of the bullets struck him in the side. He managed to stagger back to his own lines. They set him down, and did as much as they could for him. But he died a little while later.

The last and perhaps most heroic of these Burma VCs in early 1944 was Captain John Neil Randle, the Royal Norfolk Regiment, who sealed the slit of a gun-pit with his own body.

Captain Randle had not long finished his studies at Merton College, Oxford, when he was called up about a month before the war. He was in the ranks of the East Surrey Regiment for some six months before he went to an OCTU and gained his commission. Randle married soon afterwards, and was sent to India and Burma in 1942. When his wife bore his son Leslie John, the baby was named after Mrs Randle's brother, Flying Officer Leslie Manser, who was awarded the VC, posthumously after the first 1,000-bomber raid on Cologne. Now, in 1944, her husband was also to win it.

4 May 1944, at Kohima, in Burma, a battalion of the Norfolk Regiment attacked the Japanese positions on a ridge. When the company commander was severely wounded Randle took over command of the company, which was leading the attack. He handled a difficult situation in a masterly way under deafening gunfire.

At one stage Randle was wounded in the knee by grenade splinters, but he did not allow this painful blow to interfere with his leadership until the company had captured its objective and consolidated.

After this, Randle thought first of his men, limping forward to bring in all the wounded who were lying outside the perimeter. Despite the agony of his knee, Randle refused to be evacuated even then, and insisted on carrying out a personal reconnaissance in bright moonlight before a further attack by his company on the positions to which the enemy had withdrawn.

Dawn, 6 May. Led by Randle, the attack began. One of the platoons reached the crest of the hill held by the Japanese, but another platoon ran into heavy medium machine-gun opposition from a bunker on the reverse slope of the particular feature. Randle realized that this bunker covered not only the rear of his new position but also the line of communication of the whole battalion, and therefore its destruction was imperative if their operation were to succeed.

A time to live and a time to die.

Randle charged the Japanese machine-gun post quite alone, with just his rifle and bayonet. He ran straight at it. They fired straight at him. Before he got to it bullet after bullet had hit him. But, though bleeding in the face and already mortally wounded, he reached the bunker, and stilled the gun with a grenade thrown through the actual slit.

Then, with one last heave, he flung his body across the same slit so that the aperture should be completely sealed. There he died.

'The bravery shown by this officer could not have been surpassed, and by his self-sacrifice he saved the lives of many of his men and enabled not only his own company but the whole battalion to gain its objective and win a decisive victory over the enemy.'

In 1936 one of Randle's best friends was Leonard Cheshire. Now they both had the VC only Randle was no longer alive.

There is one more postscript to the story. About the time that Randle's VC was announced, a memorial was unveiled on the lonely hills around the town of Kohima, in the wild Manipur country. It honours the memory of men of the Norfolks who died in that area during May and June, 1944; men killed in battles which helped to drive the Japanese from the long stretch of the Dimapur-Imphal road.

The men of the Norfolks themselves built the memorial, in the form of a big teak cross cut from one of the great jungle trees. On its crosspiece is carved *The Royal Norfolk Regiment*, and on its plaque the three battle honours won during the campaign.

CHAPTER FORTY-THREE

From Salerno to Anzio

PETER WRIGHT, PAUL TRIQUET, WILLIAM SIDNEY (LORD DE L'ISLE AND DUDLEY)

Sicily was invaded on 10 July 1943, and fell to the Allies on 17 August. This was the stepping-stone to Italy —the next new battlefront in Europe. The following month marked the start of the long and costly campaign in the land of Hitler's southern Axis ally. It was a campaign that in most men's minds started at Salerno, and aptly enough the first VC in Italy was won there.

'If ever a man deserved the VC, it is this man to whom I have awarded the DCM.'

HM King George VI said this to General Alexander when he visited the Italian battlefield and decorated Company Sergeant Major Peter Harold Wright. The King then asked Alexander to check all the facts of Wright's great gallantry and report to him personally. The general did this, with a result that the Distinguished Conduct Medal was cancelled and the Victoria Cross bestowed instead.

So Wright became the Salerno VC, commemorating that bloody beachhead where the Allies landed to liberate Italy. Salerno —a place of slaughter and splendour.

On 25 September 1943, the 3rd Battalion, Coldstream Guards, were attacking the Pagliarolli feature, a steep wooded hill near Salerno. The combination of the slope and the trees could scarcely have been worse. Before the battalion reached the crest, the right-hand company, not surprisingly, became bogged down by slashing Spandau and mortar-fire.

All the officers were casualties.

Wright realized that his company was badly held up, so went forward to see what could be done about it. Finding that there were no officers left active, he at once assumed command, and crawled ahead all alone to examine the exact strength of the enemy there. He returned with the vital news that three Spandau posts were blocking their advance.

Wright put a plan to the immediate test. He collected a section and placed it where the guards could give some covering fire. Then, singlehanded, he set about attacking each Spandau post in turn with hand grenades and bayonet —a deadly blend. He silenced each one. Next he led the company on to the crest of the hill,

191

but soon became aware that their job was far from finished. Enemy fire sighted on to the crest made it virtually untenable. There was nothing for it but to lead them a little way down the slope again, and try to approach the top from another direction.

Brushing aside a barrage of fire from several sources, Wright turned to reorganize what was left of the company to consolidate their gains.

Soon afterwards they beat off a German counter-attack. And later again, still oblivious of staggering shellfire falling on the area of company headquarters and the reverse slopes of the hill, Wright brought up extra ammunition, and distributed it to the company. To do this, he also had to run the gauntlet of machine-gun bullets from the commanding slopes on the left flank of their position.

It was due to his magnificent leadership and outstanding heroism throughout the whole action attacking the Pagliarolli slope that the battalion succeeded in taking and keeping this vital location.

No wonder the King asked for the DCM to be changed to the VC.

Three months later and many miles farther on, the Canadians ran into opposition as savage as at Salerno, but carved an epic of endurance out of their adversity.

'Ils ne passeront pas,' said French-Canadian Captain Paul Triquet, echoing the famous battlecry of Verdun in the First World War, 'They shall not pass'.

The epic of Triquet was the story of Dead Man's Gulch, where only nine men survived out of eighty. The battle began when Triquet took a company of the Royal 22nd Regiment into Moro Valley. To the Canadians, this soon acquired the nickname of Dead Man's Gulch, due to all the enemy paratroops and fellow Canadians who were killed there, and who, because of the battle conditions, often had to lie where they fell for days before being buried.

This was Italy in December 1943.

The capture of the key road junction on the main Ortona–Orsogria lateral line entirely depended on clearing the Dead Man's Gulch gully. Until this was done, a farther advance could not be contemplated.

It was considered that the vital factor in the neutralization of this gully was a house –hardly a hamlet –known as Casa Berardi, about half a mile from the crossroads. Possession of this building would enable the courageous Canadians to enfilade the gully.

But both the gully and the house had been turned into formidable strongpoints defended by German infantry and tanks.

On 14 December 1943, Triquet and his company, with the support of a squadron of a Canadian armoured regiment, received their orders to cross the gully and take Casa Berardi. They met mountainous difficulties right from the start.

The Germans held the gully in real strength, and on approaching it the Canadians came under the whiplash of guns and mortars. A gully must be one of the worst places to try to cross. The result: all the company officers and half of the men were either killed or wounded. At first it looked like a repetition of 'the valley of Death'.

Showing superb contempt for the enemy, however, Triquet went round the troops telling them: 'Never mind them —they can't shoot.'

Finally, the Huns had infiltrated on all sides, and Triquet made up his mind in a flash of inspiration.

'They're in front of us, behind us, and on our flanks,' he said, there's only one safe place —that's on the objective.'

So when they were surrounded they took the only course possible, and attacked. Triquet himself dashed forward from the gully, with the Canadians at his heel, and together they burst through the enemy resistance. In this action they destroyed four tanks and silenced several machine-gun nests.

Still against the bitterest barrage and defence imaginable, Triquet and the remnants of his company, in close cooperation with the tanks, forced their way forward, until they reached Casa Berardi and the houses in its neighbourhood.

By this time the eighty men in the company had been reduced to the following strength: Triquet, two sergeants, and fifteen men. Just eighteen. They were at once cut off and surrounded by fresh enemy troops who appeared on the scene.

Expecting an early counter-attack, Triquet instantly set about organizing his handful of men into as strong a defensive perimeter as possible around the remaining tanks.

He passed the *mot d'ordre*.

Ils ne passeront pas.

For he had received orders by radio to hold on at all costs.

The inevitable happened. The Germans turned tanks and men on the pitifully few Canadians. The Canadians were isolated, and for five days and nights, with little sleep or food, they had to face repeated poundings by enemy guns, and they had nothing more powerful than Piats in reply.

Triquet himself ignored all this fire focused on them, and inspired the French-Canadians to hurl back every attack. The enemy had to lick heavy losses, as Triquet and his diminishing numbers held out against really overwhelming odds. Five days and five nights. And the eighteen men became nine. From eighty to eighteen then nine.

Finally, other Canadians fought their way through to contact Triquet, and the rest of the battalion took Casa Berardi, relieving the remnant nine.

Triquet had been wounded in the leg through a burn caused by a bursting smoke-bomb, but this did not prove serious, and he survived.

What the Canadians saw was one of the worst-scarred stretches of terrain anywhere in Italy. Trees flattened, tanks tortured and torn by shellfire and men and cattle killed in the fields. That was Dead Man's Gulch.

Throughout the whole of this engagement, Captain Triquet showed the most magnificent courage and cheerfulness under heavy fire. Wherever the action was hottest he was to be seen shouting encouragement to his men and organizing the defence. His utter disregard of danger, his cheerfulness, and tireless devotion to duty were a constant source of inspiration to them. His tactical skill and superb leadership enabled them, although reduced by casualties to a mere handful, to continue their advance against bitter resistance, and to hold their gains against determined counter-attacks. It was due to him that Casa Berardi was captured, and the way opened for the attack on the vital road junction.

He said, 'They shall not pass' —and they did not.

Anzio lies thirty miles from Rome, and it was the battle for this beachhead from 26 January to 23 May 1944, that became one of the bloodiest of the whole war. Out of the agony of Anzio came Major Sidney's VC awarded for utter disregard of danger in the action near Carroceto. Major William Philip Sidney became Lord De L'Isle and Dudley. He died in 1991.

The four-day period from 6–10 February 1944, was critical to the whole Anzio landings. The Germans attacked a British division with elements of no less than six separate divisions, and a continuous series of struggles were fought locally hand-to-hand. Each one had its immediate reaction on the position of adjoining troops in the region and on the action as a whole. So it was supremely important that every inch of the devastated Italian land should be doggedly and tenaciously fought for. The area of Carroceto-Buonriposo Ridge was especially vital.

During the nights of 7–8 and 8–9 February Sidney was commanding the support company of a battalion of the Grenadier Guards, company headquarters being on the left of battalion HQ, in a gully south-west of Carroceto Bridge. Enemy infantry who had bypassed the forward-position company north-west of Carroceto heavily lumbered forward in the vicinity of Sidney's company HQ successfully penetrating into the Wadi.

Sidney collected the crew of a 3-inch mortar, firing near by, and personally led a tommy gun and hand-grenade attack which sent the Germans reeling out of the gully.

He then sent the detachment back to continue their mortar-fire while he and a handful of men took up a position on the edge of the gully to beat off the enemy, who were renewing their lunge in some strength. Sidney and his Grenadier Guards managed to keep most of the Germans at bay, but a number of them inevitably reached a ditch only twenty yards in front of them. From here they could outflank Sidney's position, and would do so soon unless something happened at once. It did.

In full view of the Nazis —less than the length of a cricket pitch away —Sidney snatched ammunition for his tommy gun, and rushed forward to engage the enemy at a very close range. It was him or them. The sight of Sidney only a few paces away and firing in their midst spread alarm among them. Those who were not killed withdrew. The major had saved the situation for the moment. But war was made up of hundreds of such situations and moments. It was a question of who would crack first.

Returning to his former position on the edge of the gully, Sidney kept two guardsmen with him, and sent the rest back for more ammunition and grenades.

While they were gone the Germans took the opportunity to attack the three men

194

mercilessly. During the assault a grenade thrown at the position struck Sidney in the face, bounced off to the ground, and exploded; pieces of metal rained down on them. One guardsman was killed, the second wounded, and Sidney was also injured in the thigh. Single-handed, Sidney kept the Germans out for a further five minutes until the ammunition party returned, when the enemy was forcibly ejected and the situation restored for a while.

Satisfied that no more attacks could be made just then, Sidney made his way to a nearby cave to have his wound dressed, but before this could be done the unexpected happened. The Nazis opened up again.

He at once left the cave and returned to his post, continuing to take part in the fight for another hour, by which time the left of the battalion position was consolidated and the foe finally driven off again.

Sidney was in a very weak state through loss of blood from his thigh wound, and barely able to walk. But only when the enemy had really been beaten did he submit to treatment.

Then came the dawn, when contacts with the enemy were so close that the company could not evacuate Sidney till after dark. A whole winter's day near Anzio. But all through it, although exceedingly weak, he continued to act as a tonic to the others. And it subsequently transpired that by his actions the battalion's position was re-established, with far-reaching effects on the entire Anzio beachhead battle.

CHAPTER FORTY-FOUR

Wounded Pilot in Defenceless Lancaster

WILLIAM REID

'Oh, hell,' said Acting Flight Lieutenant William Reid, RAFVR, No. 61 Squadron, as he was wounded. Then he set about carrying on to complete his mission.

Reid did not have a long operational career behind him on the night of 3 November 1943. Only six weeks earlier he had been posted on operational duties for the first time.

Now to the night of 3 November, with Reid pilot and captain of a Lancaster bomber, part of a force detailed to attack Düsseldorf. His plane took off all right, and reached the flat moonscape of the Dutch coast. Then 'O for Oboe' met trouble. An enemy Messerschmitt Me110 described an arc in the darkness to come within yards of the Lancaster. Its pilot pressed a stream of fire from the fighter –and Reid's windscreen was shattered in an instant. Because of a failure in the heating circuit, the rear gunner's hands were too cold for him to open fire immediately, or to operate his microphones and so give warning of danger. But after a brief delay he managed to return the Messerschmitt's fire. A hectic few moments followed before it was finally driven off, but by this time the damage was done.

Reid tells exactly what did happen as far as he was concerned behind that shattered screen:

I saw a blinding flash and lost about 2000 feet before I could pull out again. I felt as if my head had been blown off –just the sort of feeling you get at the time.

Other members of the crew shouted 'Are you all right?' It was no good telling them I felt half dead, and said, 'Yes I feel all right.'

I resumed course again, and managed to get my goggles on. The wind was just lashing through the broken windscreen. Tiny pieces of the 'Perspex' were all over my face and hands. Fortunately, I didn't get any in my eyes, although there was some in my eyelids. I suppose I instinctively ducked.

My shoulder was a bit stiff, and it felt as if someone had hit me with a hammer. Blood was pouring down my face, and I could feel the taste of it in my mouth. It soon froze up because of the intense cold. I didn't turn back because there were lots of other bombers behind us and it might have been dangerous for them.

At this stage it was ascertained that Reid and the aircraft were both hurt more than might be imagined. Reid had wounds in his head, shoulders, and hands. The plane had its elevator trimming tabs damaged by the fighter, and it became very hard to handle. The rear turret too had got badly knocked about, and the communications system and compasses were put out of action. These were all serious setbacks both to the continuation of the operation and the eventual return home.

Reid found out that the crew were so far unscathed, kept completely quiet about his own injuries still, and went on to Düsseldorf.

It was the mid-upper gunner, Flight Lieutenant D. Baldwin, who reported that Reid shouted out 'Oh, hell!' as the fighter's first bursts hit the windscreen and himself.

It was the rear gunner, Flight Sergeant A. F. Emerson, who told how his fingers had been too frozen to reply to the Messerschmitt till the German was within 150 yards. Emerson thought he hit him then.

The ordeal of 'O for Oboe' and its faithful crew was still barely beginning on this night over Germany.

Soon after the Messerschmitt was driven off, or shot down, the Lancaster was attacked again, by a Focke-Wulf 190 this time. The enemy's fire raked the bomber from stem to stern. The rear gunner replied with his only serviceable gun, but the chronic condition of his turret made accurate aiming impossible.

Reid takes up the story of this fateful flight again:

My navigator was killed, and the wireless operator fatally injured. The oxygen system was put out of action. I was again wounded. The flight engineer, though hit in the forearm, gave me oxygen from a portable supply.

I looked for the Pole Star and flew on that for a bit. I knew from the flight plan just roughly where we were. Then I could see Cologne on the starboard, and turned for the attack on Düsseldorf.

So Reid refused to be turned from his objective, and he reached the target some fifty minutes later —minutes that must have seemed like days.

After the Focke-Wulf attack, Baldwin discovered the wireless operator lying over the already dead navigator.

Meanwhile Reid memorized his course so well that even amid the holocaust the bomb-aimer thought that the plane was proceeding so normally that nothing had happened. He was cut off by the communications failure, and knew neither of the casualties to his comrades or even of the captain's injuries. The bomb-aimer was Flight Sergeant L. G. Rolton, who said that Reid gave him a good bombing run right over the centre of the target. Photographs showed that when the bombs were released the aircraft was exactly in its proper place, so they must have hit their mark precisely. What an achievement, with the navigator dead and the wireless operator dying —and the pilot still nearly fainting from loss of blood!

Steering still by the Pole Star, with the added assistance of the moon, Reid then set course for home. With the windscreen shattered, the cold grew more intense each minute, and he lapsed into semi-consciousness —fatal for the pilot of a plane. Reid continues his own narrative:

> After we had bombed I steered a little north to avoid the defences, and headed for England as best I could. I was growing weak from loss of blood, and the emergency oxygen supply had given out.
>
> Because the elevators had been shot away, we had to hold back the stick the whole of the time. That was a tough job. I held both arms round it and clasped my hands, because my shoulder was weak. The engineer also held on all the time. I did not then know that he had been wounded in the hand.
>
> The bomb-aimer also helped. We went through heavy flak near the Dutch coast, and then I saw searchlights over England.

Reid spent that time over the North Sea partly unconscious and then regaining consciousness. Several times when he came round he gave the thumbs-up sign to Rolton, and at one stage the aircraft went round three times in a flat spin until the engineer and Rolton pushed with their knees to control the stick. But at last they were really over England. Reid revived, and took over the controls again. They were losing height all the time now, but he still felt confident that they could make it safely. They spotted an airfield below them, through the silky haze of a ground mist. This mist, however, was helping to hide the runway lights, and added to that, blood from Reid's head wound was running down into his eyes now. Any exertion made it worse, so that as he tried to get the flaps down it gushed out and rushed over his face —a fantastic way in which to try to bring a bomber down, but the only one possible. It was this or not at all.

Reid circled around and flashed a distress signal with the landing-lamp. Then, as the hydraulics had been shot away, they had to use an emergency system to try and get the undercarriage down. Minutes were passing, and the crew still alive thought he was going to faint again at any moment. The bomb-aimer stood behind him, so that he could pull Reid out of the pilot's seat and take over if it became necessary. But Reid kept conscious as the defenceless, damaged Lancaster slowly circled and wheeled-in for a landing through the night and the mist —lower, lower. The runway lights leapt and danced about before Reid's blood-blinded eyes, so that the whole scene in the next few seconds seemed like a bad dream — mist, lights, darkness, the Americans' airfield. Could he bring the Lancaster down? It would be a miracle. Slowly the altimeter read less and less, till the fateful moment came.

Touchdown.

And as the Lancaster felt English earth beneath it again —an unlikely possibility a few hours earlier —one leg of the damaged undercarriage collapsed under them as the load came on it. It had been shot through, and could not support anything at all. The plane thumped along on its belly for about fifty yards, and the grinding, grating noise gradually eased till the Lancaster stopped dead. Nothing exploded or caught fire. They were down. They clambered out, still somewhat dazed by the ordeal, and the Americans at once attended to their wounds.

As the citation summed it all up:

> Wounded in two attacks, without oxygen, suffering severely from cold, his navigator dead, his wireless operator fatally injured, his aircraft crippled and defenceless, Flight Lieutenant Reid showed superb courage and leadership in penetrating a further 200 miles into enemy territory to attack one of the most strongly defended targets in Germany, every additional mile increasing the hazards of the long and perilous journey home. His tenacity and devotion to duty were beyond praise.

And he lived to fight again and survive the war: a tall, fair, smiling man with a moustache, who won the Victoria Cross on one of his first operational flights.

The engineer, Sergeant J. Norris, was awarded the Conspicuous Gallantry Medal. The navigator who was killed was Flight Sergeant J. A. Jeffreys, of Australia.

CHAPTER FORTY-FIVE

The Indian and Nepalese VCs

Premindra Singh Bhagat, Richpal Ram, Lalbahadur Thapa, Chhelu Ram, Parkash Singh, Gaje Ghale, Nand Singh, Abdul Hafiz, Kamal Ram, Yeshwant Ghadge, Ganju Lama, Netrabahadur Thapa, Agansing Rai, Tulbahadur Pun, Sher Bahadur Thapa, Thaman Gurung, Ram Sarup Singh, Bhandari Ram, Umrao Singh, Sher Shah, Parkash Singh, Fazal Din, Gian Singh, Bhanbhagta Gurung, Karamjeet Singh Judge, Ali Haidar, Namdeo Jadhao, Lachhiman Gurung

Indian and Nepalese soldiers have long been known for their valour, and this was recognized by the award of twenty-eight VCs to the Indian Army in the Second World War.

The first of these went to Second Lieutenant Premindra Singh Bhagat, Corps of Indian Engineers. In the pursuit of the Italians to Gondar, in Abyssinia, on the night of 31 January–1 February 1941, he and his men had the task of clearing a road which was thickly strewn with mines, blocks, and booby-traps. They had to do this at top speed so that the advance should not be delayed.

For forty-eight hours, non-stop, Bhagat carried out this perilous and arduous work. In all there were fifteen minefields and fifty-five miles of road to be cleared. Twice his Bren gun carrier was blown up beneath him, killing several of his men, and on a third occasion, when ambushed and under close fire, he himself carried straight on with the work. Despite having one eardrum punctured and being worn out, he refused relief until he collapsed from sheer shock and exhaustion –with both eardrums damaged by then. But not until the column could get through safely to their goal.

* * *

A week later, in Eritrea, from 7–12 February 1941, Subadar Richpal Ram, 6th Rajputana Rifles, was taking part in an attack at Keren when his company commander was wounded. The forty-three-year-old Indian took command, and led his men in a bayonet charge through two-way fire to the final objective. After its capture, however, he had to withdraw when ammunition supplies ran out, but five days later he led a second assault on the same position.

As he neared it his right foot was blown off, and soon after he suffered further wounds. As he lay helpless on the battlefield he had no thought of his own condition, remaining intent on encouraging his men. As he waved them on his last words were:

'We will capture the objective.' And they did.

The first Gurkha to win the VC in this war was Subadar Lalbahadur Thapa, 2nd Gurkha Rifles. In command of two sections at Rass La Zondi, Tunisia, 5 and 6 April 1943, he was ordered to attack and secure the only passage by which a vital commanding feature could be seized to cover the penetration of the division into the hills.

First contact with the enemy was made at the foot of a pathway winding up a narrow cleft. A series of enemy posts studded this steep cleft, the inner one brandishing an anti-tank gun and the rest machine guns. Thapa and his men killed the garrison of the outer posts by *kukri* or bayonet in a first rush, but the enemy then opened very heavy fire straight down the narrow enclosed pathway and steep arena sides.

Thapa led his men onward, fighting his way up the narrow gully – straight through the firing. With little room to manoeuvre in the face of such fire, interspersed with the liberal use of grenades, Thapa nevertheless dealt with the next post, killing two men with his *kukri* and two more with his revolver. He continued to batter his way up the narrow bullet-swept approaches to the crest, and, with two riflemen, he managed to reach the crest itself, where he killed two more men and caused the rest to flee. He went on to secure the whole feature, and covered his company's vital advance up the defile. This pathway was found to be the only route up the precipitous ridge, so that, by winning it, the company could deploy and mop up all enemy opposition.

Company Havildar Major Chhelu Ram, 6th Rajputana Rifles, also won the VC for valour in Tunisia that month. It occurred during an attack on the Jebel-Garci feature near Enfidaville on the night of 19–20 April 1943.

He was with one of the two leading companies, which ran into an enemy machine-gun post on some high ground. Armed with a tommy gun and protected only by his tin helmet, Chhelu Ram ran through the fire to silence the post by killing all its occupants.

When the leading companies were approaching their third goal the enemy brought down intense machine-gun and mortar fire on them, mortally wounding the company commander. Chhelu Ram went to the officer's aid, in an utterly

201

exposed position, and attended to him, during which he himself was seriously injured.

Ignoring this wound, he at once took command of his company and elements of the other leading company, and reorganized them. The enemy counter-attacked heavily, and in no time the Indians began to run short of ammunition. Fierce hand-to-hand fighting followed, with Chhelu Ram bleeding, but rushing from point to point, rallying his men, and driving the enemy back with the cry of:

'Jats and Mohammedans – there must be no withdrawal. We will advance. Advance.'

And he did advance, ahead of the two companies, who were so inspired by him that they struck back on this vital ground, and drove off the enemy at the point of the bayonet, with stones, and with rocks. This time Chhelu Ram was wounded mortally, but would not be carried back from the fighting. He continued to command his men till he lost consciousness and died a few minutes later.

In Burma the Indians were protecting the border to their own country, and the first of many to win the VC while fighting the Japanese was Havildar Parkash Singh, 8th Punjab Regiment.

On 6 January 1943, during an attack on enemy entrenched position at Donbaik, in the Mayu Peninsula, several Bren gun carriers were subjected to intense fire. Two were put out of action, but their crews kept firing till their ammunition was all gone, when the enemy rushed the carriers on foot. Parkash Singh saw what would happen, and in a split second decided to drive his own carrier towards his comrades, and by sheer speed managed to get to them first, and rescue them from an inevitable end.

A fortnight later, on 19 January an enemy anti-tank gun put three Bren gun carriers out of use and covered them as they lay there helplessly on the open beach of the peninsula. One of the carriers, too, had survivors; from another vehicle in addition to its own crew. Parkash Singh once more saw the fate of all these trapped men unless something was done, so he drove his own carrier over to the disabled vehicles.

Flayed by fire, somehow he got through to their exposed spots on the beach. As the waves lapped gently in the distance and the enemy guns shot at him, he rescued the combined crews from one disabled carrier and the weapons from another.

Having brought the men back to safety, he returned to the beach, still under the heaviest fire. He stopped his carrier, calmly dismounted, connected a towing-chain to another carrier, sheltering two wounded men, and then directed the towing of the injured out of that inferno of sound and sand.

To stop an advance of hordes of Japanese into the Chin Hills in Burma, the Indians had to take Basha East Hill, the key to the enemy position. After two assaults had failed, a third was mounted on 24 May 1943

Havildar Gaje Ghale, 5th Royal Gurkha Rifles, commanded one platoon. He had never been under fire before, and all his platoon consisted of young untried soldiers. The approach to their goal was along a narrow knife-edge, with sharp sides and bare jungle, whereas the enemy positions were well concealed. In places the approach was a mere five yards wide and covered by a dozen machine guns, besides being subjected to artillery and mortar fire from the reverse slope of the hill.

While preparing for the attack they came under heavy fire, but Gaje Ghale rallied his men and led them forward. Approaching to close range of the enemy, the platoon came under a solid sheet of fire, and Gaje Ghale was wounded in the arm, chest, and leg by a hand grenade. This did not stop him, nor did the arcs of fire from all sides. He closed his men, and led them to grips with the enemy in personal combat.

Dominating the whole fight with his courage, he hurled hand grenades which were covered in blood from his neglected wounds, and led one assault after another to the shout of the Gurkhas' battlecry:

'Ayo Gurkhali.'

Spurred on by this man, they somehow stormed the hill and slew most of the enemy. Then Gaje Ghale held and consolidated their hard-won position, and it was not until the situation was really secure that he agreed to go to the aid post –getting there alone.

Six times wounded in an assault, Naik Nand Singh, 11th Sikh Regiment, went on. It was now nearly a year later in Burma, on the night of 11–12 March 1944. A Japanese platoon about forty strong, armed with machine guns and a grenade discharger, infiltrated into the battalion position covering the main Maungdaw–Buthidaung road. They occupied a dominating spot, still further strengthened by foxholes and underground trenches on the steep sides of the hill.

Nand Singh commanded the leading section of the platoon ordered to recapture this spot at all costs. He led his section up a steep, razor-edged ridge, under heavy fire. Although wounded in the thigh, he rushed on ahead of the others and took the first enemy trench with the bayonet. Then he crawled forward alone, still under the same fire, and was wounded once more in the face and shoulder by a grenade which burst only a yard in front of him. He took the second trench.

Soon afterwards, with all his section killed or wounded, Nand Singh dragged himself out of the trench and took a third trench, bayoneting all inside. By storming these three trenches he enabled the rest of the platoon to follow up and seize the top of the hill. Nand Singh's VC was announced on D-Day, 6 June.

Now to a man who did not survive. His last words were:

'Reorganize. I'll give you covering fire.'

But he could not pull the trigger.

Jemadar Abdul Hafiz, 9th Jat Regiment, was one of two Indian VCs gazetted on the same day.

In the early hours of 6 April 1944, in the Burma hills ten miles north of Imphal, the enemy had attacked a standing patrol of four men, and taken a feature overlooking a company position. At first light a patrol went out and contacted the enemy, reporting that they thought some forty Japanese were there. They could not tell if the enemy had dug in during darkness.

The company commander ordered Abdul Hafiz to attack the enemy with two sections from his platoon at 09.30 hours He led the attack up a completely bare slope with no cover, which steepened still more near the crest. When a few yards below the top, the Japanese opened up. But before this Abdul Hafiz had told his men that no Japanese could stop them.

He was at once wounded, but pressed on to lead an assault on the crest, which they gained with great dash. On reaching the top, though, Abdul Hafiz was wounded again, in the leg this time, but seeing a machine gun firing from a flank in their direction, he went for it, and, seizing the actual barrel, pushed it upward while a comrade killed the gunner.

Then Abdul Hafiz snatched a Bren gun from an injured man, and led his men after the enemy. So savage was their attack that the large number of Japanese still on top of the hill ran away down the other side. Regardless of machine-gun fire spattering across at him from another feature a few hundred yards away, he chased the Japanese, firing at them as he ran.

Suddenly Abdul Hafiz was wounded in the chest from the distant machine-gun fire, and collapsed holding his Bren gun and trying to go on firing. That was when he gasped out his last words.

Announced on the same day was the VC to Sepoy Kamal Ram, 8th Punjab Regiment, fighting the war in Italy, far from Burma and his homeland. It happened on 12 May 1944 after crossing the river Gari, when an advance was held up by heavy machine-gun fire from four posts. As the capture of the position was essential to secure a bridgehead over the Gari, the company commander called for a volunteer to get round the rear of the right-hand enemy post and silence it.

Volunteering at once, and crawling forward through the wire to a flank, Kamal Ram attacked the post and shot the first gunner. A second German tried to seize his weapon, but he dispatched this one with the bayonet, and went on to shoot a German officer who emerged from the trench about to fire a pistol.

Kamal Ram went on to attack the second post, and, after shooting one gunner, he threw a grenade into the trench, causing the rest to surrender, then, seeing a havildar making a reconnaissance for an attack on the third post, Kamal Ram joined him, and, having first covered his companion, went in and finished off the post. All this enabled his company to secure the ground vital to establishing the bridgehead and completing work on two bridges.

Also in Italy, on 10 July 1944, Naik Yeshwant Ghadge, 5th Mahratta Light Infantry, came under heavy fire at zero range. He rushed at the machine-gun post, threw in a grenade which knocked out the gun and its firer, and then shot one of the crew with his tommy gun. Having no time to change the magazine, he grasped his gun by the barrel and beat to death the remaining two men of the gun crew. Tragically, though, he was shot in the chest and back by snipers, and died in the post he had captured.

Like many other Nepalese in the Burma campaign, Rifleman Ganju Lama will never forget the Imphal Plain. It was here at Ningthouknong that he added the VC to the MM won a month earlier for knocking out an enemy tank with his Piat gun.

On the morning of 12 June 1944, the enemy put down an intense artillery barrage on positions north of the village, causing heavy losses. They at once followed this with an attack supported by five medium tanks. After fierce hand-to-hand grappling they drove in the perimeter in one place, and enemy infantry plus three tanks charged through, pinning the Indians to the ground with fire.

B Company, 7th Gurkha Rifles, received the order:

'Restore the situation.'

Soon after passing the starting line B Company came under fire from machine guns entrenched and also mounted on tanks —at point-blank range This was the rifleman's moment.

Ganju Lama, the No. 1 of the Piat gun, on his own initiative, crawled forward and took on the tanks all alone. Concentrated crossfire met around him, breaking his left wrist and wounding him in his right hand and a leg. But he brought his Piat into play within thirty yards of the enemy tanks looming above him. He knocked out first one, then another, and a third was destroyed by an anti-tank gun.

Despite his three wounds, he moved forward again, and threw grenades at the tank crews trying to escape. Not until he had killed or wounded them all would he let himself be taken away for treatment.

Ganju Lama was decorated with the VC by Lord Wavell, Viceroy of India, on 24 October 1944, beside Kamal Ram and the widow of Abdul Hafiz.

Water Picquet and Mortar Bluff were the names of two posts forming the scene of the next two VCs in Burma. On 24 and 25 June 1944, the enemy took the two posts, which were well sited and mutually supporting. Their possession threatened Allied communications.

Subadar Netrabahadur Thapa was in command of a garrison of fifty-one men who took over Mortar Bluff, on its hillside commanding the base of Bishenpur, during the afternoon of 25 June. The picquet position was devoid of any cover, and Water Picquet, a short way off to the south, was still in enemy hands. The retention of Mortar Bluff was essential to the safety of the other positions farther down the ridge.

The relief had been harassed by enemy snipers at close range, but was completed at 18.30 hours without loss. But soon after seven o'clock the enemy attack came. A 75-mm and a 37-mm gun were brought up on the high ground overlooking the post, and these poured shell after shell at point-blank range into the narrow confines of the picquet for ten endless minutes. A company of Japanese then attacked.

A fierce fight ensued, with Netrabahadur Thapa and his men holding ground against huge odds. He moved around all the while, encouraging his young NCOs and riflemen, and tending the wounded.

A short lull followed, enabling him to give a clear report on the telephone to his CO and to ask for more artillery defensive fire. Then he made preparations to meet the next onslaught.

Under cover of the pitch-dark night and Burma-strength rain, the enemy moved round to the jungle and launched their next attack from its cover. Still in strength and as ferocious as ever, the Japanese poured out of the jungle across the short space of open ground to the picquet defences. For a time the Indians held on, until they had the appalling ill-luck of suffering two jammed machine guns.

With much reduced fire power, this section could not hold on, and the Japanese overran two sections, killing or wounding twelve of the sixteen men. Having no reserve, Netrabahadur Thapa went forward from his headquarters, and stemmed any further incursions with well-flung grenades.

But the situation was critical, as the rain still soaked everything and every one. With more than half of his men casualties, ammunition low, and the enemy in possession of part of his perimeter, he would have been justified in withdrawing, but in his report to his CO he said that he intended to hold on, and asked for reinforcements. So fine were his plans for defence, and so fine the example of this gallant Gurkha officer, that not a man moved from his trench and not a yard more ground was gained by the enemy despite their desperate attempts.

Thus the night passed, until at 04.00 hours a section of eight men with grenades and small arms ammunition arrived. Their presence inevitably drew fire, and soon all eight were casualties. But, undismayed, the subadar retrieved the ammunition himself, and with his platoon-headquarters men took the offensive, armed with grenades and *kukris*. While doing this he received a bullet in the mouth, followed by a grenade which killed him outright.

They found him later, *kukri* in hand and a dead Japanese by his side with a cleft skull. He had fought against the greatest odds imaginable for eight hours before being killed.

On the morning of 26 June a company of the same 5th Royal Gurkha Rifles was told to retake the two picquets at all costs.

They went into the attack after an artillery barrage, but, on reaching a false crest about eighty yards from their objective, they were pinned down by a machine-gun in Mortar Bluff and a 37-mm gun in the jungle. The Nepalese suffered severe losses.

Naik Agansing Rai realized at once that more delay would mean more losses, so he led his section straight through the fire, directly at the machine gun. Shooting as he ran, he charged the position, killing three of the crew of four. The fourth was too petrified to fight. Inspired by Agansing Rai's courage, the section surged across the bullet-ridden ground, and routed the whole garrison of Mortar Bluff.

That was just the start.

Their position now came under intense fire from the gun in the jungle and from Water Picquet. Agansing Rai again advanced towards the gun, his section following. They were decimated to three men before half the distance had been trodden, yet they pressed on to reach the goal. Arriving at close range, Agansing Rai killed three of the crew, and his men accounted for the other two.

The party then returned to Mortar Bluff, where the rest of their platoon were forming up for the third thrust at Water Picquet. In the ensuing advance more machine-gun fire and showers of grenades wiped out many more Indians.

Once more Agansing Rai, covered by his Bren gunner, went on alone, clutching a grenade in one hand and his Thompson sub machine gun in the other. Devastating fire flew all around him, but he reached the enemy post; his grenade and bursts from his gun killed all four occupants of the bunker. Demoralized by this complete contempt for danger, the enemy fled before the onslaught on Water Picquet, and so it was recaptured according to orders.

Rounding off this Burma group, Rifleman Tulbahadur Pun won his VC in the same action at Mogaung as Captain Michael Allmand. In the same week of June 1944, as the previous two VCs, a battalion of the 6th Gurkha Rifles were told to attack the railway bridge at Mogaung. As soon as the attack developed the enemy opened concentrated crossfire from a position known as the Red House and from a strong bunker 200 yards to the left of it. So intense was this crossfire that both the leading platoons of B Company, one of them Tulbahadur Pun's, became pinned to the ground, and the whole of his section was wiped out except for himself, the section commander, and one other man. The section commander led the remaining two men in a charge on the Red House but was at once badly wounded.

Tulbahadur Pun and his remaining companion continued the charge, but the latter too was hit. So Tulbahadur Pun seized the Bren gun and, firing from the hip as he went, continued the charge on this heavily bunkered position alone, in face of the most shattering automatic fire aimed straight at him.

With the dawn coming up behind him, he presented a perfect target. He had to move thirty yards over open ground —ankle-deep in mud, through shell-holes, over fallen trees. Despite these odds, he reached the Red House, and closed with the Japanese inside. He killed three of them, put five to flight, and captured a couple of light machine guns and ammunition. Then he gave accurate supporting fire from the bunker to the rest of his platoon, enabling them to reach their goal.

The opening pair in the second group of fourteen Indian and Nepalese VCs were both awarded for action in Italy. On 18–19 September 1944, a battalion of the 9th Gurkha Rifles was fighting its way into the state of San Marino against a bitter German rearguard from prepared positions dominating the river valley.

Rifleman Sher Bahadur Thapa was No. 1 Bren gunner in a rifle company, which came under heavy enemy observed fire just before dawn. He and his section commander charged an enemy post, killing the machine gunner, and putting the rest to flight. Another group of Germans attacked the two Gurkhas, and the section commander was at once badly hurt by a grenade. At this, Sher Bahadur Thapa rushed at the attackers, reached the crest of the ridge, and swung his Bren gun into action.

Disregarding suggestions that he should withdraw to the cover of a slit trench, he lay in the open under a hail of bullets. By the intensity and accuracy of the fire he could bring to bear only from the crest, he silenced several enemy machine guns, and checked a number of Germans trying to infiltrate on to the ridge.

At the end of two hours both forward companies ran out of ammunition, and, as they were practically surrounded, they received orders to withdraw. The rifleman covered their withdrawal as they crossed the open ground to position in the rear, and remained alone at his post until he too had no more bullets. He then dashed forward under accurate enemy fire, and rescued two wounded Gurkhas lying between him and the advancing Germans. While returning the second time, he fell, riddled by bullets. His was a case of a life sacrificed for his comrades,

Three weeks later another Gurkha gave his life to save his comrades in circumstances just as heroic. On 10 November 1944, a company of the 5th Royal Gurkha Rifles sent a fighting patrol on to Monte San Bartolo, an objective of a future attack. In this patrol were two scouts, one of whom was Rifleman Thaman Gurung.

By skilful stalking, both scouts reached the base of the position undetected. Thaman Gurung then started to work his way to the summit, but suddenly the second scout attracted his attention to Germans in a slit trench just below the crest, about to open machine-gun fire on the leading Gurkha section. Thaman Gurung leapt to his feet and charged them so surprisingly that they surrendered.

Then he crept forward to the summit of the position, from which he saw a group of Germans on reverse slopes preparing to throw grenades over the crest at the leading section. Although the skyline had no cover at all and was under close fire, he crossed it and attacked them with his tommy gun, thus allowing the forward section to reach the summit. Due to heavy fire from the enemy, however, the platoon had subsequently to be withdrawn.

Again Thaman Gurung crossed the skyline, and in full view of the enemy he put burst after burst of tommy gun fire into the German slit trenches till he had no more bullets left. Then he hurled two grenades in for good measure. Rejoining his section, he collected two more grenades and once more doubled over the crest of the hillock and hurled them at the surviving Germans. This diversion enabled both rear sections to withdraw without further loss.

Meanwhile the leading section, which had remained behind, was still on the summit. He told them to withdraw, seized a Bren gun and a number of magazines, and yet again ran to the top of the hill where, although he knew that his action meant almost certain death, he stood up in full view of the enemy and opened fire. It was not until he had emptied two complete magazines, and the remaining section was well on its way to safety, that he fell, shot dead.

The story of the Indian VCs returns east to Burma for ten more awards.

Subadar Ram Sarup Singh was in charge of a platoon of the 1st Punjab Regiment, who were ordered on 25 October 1944, to put in a diversionary attack on the flank of an enemy position. This feature was defended by a large force of fresh Japanese troops who had turned the hill into a fortress, every approach being covered by machine guns sited in bunkers.

The platoon of Ram Sarup Singh charged this fortress, so bewildering the enemy that they fled from it, suffering casualties in their haste. The subadar was wounded in the legs during this phase too, but took no notice of the injuries. While he was consolidating, the enemy opened ferocious fire with grenade dischargers, and put in a strong thrust in three waves of twenty men each from a flank. It seemed that the platoon must be overwhelmed, but Ram Sarup Singh got another light machine gun into position and led a charge, bayoneting four of the enemy himself. Although badly hit in the thigh this time, he got up, and again went for the Japanese, calling encouragement to his men. He bayoneted and shot two more enemy, but then fell mortally wounded by machine-gun fire. The result was a rout of the Japanese.

In the same gazette as Ram Sarup Singh's award came news of the VC for Sepoy Bhandari Ram, at East Mayu, Arakan, during an attack on a strong enemy bunker on 22 November 1944. He was in the leading section of a platoon of the 10th Baluch Regiment, and to reach their goal they had to climb a precipitous slope by way of a narrow ridge with sheer sides.

When fifty yards from the top of the slope the leading section came under withering fire. Three men were wounded, including Bhandari Ram, hit in the left shoulder and the leg. The platoon was pinned down.

He then crawled up to the Japanese light machine gun and got to within fifteen yards of the enemy position. The Japanese aimed grenades at him, one of which exploded so near that it wounded him severely in the face and chest.

Now he had been hit in the shoulder, leg, face and chest.

Undeterred although so terribly wounded and bespattered with blood, he crawled to within five yards of his objective. Pausing a moment to draw strength, he threw a grenade into the position, killing the enemy gunner and two other men. Then the Indian platoon took the position –and Bhandari Ram survived to receive his VC.

The next two VCs showed the Japanese that the Indians could fight just as fanatically as themselves. In the Kaladan Valley of Burma, on 15 and 16 December 1944, Havildar Umrao Singh of the Indian Artillery had charge of a gun in an advanced section of his battery when it became subjected to 75-mm gun and mortar-fire for ninety minutes on end.

Though twice wounded by grenades in a first attack, he held off a second thrust by skilful control of his men's small-arms fire, and by manning a Bren gun himself, which he fired over the shield of his gun at the enemy –who had got to five yards off.

Again the Japanese were beaten back, and two more attacks received the same treatment. By this stage all his gun detachment had fallen killed or injured except for himself and two others.

When the final attack came the other heavy gun had been overrun. All his ammunition was gone too, so, seizing a gunbearer, he closed with the enemy in furious fighting, and was seen to strike down three Japanese in a desperate effort to save his gun. Finally, he fell overwhelmed and knocked senseless.

That was not the end though.

Six hours later a counter-attack restored the position, and he was found by colleagues in an exhausted state beside his gun and almost unrecognizable, with seven severe wounds, and ten dead enemy round him. Umrao Singh recovered in hospital.

In the same region on the night of 19–20 January 1945, Lance Naik Sher Shah was commanding the left forward section of a platoon of the 16th Punjab Regiment.

At 19.30 hours an enemy platoon attacked their post. Realizing that over-whelming numbers would probably destroy his section, Sher Shah stalked the enemy from their rear and broke up their attack by firing into their midst. He killed the platoon commander and six other enemy, and after their retreat he crawled back to his post.

At 00.15 hours the enemy returned reinforced. Sher Shah heard the voice of their officers giving orders through the night, and the ghastly sound of bayonets being fixed. Again he left his post, and, in spite of Japanese covering fire, crawled forward till he could make out an enemy group. He fired into them, and again they broke up and withdrew in disarray.

While on his way back for the second time, he was hit by a mortar bomb, which shattered his right leg. He regained his position, however, and, propping himself against the side of the trench, went on firing. When asked whether he was hurt he said it was only slight.

Some time afterwards two colleagues found that his right leg was missing.

The Japanese again started forming up for another attack. In spite of his severe wounds and loss of blood, Sher Shah somehow left his post and crawled forward, firing into them from a close range. He went on till the third attack broke up and until he was shot through the head. This gallant Punjabi had killed twenty-three enemy and wounded four more. They were all found at daylight immediately in front of his post.

There seemed no end to the Indians' valour, and on the night of 16–17 February 1945, at Kanlan Ywathit, Jemadar Parkash Singh added to their laurels. At about 23.00 hours the Japanese fiercely attacked the 13th Frontier Force Rifles position in strength and supported by every weapon imaginable, even flame-throwers that stabbed the jungle dark like some strange nightmare.

Parkash Singh was severely wounded in both ankles and could not walk, so he crawled forward, dragging himself on his hands and knees to his platoon sector, and took over command again.

Soon after midnight his company commander found him propped up by his batman, who had also been wounded, firing his 2-inch mortar –the crew of which had both been killed. Parkash Singh was rallying his men, directing their fire, and crawling round collecting and distributing ammunition.

As one complete section had by now become casualties, he took over their Bren gun, and held the sector singlehanded until reinforcements were rushed up to him.

Again he was wounded in both legs, above the knees, by a burst of machine-gun fire. Despite the ultimate agony and much loss of blood, he went on firing his Bren, dragging himself about by his hands as his legs had been smashed. He regrouped the remnants of his platoon so that they successfully held an enemy charge.

At 01.45 hours Parkash Singh was wounded for the third time in the right leg, and was now so weakened from loss of blood he literally could not move. Yet he continued to direct his men's fire.

Although it was obvious to them that he was now dying, he shouted out the Dogra war cry, which was taken up by the rest of the company in a wave of inspiration, and they drove off the enemy.

02.30 hours: Parkash Singh was wounded for a fourth time, in the chest, by a grenade. He died a few minutes later, after telling his company commander not to worry about him, for he could look after himself.

Two more VCs on a single day: 2 March 1945. Naik Fazal Din's section of the 10th Baluch Regiment found themselves in an area flanked by three bunkers on one side and a house and bunker on the other. Machine-gun fire and grenades greeted them from the bunkers, so Fazal Din replied on his own with grenades at the nearest bunker. Suddenly, six Japanese, led by two officers wielding swords, rushed from the house. The Bren gunner shot one of them and another man, but by then had hardly any ammunition left. He was almost simultaneously set on by the second enemy officer, who killed him with his sword.

Fazal Din tried to help his colleague, but was run through the chest by the officer's sword, the point appearing through his back.

The officer withdrew the sword, but Fazal Din was not dead yet. He tore the sword in a frenzy from the Japanese and killed him with it. Then he attacked and killed another enemy soldier. Then went to help a Sepoy who was struggling with yet another enemy, and killed this Japanese with the same sword. Then he waved the sword to rally his men. Then he staggered to platoon headquarters, about twenty-five yards away, to report. He died soon after. His indescribable courage sparked the rest of his men to annihilate the garrison of fifty-five Japanese. Fazal Din was an NCO with an unquenchable spirit.

While this action was going on, another Naik was winning the VC not far away – and surviving. Naik Gian Singh was in command of a leading section of the 15th Punjab Regiment, trying to dislodge the enemy from foxholes along cactus hedges. Suddenly he saw them, exactly the length of a cricket-pitch ahead. Telling his machine-gunner to cover him, he rushed the foxholes firing his tommy gun. A hail of fire hit him in the arm, but he ploughed on, pitching grenades as he went. He killed several enemy, including four in one of their main weapon-pits.

By this time a troop of tanks had moved up in support of the Indian platoon, but the vehicles came under fire from a concealed anti-tank gun. Gian Singh saw their danger, and dashed forward to kill the crew and capture the gun. His section followed him down a lane of cactus hedges, clearing the enemy on their way. Twenty Japanese fell to them. Gian Singh was ordered to the aid post for his wounds, but did not go until the whole action was over.

On the first anniversary of D-Day in Normandy the news was heard of the next Nepalese VC won in Burma on 5 March 1945, by Rifleman Bhanbhagta Gurung of the 2nd Gurkha Rifles.

A company of Gurkhas were attacking a position known as Snowden East when one of the sections were forced to ground and unable to move. Then they came under deadly accurate fire from a tree-sniper some seventy-five yards off. As this Japanese was causing losses to the Gurkhas, Bhanbhagta Gurung stood up fully exposed to the general heavy fire, calmly took aim, and killed the sniper with a perfect shot from his rifle.

The section then advanced again but when within twenty yards of their goal they were met by murderous fire once more. He dashed forward alone, and attacked the first enemy foxhole with grenades, and the next one with his bayonet.

Two further foxholes were still firing on the Gurkhas, so he dived forward again to do exactly the same thing with grenade and bayonet. While attacking all four foxholes he was in the line of continuous fire from a bunker —which he then set out to attack.

He doubled forward, leapt on to its roof, and flung two No. 77 smoke grenades into the bunker slit. Two enemy rushed out, and he killed them with his *kukri*. A remaining Japanese was still firing inside, so he crawled inside the bunker, killed him, and captured the machine gun. Five positions taken single-handed.

Lieutenant Karamjeet Singh Judge was a platoon commander in a company of the 15th Punjab Regiment on 18 March 1945, when they were ordered to take the cotton-mill area on the outskirts of Myingyan. Nearly 200 enemy shells fell around the tanks and infantry during the attack, and the ground over which it took place was very broken and unsuitable for tanks.

All through this struggle the Lieutenant dominated the whole battlefield by his continued superb courage. Time and again the infantry were held up by fire from bunkers not seen by the tanks. Every time he coolly went forward through a maze of bullets to recall the tanks by the house telephone.

Cover around the tanks did not exist, but he ignored both the small-arms fire and the heavy shelling. He always managed to recall the tanks to tackle bunkers which he personally indicated to them, thus allowing the infantry to proceed again.

In each case, too, he led these charges against the bunkers, invariably arriving first. No fewer than ten bunkers were wiped out in this way. Once two Japanese suddenly rushed at him from a small nullah with fixed bayonets, but at a distance of only ten yards he killed them both.

About a quarter of an hour before the battle ended a last nest of three bunkers was located, which was difficult for the tanks to approach. Also an enemy machine gun was firing at the infantry. Karamjeet Singh Judge directed one tank to within twenty yards of the first bunker at great personal risk, and then threw a smoke grenade as a means of indication.

After some minutes of fire, using the house telephone again, he asked the tank commander to cease fire while he took a few men in to mop up. He got within ten yards of the bunker before an enemy light machine gun opened up and struck him in the chest. By this time, though, the remaining men of the section could storm the strongpoint and so complete their mission.

✱   ✱   ✱

In the last month of the active war in Italy the Indians added a final pair of VCs, won on the same day, 9 April 1945, and in the same spot, the River Senio. During the crossing of the river near Fusignano in daylight a company of the 13th Frontier Force Rifles had to assault the strongly entrenched enemy on the far bank. These positions had been prepared and improved over many months and were mainly on the steep flood banks, some twenty-five feet high.

Sepoy Ali Haidar's section soon came under heavy fire from two posts about sixty yards distant, and only three men, including himself, managed to get across. The rest of the company, too, were temporarily held up. Ali Haidar left the other two men to cover him, and charged the nearest post, now thirty yards away. He threw a grenade, but almost at the same instant a German threw one at him, wounding him severely in the back.

Nevertheless, Ali Haidar kept on, and destroyed the post, four enemy surrendering. Oblivious of his wounds, he went for the next post, in which the enemy had a Spandau and three automatics. Not surprisingly, he was wounded once more, in the right leg and right arm. But, though very weak, he crawled closer, and, in a final effort, raised himself off the ground, lobbed a grenade, and lurched into the post. Two Germans were wounded and two surrendered. Taking advantage of his dauntless dashes, the rest of the company charged over the river and made a bridgehead, before picking him up and bringing him back. As a result of his deeds, the battalion took 220 enemy and gained their goal. And Ali Haidar lived.

That same evening a company of the 5th Mahratta Light Infantry assaulted the east flood-bank of the Senio north of St Polito. Three minutes later another company was to pass through and assault the west flood-bank.

In this sector the Senio was about fifteen feet broad, four to five feet deep, and flowed between precipitous flood-banks thirty to thirty-five feet high, honeycombed with an intricate system of dugouts and defences —and with a mine-belt on the inner face of the east flood-bank.

Sepoy Namdeo Jadhao was a company runner, and when his company crossed the river he was with his commander close behind one of the leading sections.

When wading the river and emerging on the west bank the party came under heavy fire from three posts, wounding the company commander and two men.

All the rest except Namdeo Jadhao were killed.

This Sepoy then carried one of the wounded men through the deep water and up the steep slope of the bank, through the mine-belt, to safety. Then he made a second trip to bring back the other wounded man —again under the constant chatter of machine-gun fire.

Having done this, he next determined to wipe out the enemy posts and so avenge his dead comrades. Crossing the exposed east bank yet a third time, he dashed at the nearest post and silenced it with his tommy gun. As he was wounded in the hand, however, and unable to fire it further, he threw it away and resorted to grenades. With these, he successfully charged and wiped out two more posts, at one time crawling to the top of the bank to replenish his stock from his comrades on the reverse slope.

Having silenced all fire from the east bank, he then climbed on to the top of it, where, in spite of heavy mortars, he stood in the open, shouting the Mahratta war-cry, and waving the rest of the companies over the river.

After these two Sepoys came the last Indian VC, won fittingly in Burma. He was the rifleman who held an exploding grenade –and lived.

At Taungdaw, on the west bank of the Irrawaddy, during the night of 12–13 May 1945, Rifleman Lachhiman Gurung was manning the most forward post of his platoon. At 01.20 hours, some 200 enemy assaulted his company position. His section, and post in particular, bore the brunt of this onslaught. The post dominated a jungle path leading up into his platoon locality.

Before actually assaulting, the enemy hurled innumerable grenades at the position. One fell on to the lip of his trench. He at once grasped it, and flung it back at the Japanese. Almost immediately another grenade fell directly inside the trench. Again he snatched it up, and threw it back before it could go off. A third then fell in front of the trench. He tried to throw it back, but it exploded in his hand, blowing off his fingers . . . shattering his right arm . . . ripping his face, body, right leg. His two comrades were also badly wounded, and lay helpless in the bottom of the trench. The enemy, screaming and shouting, formed up shoulder to shoulder and tried to rush the post by sheer weight of numbers.

But he did not die.

Regardless of his appalling wounds, Lachhiman Gurung fired and reloaded his rifle with his left hand, maintaining a steady rate. Wave after wave of fanatical attackers were thrown in by the enemy, and all were repulsed with casualties.

For four hours, after being so severely torn to pieces, Lachhiman Gurung remained alone at his post, waiting with complete calm for each attack, which he met with fire at point-blank range from his rifle. Of the eighty-seven enemy dead counted in the immediate vicinity of the company locality, thirty-one lay in front of his section –the key to the whole position.

If the enemy had overrun his trench the entire reverse slope would have been turned. As it was, Lachhiman Gurung so inspired his comrades to resist the Japanese that, although surrounded and cut off for three days and two nights, they held and smashed every attack.

And he did not die.

CHAPTER FORTY-SIX

I Hope You Never Receive This . . .

CYRIL BARTON

C yril Barton believed in God. He was born on 6 June 1921, in Suffolk, but his family soon moved to Surrey, where he went to school. After leaving Kingston-on-Thames Technical College he became apprenticed to an aircraft factory in the district, and continued to study in the evenings, while living at nearby New Malden.

This time marked the start of his conscious Christian experience. He attended Bible Class regularly, and also the local church. Once his class leader asked Cyril, 'Do you know Christ as your personal Saviour?'

Barton answered, 'Yes.'

And during one of the special Youth Services on Sunday evenings he gave his witness for Christ before his friends. Throughout the summer months he eagerly joined in the open-air meetings, and later on he became a teacher in the Sunday School. The Boys' Club at the church provided him with another outlet for his energies. At services to attract new members for the church, Barton tackled some of the toughest types in the area, bringing them into the services.

When war broke out Cyril was eighteen. A year later came the Blitz, with the result that his mother moved from New Malden with her younger children.

During the winter of 1940-41, when the blitz was at its height, Cyril went to live with his Bible Class leader at Surbiton, and they both decided there and then to join the RAF. It had always been his ambition to fly. Now the chance came.

He joined up in the early part of 1941, and returned to England after a period of training in the United States in 1942. Then, in July 1943, he made his first operational flight. But before he did this he deposited with his younger brother, Kenneth, a letter for his mother, to be given to her if he died.

And earlier still, in February, he told of an experience he had had while stationed in Yorkshire. The first Sunday he was there he went to the local Methodist church, and took one of his oldest room-mates. The attendance, the singing, and the sermon were all poor. After the service they had a social hour of solos and other turns. Towards the end no one was keen on saying anything, so

215

Barton took the opportunity to give his testimony. It rather took the breath away from his pal, who knew that he read the Bible, and did not smoke, drink, or gamble, but this was the first time that Barton had really told him exactly what he believed. The next Sunday, Barton preached the sermon, and his pal read the lesson!

Barton was promoted Flight Sergeant in September 1943, soon after his initial operations, and was commissioned the same month. During a flight to Leverkusen in November 1943 his navigator and bomb-aimer were both injured by flak. Although the aircraft was damaged, Pilot Officer Barton brought it successfully back to England for further operations. He was posted to No. 578 Squadron in the following January, by which time he was making trips to Berlin —four altogether —and other heavily defended targets.

On 13 March 1944, Cyril wrote to a friend after leave:

After I left you on Monday I had a whole lot to think about. During the rest of my leave I decided that when I went back to camp I would openly kneel by my bed in prayer every night —something I have funked since my first day in the RAF.

As perhaps I told you, I share a room with W—, my bomb-aimer, and J—, my wireless operator, the only other two officers in the crew. They know what I believe to a certain extent, and take care not to offend me. However, I felt that my witness was not as vigorous as it should be, and I knew if I didn't do anything about it I would only slip back —and if I did, it would cost me a lot. I could not face the one any more than the other; but I think that the Lord made up my mind for me.

I was still undecided on Friday evening, when I met Doreen at the station at Harrogate. Just before the train went, I asked her to pray that the Lord would give me strength when I got back to camp to do something that I had failed to do since I joined up, but did not say what. She promised —and kept it.

After that I could not go back on it; but I was rather disappointed when neither W— nor J— were back when I arrived. Next day W— and I were in the billet together and when I went to bed W— was busy writing; but although I was on my knees for about ten minutes I'm sure he did not even notice me.

The third night I went to the local Methodist church with all the crew except J— and W—. When I got back they were sound asleep! You don't know how it took it out of me, being the third night in succession that the opportunity had been taken away.

However, last night, I was on my knees and at prayer when W— came in. I've been in some tight corners over Germany (and I am not shooting a line, I really have!) but my heart never dropped with such a bump as when that door opened! I never felt so lonely in my life. W— made no comment that I could hear, but tip-toed round the room until I got up.

When I did so I was in a cold sweat, but W— broke into conversation as if nothing had happened —I'd like to ask you to pray on that I may find His grace to see this thing through.

A fortnight later, on 28 March, he wrote:

Nine days after I came back from leave I got the opportunity that I had been waiting for. I had been to church and when I got back J——and W——were in and listening to the radio. It was fairly late, so I got undressed and excused myself from conversation by saying that I would be off the 'intercom' for ten minutes, and knelt by my bed. J——very reverently turned down his favourite radio programme and an awkward hush settled on the room. The Lord was very real to me for a few minutes, and I was very thankful to Him for bringing me through, whatever the consequences might be.

When I got up, they both tried to carry on as though nothing had happened, and made no comment. However J——was so badly shaken that he left his radio on (just humming) until after he had got into bed and would have forgotten it altogether if I had not reminded him that it was on –It still seems difficult to believe that something I had almost given up as hopeless had actually been achieved after three years.

I have now done eighteen ops and am looking forward to finishing within a reasonably short time –DV.

Two nights later, on 30 March 1944, no less than ninety-six bombers were reported missing from the night's raid on Germany. It was one of the heaviest Allied losses of the war.

This raid took place on the very day that the above letter was received.

Pilot Officer Cyril Joe Barton was captain and pilot of a Halifax bomber detailed to attack Nuremberg. Seventy miles short of the target, a Junkers Ju88 swooped on the plane. The very first burst of fire from it made the entire inter-communication system quite useless. A Messerschmitt Me210 joined in the affray and damaged an engine. It was the old familiar story –the bomber's machine guns went out of action, so the gunners could not return the German fighter's fire.

Barton kept his Halifax on course, covering those seventy miles to Nuremberg, as fighters continued to attack him all the way to the target area. In the confusion caused by the failure of the intercom system at the height of the battle, a signal was misinterpreted, and the navigator, air bomber, and wireless operator left the aircraft by parachute.

Barton then faced a situation of dire peril. His aircraft was damaged, his navigational team had gone, and he could not communicate with the rest of the crew. If he continued his mission he would be at the mercy of hostile fighters, when silhouetted against the fires in the target area; and if he happened to survive that, he would have to make a four-and-a-half-hour journey home on three engines across the usual heavily defended territory. Barton determined to press home his attack at all costs, so he flew on, reached the target, and released the bombs himself.

As Barton wrenched the heavy Halifax round to head for home, the propeller of the damaged engine –which had been vibrating badly –flew off. Two of the bomber's petrol-tanks had also suffered damage, and were leaking. Barton remained aloof to all these dangers, and concentrated on the task of holding to his course without navigational aids and with strong head winds. Somehow he successfully avoided the most dangerous defence areas on his route. He could not know then of the disastrous number of ninety-six Allied planes to be lost on the entire mission.

Using just his own judgement, he eventually crossed the English coast only ninety miles north of his base.

Now the worst part was about to begin. The leaks in the petrol-tanks had their inevitable outcome, so that fuel was nearly non-existent. He was almost literally flying on a wing and a prayer.

The port engines stopped with a sickening, intermittent chug. Barton saw a suitable landing-place, but the aircraft was now too low to be abandoned successfully.

'Take up crash-stations,' Barton ordered the three remaining members of the Halifax. The plane lost height rapidly now. With only one engine working, he struggled gamely to land clear of a group of houses just below them. The last seconds now, as the Halifax fell, for a crash-landing. The three members of the crew survived, but Barton was killed in the crash.

The three who baled out over Germany were safe too, as prisoners of war, so he alone died, while the other six survived.

Mrs Barton read the letter Cyril had written in case this ever happened:

Dear Mum,

I hope you never receive this, but I quite expect you will. I'm expecting to do my first operational trip in a few days. I know what ops over Germany mean, and I have no illusions about it. By my own calculations the average life of a crew is 20 ops and we have 30 to do in our first tour.

I'm writing this for two reasons. One, to tell you how I would like my money spent that I have left behind me; two, to tell you how I feel about meeting my Maker.

1. I intended, as you know, taking a university course with my savings. Well, I would like it to be spent over the education of my brothers and sisters.

2. All I can say about this is that I am quite prepared to die. It holds no terror for me.

At times I've wondered whether I've been right in believing what I do, and just recently I've doubted the veracity of the Bible, but in the little time I've had to sort out intellectual problems I've been left with a bias in favour of the Bible.

Apart from this, though, I have the inner conviction as I write, of a force outside myself, and my brain tells me that I have not trusted in vain. All I am anxious about is that you and the rest of the family will also come to know Him. Ken, I know, already does. I commend my Saviour to you.

I am writing to Doreen separately. I expect you will have guessed by now that we are quite in love with each other.

Well, that's covered everything now I guess, so love to Dad and all,
Your loving son,
Cyril

CHAPTER FORTY-SEVEN

Firefighting Outside
a Lancaster

NORMAN JACKSON

N ow the allies really began to put the pressure on the Fatherland, with the inevitable result that most of the Victoria Crosses won at this stage went to Bomber Command. Sergeant Norman Cyril Jackson was no more exceptional than his fellows, but his exceptional claim to fame was that he became the first RAF Flight Engineer to be awarded the Victoria Cross.

Jackson wasted a bare month of the war before enlisting on 10 October 1939. When training as a flight engineer Jackson was involved in a crash-landing at a conversion unit. In spite of a broken ankle he continued the course for several weeks with his limb in plaster. Starting so early on, it was not surprising that he completed a whole tour in Coastal Command during the first three years of the war. Then in July 1943 Jackson joined No. 106 Squadron, Bomber Command, as part of the personnel for the mounting offensive on Germany. This next spell was a concentrated tour of thirty operations between August 1943 and April 1944, each operation possibly his last. All aircrew knew this, of course, but the more 'ops' they did, the greater the odds on their not returning. But Jackson did come back from these thirty flights, which included a comparatively peaceful sea-mining trip to the Baltic, ten attacks on Berlin, six on Nuremberg, five on Stuttgart, and two on Munich. These were really hitting the heart of Hitler's diminishing empire. This tour totalled 201 operational-flying hours –just 201 hours of 'ops'.

The nearest Jackson got to any accident on these trips came on the night of 2 December. He was flight engineer of a Lancaster severely damaged by flak. Then three minutes later the bomber came in combat with an enemy fighter. Things happened like that sometimes. The starboard engine was already on fire when the fighter closed, but the enemy was shaken off somehow –a near thing that time. It was the familiar story from then on. The bomber returned to England flying on three engines, with the wireless telegraphy, radio telegraphy, intercom and both turrets out of action. You could call it an aircraft –just, but hardly a warplane.

So 26 April 1944, dawned. D-Day was approaching. Things were getting tenser with the mounting tempo of air operations. That morning Jackson got a telegram

219

telling him of the birth of a son to his wife. The crew were jubilant and excited about this, Jackson too, especially since the night's operation against the stiff target of Schweinfurt was to be the last of his Bomber Command tour. That would be two tours completed, once the night of 26 April was over.

The date of 26 April 1944, was destined to be more than the day he heard of his son's birth.

Jackson flew as flight engineer of the Lancaster that night. Despite the expected opposition, they had a reasonable approach to the target. They dropped their bombs successfully, and the aircraft was climbing out of the inferno of the target area when it happened.

The Lancaster throbbed along at 20,000 feet —four miles up —when an enemy fighter pounced on it. The captain reacted instinctively, and took evasive action within the second, but the fighter secured hit after hit on the heavy Lancaster. Fire —that eternal enemy in a bomber —broke out near a petrol-tank on the upper surface of the starboard wing, between the fuselage and the inner engine.

The evasive tactics during the engagement threw Jackson to the floor, where he sustained a series of wounds from shell splinters in the right leg and shoulder. He recovered himself quickly, and said he could deal with the fire on the wing. He got the captain's permission to try and put out the flames. He knew they could not fly back to England in that state; could not fly for long at all, in fact, unless something were done.

Stuffing a hand fire-extinguisher into the top of his life-saving jacket, and clipping on his parachute pack, Jackson jettisoned the escape-hatch above the pilot's head. Then he started to climb out of the cockpit and back along the top of the fuselage to the starboard wing. Out into the fiery black night.

But before he could leave the fuselage, his parachute pack opened, and the whole canopy and rigging-lines streamed and spilled into the cockpit.

Undeterred, Jackson went on. The pilot, bomb-aimer, and navigator gathered the parachute together, and held on to the rigging-lines, paying them out as the airman crawled aft; all this still four miles high above the hostile country. Eventually Jackson slipped, and falling from the fuselage to the starboard wing, in some way completely incredible, grasped an air intake on the leading edge of the wing. Every sinew strained beyond the normal limit, he succeeded in clinging on, but inevitably lost the extinguisher, which was blown away with the piercing wind-stream in the middle of the night.

By this time the fire had spread alarmingly, and continued to do so progressively faster. Jackson himself was involved in it. His face, hands, and clothes were severely burned. Charred and in agony, he could not keep his hold, and was swept through the flames and over the trailing edge of the wing. When the rest of the crew last glimpsed him on that terrible night he was dragging his parachute behind him. It was only partly inflated, and burning in a number of places.

The captain realized that the fire could not possibly be controlled now, and gave the order automatically. 'Abandon ship'.

Four members of the crew baled out safely, and were taken prisoner, but the captain and rear gunner failed to get out. So Flying Officer Fred Mifflin and Flight

Sergeant Hugh Johnson 'bought it' as the blazing Lancaster crashed. Two dead, four alive. And what about Jackson?

The wind whipped through the nylon and the lines of the parachute, spreading the patches of fire as he fell. His speed increased more and more with the area of flames. Jackson could not control his descent at all, but thankfully it did not reach a fatal speed. He landed heavily, and broke his ankle; so with a broken ankle, his right eye closed through burns, other burns scarring and hurting him, and with his hands useless, he was reduced to a pitiable state. All he could do was wait for daybreak, when he crawled to the nearest village, and rapped on the door of the smallest cottage he could see. An old woman and her daughter took him in and gave him first aid. Then, after rough medical treatment at a nearby hospital, he was paraded through the village. People turned out to jeer and throw stones at him, but he was too far gone to care much about them.

Then he was made a prisoner of war, and bore the intense agony and discomfort of the journey to a Dulag Luft with fortitude. This was far from the end of Jackson's ordeal. Perhaps the night of 26 April 1944, marked the most concentrated nightmare, but then there followed ten months in hospital, where he made a good recovery.

But before all this the whole crew had been posted as missing. Two-and-a-half weeks went by until the German radio announced that Jackson was a prisoner of war with the four others.

All that remained in 1945 was for them to be returned home soon after VE day, when it was found that his hands needed still further treatment, and were only of limited use to him. It was at this stage too that the whole story was pieced together by the reports of the rest of the crew. How he ventured out of the bomber travelling at 200 miles an hour at a great height and in intense cold; how he ignored the extra hazard of his spilled parachute; and how, if he had managed to subdue the flames, there would have been little or no prospect of his getting back into the cockpit.

After this 'almost incredible feat', as it was officially called, Jackson was awarded the Victoria Cross on 26 October 1945. And the next day after the announcement he was looking for a house for his wife and baby son, Brian, the boy who was born the day before the raid on Schweinfurt.

They did find a bungalow eventually, and outside it, in Burton's Road, Hampton Hill, Middlesex, at night passers-by could see the silhouette of a Lancaster bomber lit up in the porthole-shaped window. There is no need to ask Jackson what it means or why he put it there.

CHAPTER FORTY-EIGHT

Cassino and After

Richard Wakeford, Arthur Jefferson, John Mahony, Maurice Rogers

The fiercest fighting of the entire Italian campaign took place at Cassino and Monte Cassino, crowned with its ancient abbey. After three major Allied assaults, the positions were finally won on 18 May 1944. The second VC for the Hampshires was won by Captain Richard Wakeford in the battle for Cassino on 13 May.

The battalions in the bridgehead spent nearly the whole of 12 May pinned down, deafened by the constant explosion of shells and mortar-bombs, and by very heavy machine-gun fire. During the day it was decided that the Hampshire Battalion should come under command of 12th Infantry Brigade and cross the river farther upstream by way of Amazon bridge, which had been completed after an epic night's work by the sappers. Accordingly, at three o'clock on the morning of 13 May, the battalion began to move to its new start-point. The crossing was to have been made at 06.45 hours, but owing to delays by other units they did not start until 13.30 in the afternoon. The area in which they had to wait was under intense fire, and there were some casualties.

The battalion advanced over Amazon bridge in brilliant sunshine, but in spite of the heavy enemy barrage the casualties were light. Three hundred yards across the river the battalion found what cover they could in shell-holes and small ditches while Colonel Fowler-Esson coordinated his plan with OC Troop, 17th/21st Lancers (with Sherman tanks) and with the gunners. The plan was for the battalion to wheel left along the river and then to proceed towards the original objectives. Zero hour for the advance was 14.30 hours, preceded by a fifteen-minute artillery concentration on the first objective. As the battalion waited in the scanty cover they were under constant HE fire, but spirits were high. The company commanders dis-regarded the enemy fire and walked round encouraging their men.

At 14.30 on the afternoon of 13 May the 2nd/4th Battalion was ordered to advance. The companies stood up, formed into extended line, and with fixed b-ayonets walked grimly forward beside the river, accompanied by the Sherman tanks of the 17th/21st Lancers. At once enemy machine guns in 'Square Wood' opened fire; the tanks swung their guns round and roared in reply, and then No. 8 Platoon, under Lieutenant Bowers, stormed into the wood, overwhelmed the enemy, and came out with seventy-three prisoners. The battalion crossed the River Pioppeta, but the tanks were unable to cross at once as the route was blocked by an AFV carrying bridging-equipment. The battalion, however, waded the river and continued the advance under covering fire from the tanks.

The enemy were nonplussed by this flank attack, and daunted by the resolute advance; finding themselves between the Hampshire Battalion and the river, they began to surrender. Soon long lines of Germans were seen doubling towards the battalion with arms raised. The prisoners were quickly passed back, and A and C Companies, on the left, continued to move along the line of the river, systematically dealing with all enemy resistance, while B and D Companies, on the right, worked away from the river and soon began to meet stronger opposition. But they continued to press forward relentlessly, mopping up as they went.

B and D advanced up the slope beyond the Pioppeta and, having topped the ridge which had been their original objective, they pressed on. Captain Wakeford, accompanied only by an orderly and armed only with an automatic pistol, was leading B Company, on the right. He reached the objective first, killed a number of Germans, and when his company caught up with him he handed over no fewer than twenty prisoners.

The success of the battalion was such that there was no stopping them, and Colonel Fowler-Esson, who was with the leading companies throughout, kept them going. A strong-point in a house in the line of advance was vigorously defended, but Captain Wakeford once more led B Company in the assault with grenades and tommy guns. Captain Wakeford was himself twice driven back by grenades, but with a final rush he reached a window and flung in grenades. Five Germans surrendered at once; a sixth came out, as though to surrender, and suddenly shot one of B Company. He was immediately disposed of.

By five o'clock in the afternoon the companies had taken up positions well beyond their objectives on Brown Line. The whole operation was a fine example of a 'set-piece' attack, with infantry, tanks, and artillery cooperating to the finest degree. It was like a model exercise at a battle school. At the cost of comparatively slight casualties, the battalion had cleared Brown Line across the whole front of 28th Brigade's sector and beyond. The battalion were in the highest spirits; they had taken some 200 prisoners, and the battlefield was scattered with German corpses. Thus ended the first phase of the attack on the Gustav Line. There had been one tragic incident when the RAP following up the advance set off an AP mine, and one stretcher-bearer was killed and the MO was so badly wounded that he died after evacuation. There were many casualties in the party.

It took the enemy some little time to get over the shock of this most successful operation, but before long the company positions came under concentrated shell-fire, but fortunately, casualties were only slight. The next task for the battalion was to advance to Blue Line, 1,000 yards to the west. This began at 02.45 hours on the morning of 14 May, a silent attack without any barrage. The battalion advanced in extended order, keeping direction by compass, and with tracer-bullets to guide them along their general axis of advance.

A combination of mist and cordite fumes made visibility poor, but the advance was admirably maintained, and the companies made such steady progress that by seven o'clock all objectives had been reached with but little opposition. The enemy had, it appeared, straightened out his line, because of a thrust that seemed to be developing on the right from the Royal Fusiliers and the Black Watch. There was confused fighting on either flank, but it did not develop on the battalion's front, though one flanking company assisted with machine-gun fire. By midday all fighting on the battalion front had died down except for exchanges of mortar-fire. By this stage of the operation the battalion's casualties were some fifty killed, wounded, and missing.

For the third phase of the attack, which was to take the battalion to Red Line, it returned from the command of the 12th to the 28th Brigade. Their position at the end of the second phase was along the track between the Casa Petra, on the right, and the Casa Pagezzani, on the left. In front of them an easy slope descended to the Pioppeta 300 yards away, and 500 yards beyond the ground rose to their objective, Massa Vertechi.

At 17.45 hours on the evening of 14 May the barrage opened up, and at 18.00 hours the companies moved forward down the slope towards the river. The pioneers rushed down a carrier loaded with light bridging-equipment, in an attempt to build a tank-crossing, but the bridge sank in the soft mud beside the river so that the tanks were unable to cross.

The companies advancing down the slope ran into very heavy defensive fire, and lost more than 100 men in two minutes, and as a result the attack began to lose its momentum. Then Colonel Fowler-Esson got out of the tank from which he was directing the battle, and, with Major Mitchell and RSM Newsom, rallied the companies and led them forward across the stream in the teeth of fierce fire. The enemy were bringing down everything they had on the advancing troops, and casualties were very heavy, including both Captain Dent, commanding D Company, and the adjutant. But in spite of the inferno of fire the advance was maintained up the slopes towards the objective.

It was at this point that Captain Wakeford came so splendidly to the fore. He was already wounded in the face and both arms, but he led B Company up the slope on the left of the battalion, keeping them under perfect control through the withering fire. Half-way up the hill his company came under heavy Spandau fire; Captain Wakeford organized and led a party which charged and silenced the machine guns.

As the company advanced again mortar-bombs were bursting among the men, and Captain Wakeford was wounded in both legs. But he still led on, reached the objective, organized and consolidated the remainder of his company, and reported to his commanding officer before submitting to any personal attention. For his extreme gallantry Captain Wakeford was awarded the Victoria Cross, and the citation ends with these words:

> During the seven-hour interval before stretcher-bearers could reach him, his unwavering high spirits encouraged the wounded men around him. His selfless devotion

to duty, leadership, determination, courage, and disregard for his own serious injuries were beyond all praise.

Following Wakeford's wonderful example came three more VCs in Italy, before the Allies launched the long-awaited invasion from the north. The first of these went to Fusilier Francis Arthur Jefferson of the Lancashire Fusiliers on the very day after Wakeford had been rescued by his stretcher-bearers.

On 16 May 1944 during an attack on the Gustav Line, an anti-tank obstacle held up some of our tanks, leaving the leading company of Fusilier Jefferson's battalion to dig in on the hill without tanks or anti-tank guns. The enemy counter-attacked with infantry and two Mark IV guns, which opened fire at short range, causing a number of casualties and eliminating one Piat group entirely.

As the tanks advanced towards the partially dug trenches, Fusilier Jefferson, entirely on his own initiative, seized a Piat, and, running forward alone under heavy fire, took up a position behind a hedge.

As he could not see properly he came out into the open, and, standing up under a hail of bullets, fired at the leading tank which was now only twenty yards away. It burst into flames, and the crew were killed. Fusilier Jefferson then reloaded the Piat and proceeded towards the second tank, which withdrew before he could get within range. By this time our own tanks had arrived, and the enemy counter-attack was smashed with heavy casualties.

Fusilier Jefferson's gallant act not merely saved the lives of his company and caused many casualties to the Germans but also broke up the enemy counter-attack, and had a decisive effect on the subsequent operations. His supreme gallantry and disregard of personal risk contributed very largely to the success of the action.

A week later it seemed that the former journalist Major John Keefer Mahony was the target of every German gun on the Italian line, for it was as though the enemy singled him out as the soul of the defence there.

On 24 May 1944, A Company of the Westminster Regiment (Motor), under Major Mahony, was ordered to force the first bridgehead across the River Melfa.

The enemy still possessed strong forces of tanks, self-propelled guns, and infantry holding defences on the east side of the river. Mahony knew this, of course, yet personally led his men down to the river and across it. Mahony accompanied the leading section of the company.

Although they made their crossing in devastatingly clear view of the enemy, and subjected to shattering machine-gun fire from posts on the right rear and left front, Mahony directed each section into its proper position on the west bank with coolness and confidence. The crossing was made, and a small, shaky bridgehead built on ground where it was only possible to dig shallow weapon-pits. The company maintained itself there, virtually inviting drastic casualties, from 15.30 hours till 20.30. At this stage the remaining companies and supporting weapons were able to cross the river and reinforce them.

It was in those five hours that Mahony won the VC.

The Germans enclosed the bridgehead on three sides by an 88-mm self-propelled gun 450 yards to the right and a battery of 42-mm AA guns 100 yards to the left, a Spandau 100 yards to the left of it, a second 88-mm self-propelled gun to the left of the Spandau and approximately a company of infantry with mortars and machine guns on the left of the 88-mm gun. From all these weapons, Mahony's company was constantly under fire, till he eventually succeeded in knocking out the self-propelled equipment from the infantry on the left flank.

Very soon after the bridgehead had been established the enemy threw infantry at it backed by tanks and guns. The Westminsters beat them off with its Piat, 2-inch mortars, and grenades, solely due to the skilful way Mahony had organized his defences.

Mahony personally supervised the Piats. By this time, though, the strength of the company had fallen to sixty men, and all except one of the platoon officers had been wounded. Scarcely an hour later enemy tanks formed up again about 500 yards in front of the bridgehead with a company of infantry. Mahony comforted the wounded, exhorted the rest, then prepared to meet the savage slash at the bridge-head.

Machine guns smote them into stupefied stillness. But Mahony crawled forward to the position of a section pinned down. By throwing smoke grenades to hide their movement from the stricken site, he was able to extricate them from the vulnerable hot spot with the loss of only one man.

Forming and holding the bridgehead across the river was vital to the whole Canadian Corps action, and failure would have meant delay and a repetition of the attack, probably involving heavy losses in men, material, and time —all priceless. It would also have given the enemy a breathing-space which might have broken the impetus of the corps advance.

Mahony instinctively knew all this, assimilated it, and never let the thought of failure enter his head. And at the first sign of faltering among men in this three-sided onslaught he was there to shout some words to help them carry on.

The Germans —especially those only 100 yards off —perceived that Mahony was the pivot of the defence, and consequently fired at him constantly with all the weapons in their armoury, from rifles to 88-mm guns. Mahony ignored the lot, and, although outnumbered so dramatically, the Canadians finally drove off the German three-pronged counter-moves, with the destruction of three self-propelled guns and a Panther tank.

Mahony's behaviour would have been remarkable if he had been wholly fit throughout those five horror-laden hours. But, in fact, quite early on he was wounded in the head and twice in the leg. He brushed aside all suggestions of medical aid in spite of loss of blood, and went on with the work of directing the defence of the bridgehead, though movement of any kind must have caused him the acutest pain.

It was only when the other companies of the Westminsters had crossed the river to support him that he allowed his wounds to be treated, but even then he stayed with his Canadian comrades, and would not be evacuated.

*   *   *

The fourth and final VC of this Cassino and after group was Sergeant Maurice Albert Wyndham Rogers, a man of 'great gallantry' whose citation said :

On June 3, 1944, in Italy, a battalion of the Wiltshire Regiment was ordered to attack high ground held by the enemy. The leading company had taken their first objective but were unable to reach their final objective owing to the heavy enemy fire and casualties.

The carrier platoon, dismounted, were ordered to capture the final objective supported by fire from the company and a troop of tanks. The objective was wired and mined and strongly defended by the enemy. The carrier platoon advanced through the machine-gun and mortar-fire until they reached the enemy's wire, which was 70 yards from the objective.

At this point the platoon was under the intense fire of seven machine-guns, firing at ranges of from 50-100 yards, and sustained a number of casualties. The platoon, checked by the enemy's wire and the intensity of his machine-gun fire, took cover and returned the fire, preparatory to gapping the wire.

Sergeant Rogers, the platoon sergeant, without hesitation, continued to advance alone firing his Thompson sub-machine-gun. He got through the enemy's wire, ran across the minefield, and destroyed two of the enemy machine-gun posts with Thompson sub-machine-gun and hand grenades. By now Sergeant Rogers was 100 yards ahead of his platoon, and had penetrated 30 yards inside the enemy's defences. He had drawn on to himself the fire of nearly all the enemy's machine-guns, and threw their defence into confusion. Inspired by the example of Sergeant Rogers, the platoon reached the enemy's wire and began the assault.

Still alone, and penetrating deeper into the enemy position, Sergeant Rogers, while attempting to silence a third machine-gun, was blown off his feet by a grenade which burst beside him and wounded him in the leg. Nothing daunted, he stood up, and, still firing his Thompson sub-machine-gun, ran on towards the enemy post, but was shot and killed at point-blank range.

This N.C.O.'s undaunted determination, fierce devotion to duty, and superb courage carried his platoon on to their objective in face of a determined enemy in a strongly defended position. The great gallantry and heroic self-sacrifice of Sergeant Rogers were in the highest traditions of the British Army.

CHAPTER FORTY-NINE

Triumph in Normandy

STANLEY HOLLIS, SIDNEY BATES, DAVID JAMIESON, TASKER WATKINS, DAVID CURRIE

The grimness and the glory of D-Day, 6 June 1944 –the greatest invasion in the history of warfare. On one of the Normandy beaches where the British landed, snipers had stopped the 6th Green Howards in their tracks. They dug in wherever they could, but until the Armoured Vehicles Royal Engineers drove ashore they were at a standstill. From behind the shelter of a wall the Germans mixed grenades with snipers' fire. Then the AVREs reached the upper beach, and, covered by two of them, the infantry stormed up to the wall, and hit the enemy point-blank on the once peaceful sea road. After a brief period of resistance the sight of the demolition vehicles startled the enemy, who began to retreat. So the value of armour was beginning to be apparent all along the British line.

One company of the Green Howards negotiated a minefield, with only minor losses, and then found themselves confronted by stronger enemy resistance. They were on their way to take the important Mont Fleury battery, which had already been well pasted by both the RAF and the Navy.

Despite resistance, they were making good headway towards the battery, when the company commander noticed that two of the enemy pillboxes on the route had been bypassed by the leading platoons.

Thus started an action which earned the one Victoria Cross of D-Day.

Taking Company Sergeant Major Stanley Hollis with him, the commander advanced to try and clear them. When they were only twenty yards from this live pillbox a machine gun opened fire from the slit, and Hollis instantly rushed straight at it, firing his Sten gun through the grid. In a split second Hollis jumped on top of the actual pillbox as he recharged his magazine and forced it home. At the same time he wrenched out a grenade and threw it through the door, following it with Sten fire. Two Germans dropped dead, and Hollis rushed in, holding up the rest as prisoners.

As soon as they were safely taken he ran over to a neighbouring trench, and cleared several of the enemy out of it. By this action he certainly saved the rest of his company from being heavily fired on from the rear, and so enabled them to open the main beach exit from this end of their sector.

Taking the VC story to its end, later on D-Day, in the village of Crepon, the

228

company encountered a field gun and crew armed with Spandaus, at 100 yards' range. Hollis was put in command of a party to cover an attack on the gun, but the movement was held up. Seeing this, he pushed right forward to engage the gun with a Piat from a house at fifty yards' range. He was observed by a sniper, who fired; the bullet grazed his cheek. At the same second the enemy gun swung round and fired at point-blank range into the house. Masonry started to fall all around them, so Hollis moved his party to another position. Two of the enemy gun crew had by this time been killed, and the gun itself was destroyed soon afterwards.

But Hollis then learned that two of his men had stayed behind in the house. He at once went to try and get them out. In full view of he enemy, who continually fired at him, he went forward quite alone, using a Bren gun to distract their attention from the two other men. Under cover of this heroic diversion they were able to run back to the company —and Hollis too got back safely.

Wherever the fighting was heaviest throughout D-Day Hollis displayed daring and gallantry, and on both these occasions he alone prevented the enemy from holding up the advance of the Green Howards at critical stages.

Two months after D-Day, on 6 August 1944, the British 3rd Division were engaged in the struggle to break out of the Falaise pocket of the Normandy bridge-head, but they sustained a setback when the 10th SS Panzer Division counter-attacked at Sourdeval, a small hamlet half-way between Burcy and Chenedolle. Luckily, however, this enemy counter-stroke began just as the Norfolks were actually relieving the 3rd Monmouths of 11th Armoured Division, with the result that both battalions were there together. The two forces formed into a single striking-power, nicknamed 'the Normons' and then set about resisting the counter-attack.

This was when Corporal Sidney 'Basher' Bates came into action. Born at Camberwell, Bates had joined the Norfolks soon after the days of Dunkirk, when he was just nineteen, and he had risen to lance corporal on 13 July 1944, and acting corporal a fortnight later.

His last words to his mother, as he left their blitzed house at 23 Councillor Street, were: 'Don't think I'm brave, Mum. I'm scared.' Now it was 6 August, and the Panzers were on the attack. It was a Sunday. A heavy and accurate artillery-and-mortar programme heralded the onslaught, and the battalion's position had been well pinpointed.

Half an hour later the Germans' main attack developed, with heavy machine-gun and mortar-fire concentrated on the point of junction of the two forward companies.

Nine days a corporal, Bates was commanding the right forward section of the left forward company. Casualties started to appear all around him, so he decided to move the remnants of his section to an alternative position, where he thought he would be able to counter the enemy thrust with less difficulty. But instead, the enemy, wedged into their whole area, deepened, until some sixty Germans supported by fire were coursing through the British-held ground.

Bates's great friend, his Bren gunner, was killed beside him. Bates had always been known as a cheerful chap, but something seemed to snap inside him when he saw that the man was dead. His mind was swamped by sudden fury and an awareness of the desperate situation.

Bates did not care any more. Seizing the Bren gun from the man's hands, he left his slit trench, and charged into the enemy, firing furiously as he ran. The bullets sprayed out in an arc from the gun, but enemy fire streamed back towards him, shell-splinters ripping the air round.

'Take that, you bastards,' he shouted.

Almost at once the inevitable happened, and he fell, hit by machine-gun fire. After slumping to the ground he somehow dragged himself up again, and actually advanced on the enemy, still firing from the hip. The spread of his bullets began to have an effect now on the Nazi riflemen and machine gunners, but mortar bombs continued to fall perilously near to his running form.

For the second time they hit him, much more seriously. Blinding pain scorched through Bates's body, but instinctively he staggered to his feet again, tottering towards the enemy yet once more, and still firing. As he covered the first five yards the Germans began to get panicky because they could not halt him, and some of them started to run.

At this instant bomb splinters struck him. The third hit. This time he fell to the ground, dying but not yet dead. Bates pressed the Bren to his body, twisted round on the ground, and went on and on firing from his final position. His strength ebbed away, but not before the Germans withdrew from their wedge and the position was restored. The enemy were no longer in sight now, and singlehanded Bates had saved the critical situation. Then he died.

On the next day another man of the Royal Norfolks featured in the chronicle of courage.

The tallest man in the Royal Norfolk Regiment, Captain David Auldgo Jamieson stood 6 feet 5 inches. Two months after D-Day Jamieson was wounded in the right eye and left arm, but he fought on to hold his position in a bridgehead over the River Orne. Still only twenty-three years old, he had been in the pre-Dunkirk stand at St Valery in 1940, when he was not yet twenty. And in 1944 he trained 1,250 recruits, whom he took to France on D-Day.

Now it was D+62. The young captain with the long, straight nose and direct eyes, from Thornham, near King's Lynn, was now commanding a company of the Norfolks which had established that bridgehead over the Orne, south of Grimbos.

7 August 1944. They repulsed three enemy thrusts, with heavy losses to the Germans. The last of these came at 18.30 hours, when a battle group with Tiger and Panther tanks roared out of the evening air to lash the little bridgehead. The brunt of their force fell on Jamieson's company. For four hours the Norfolks flung them back, accounting for three tanks and an armoured car. Jamieson exercised courage and judgment and decisively swayed the conflict.

They won respite only for the rest of the night though, for on the morning of 8 August the Nazis threw in a fresh battle group against the far from fresh Norfolks. This move succeeded in doing just what it intended, penetrating the defences surrounding the East Anglian soldiers on three of their four sides.

Moreover, during the attack two of the three tanks supporting the hard-pressed Norfolks were wiped out, leaving one still intact. Jamieson knew that he had to try and get to the last tank to direct its fire, so he left his trench at the height of the fighting. Close-range fire from a selection of weapons started to spit across at him, but he did his best to dodge it. He reached the tank, but, as he could not get in touch with its commander by the outside telephone, Jamieson climbed on to it in full view of the Germans.

They could not fail to spot the tall figure of the captain. Their shooting was soon stepped up in intensity, as Jamieson stayed there directing the tank's fire. Inevitably, he was wounded in the right eye and left forearm. But that was not the end of Jamieson. When his wounds had been dressed he positively refused to be evacuated from the bridgehead which had been so dearly won.

By now all the other officers had become casualties, so he knew it still remained up to him to carry on the opposition. Reorganizing his men in full vision of the frustrated Nazis, he ignored the lack of cover, eventually tipping the scales by his very disregard of the danger. After several hours the Germans had to yield and retire.

The conflict was rejoined three more times during that day, with infantry and tanks trying to force a decision. The wounds throbbed sickeningly, but Jamieson continued in command. He arranged for the artillery support over his radio, and, going out into the open, he made sure that the men were in good heart.

There were moments and minutes when their whole position seemed hopeless, but he never hinted at it to the men. He was determined to hold the bridgehead over the Orne, and hold it he did. Seven counter-attacks he resisted altogether in the thirty-six hellish hours. By the evening of 8 August the Germans had had enough and withdrew, leaving a ring of dead men and burnt out tanks round the three sides of the Norfolks.

A week later, still in Normandy, this was just one of several terrible moments endured by Lieutenant Tasker Watkins: his Sten gun jammed when faced by a German.

He was commanding a company of the Welsh Regiment on the evening of 16 August 1944; a summer evening, though far from peaceful.

The battalion had been ordered to attack objectives near the railway at Bafour, and Watkins and his company had to cross open cornfields in which they knew that booby-traps had been set. Spasmodic explosions confirmed this early on. It was not yet dusk, and they also soon came under fire from German machine guns, cleverly concealed in the high corn and also farther back. An 88-mm gun joined in as well, and the Welsh Regiment started to suffer catastrophic casualties. Their advance slowed up, and stopped.

Watkins was the only officer left.

He placed himself at the head of his men, and under severe short-range fire they charged two posts in succession. He personally killed or wounded all the occupants with his Sten gun.

Reaching his real objective, he stumbled on an anti-tank gun manned by a single

German soldier. For a split second they faced each other before Watkins triggered his Sten. It jammed.

The German delayed acting for a moment, and Watkins at once threw the Sten in his face, and shot him with a pistol before he had time to recover. How could a man get nearer to death?

Watkins and his company numbered only some thirty men when they were set on by fifty German infantry. Watkins did not waver. He directed the fire of the surviving thirty, then led a bayonet charge into gathering gloom, almost entirely destroying the Germans.

After dusk, orders were given for the battalion to withdraw, but, as the radio of Watkins's company had been destroyed, they did not receive the command. Consequently, they now found themselves suddenly surrounded in depleted strength and failing light.

Watkins made up his mind to rejoin the battalion by passing around the flank of the enemy position through which he had advanced. So they started. But while in the eerie depths of the cornfield, with the tall stalks deathly still, he was challenged by an enemy post at point-blank distance.

'Scatter,' he whispered to his men.

Then he went in alone with a Bren gun, and silenced the post by a burst that cracked out into the night. Watkins at last led the remnants of his company back to battalion headquarters.

The liberation of France went on.

So to the last stage of the Normandy narrative, a day or so after Watkins's exciting exploit. This VC was won by Major David Vivian Currie, 29th Canadian Armoured Reconnaissance Regiment, Canadian Armoured Corps.

With a mere handful of men, Major Currie closed the Falaise Gap in Normandy, while the trapped Germans were destroyed as a fighting force.

It started on 18 August 1944, when Currie was commanding a small mixed force or Canadian tanks, self-propelled anti-tank guns, and infantry. His orders: to cut one of the main escape routes from the Falaise pocket.

Not surprisingly, they were held up strongly in the village of St Lambert-sur-Dives, and 88-mm guns knocked out two of their tanks. Currie at once decided to enter the village alone, on foot, at dusk, through the enemy outposts. His intention was to reconnoitre the German defences and to extricate the crews of the two disabled tanks. Heavy mortar-fire greeted him most of the way, but he succeeded in doing exactly what he wanted.

Early next morning, 19 August, without any previous softening-up bombardment, Currie personally led an attack on the village, advancing right through fire from enemy tanks, guns, and small arms. By noon, on that hot summer day, he had seized and consolidated a position half-way inside the vital village.

The next thirty-six hours were no summer picnic. The Germans hurled a succession of severe attacks at the courageous Canadians, but Currie had organized his defensive position so skilfully that the enemy were the ones to suffer most in the end.

At dusk on 20 August they tried to mount a final paralysing punch at the Canadians, but found themselves routed before it could even be deployed. Seven enemy tanks, twelve 88-mm guns, and forty vehicles were destroyed; 300 Germans were killed and 500 wounded; 2,100 captured. Currie did not stop at that. He promptly ordered an attack, and completed the capture of the village, thus denying the Chambois-Trun escape to the remnants of two German armies cut off in the pocket.

Three days and three nights the fierce fighting lasted altogether. Once Currie personally directed the fire of his command tank on to a Tiger tank, which had been harassing his position, and knocked it out. During another attack, while the guns of his command tank were taking on other targets at longer ranges, Currie used rifles from the turret to deal with individual snipers who had infiltrated to within fifty yards of his headquarters.

The only time that reinforcements were able to get through to his force, he himself led the forty men forward into their positions, and explained the importance of their job. During the next attack these new reinforcements had to withdraw under intense fire, but Currie collected them together again, and led them back into position, where they held on.

His employment of the artillery support, which became available after his original attack went in, was typical of his cool calculations of the risks involved on every occasion. At one spell, despite the fact that short rounds were falling within three yards of his own tank, he ordered fire from medium artillery to continue, because of its devastating effect on the attacking enemy.

Throughout the operation the casualties to Currie's force were heavy, but he never let the possibility of failure enter his men's minds. As one NCO said :

'We knew at one stage that it was going to be a fight to a finish but he was so cool about it, it was impossible for us to get excited.'

Since all the officers under him were either killed or wounded, Currie had no respite from his duty, in fact obtained only one hour's sleep the whole time. Yet he hid his fatigue from the troops, and took every chance of visiting their weapon-pits and other defences, to talk to them. When his force was finally relieved, and he felt satisfied that the turnover was really complete, Currie fell asleep on his feet and collapsed.

The successful stand at St Lambert-sur-Dives could largely be attributed to Currie's cool, inspired leadership.

CHAPTER FIFTY

Hitting Back in Burma

HANSON TURNER, MICHAEL ALLMAND, FRANK BLAKER, SEFANAIA SUKANAIVALU

Now the Allies were attacking on all fronts from Normandy to New Guinea, from Italy to Burma. And on D-Day itself, as they clawed a beachhead in northern Europe, the VC story swung east again to Burma, and to Sergeant Hanson Victor Turner, the West Yorkshire Regiment.

Carrying only hand grenades, he charged a Japanese army all alone, and stopped an enemy tank.

Sergeant Turner belonged to the 5th Indian Airborne Division, whose spectacular landings in Burma foiled the Japanese plan to invade India.

This happened at Ningthouknong, in Burma, soon after midnight on 6–7 June 1944, when an attack was made in substantial strength by the Japanese, using machine guns.

At first the attack fell largely on the south-west corner of the position, held by a weak platoon of about twenty men, of which Turner was one of the section commanders. By creeping up under cover of a nullah, the enemy were able to toss grenades with deadly effect against this portion of the perimeter. Three out of four light machine guns in the platoon were soon destroyed, and the platoon itself was forced to give ground.

Turner at once regrouped his party, and withdrew just 40 yards. The Japs tried with their customary persistence to dislodge them, and concentrated every bullet they could to try and reduce the position, and so extend the penetration. For more than two hours they fired on Turner and his dwindling party, but achieved no further success in this sector. Turner held on all night.

When it became clear that the Japs were trying to outflank the position Turner determined to take the initiative, although he was strictly very much on the defensive. The men left under his command represented the absolute minimum to maintain the position he had built up so painstakingly. No party for a counter-attack could therefore be mustered: they did not exist. And speed was a key factor if the enemy were to be frustrated.

So Turner, boldly and fearlessly, set out from the position alone, and armed only with all the hand grenades he could carry. Into the attack. One man against an army. He used every one of them with devastating result, and returned for more.

234

The Japanese were keeping up fire on him all the while, but he survived.

Turner made five journeys altogether for further stocks of grenades. It was on the sixth sortie, still alone, while throwing a grenade at an enemy point, that Turner was killed.

> His conduct on that night will ever be remembered by the regiment. His superb leadership and undaunted will to win in the early stages of the attack were undoubtedly instrumental in preventing the enemy plan from succeeding. The number of enemy dead the next morning was ample evidence of the deadly effect his grenade-throwing had had. He displayed outstanding valour, and had not the slightest thought of his own safety. He died on the battlefield, in a spirit of supreme self-sacrifice.

Burma seemed to breed courage. One of Wingate's Chindits in the 'forgotten' Fourteenth Army, Captain Michael Allmand, charged Japanese machine-gun nests on the Burma front on three separate days of June 1944.

The now-famous Fourteenth Army were fighting on a 700-mile front of forests, mountains, swamps, and jungle, in three main regions. One was down on the Bay of Bengal, the next in the central Imphal area and the third nearest to China, and centred on Mogaung. Close to here, Allmand's action took place.

Allmand was commanding the leading platoon in a company of the 6th Gurkha Rifles on 11 June 1944, when the battalion received orders to attack the Pin Hmi road bridge. The Japanese had already successfully held up the advance at this point for twenty-four hours. This whole sector was at an altitude of over a mile above sea-level, in about as remote a region as could be imagined.

The approach to the Pin Hmi bridge was extremely narrow, with the road banked up. Swampy patches and densely covered jungle marked the low-lying land on either side of the road. The Japanese, as usual, were well dug in along the banks of the road and in the jungle, where they continued to put up fanatical resistance with machine guns and small arms.

The platoon edged and inched its way to within twenty yards of the bridge; less than the length of a cricket-pitch. At that stage the enemy opened heavy and accurate fire, inflicting severe casualties, and forcing them to seek cover. Allmand, however, refused to be daunted by this close-range maelstrom, and charged on by himself, hurling grenades into the enemy gun positions, and slaughtering three Japanese with his *kukri*. This inspired the surviving men, who followed their platoon commander, and went on to take the objective.

Just two days later Allmand took over command of the company, due to casualties among other officers. This time their objective was a ridge of high ground. Allmand led his company by dashing thirty yards ahead through long jungle grass and marshy ground, swept by murderous machine-gun fire. He personally killed a number of enemy machine gunners, and then went on to lead his men on to the ridge they had been ordered to seize.

Ten more days passed before the final attack on the railway-bridge at Mogaung. By now, 23 June, Allmand was suffering from trench foot, which made it difficult and painful for him to walk. Despite this, he moved forward alone through thick mud and shell-holes towards the vital railway bridge. The pain stabbed through his foot, but he put it out of his mind, and charged a Japanese machine-gun nest single-handed. He was hit by a bullet and mortally wounded.

But as one man died there was always another to follow his footsteps. This time it was Major Frank Gerald Blaker, of the Highland Light Infantry.

The machine guns were the pivot of the Japanese defence on an important hill in Burma. His company pinned down by raking fire, Major Blaker charged the guns alone. Then, lying wounded on the ground, he raised himself to cheer on his men.

Blaker's regiment was attached to the 9th Gurkha Rifles of the Indian Army on 9 July 1944, when a company of the Gurkhas were ordered to carry out a wide, encircling movement across completely unknown and precipitous country marked by dense jungle. The aim; to attack a strong position on the summit of an important hill overlooking Taungni. Blaker's company was operating with the Gurkhas on this hazardous encirclement, and he carried out the movement with the utmost precision, taking up a position with his company on the extreme right flank of the Japanese. This in itself represented a feat of considerable military skill.

Another company encountered bitter opposition, but succeeded in taking the forward edge of the enemy position by a flat-on frontal assault, though failing to reach the main crest of the hill due to the fierce, verging on fanatical, opposition.

At this crucial moment Blaker and his company came under devastating fire from a medium machine gun and two lighter ones at deadly close range, which almost completely stopped their advance. The major quickly appreciated the significance of being stopped, so advanced ahead of his men through the sound of the Japanese guns.

One of the enemy bowled a grenade towards the advancing officer. It exploded with a weird, convulsive sort of noise amid the Burma foliage, and gashed a great hole in Blaker's arm. Blaker went on to locate the machine guns, which were the pivot of the enemy defence in the area and, with a superhuman effort, charged the position all alone.

Three rounds ripped into his already wounded body, driving him to the ground. Blood began to drain away from him, but he did not lose heart. In fact, while lying there, he tried to prop himself up a little on his uninjured arm, and cheered on his company. The sight of his riddled uniform and the sound of his voice rallied the men marvellously, so that they stormed the hill, forcing the enemy to flee terror-stricken into the thicker jungle.

As soon as they could pause, they evacuated Blaker from the battlefield, but it was already too late, and he died of his four wounds: the eighth VC to be awarded for actions in Burma, and one more medal to the immortal Chindits.

Meanwhile farther east still, in the Solomons, one of the most poignant sacrifices of the war had been made by the man with the honour of being the only Fijian VC.

To stop his men trying to rescue him after he had been wounded, he raised himself up deliberately in front of Japanese fire, and was riddled with bullets.

On 23 June 1944, at Mawaraka, Bougainville, in the Solomon Islands, Corporal Sefanaia Sukanaivalu crawled forward to rescue some men who had been wounded when their platoon was ambushed and some of the leading elements had become casualties.

After two wounded men had been successfully recovered, this NCO, who was in command of the rear section, volunteered to go on farther alone to try to rescue another one, in spite of machine-gun and mortar-fire, but on the way back he was seriously wounded in the groin and thighs, and fell to the ground unable to move any farther.

Several attempts were then made to rescue Corporal Sukanaivalu, but without success, owing to heavy fire being encountered on each occasion and further casualties caused.

This gallant NCO then called to his men not to try to get to him as he was in a very exposed position, but they replied that they would never leave him to fall alive into the hands of the enemy.

Realizing that his men would not withdraw as long as they could see that he was still alive, and knowing that they were themselves all in danger of being killed or captured as long as they remained where they were, Corporal Sukanaivalu, well aware of the consequences, raised himself up in front of the Japanese machine guns, and was riddled with bullets.

This brave Fijian soldier, after rescuing two wounded men with the greatest heroism and being gravely wounded himself, deliberately sacrificed his own life, because he knew that it was the only way in which the remainder of his platoon could be induced to retire from a situation in which they must have been annihilated had they not withdrawn.

CHAPTER FIFTY-ONE

Polish-Canadian Hero

ANDREW MYNARSKI

Two men are the main figures in this action which resulted in one living and one dying. And the Victoria Cross went to one of them. It occurred on D-Day+6, 12 June 1944, over France, but began many years earlier.

Pilot Officer Andrew Charles Mynarski was born at Winnipeg, Manitoba, in 1916, and joined the Royal Canadian Air Force in September 1941, as a wireless operator air gunner. Just over a year's training was spent in his home country, and then this Polish-Canadian airman came to England at the beginning of 1943. His service career after that followed the usual pattern of operations and leave, but mainly 'ops'. Then, as the great invasion was actually being launched during the first week of June 1944, Mynarski was commissioned as a pilot officer. It seemed as if it were to justify that promotion that he carried out his Victoria Cross action only a few days later.

D+6. The night of 12 June. Mynarski, wearing the thin blue ring of pilot officer, was the mid-upper gunner of a Lancaster detailed to attack a special target at Cambrai, in France. So the Lancaster of No. 419 Squadron, RCAF, took off after dark. Over the Channel they flew, where supply craft still plied to and fro reinforcing the troops who were grappling to enlarge their beachhead established the previous week. Flying Officer George Brophy surveyed the scene below and above from his perch of rear gunner in the bomber. While they were still over the water, the night seemed almost idyllic. But you never knew what the next moment might bring on a bombing raid. This was the quiet before the storm. And, unknown to him, at that precise second, Brophy was destined to be one of those two men figuring in the Victoria Cross action soon to take place. And the other? Mynarski, of course. One would live, the other die. And, as yet, neither of them knew anything about it. Yet they would before many more minutes. That was the strange part of life, especially on operations. One could not perpetually expect death or destruction every moment.

The Lancaster kept its place with No. 419 Squadron well. They were over France now. The bloody beaches of 6 June were behind them, and still they did not know. The bomber began gliding in on the target at Cambrai, when out of the invisibility of the night a Junkers jumped practically on them, riddling them with

238

cannon-shells. It all happened in a fraction of a minute. Both port engines failed at once. Only the two on the starboard were left for flying.

Fire broke out between the mid-upper turret and the rear turret —or between Mynarski and Brophy. The situation seemed desperate. More fire along the port wing, with its pair of useless engines licked by the orange-yellow sizzling sheets. The order to abandon had to come any second. It could not be delayed without disaster. As the flames grew fiercer the captain gave it.

'Abandon ship.'

Mynarski heard the phrase over the intercom; so did Brophy; so did the others. But Brophy and Mynarski were the principal players in the next seconds. As the crew began to bale out, Mynarski too left his turret and clambered along towards the escape-hatch. He stopped short though, for looking after, he saw through the smoke and utter confusion that Brophy was still in his rear gun turret, and apparently unable to leave it. In fact, the turret had become completely immovable. The hydraulic gear had been put out of action when the port engines failed, and in his attempt to escape Brophy had broken the manual gear.

All this time the fire between the two men's turrets blazed worse and worse. But as soon as he saw the situation Mynarski choked and stumbled his way through the flames in an endeavour to reach the rear turret and release the gunner trapped there. It was an awful moment for both the men. Brophy trapped and doomed to die, so it seemed, in his transparent coffin. And Mynarski now himself on fire up to the waist, with both his clothes and parachute burning, and beating their ghastly heat into him. As he got hotter he tried again to move the rear turret and free the gunner. But Brophy was still there. As well as the flames surging around his lower half, Mynarski was covered in hydraulic fluid. Because he had no axe or crowbar, he fought madly with just his hands to release the turret and its occupant, but it was obviously hopeless. Mynarski was frenziedly trying to find some way out, but there was none.

Their eyes met. Brophy shouted, 'Get going. You can't help me, anyway. I've had it.'

The rear gunner motioned for Mynarski to leave him and try to save his own life. Time was running out now. The plane lost height inexorably. So Mynarski went back reluctantly, defeated, through the flames.

Then at the escape-hatch, as a last gesture to the trapped Brophy, he turned towards him, stood to attention in his flaming clothing, and —though in agony — he saluted.

But by this late stage in the action his parachute and clothes had burned up badly. Nevertheless, he jumped out of the aircraft. French people on the ground stood helplessly watching his burning descent —as if a human torch were tracing a message, or looking almost like one of the Pathfinders' flares. The Resistance pointed to him as he fell, trying to mark his course. Meanwhile the bomber flew on for a few minutes, its two starboard engines protesting all the while. The fire had spread right across the port of the plane, and it could not stay aloft much longer. At this second both men were still alive —Brophy still trapped in his turret, Mynarski falling too quickly to earth.

Mynarski came to ground at a considerable speed, his chute a fireball in the French night sky. A thump, and he was down; terribly badly burned and charred from his fight through to the rear turret and his delay in leaving the aircraft. Then the Lancaster crashed, with a hideous noise in the night.

As the bomber hit the earth, it burst asunder, and those of the crew who had not already jumped were hurled clear of the charnel-house scene. In a few seconds it had burnt out. But Brophy lived, saved by some miracle of deliverance at that last impact; thrown clear, and not badly injured.

And Mynarski? So severely burnt was he that the gallant Polish-Canadian died from his injuries.

He must have known, of course, that when he was trying to free the rear gunner he was, with every precious tick of his watch, losing his last chance of getting away from the scorching ship.

A sad story, but at least Mynarski's sacrifice turned out to be not entirely in vain. The experience of Brophy seemed almost as if a miracle had crowned the efforts of the mid-upper gunner. The list of VCs of the air continued to grow, and their courage seems almost beyond belief.

CHAPTER FIFTY-TWO

Coastal Command Epic

DAVID HORNELL

The next two air VCs are both Coastal Command, and each won the honour in a Catalina flying boat. The first: Flight Lieutenant David Ernest Hornell. The second: Flying Officer John Alexander Cruickshank. Both too were as the result of anti-submarine patrols in northern waters.

Hornell came first. Like Mynarski, he was a Canadian; one with an athletic background. His career notes include such sports achievements as High School senior track champion. He was also a swimmer and tennis player of repute. He helped to form the Lakeshore Tennis Club, near Toronto. Hornell was also at that time a Sunday School superintendent. After his RCAF training, he was posted to the northern part of Vancouver Island, where he flew Stranraers on coastal patrol; good experience for what was to follow on a front nearer the active war. Then in 1943 Hornell went over to another part of the west coast of Canada, as a tester of Boeing aircraft. After this came the move to Britain, where his younger brother, Bill, was also serving in the RCAF with an RAF Albemarle squadron engaged in glider-towing and troop work.

Hornell's own operational missions now numbered sixty, involving 600 hours' flying. These coastal patrols meant long hours in the air, as the average time per operation indicates —ten hours. He did not complain, but just got on with his job day in, day out.

This particular day was 24 June 1944. Hornell was now captain and first pilot of a twin-engined amphibian aircraft, the faithful friend of many seamen —a Catalina. His anti-submarine patrol in these very northern Atlantic waters had already lasted some hours, but not the average ten.

Suddenly, from an empty seascape, a fully surfaced U-boat appeared, travelling at high speed on the port beam. Hornell at once turned to attack the raider. But he had been seen, so there could be no element of surprise. This inevitably tipped the scales strongly in favour of the U-boat.

The vessel altered course within a minute, tracing an arc of white wake in the grey waters. Then the submarine opened up with anti-aircraft fire as soon as she could reach the range of the Catalina. As the flying boat flew nearer, this fire intensified. Misses became near misses; and near misses turned into hits.

The two front guns of the aircraft replied as best they could, but early on the

241

starboard gun jammed —leaving only one weapon effective against a fully armed U-boat. Hornell and his crew registered hits on and around the conning-tower of the U-boat. But the hits on the aircraft were worse, two large holes appearing in the starboard wing. Two holes and a jammed gun. The whole starboard side had become a liability.

Ignoring the enemy's concentrated fire focused on him and the Catalina as it flew in manoeuvring for an attack, Hornell did his best to cope with the situation. But it was a situation changing for the worse all the time.

Oil poured belching black from his starboard engine, which had by now caught fire. The same wing was ablaze as well, and the petrol tanks looked dangerously near to the flames leaping and licking spitefully along the wing.

While this deteriorated the poor Catalina was hit and hit and hit by the pom-pom guns of the newly commissioned U-boat. Holed in many places, so that the Atlantic gale howled through it, the flying boat was vibrating violently. Hornell had all he could cope with just controlling it. Nevertheless, he had gone this far and decided to go the whole way. He would 'press home his attack'. How inadequate this official phrase seems for such determination! Irrespective of the slender chance he had of escaping from this desperate position, Hornell brought his plane down very low indeed. The U-boat's fire volleyed to a fearful frenzy. This was really fighting to the death —like two great animals —one a sea serpent, the other an amphibian. But many men's lives were involved as well. Hornell coaxed the shreds of his plane into position, and released his depth charges in a perfect straddle across the struggling U-boat. The German gunners looked like death for an instant. Then the bows of the vessel were heaved out of the Atlantic waves, and she sank without so much as a protest. The final strike had been decisive. Some of her crew struggled in the sea.

Soon the cruel sea would take its toll. Always there was the sea, waiting, subdued, to swallow men unwise enough to fight on it —or above it. The enemy knew, and so did Coastal Command, for although theirs was an air force, their whole operations were so closely connected to the sea that they felt truly amphibious.

But for the moment Hornell was still airborne. By some sort of superhuman efforts at what was left of the Catalina's controls, Hornell managed to gain a little life-giving height. But he was only borrowing time. He knew that full well. Yet it was the best he could do just for the moment.

He looked out. The fire in the starboard wing had grown more intense and complete. And the infernal vibration was worse too.

Then the burning engine fell off.

Hornell and all of them knew that their plight was critical. The Catalina could not really be expected to keep them airborne any longer. It was surprising the poor plane had lasted so long. It seemed to be held together by Hornell's will power and little more.

That engine dropping off was the final factor. They had to ditch. Hornell got the plane into the wind and the swell, and both pilots had to pull out all they knew to get it down without drowning them all. The first time they hit the crest of a wave and leaped 150 feet; the second time they still bounced, but the power was off now; the third time they stayed on the sea.

Eight men in the middle of nowhere: Flight Lieutenant David Hornell; Flying Officer B. C. Denomy; Flight Lieutenant S. E. Matheson; Flying Officer G. Campbell; Flight Sergeant I. J. Bodnoff; Flight Sergeant S. R. Cole; Sergeant D. S. Scott; Sergeant F. St Laurent.

Matheson and Cole had been injured in the attack, but all eight somehow got away from the plane, and Scott and St Laurent launched the dinghies. Everyone except St Laurent were with the first dinghy, while he was having some trouble blowing the other one up. Then it blew up really. It exploded. So St Laurent joined Scott, Campbell, Bodnoff, and Cole in the remaining inflated dinghy, while the other three, including Hornell, stayed in the sea, hanging on to it for dear life.

The heavy swell had already swept the U-boat's crew away to their graves. The aircraft settled rapidly as this swell sucked her down.

So that was the end of the air phase of Hornell's Victoria Cross operation. The crew as well as their plane had to be amphibious, for after ordeal by fire in the air came worse ordeal by water in the icy Atlantic.

This is Denomy's own account of the next twenty-and-a-half hours:

This is the way we stayed for the first two hours. Campbell took Hornell's trousers and tied the legs together to make a bailing bag. I took Matheson's flying helmet, and hanging on with one hand, bailed with the other. After two hours, when we were becoming numb, Hornell and I got into the dinghy and Scott and Campbell got into the water. I then started to bail with a regular bailing bag. After about one hour we decided it was necessary to get every one into the dinghy for survival. We were successful in getting every one in except Scott who had to leave his feet trailing in the water. As we carried on in this matter, I would bail for ten minutes and rest for five. To give room and allow free movement to bail, someone had to slip into the water. This continued for 12 hours.

About four hours after we ditched, an aircraft, a Catalina flown by Lt. Johansen, a Norwegian, was sighted. Campbell fired three of the two-star cartridges provided in the dinghy. It was our third and last flare that the aircraft saw. The aircraft dropped sea markers or smoke floats periodically to keep us in sight. At this stage, the waves were about 18 feet high and the wind about 20 knots. After about 30 minutes, the aircraft flashed to us:

'Courage –H.S.L. on way –help coming.'

It then went about two miles away, and returned flashing 'Vs', also 'U-boat killed.' This, of course, gave us considerable courage and Matheson, our navigator, kept working out an ETA for the high speed launch.

After about eight hours in the dinghy . . . we threw over our ration box and oars etc., keeping only the water can. The waves were now about 25 feet high and wind about 30 knots. Hornell and Campbell were seasick and Hornell began to suffer noticeably from cold. Campbell had a half package of dry cigarettes which we rationed to the entire crew. Someone else had a few barley candies which helped considerably. During the next few hours, the waves and wind increased greatly until at one stage the wind was between forty-five and fifty knots and the waves 50 feet high. To keep the dinghy upright, we invented a game, 'Ride 'em Cowboy,' to ride the waves. We would shift our weight from one side to the other as we went up and down the high waves.

Unfortunately, after 14 hours at sea, a wave broke as we were at the top of it, and capsized us. We all managed to re-enter the dinghy, but we had lost our bailing bag and water can. This left us at the mercy of the seas entirely. At this point, St Laurent and Hornell showed serious signs of weakening. Hornell, suffering from intense cold, became temporarily blind. St Laurent became delirious and soon passed away. We slipped his body out of the dinghy to make room for Scott, who had remained partly in the water.

After about 16 hours in the dinghy, a Warwick was successfully homed to us and attempted to drop an airborne lifeboat. However, the winds were too strong and it drifted away. It was about 500 yards away and could only be seen when both it and we were on the crest of a wave. Despite the state of the sea, the distance, and his own physical condition (very weak and blind), Hornell wanted to swim for it. I refused to let him because I considered it impossible. At this stage, winds and waves were gradually decreasing in strength and size.

Scott, who had been in the water for such long times, grew very weak, and, about 19 hours after our ditching, died. We also slipped his body out of the dinghy.

We were all very weak and becoming discouraged; however, we carried on by exercising ourselves as much as possible. Cole and Bodnoff seemed to regain strength from nowhere; Campbell and Matheson seemed to lose strength rapidly. Cole worked on Matheson, Bodnoff on Hornell, and I on Campbell. Cole attempted to make a sea drogue with his field service cap but this did not prove a success.

We continued to work on one another until, after 20 hours and 35 minutes in the dinghy, the rescue launch was sighted by Cole. In about ten minutes, the launch was alongside and hauled up Matheson, Campbell, and Hornell. Bodnoff and Cole climbed up the rope ladder with the assistance of the sailors. I managed to get up by myself. On board, they immediately began work on us. They worked on Hornell for about three hours, but were not successful. He never regained consciousness. The launch took us to a military hospital in the Shetland Islands. F/L Hornell is buried there in a military plot. Cole, Bodnoff, and Campbell were discharged from the hospital in four days, Matheson and myself after eight days.

Outstanding about F/L Hornell was his marvellous ability in flying such a badly damaged aircraft, especially in the face of strong enemy fire. His courage and bravery throughout marked him as a great man. Words cannot do justice to the fine job he did.

Hornell was awarded the Victoria Cross posthumously. Denomy whose account of the ordeal at sea was so graphic, received the DSO, Campbell and Matheson the DFC, and Bodnoff and Cole the DFM.

CHAPTER FIFTY-THREE

Struck in Seventy-two Places by Flak

JOHN CRUICKSHANK

S truck in seventy-two places by pieces of flak —this was the fantastic experience of Flying Officer John Alexander Cruickshank, RAFVR, No. 210
Squadron, the second VC of Coastal Command piloting a Catalina flying
boat. Could a man survive such incredible injuries?

A Scotsman from Edinburgh, Cruickshank was employed at the Commercial
Bank of Scotland, and had been a member of the Territorial Regiment of the Royal
Artillery for some time before the war. It was with this unit that he served until
June 1941, when he decided to transfer to the RAFVR. Volunteering as a pilot,
he underwent training in Toronto and Pensacola, returning to Britain the following
year. A staunch-looking Scot with a dark moustache, Cruickshank started flying
with Coastal Command early in 1943. Eighteen months' steady work took him till
17 July 1944. And as a result of what he did on this day he would be called in the
Press 'the good-looking boy from the bank who won the VC'.

Cruickshank was piloting his Catalina between 69 degrees and 70 degrees north-
west of the Lofoten Islands on a normal anti-submarine patrol. He had heard what
had happened to Hornell quite recently. But now all seemed peaceful enough. Then
came this:

'Blip up, skipper —'bout sixteen miles away.' Flying Officer 'Joe' Cruickshank
was roused from a reverie by this shout from his navigator who was operating the
radar. This U-boat patrol was now inside the Arctic Circle —no place to be ditched
in the drink. The navigator's shout seemed to mean business.

'O.K. Home us on to her,' he called back.

The aircraft made its way towards the spot, and then, slightly to starboard, the
crew saw the telltale plume of foam. The submarine surfaced —one of the latest
type of U-boat, with a tonnage five times as great as the standard model; almost a
warship. Attacking this sort of sub was no picnic nowadays. From his pilot's seat,
Cruickshank could see 37-mm and 20-mm anti-aircraft cannon behind the
conning-tower.

'Pilot to crew. It's a U-boat. We're going in.'

He flew into the wind that whistled around the Arctic even in July, so that his engine noise could be carried away from the U-boat. There was not a single sign that the 'Cat' had been seen. Nearer and nearer it dived on to the German sub —a 'Cat' about to pounce on prey much bigger than itself.

Click! The bomb-aimer's thumb stabbed the release button. But nothing happened. The depth charge had jammed. A double danger at once, from the submarine and the weapon.

By now the aircraft had been well and truly spotted. The formidable fierce guns of the craft came into action with electrifying effect. Levelling up at fifty feet above the Arctic, Cruickshank cursed his luck and began a turn for another run. There was no thought to giving up at this stage. Within seconds the shells streamed past the cumbersome Catalina, as she made her laborious turn. He banked heavily.

'Hold on, we're going back,' he shouted into the mouthpiece of his intercom. It was Cruickshank's twenty-fifth Coastal Command patrol —and the first time he had sighted a U-boat. He did not intend to let her go. He began his second run over the vessel. The whole armoury belched up at the 'Cat' as it came down to depth charge dropping height —which meant right in the teeth of the cannon. Shells spat up. They had to hit. The gunners would have had a hard job to avoid it.

And they did hit.

The firing flailed into the Catalina, killing Dickson, the navigator bomb-aimer outright.

This is what happened next, narrated by the twenty-year-old wireless operator, Flight Sergeant John Appleton: 'The skipper called 'Everybody ready?" and then "In we go again." We made a perfect run-in at low level. When almost on top of the U-boat another shell burst in the aircraft. Everything seemed to happen in a flash. I was hit in my head and hands. Cruickshank took no notice. He continued straight on.'

There were explosions in the plane, and the second pilot and two others of the crew fell injured. The nose-gunner had his leg riddled with red-hot shrapnel. Fire broke out, and the aircraft filled with the fumes of exploding shells. The whole frame of the plane was devastatingly damaged as the anti-aircraft fire concentrated in a climax.

Cruickshank was hit in seventy-two places, by seventy-two separate pieces of flak. He received two serious wounds in the lungs and ten penetrations in the lower limbs. But he did not die. He did not even falter. He flew the Catalina on, right over the enemy, released the depth charges himself, and straddled the submarine perfectly.

A gunner fought the flames with an extinguisher all the time Cruickshank was making his attack.

The U-boat sank, vanishing in a frothy white sea.

But the fire blazed still. At this moment Cruickshank collapsed, and the second pilot took over the controls. This pilot was Flight Sergeant Jack Garnett, and though wounded he managed to steady the plane sufficiently to keep the 'Cat' airborne. Soon afterwards Cruickshank came to again, and although he was

246

bleeding profusely, he insisted on resuming command and taking over the controls. He took over, and retained his hold until he was satisfied that the damaged plane could be kept under control, that they had set a course for base, and that all the necessary signals had been sent.

Only after all this could Garnett persuade him to consent to have medical aid. Despite the seventy-two stabs, he refused morphia in case it might prevent him from carrying on if and when he was needed.

Then came the long run home. The attack had been made at almost maximum distance from base. Now the questions were: could the plane keep going? and could Cruickshank live long enough to get back for proper medical attention? Only time would answer either of these.

They carried Cruickshank aft, and put him on the only serviceable bunk —the others had been on fire. Fortunately, the fires were all under control fairly soon.

Wireless operator Appleton dressed his wounds, and they kept him warm with their Irvin jackets. He recovered fairly quickly, and asked for a cigarette and something to drink. He was extremely thirsty. He kept asking if everything was all right, and insisted on periodic checks.

So the hours started to pass. They left the Lofotens behind, and aimed away from that weird world of the Arctic, heading for the Shetlands. One, two, three, four, five, five and a half hours it took altogether. Several times Cruickshank lapsed into unconsciousness without the morphia. He lost a lot of blood. Yet when he came round each time his first thought was for the safety of the aircraft and crew. It still seemed touch-and-go whether he could last out till they saw the Shetlands.

Then the ordeal produced one more extension that no one who had gone through so much already should have had to face.

The hobbling Catalina eventually flew right through the evening till about 22.00 hours, British double summer time. It was dusk. The glorious sight, the Shetlands, became dimmed by the dark. Cruickshank realized that with the plane in its present condition they had to take great care in bringing her down on the water, especially for the second pilot, who had also been wounded —although less badly.

Cruickshank could only breathe now with the greatest agony, but he insisted — with the sweat streaming down his face —on being carried forward and propped up in the second pilot's seat. The blood still oozed away, and with it went his strength. Somehow he stayed conscious.

Sullom Voe lay below now. They had only to get down. But he refused to rush it. For a full hour, in spite of his rapidly ebbing strength, he gave orders as they were needed. He was not going to bring that plane down until the conditions of light and sea made it possible without more risk than could be avoided.

With his help, the Catalina landed safely on the friendly waters off Sullom Voe. Even now Cruickshank would not yield. He remained captain of his aircraft, and directed it while it taxied across the bay and beached, so that it could be easily salvaged.

The base had received their signals, and a medical officer was waiting to go on board as soon as the big flying boat ground to a halt on the shingle of the Shetlands. As it did so Cruickshank collapsed. This was the reaction. He should have passed out hours before. Only indomitable willpower had kept him going and had sunk the sub.

The medical officer gave him a blood transfusion on the spot, and life flowed slowly back again. Then they removed him gently to hospital, where he had to remain for a long time. The attack was on 17 July. The Victoria Cross award was dated 1 September. He was still in hospital then, and it would be a considerable time after that before he was well again, which was not surprising in view of his seventy-two wounds. The surprising fact was that he had lived at all.

Three weeks later, on 21 September, HM King George VI held an investiture at the Palace of Holyroodhouse. The ceremony took place in the picture gallery, and awards were made in the presence of a large gathering of relatives of the recipients of various honours.

The King presented the Victoria Cross to John Cruickshank, shook hands with him, congratulated him on his devotion to duty, and told him that he had put up a tremendously fine show.

Flight Sergeant John Garnett, the second pilot, received the Distinguished Flying Medal and he, too, was cordially congratulated by the King.

So both men had survived their Arctic ordeal, with honour.

CHAPTER FIFTY-FOUR

Pathfinder Supreme

LEONARD CHESHIRE

When he had completed 100 bombing missions over Europe, Leonard Cheshire received the Victoria Cross. By October 1943, he had won the DFC, DSO, and two Bars. And it was in this month that Cheshire took command of No. 617 Squadron, and opened his fourth operational tour. His first impact came when he began to devise a fresh way of ensuring accurate attacks against comparatively small targets. This developed as the new marking system by an aircraft flying lower than the rest of the force. Cheshire pioneered this 'Master Bomber' technique with No. 617 Squadron, confirming its effect in practice by attacks on the flying-bomb sites in the Pas de Calais. The method was then later adopted for a series of small, specialized raids on targets in France vitally associated with the German aircraft production. By the end of March 1944 eleven of these dozen targets had been destroyed or damaged, using the new marker system of attack and a 12,000lb blast bomb.

The very first raid with this remarkable bomb was on an aero-engine factory at Limoges, on 8 February. Cheshire led twelve Lancasters through cloud to reach the target in moonlight. Cheshire then dipped his marker Lancaster down to a mere 200 feet over the factory, and dropped a load of incendiaries right in the middle of it. These burst at once, throwing up vast volumes of smoke. After the deputy leader had then dropped two red-spot fires from 7,000 feet into the incendiaries, the rest were given a perfect point at which to aim. Four of the five gigantic 12,000lb monsters fell bang on the factory, each actually obtaining direct hits on separate buildings. The damage was therefore quite devastating.

Cheshire soon saw that for the marker plane something more manoeuvrable than the Lancaster was needed, and got two Mosquitoes for this low-level marking task.

The 'Master Bomber' technique quickly established itself as adaptable to all conditions, where more normal methods would have failed. On 10 March, the squadron's target was a needle-bearing factory comprising an area only 170 by 90 yards. Despite the weather forecast of a full moon and clear visibility, a screen of cloud obscured practically all the moonlight. Cheshire and his deputy tried repeatedly to pick out and mark the target, but decided it was no good using the red-spot fires or green indicators, as intended. Improvising brilliantly, Cheshire dropped incendiaries on the eastern and western edges of the target, and then told the force to bomb between these twin glows. Although their success seemed doubtful, later daylight reconnaissance proved that they had succeeded beyond all their expectations, and almost entirely destroyed the vital small factory.

Still operating over France, one of Cheshire's next targets called for bigger-scale bombing altogether: the railway marshalling yards at La Chapelle, just north of Paris. 20 April was the night chosen for the attack, as part of the general pre-invasion softening up and dislocation of communications in the entire northern France region. No. 617 was only one of many squadrons participating, and the plan called for separate attacks on two aiming points within the overall target of the marshalling yards. More than 250 aircraft were to be employed.

The entire technique of bombing had developed by now into a highly scientific operation. First of all, at 00.03 hours, six Mosquitoes reached the target area two minutes ahead of the time for the start of the attack. These aircraft dropped strips of metal-covered paper to confuse the enemy's radar-directed air and ground defences.

Aircraft from a group other than Cheshire's were due to drop green target indicators first of all, but although these were released they failed to cascade at once, so that little time remained for Cheshire to find and mark the exact bombing point. Cheshire operated rapidly, however, and located the aiming point, marked it with red-spot fires, and told his deputy to add more fires for a clear indication. He gave orders for the controller of the force to instruct bombing to begin, but a further delay occurred due to a failure in the VHF radio telephone between Cheshire and the controller, who did not receive the instructions till after the main force of bombers were actually in the La Chapelle area. Despite the delay and congestion, the plan proceeded smoothly from then on, and reconnaissance revealed that the entire area around the two aiming points lay utterly irreparable –further proof of the marker technique, which survived even setbacks such as the delay of the first indicators to cascade, and then the interruption of the communication between Cheshire and the attack controller.

Much of the bombing potential was naturally being directed against the invasion areas and the links with it, but Cheshire fulfilled his wish to try out the marker technique where it would be most severely tested –against targets in Germany itself. Two raids especially proved it during April and both –more particularly the second –later earned him the Victoria Cross. The first was on Brunswick, the second on Munich.

Chesh's group –No. 5 –received orders to bomb Brunswick on 22 April with a maximum force, which turned out to be 265 aircraft. Only three of the whole 265 planes were lost; a remarkably low proportion for a raid so deep into enemy territory.

Directly after Brunswick followed the famous Munich raid, for which Cheshire won the Victoria Cross by his 'cold and calculated acceptance of risk'. Munich was selected for this experimental attack at Wing Commander Cheshire's own request, to test out the method of marking at low level against a heavily defended target in the heart of the Reich; and because of the fierce nature of its anti-aircraft and searchlight defences. The number of guns in the immediate area of Munich was thought to number a couple of hundred: nearly one for each aircraft.

It was only two nights after the Brunswick bombing, on 24 April, that exactly the same number of aircraft aimed for the city so dear to Hitler. All but ten of these actually attacked. The scientific approach reached one stage farther with the inclusion of a feint raid on Milan by half a dozen Lancasters of Cheshire's squadron to lure enemy fighters from Munich.

The main force flew via south-west France to avoid some enemy defences. But four Mosquitoes, carrying out the marking, flew direct. From Augsburg to Munich they endured continuous ack-ack fire, yet they reached Munich precisely on time. Cheshire's plane was caught in a cone of searchlights and every gun within range opened fire on him. He dived to 700 feet, identified the aiming point and dropped his red-spot fires at 01.41 hours. The other three marker Mosquitoes did the same.

The main force then flew into the attack. Cheshire continued to fly over the city at a mere 1,000 feet as the bombs were falling. Shell fragments hit his aircraft but he went on with his control of the operation. Searchlights so blinded him at one stage that he nearly lost control. Still at only the height of the Empire State Building, he stayed until he was sure he could do no more. But extricating himself to head for home was worse than flying in. He had to suffer withering fire for twelve minutes before he finally got clear.

Out of the 265 aircraft taking off, nine were lost —a proportion of 3·5 per cent, or one in thirty.

The damage done was out of all proportion to the size of the force, and much of Munich seemed to be affected, including buildings of the Nazis.

'Chesh' had done it again.

Now the searchlights were switched on over France again for those final withering weeks before the invasion. And to Cheshire that meant more 'ops' with his marker method. During his fourth tour of 'ops' he led No. 617 Squadron on *every* occasion, always undertaking the most dangerous and difficult task of marking the target alone from a low level in the face of strong defences.

One such 'op' early in May, was against the large military depot and tank-park at Mailly-le-Camp where thousands of enemy troops were believed to be located. Cheshire's Mosquito hummed over the area in dazzling moonlight, but despite the fact that this was the only operation of the night, and so all enemy fighters could be made available against them, he managed to mark it correctly. The attack went ahead as planned, but because of the bright night and the fighters on tap, forty-two bombers were lost out of the 338 that set out from England. The effect of the shattering raid, however, offset these tragic losses. Literally hundreds of buildings in the region were wiped out, and the entire camp cratered by the bombs. Enemy troop casualties too were severe. So Mailly-le-Camp no longer remained as an operational headquarters of the 21st Panzer division —as believed by Intelligence prior to the attack. Nothing could stop Cheshire now. No matter how heavy the odds against him, he seemed to survive.

D-Day came and went. And with it came a new weapon to No. 617 Squadron, an even bigger one than the blast bomb. This was the terrific and terrifying

'Tallboy,' a 14,000-pounder which reached the ground at a speed far faster than that of sound —so no warning preceded its arrival. It was developed for targets where deepest penetration was wanted, and extreme accuracy would be needed in releasing it.

It made its debut on 8 June, when No. 617 Squadron attacked the Saumur railway tunnel, which ran north-east to the Normandy front. Four Lancasters of another squadron helped by being detailed to drop flares for Cheshire to lead the assault by marking the target. This small flare force encountered difficulty, but, although many flares dropped wide, Cheshire could make out his whereabouts just sufficiently to release his red-spot fires into the cutting leading to the tunnel, only forty yards from its actual mouth. Nineteen Lancasters made the attack with 'Tallboys' after several dummy runs to be sure they were in the precise position. Here they had to be exact, but it could hardly be expected that many of their giant bombs would drop in so small an area.

In fact, one exploded in the cutting, while another fell on the roof of the tunnel. The crater caused by the latter was 100 feet wide. Two more erupted in the deep cutting approaching the Saumur tunnel, and blocked the whole railway with craters still wider than the one on the roof. And the main line stayed blocked until the Allied armies occupied the area. So the operation succeeded, even if the actual entrance to the tunnel was not definitely blocked. The railway *was* the whole object of the operation after all.

Jubilant at the dramatically devastating impact of these 'Tallboy' bombs, No. 617 Squadron looked forward to the next chance to use them. It soon came, five days later. On 14 June, Cheshire led a small section of Lancasters of No. 617 Squadron to attack the E-boat pens at Le Havre, and try to stop the activities of these vessels against the supply line of the Normandy beachhead. They carried 'Tallboy' bombs to penetrate the thick concrete roofs designed to protect these pens from the air. The marker for this dangerous mission was, once more, Leonard Cheshire.

Cheshire was as determined as ever to leave an accurate mark for the following bombers, so he dived well below the altitude range of the anti-aircraft guns which peppered the plane. This brutal barrage geared up to a great crescendo as he descended lower, lower. They hit his plane, but still he dived down, in broad daylight, and without any cloud cover. Closer still he came to them, only releasing his markers when he felt sure they would do their job. The plane was blazing, but still he flew on, and somehow got out of that holocaust of Le Havre and eventually to England again. The following force made several direct hits on the E-boat pens, and one of the 'Tallboy' bombs pierced the roof, destroying part of the wall.

Cheshire had done his duty, and lived to win peace.

CHAPTER FIFTY-FIVE

Pathfinder's Sacrifice

IAN BAZALGETTE

Three of the last six VCs of the air were members of the famous Pathfinder force of RAF Bomber Command. The awards were made in recognition of the vulnerable and vital work they did in leading the mass air attacks on the enemy in the later stages of the war.

First in order of operations, but the third of the trio to receive the award, was Acting Squadron Leader Ian Willoughby Bazalgette, DFC, RAFVR, No. 635 Squadron.

Bazalgette, like Cruickshank before him, had started his war in the Royal Artillery, receiving a commission in September 1940. This was not quite what he wanted, however, and a year later he entered the RAFVR. Another year passed, and he was at last with No. 115 Squadron, for flying duties.

During his first tour of operations he gained an immediate award of the DFC for a low-level attack on Milan in a Wellington. He survived the tour to become a Flight Commander at an operational training unit in Scotland, but he lived for danger, and always longed for the day when he could get back on 'ops' again. In fact, when he did finally return to an operational squadron he was told that his stay at an operational training unit was one of the very shortest on record.

As an instructor in Scotland, incidentally, he had as his deputy in the flight Squadron Leader R. A. Palmer, another Pathfinder to win the Victoria Cross. It was a strange twist that these two, who later became VCs, should have worked together at the same OTU at the same time.

'Baz', as he was known among his friends, was a good mixer, in the opinion of his wireless operator, Flight Lieutenant C. R. Godfrey, DFC. He had a dry sense of humour at that time which made him one of the most popular members of the mess. Before a difficult operation he would get his crew together and tell them the job they had to do, and no matter how tough it might be, he knew that they would back him all the way. He inspired that sort of confidence; so much so that when-ever aircrews talk about their old days in the mess at Downham Market, Norfolk, the name of Baz is bound to be one of the first on their list.

But Baz was a many-sided man. His greatest hobby, when he could find time, was collecting recordings of music he loved best. Before buying them he compared one recording with another, one orchestra and conductor with a second, and even a third. Each work had to be made and played by the performers he considered most suited to that particular composer. This showed not only a deep love of music, but a sense of perfection as well, which was soon to be revealed in his service career.

Now, Bazalgette –'Will' at home –was well on towards the end of his second tour. His first had been prolonged at his request from thirty to thirty-three. Now he had done fifty-four.

With the Second Front now well established, Bazalgette went out as 'Master Bomber' of a Pathfinder squadron detailed to mark an important target at Trossy St Maximin for the main bomber force: a vital rocket and bomb site.

The date was 4 August 1944, the thirtieth anniversary of the outbreak of the First World War.

When nearing the target his Lancaster came under heavy ack-ack fire. Both the plane's starboard engines spluttered to a standstill, ominous in their finality. Serious fires erupted in the fuselage and the starboard mainplane. The bomb-aimer was badly wounded. This was the usual terrible time when a bomber had been hit. But now it became far more serious, for as the deputy 'Master Bomber' had already been shot down, the success of the entire attack devolved on one man –Bazalgette. This he knew. He had known it as soon as he glimpsed the deputy Lancaster dive in flames.

Now it was up to him. The conditions deteriorated from appalling to impossible. Fire swept the fuselage, and the whole plane was plunged into its fatal grip. But through it all Bazalgette did not waver an inch. He was the Pathfinder. He reached the target, marked it for the main force, and then bombed it himself. The success of the ensuing raid was due entirely to him.

But although he appeared calm, to try to control the Lancaster was by now really out of the question. After he had dropped his bombs the Lancaster took a dive, virtually out of all semblance of control. But by supreme skill and strength, Bazalgette forced his will on it still –and regained some sort of control for a few moments. He was thinking quickly all through that brief time, trying to decide on the best thing for his crew's safety.

Then the port inner engine failed. Three out of four had gone.

Then the whole of the starboard mainplane melted into a mass of flames.

Even now Bazalgette did not admit defeat. He fought bravely to bring the aircraft and his precious crew to safety. The mid-upper gunner was overcome by fumes. The captain then decided the time had come to order all those of the crew who could do so to bale out –quickly.

So now the black dots of men began to emerge from the blazing Lancaster. Their parachutes jerked them to a stop in mid-air, and they floated across the French landscape.

But back in the plane Bazalgette refused to quit. He knew that the wounded bomb-aimer and helpless gunner, unconscious under the fumes, could never get out by parachute. He had to try and land the ship. This was his last effort: an almost hopeless task of getting the great Lancaster down somewhere.

With superb skill, he controlled the blazing monster. It drifted down over a small French village near by. He knew he had to avoid this, and he did. Swinging the aircraft clear of the cluster of houses, he literally landed it with sheer strength and guts and airmanship. All his many missions led to this last supreme effort: to land a blazing plane on one engine, with no crew to help him. But he did it —and avoided the village.

The sequel came a few seconds later. The Lancaster jerked to a halt —and exploded.

Bazalgette and the two men he tried to save all perished.

The little village was Senantes. The local inhabitants watched the drama over-head with intense emotion. They saw the searing fire spreading throughout the Lancaster, and then the four parachutes billowing out of the burning plane. Despite the German occupation troops, they hurried to the area where the aircrew had fallen, found that all four were safe, and hid them from the Germans.

Soon after the plane exploded the enemy recovered the bodies of the bomb-aimer and mid-upper gunner. The Frenchmen wanted to keep them, but the Germans would not leave them. The next day the patriots succeeded in freeing Bazalgette's body from the wreckage, and fiercely guarded it in order to be able to honour him as free and grateful Frenchmen.

Some time afterwards the village was vacated by the enemy, and by a strange coincidence Bazalgette's sister, Ethel, who was secretary to the commanding officer, Intelligence Section, 9th American Air Force, was stationed not far from Senantes. When she heard of her brother's heroic death she went to the village, and the French people arranged a service for him which she could attend. Bazalgette was given full military honours, and people from many miles around there came to pay homage.

As the citation to his Victoria Cross stated: 'His heroic sacrifice marked the climax of a long career of operations against the enemy. He always chose the more dangerous and exacting roles. His courage and devotion to duty were beyond praise.'

Finally, in memoriam came a few lines in a newspaper on the anniversary of his death:

In loving memory of Will, Squadron Leader Ian Willoughby Bazalgette, VC, DFC, killed during air operations against the enemy, Aug 4, 1944.

'In all things young and transient you fly
Still gay and splendid, riding through the sky.'

CHAPTER FIFTY-SIX

Busting Gothic Line

GEORGE MITCHELL, GERARD NORTON, RICHARD BURTON

The London Scottish, the Hampshires, the Duke of Wellingtons –they were all in the Italian campaign. And a man from each of these regiments won the VC there during 1944, by Monte Damiano, Monte Gridolfo and Monte Ceco. It was no accident that these three were all uplands, for the fighting in Italy was a war among the mountains.

After amazing gallantry which won him a posthumous VC, Private George Allan Mitchell, the London Scottish, was killed by a German who had surrendered to him.

Mitchell was just one soldier forming part of the 56th Division, and he had been with them since their first action in the final stage of the Tunisian campaign at Enfidaville.

The regiment's second engagement proved to be far more arduous, as they had to take part in one of the most daunting operations imaginable: a landing in face of powerful opposition.

This was Salerno.

The Allied force, landing in Salerno Bay on 9 September1943, had to meet an enemy force, not only of equal strength but with the great advantage of a good defensive position and land supply routes. On 13 September the 56th Division was temporarily forced back from Battipaglia, won at such cost, but retook it in a fierce counter-move. Then the division began to force its way through the defiles leading towards Naples and the north.

In mid-October the division crossed the Volturno, and in the first week of January took the desperately defended town of Calabritto. There followed a series of struggles for hill-features, unimpressive to the world because they were known only by their heights in metres. But bigger strain and sacrifice were needed to take these positions than to enter many towns with much more historic names. Later in the month the division thrust its way across the wintry, swollen River Garigliano, and on to the slopes of Monte Damiano, which proved to be the setting for Mitchell's VC.

On the night of 23-24 January 1944, a company of London Scottish initiated a local attack to try and restore a serious situation on a portion of the main Damiano ridge.

The company attacked with two platoons forward and a composite platoon of London Scottish and Royal Berkshires in reserve. The company commander was wounded in the very early exchanges of the attack, and the only other officer with the company was wounded soon afterwards.

A section of this company was ordered by the platoon commander to carry out a right-flanking movement against some enemy machine guns which were rasping out into the night and holding up the advance. Almost as soon as he had issued the order, the platoon commander was killed. There was no platoon sergeant. The section itself consisted of a lance corporal and three men, who were shortly joined by Mitchell, the 2-inch mortar men from platoon headquarters, and one other private. During the advance the enemy opened heavy machine-gun fire at point-blank range. Mitchell immediately dropped the 2-inch mortar he was carrying, and, seizing a rifle and bayonet, went charging up the hill all alone through a metallic hail of Spandau fire.

He reached the enemy machine gun unscathed, leapt into the weapon-pit, shot one of the crew, bayoneted another, and so silenced the gun. As a result of this heroism, the advance of the platoon was able to continue.

But soon afterwards the leading section was again held up by fire from about two German sections strongly entrenched. Mitchell realized for a second time that prompt action was the only hope, so he rushed forward into the assault, firing his rifle; oblivious of the bullets interlacing the air in that area. The rest of his section followed him, and arrived in time to complete the capture of the position. Six Germans were killed and twelve were made prisoners.

Just as the section was reorganizing, yet another machine gun cracked out at them from very close. Yet again Mitchell ran on with his rifle and bayonet, killing the crew.

Now the section found themselves right below the crest of the hill, from which a host of rifle fire peppered them like an irregular outburst from the exhaust of a car. Grenades, too, came down towards them; altogether, not an ideal place to stay for long. Mitchell had used all his ammunition, but, despite this, he called on the others for one further heave up the hill. He personally led the way up the steep, rocky slope. Dashing to the front, he was the first man to reach the enemy position, and through his lead they were able to force the rest of the Germans to surrender.

Throughout this entire operation, carried out on a jet-dark night up a slope strewn with rocks and scrub, Mitchell proved to be the power behind their success.

Then, a few minutes later, just as they thought nothing else would happen that night, one of the Germans who had surrendered snatched up a rifle and shot Mitchell through the head.

The third of the three VCs for the Hampshires, like the second, was won in Italy. The Hampshire Brigade were now at the Gothic Line proper, with the River Foglia before them and the grim mass of Monte Gridolfo a couple of miles beyond. Monte Gridolfo was indeed a formidable objective; all houses had been pulled down, trees felled, and avenues prepared between extensive minefields for machine-gun fire. Gullies which could have given cover had been filled in with logs, and the assault of the bare slopes of the hill looked suicidal. It required courage of no mean order to assault those formidable slopes in the broad light of an August day.

Yet they were assaulted. The 2nd Battalion advanced on them with great determination, crossing the Foglia at 13.00 hours in the afternoon of 30 August 1944, with little opposition. The road below Belvedere Fogliensi was crossed, and then the two leading companies were held up by very intense mortar and machine-gun fire, and forced to take what cover they could until darkness came down. Then they moved forward again, and attacked and cleared the fortified houses on the first ridge, in spite of very bitter opposition. Major Brehaut and Major Hutchinson led their companies with great spirit, and dealt with one machine-gun post after another. By dawn on 31 August the first height was captured and held by the 2nd Battalion.

Then the 1st/4th Battalion passed through, and carried on the furious assault. Nothing could stop them, and with great heroism they dealt with strongpoint after strongpoint, driving deeper into the Monte Gridolfo feature. The battalion was at the top of its form, but D Company, led by Major Baillie, was outstanding, and Lieutenant Gerard Ross Norton, MM, commanding a platoon of that company, fought with such gallantry that he won the Victoria Cross.

Lieutenant Norton was one of the officers seconded to the brigade from the Union Defence Force. He had joined the Army at the beginning of the war, in company with a colleague of his from a bank in East London, South Africa. This colleague was Major Baillie, his company commander at the battle of Monte Gridolfo. They had fought together in Tobruk, escaped together when it fell, and had walked 500 miles to Alamein. Lieutenant Baillie, as he was then, had won the MC, and Sergeant Norton the MM. When Lieutenant Norton joined the 1st/4th Battalion in July 1944, he found that his old colleague was now his company commander.

The action in which Lieutenant Norton won the Victoria Cross was on 31 August. Major Baillie's company attacked strongly-held German positions protecting the village of Monte Gridolfo. Lieutenant Norton led his platoon in an attack on one of the strongpoints, which was constructed with well-sited concrete emplacements, and it was soon pinned down by heavy machine-gun fire from a valley on the right flank of the advance.

On his own initiative, Lieutenant Norton at once went forward alone, and engaged a series of enemy positions in this valley. He attacked the first machine-gun position with a grenade, killing the crew of three. Then, still alone, he worked his way forward to another enemy position containing two machine guns and fifteen riflemen. After a fight lasting ten minutes he wiped out both machine guns with his tommy gun, and killed or took prisoner the rest.

Throughout these engagements Lieutenant Norton was under direct fire from an enemy self-propelled gun and, still under fire from this gun, he led a party of men who had come forward against a house and cleared the cellar and upper rooms, taking several more prisoners, and putting the rest to flight. Although by this time he was wounded and weak from loss of blood, he went on calmly leading his platoon up the valley, and captured the remaining enemy positions.

The official citation said:

> Lieutenant Norton displayed matchless courage, outstanding initiative, and inspiring leadership. By his supreme gallantry, fearless example, and determined aggression, he assured the successful breach of the Gothic Line at this point.

There is a charming postscript to his tale of gallantry. When Lieutenant Norton was taken back to the base hospital he discovered that the nurse who was to look after him was his twin sister. The next day was his birthday.

With the capture of Monte Gridolfo, the Gothic Line was breached, and within thirty hours of the beginning of the assault the three battalions of the Hampshire Brigade were within the enemy defences. The 5th Battalion, which had been in support, took up the lead early on 1 September, and made good progress until they came up against strong resistance at a road junction. They called for tank support at first light, the resistance was cleared, and the battalion took up forward positions above Meleto, just north of Monte Gridolfo, from which they fought off several enemy counter-attacks, and captured Meleto by the evening of 2 September.

This successful breaching of the much-vaunted German Gothic Line gave the men of the Hampshire Brigade ample reason to be pleased with themselves. They had been splendidly helped by the squadrons of the North Irish Horse; their Churchill tanks had always been there, supporting the battalions over appalling tank country. Squadron leaders on foot led their tanks up seemingly impossible slopes; nothing daunted them.

The General Officer Commanding Eighth Army, General Sir Oliver Leese, sent a signal to the Commander, 128th Brigade :

> My best congratulations to you and your brigade on your hard-fought four days' advance, including the capture of Monte Bartolo and culminating in the forcing of the Gothic Line, and the capture of Monte Gridolfo. This was a fine achievement.

It was not only a fine achievement by the rifle companies; the whole brigade threw themselves passionately into those violent and exhausting days. The advance was so fast at first that supporting supply echelons had great difficulty in keeping up. They raced through the thick clouds of dust, often under shell-fire, and got the rations and ammunition up in spite of very great difficulties.

Drivers, cooks, quartermasters' staffs, all suffered casualties, and all kept hard on the go with only a couple of hours' sleep snatched here and there. It was a fully concentrated effort by every one. The orders were to 'Bust the Gothic Line.' It was duly busted.

And now Private Richard Henry Burton's experiences contain most of the story of Sicily and Italy.

'I must have been bomb-happy or mad, but they say they are going to give me a medal,' wrote Burton to his mother, in Melton Mowbray. 'Anyway, I have paid the Boche back for my wounds.'

The wounds he referred to were received on three separate occasions. This 6-feet 3-inch giant of a Leicestershire man fought in the invasion of Sicily and at the Anzio bridgehead, before pushing his way northward up Italy to reach Monte Ceco on 8 October 1944.

That was the day of mud and continuous rain, when Burton gained his VC, and lived. The Germans held the 2,300 feet hill, nearly a mountain, and from it they overlooked the entire Allied advance northward. Here was one of those almost insoluble dilemmas of war. It could not be taken. It had to be taken. Two companies of the Duke of Wellington's Regiment received orders to take it.

The assaulting troops got to within twenty yards of the ridge at the top. A ridge from which spat a stream of Spandau fire. Certain sudden death, it seemed to say, as it chattered and spluttered noisily down the decline towards the leading platoon. And with the platoon commander soon wounded, the rest of the men were held up.

At once another platoon was taken through the two companies, to try and assault that impregnable ridge. Four Spandaus shot away steadily at this little line of British troops. This was when Burton said he must have been bomb-happy or mad. The runner of the second platoon, he took size 11 army boots, and on these he heeled his way upward with a tommy gun. Engaging the first Spandau position, he killed its crew of three.

Again the assault became bogged down by flailing fire from two more machine guns. Again Burton dashed forward up Monte Ceco, till his ammunition was all gone. Somehow he managed to snatch up a Bren gun, which he fired from the hip as he went, killing or wounding the crews of both these guns.

The company could then consolidate on the forward slope, while the rain rolled down the hillside in small rivulets, soaking everything and everyone there. Burton's actions were not yet over.

The enemy punched back without pause, but Burton, with most of his comrades in the platoon either dead or wounded in the wet, dashed forward again to direct such staggeringly accurate fire on the Germans above that they retired. Burton combined with the weather was more than they could face, and they left the feature firmly in British hands.

More blurring, blinding rain, and another counter-stroke. The enemy tried to weaken the adjoining platoon position, and Burton was somehow in the thick of things yet again. He had placed himself on the flank, and once more brought such deadly fire to bear that the attack failed to dislodge the company from their precious hill. So the day ended at last as it had begun, with rain drenching down relentlessly on the Duke of Wellington's Regiment. Despite this, however, Burton felt glad to be alive. They were all a little nearer the end in Italy.

CHAPTER FIFTY-SEVEN

The Glory that Was Arnhem

JOHN GRAYBURN, LIONEL QUERIPEL, JOHN BASKEYFIELD, ROBERT CAIN

Arnhem. Only that one word is needed to identify the setting and spirit of the next four VCs. Arnhem, where triumph and tragedy were so indissolubly intermixed.

Lieutenant John Hollington Grayburn was a platoon commander of the parachute battalion dropped ahead of the Allied armies, on 17 September 1944, with the task of seizing and holding the bridge over the River Rhine, at Arnhem.

The north end of the bridge was captured and, early on the same night, Grayburn was told to assault and take the southern end with his platoon. He led his platoon on to the precious bridge and began the attack, but the paratroops met a horrifying hail of fire from two 20-mm quick-firing guns, and also from the machine guns of an armoured car. Almost at once a shot ripped through Grayburn's shoulder. Despite his wound and the total absence of cover on the bridge, he pressed forward with wonderful spirit till his casualties became so alarming that he had no option but to withdraw. Grayburn directed this withdrawal from the bridge personally, and he was the very last man to leave the embankment and return to a semblance of cover.

They had tasted the mood of Arnhem.

Later on Grayburn's platoon was ordered to take a house vital to the defence of the bridge, and he personally organized its occupation, again in spite of his wound. Occupying it was one thing; holding it, another.

Throughout the next day and night the Germans slung ceaseless attacks at this house, using not only infantry firing mortars and machine guns, but tanks and self-propelled guns. The house was extremely exposed and difficult to defend. With all the forces at their disposal, it seemed miraculous that the enemy did not destroy or take the house. The credit for their failure went to Grayburn's great courage. Constantly he exposed himself to their fire as he moved among the men, already seeming as if he had learnt the lesson of complete fatalism that most of them had to accept sooner or later at Arnhem.

On 19 September, two endless days after the drop, the Nazis renewed and increased their intense grabs at the house. They knew as well as Grayburn its vital place in the defence of the bridge. Bullets, shells, and mortars merged into a mesmerizing foreground of noise as the Germans battered away at the house. Eventually they managed to set the place on fire, and Grayburn had to evacuate it.

Grayburn straightway took over all remaining men and reformed them into a fighting force. He spent the night organizing a position to cover the approach to the bridge.

20 September now. They met it, tired, bullet-wracked. Grayburn extended his defence by a series of fighting patrols, which stopped the enemy penetrating to the houses around them.

The next move in this struggle to the finish: enemy tanks to the fore. These shook Grayburn's defences so wildly that he had to withdraw farther north. The enemy were on the threshold to the bridge, and tried to lay demolition charges under it. The whole situation quickly became critical. Grayburn realized it.

Still ignoring his wounded shoulder, he organized and led a fighting patrol that actually drove off the enemy temporarily, and gave time for the fuses to their demolition charges to be removed. Already they had partly burned through, and the operation could not have been more hazardous.

Grayburn was wounded again, this time in the back, but he would not be evacuated. Not that any of them could be evacuated far from Arnhem.

Finally, an enemy tank rolled remorselessly towards his position. He had no defence against it, so admitted the position untenable. Grayburn stood up in full view of the oncoming tank, and personally directed the movement of his men to the main defensive perimeter, where he had been ordered.

He was killed that night.

In constant pain and weakened by his wounds, short of food and without any sleep throughout the seventy-two hours and more, Grayburn never flagged for a moment. Without his efforts, the Arnhem bridge could not have been held for those first three days.

While the German contingent were hammering at the house Grayburn had taken over, on 19 September, Captain Lionel Ernest Queripel, the Royal Sussex Regiment, was acting as commander of a composite company of three parachute battalions.

Queripel was with the 2nd Battalion in the desert, and after El Alamein he volunteered for the 10th Parachute Battalion.

'Determined –rather dour, but with a quiet wit which soon endeared him to all of us,' says a brother officer. 'There was no stopping him once he had decided to do something.'

Here was his chance at Arnhem.

19 September 14.00 hours: his company were advancing along a main road which ran on an embankment towards Arnhem. The advance had an accompaniment of medium machine-gun fire which grew so much that they became split up on either side of the road. Many men were killed.

Queripel at once reorganized his force. To do this, of course, meant crossing and re-crossing the road while under very accurate fire. As he carried a stricken sergeant to the regimental aid post Queripel was himself wounded in the face.

With his force reorganized, the captain next led a party of men against this strongpoint that was holding up their imperative advance. The post comprised a captured British anti-tank gun and two machine guns. These all fired with maximum frequency at the group daring to try and attack them. Queripel killed the crews of the machine guns and recaptured the anti-tank gun, which had thus already been on three sides in two days. The advance continued.

Queripel's face wound really hurt him.

Later that day, Queripel received further wounds in both arms. He found himself cut off with a small group of his men, and took up a position in a convenient ditch. Mortars and Spandaus got their measure, and made the place impossible. Regardless of his agonizing wounds, Queripel continued to inspire his men to resist with anything they had —hand grenades, pistols, and the few remaining rifles.

Through the pain he could still think clearly, and he realized that as enemy pressure on them mounted they would have to withdraw. Despite the men's protests, Queripel ordered them to get away, while he covered their movement with his automatic pistol and a pitifully few hand grenades. This certainly saved their lives. It was the last time any of them saw him. On 1 February 1945, the date of his citation, he was officially reported wounded and missing.

He died in captivity.

Baskeyfield became a legend to his comrades even while they were still struggling in that cauldron called Arnhem. In fact, some say that it was the one day's deeds of this twenty-one-year-old Burslem man which inspired them to hold out for a further six days.

On 20 September 1944, the day Grayburn died, Lance Sergeant John Daniel Baskeyfield, the South Staffordshire Regiment, was the NCO in charge of a 6-pounder anti-tank gun at Oosterbeek. The enemy developed a vicious attack on this sector with everything they had: infantry, tanks, self-propelled guns. Their obvious intention was to break into and overrun the battalion position.

During the earlier stages of the action, the crew commanded by Baskeyfield destroyed two Tiger tanks and at least one self-propelled gun. These successes were due to his coolness and daring in allowing each tank to thunder up to well within 100 yards of them before opening fire. He did this fully realizing the risk he ran. The general Arnhem situation, however, was so desperate already that Baskeyfield knew that they had to accept such risks. The result; he was badly wounded in the leg, and the rest of his crew also received fatal or serious injuries.

Arnhem, September 1944. Another world from the Burslem butcher's shop he managed before joining up.

Although this marked the start of a major German assault on their defences, they did get a short respite after this engagement. But Baskeyfield refused to be carried to the regimental aid post, despite his severe leg injury. Instead, he spent the time attending to his precious gun, and calling encouragement to his comrades in neighbouring trenches.

Then the Germans lashed and lunged with greater ferocity still. A mass of mortar-fire; deadly shell-splinters. Manning his gun quite alone, Baskeyfield calmly continued to fire round after round at the enemy until they put his weapon out of action altogether.

By this stage his solitary gunfire had become the main factor in keeping the enemy tanks at bay. It was virtually one man versus the Panzer tanks.

This magnificent rearguard fight by Baskeyfield held together the men still surviving in his area, and inspired them to go on. Time after time the enemy launched tank attacks, only to be beaten back brutally, brilliantly, by the wounded lance sergeant.

At last, when the inevitable happened, and they knocked out his gun, Baskeyfield still was not finished. Under intensified fire he crawled to another 6-pounder nearest to him, the crew of which had been killed. This he also manned single-handed.

Getting it into operation at once, he engaged an enemy self-propelled gun which was approaching to attack once more. Another soldier started to claw and crawl a way across the open ground to help him. He was killed almost at once. Certainly before he reached the lance sergeant. The action had got to epic proportions already. Baskeyfield managed to fire two rounds at the advancing self-propelled gun, one scoring a sufficiently direct hit to put it out of action. He was just preparing to fire a third shot as a supporting enemy tank lumbered up into the sector. It loosed a shell straight at the 6-pounder gun, struck it, and killed Baskeyfield.

During the days ahead at Arnhem stories of his valour inspired all ranks of this gallant group. He spurned danger, ignored pain, and epitomized the essence of Arnhem.

Major Robert Henry Cain, the Royal Northumberland Fusiliers grew his fierce-looking black moustache to frighten the Italians in North Africa. But that was a long time ago, and now he found himself at Arnhem –and destined to be the fourth of the VCs of that triumphant tragedy.

Cain's qualities became evident, not in a single action at Arnhem, but throughout every hour of the week from 19-25 September 1944.

He was commanding a rifle company of the South Staffordshire Regiment on 19 September when his company was completely cut off from the rest of their battalion. For that next week, therefore, the Germans hurled every conceivable weapon and device at them in an attempt to break them; tanks, self-propelled guns, and infantry. The Nazis tried to infiltrate into the company's lines innumerable times, and if they had succeeded the whole situation of the gallant airborne forces would have been directly jeopardized. And by his wonderful devotion to duty –an overworked phrase –Cain was personally responsible for saving a vital sector from falling into the hands of the enemy.

The events of that week began on 19 September. On 20 September the day after the cut-off, a Tiger tank trundled near to the area held by Cain's company. Armed with a Piat, Cain went out to tackle it quite alone. He took up a position in the path of the tank, and just waited, holding his fire. This needed nerves stronger than those of most men. Closer it came, forty, thirty, twenty yards. Only then did Cain open up with his Piat. The tank stopped suddenly, and swung its guns round on him. Cain was lying down to operate his Piat, and the tank shot away a corner of the house near him.

He was hit by machine-gun bullets, and then the falling masonry battered and buried him further, but he forced his teeth together, and went on firing. Cain scored several direct hits at the on-coming tank, through the dust and confusion all around him, and actually immobilized it. Then he supervised an operation to bring up a 75-mm howitzer very rapidly, which completely disintegrated the enemy tank. Only then would he agree to have his wounds dressed.

The next morning, 21 September, Cain was up and about again as three more tanks tried to make incursions into the British line. Each time he left cover, and took up a position on open ground to fire his Piat at them. Each time he managed to drive off the tanks. Each time the odds were on his being killed, but he survived.

His wounds were not superficial the previous day, yet during the next four days Cain seemed to be everywhere that danger threatened. From his constant confidence, the men held out with him. He refused rest or medical attention all the time, though his hearing had been seriously impaired because of a perforated eardrum, and he was also still suffering from multiple wounds.

On 25 September the Nazis flung a ferocious concerted attack on Cain's position, using self-propelled guns, flame throwers and infantry. The air of Arnhem reeked, and tongues of flame flashed. By then, the last Piat had been put out of action, and Cain was armed with only a light 2-inch mortar. Miraculous as it seemed, in a death-or-glory three hours' battle, Cain and his men and this mortar so demoralized the Germans that they withdrew in disorder.

It was Cain's combination of skill and daring that achieved the impossible. And as his citation ended: 'His coolness and courage under incessant fire could not be surpassed.'

CHAPTER FIFTY-EIGHT

Dakota Captain at Arnhem

DAVID LORD

T he first member of the RAF Transport Command to become a VC; this honour belongs to Flight Lieutenant David Samuel Anthony Lord, DFC, No. 271 Squadron.

Lord enlisted in the ranks in 1936, and was commissioned six years later, in the middle of the war. He served with Nos. 31 and 271 Squadrons. When he was awarded his DFC in July 1943 it was stated that he had completed his very large number of operational sorties in Iraq, the Western Desert and Burma. His duties in Burma included the evacuation of casualties, women and children, often in the face of severe opposition. During the early summer of 1943 he did especially admirable work there, dropping food supplies to troops in the field. His sorties often took him deep into enemy territory without fighter escort, calling for courage and endurance. It was not only Bomber, Fighter, and Coastal Commands that took guts. This job of Transport Command was just as bad, for the planes were always vulnerable targets for the enemy.

So to Arnhem, that immortal name made more so by the citation that follows. This is exactly as it was issued by the Air Ministry on 13 November 1945. Nothing need be added or altered:

Flight Lieutenant Lord was pilot and captain of a Dakota aircraft detailed to drop supplies at Arnhem on the afternoon of 19 September 1944. Our airborne troops had been surrounded and were being pressed into a small area defended by a large number of anti-aircraft guns. Aircrews were warned that intense opposition would be met over the dropping-zone. To ensure accuracy, they were ordered to fly at 900 feet when dropping their containers.

While flying at 1,500 feet near Arnhem, the starboard wing of Flight Lieutenant Lord's aircraft was twice hit by anti-aircraft fire. The starboard engine was set on fire. He would have been justified in leaving the main stream of supply aircraft and continuing at the same height or even abandoning his aircraft. But on learning that his crew were uninjured and that the dropping-zone would be reached in three minutes, he said he would complete his mission, as the troops were in dire need of supplies.

By now the starboard engine was burning furiously. Flight Lieutenant Lord came down to 900 feet, where he was singled out for concentrated fire of all anti-aircraft fire. On reaching the dropping-zone, he kept the aircraft on a straight and level course while supplies were dropped. At the end of the run, he was told that two containers remained.

Although he must have known that the collapse of the starboard wing could not be long delayed, Flight Lieutenant Lord circled, rejoined the stream of aircraft, and made a second run to drop the remaining supplies. These manoeuvres took eight minutes in all, the aircraft being continuously under heavy anti-aircraft fire.

His task completed, Flight Lieutenant Lord ordered his crew to abandon the Dakota, making no attempt himself to leave the aircraft, which was down to 500 feet. A few seconds later, the starboard wing collapsed and the aircraft fell in flames. There was only one survivor, who was flung out while assisting other members of the crew to put on their parachutes.

By continuing his mission in a damaged and burning aircraft, descending to drop the supplies accurately, returning to the dropping-zone a second time and finally, remaining at the controls to give his crew a chance of escape, Flight Lieutenant Lord displayed supreme valour and self-sacrifice.

The one man to survive was Flying Officer H. A. King who was subsequently taken prisoner.

So Transport Command takes its place proudly among other Commands with VCs to their credit.

CHAPTER FIFTY-NINE

Into the Low Countries

JOHN HARPER, GEORGE EARDLEY, DENNIS DONNINI, HENRY HARDEN, AUBREY COSENS, FREDERICK TILSTON, JAMES STOKES

France was freed, but a lot of lives still had to be lost before the Germans were beaten back into their own country and finally just beaten. A lot of lives like that of Corporal John William Harper. Three times Harper clambered over a wall, right in the sights of German guns.

It happened in north-west Europe on 29 September 1944. when the York and Lancaster Regiment attacked the Depot de Mendicité, a natural defensive position surrounded by an earthen wall, and then a dyke. And, naturally, such a spot was being strongly held by the Nazis.

Harper was commanding the leading section in the assault. The enemy had got really well dug in, with a perfect field of fire across 300 yards of completely flat and exposed terrain.

Despite this unpromising state, and with disdain for the storm of metal in mortar bombs and rifle fire brought to bear on this open ground, Harper led his section straight up to the wall, and killed or captured the enemy holding the near side. During this stage of the attack the platoon commander was seriously wounded, and could take no further part in it. Harper took over control of the platoon.

As the enemy on the far side of the wall were now throwing grenades over the top, Harper climbed over alone, also throwing grenades. In the face of close-range small-arms fire he personally routed the Germans directly opposing him. He took four prisoners and shot several as they fled.

Still seeming to ignore the heavy Spandau and mortar-barrage which was punishing and pulverizing the area, once again he climbed over the wall alone, to find out whether it would be possible for his platoon to wade the dyke that lay beyond. He found the dyke too deep and wide to cross, and so he came back, when he received orders to try and establish his platoon on the enemy side of it.

For the third time Harper climbed over alone, found some empty enemy weapon-pits and, providing the necessary cover-fire, urged and encouraged his section to scale the wall and then dash for cover. By this action he was able to bring down enough covering fire to enable the rest of the company to cross the open ground and surmount the wall with the loss of only one man.

Harper then left his platoon in the charge of his senior section commander and walked alone along the banks of the dyke, attracting vicious Spandau-fire all the time, to try and find a crossing-place for the men. Eventually, he made contact with the battalion attacking on his right, and found that they had located a ford.

Back he came again across the pitilessly open country, and, while directing his company commander to the ford, he was struck by a bullet which fatally wounded him.

He died on the bank of the dyke.

The success of the battalion in driving the enemy from the wall and back across the dyke must be largely ascribed to the superb self-sacrifice of Harper.

Soon after Harper's heroism, Acting Sergeant George Harold Eardley, of the King's Shropshire Light Infantry, received the bronze cross for the following action:

In North-west Europe on October 16, 1944, during an attack on a wooded area east of Overloon, strong opposition was met from well-sited defensive position in orchards. The enemy were paratrooped and well equipped with machine-guns.

A platoon of the King's Shropshire Light Infantry was ordered to clear these orchards and so restore the momentum of the advance, but was halted some 80 yards from its objective by automatic fire from enemy machine-gun posts. This fire was so heavy that it appeared impossible for any man to expose himself and remain unscathed.

Notwithstanding that, Sergeant Eardley, who had spotted one machine-gun post, moved forward, firing his Sten gun; he killed the officer at the post with a grenade. A second machine-gun post beyond the first immediately opened up, spraying the area with fire. Sergeant Eardley, who was in a most exposed position, at once charged over 30 yards of open ground and silenced both the enemy gunners.

The attack was continued by the platoon but was again held up by a third machine-gun post, and a section sent in to dispose of it was beaten back, losing four casualties. Sergeant Eardley, ordering the section he was with to lie down, then crawled forward alone, and silenced the occupants of the post with a grenade.

The destruction of these three machine-gun posts single-handed by Sergeant Eardley, carried out under fire so heavy that it daunted those who were with him, enabled his platoon to achieve its objective, and, in so doing, insured the success of the whole attack.

His outstanding initiative and magnificent bravery were the admiration of all who saw his gallant action.

That last winter of the war in Europe was tough, often tragic, and fought in appalling weather, worse than Fusilier Dennis Donnini had been used to in his home county of Durham.

On 18 January 1945, a battalion of the Royal Scots Fusiliers, supported by tanks, found themselves the leading battalion in an assault on the German position between the Rivers Roer and Maas. This position consisted of the unpleasant combination of a broad belt of minefields and barbed wire, on the other side of a stream.

As a result of a thaw in the freezing weather the stream had become swollen so much that the Allied armour could not cross it. So the infantry had no choice but to continue the difficult assault without the vital support of the tanks.

Donnini's platoon was ordered to attack a small village. As they left the temporary safety of their trenches the platoon came under concentrated fire from the houses ahead of them, and a bullet hit Donnini in the head. He fell down, stunned for a few minutes, but not dead. Soon afterwards he recovered his senses, and realized at once his whereabouts and orders. It was as if he had been whipped into a frenzy. He got up, charged down thirty yards of open road, and delivered a grenade into the nearest window.

The enemy inside the house fled through the gardens of four houses, followed by Donnini and the survivors of his platoon. As the chase continued they came under bursts of fire from seventy yards' range. This did not stop them, though, and Donnini, with two colleagues, crossed an open space to reach the cover of a wooden barn, thirty yards from the enemy trenches that were the source of the firing.

Blood had been pouring from Donnini's head wound all the time, and he was weakening. But not noticeably. One of his colleagues had been wounded as well, so Donnini ran into the open, under the most intense close fire, to carry the man into the barn. With the wounded man safely behind cover for the moment, Donnini dashed out into the open again, taking a Bren gun with him as he went.

The blood streamed from his head. He was hit and wounded a second time. He went on firing his Bren in a daze, scarcely seeing anything any longer. Suddenly, a third enemy bullet hit a grenade Donnini was carrying . . . He was killed.

The self-sacrifice of the fusilier drew the enemy fire away from his colleagues to himself, with the result that the platoon went on to take the position, accounting for thirty Germans and two machine guns. So this point-blank battle in miniature ended in death for Donnini, but his action enabled the rest of them to overcome an enemy twice their own number.

That winter evoked every kind of courage from the Allied armies, like the brand of Lance Corporal Henry Harden, Royal Army Medical Corps. This man won the VC with a stretcher instead of a gun, saving the lives of two wounded commandos.

In north-west Europe, on 23 January 1945, the leading section of a Royal Marine Commando troop had been forced to the ground by fierce fire. As it was clearly impossible to engage the enemy from the open, they decided to make for some nearby houses. The commandos managed this move successfully, despite the hail and holocaust of fire –but left lying in the open were an officer and three other men all injured.

At this stage shells and mortars were falling on the entire troop, so it seemed out of the question to try and rescue the four wounded men in the foreseeable future.

Lance Corporal Harden thought quite the reverse. This medical orderly attached to the troop at once set out across the 120 yards' distance. Fire concentrated on him from four separate positions, all within 300 yards of his scurrying figure. Quite oblivious to it all, Harden moved through this fire and lived. That was the most amazing thing of all. Picking his way from one casualty to another, he crouched beside each, dressing their wounds.

After he had attended to three like this, he decided to carry one of them back to cover. Again meeting machine guns, he somehow managed to drag the man to safety.

An officer then ordered Harden not to go forward again, and they tried to bring in the other casualties with the aid of tanks. But where Harden had succeeded, tanks failed, due to bitter barrage of enemy anti-tank weapons. A further shot was then made to reach and recover the remaining three men under cover of a smokescreen, but this, too, failed, and brought about an increase in enemy fire all around the area of the injured commandos.

With a volunteer stretcher-party, Harden insisted again on going to get them, and by some fortune they came back across that 120 yards of open ground with a badly wounded man on the stretcher. All that way they were as vulnerable as anyone could ever be, lifting the stretcher and quite unable to defend themselves at all.

Two men saved, two more still out there. There was no question in Harden's mind of leaving them there. He saw his job as bringing back the wounded, whatever the circumstances happened to be. Again with a stretcher-party, he set out for the third time. They got there all right, reaching the commando officer. The enemy rifle and mortar-fire seemed stronger than ever as they heaved the man on to the stretcher; and then came the return to cover. Harden's charmed life could not be expected to go on much longer, and sure enough, when they were part of the way back towards the troop, he was shot and killed.

It goes without saying that Harden showed superb devotion to duty, and certainly saved the lives of the wounded brought back. But there was more to it than that. The commandos could witness what he achieved at this nerve-wracking period, and in this manner he helped steady the whole troop. Courage, like fear, can be catching, and if any of them felt in need of a little extra just then they gained it from Harden's selfless spirit.

Two courageous Canadians symbolized their countrymen's part in the push into the Low Countries.

Sergeant Aubrey Cosens came to fight from the mining town of Latchford, near Cobalt, Ontario, and he got as far as Mooshof, Holland, before being killed.

On the night of 25-26 February 1945, the 1st Battalion, the Queen's Own Rifles of Canada, launched an attack on the hamlet of Mooshof to take ground vital for future advances. Sergeant Cosens's platoon, with two tanks to help them, went for enemy strongpoints in three typical Dutch farm buildings. The scene should have been one of peace, but this was war on a fanatical scale. Twice the Germans threw them back, and then the maddened enemy themselves attacked, inflicting chaos and casualties on the platoon, whose commander was killed.

Cosens at once assumed command of the only other four survivors of the platoon. These he placed to give him covering fire while he ran across the open farm ground under the thud of heavy mortar-fire and screech of shells. Cosens's aim was the one remaining tank, where, heedless of risk, he took up an exposed position right in front of the turret, and directed its fire towards the Nazis.

Another counter-attack had been repulsed by the Canadians when Cosens ordered the tank to attack the idyllic cluster of farm buildings, while the four survivors of his platoon followed in the closest support possible. After the tank had rammed the first building Cosens jumped down and entered it alone, taking prisoner those defenders he did not kill. Still alone, he next entered the second and third farm buildings, personally killing or capturing all the enemy there. This he did despite deafening fire.

Just after these important points were reduced, an enemy sniper, still surviving somewhere, shot him through the head. Cosens had taken on forty or more Germans and killed at least half that number before he himself was killed.

Forty-eight hours later, on I March, the second Canadian had made his contribution to victory in Europe.

Canada's legless VC Major Frederick Albeit Tilston, made six or more 'death' trips to carry ammunition and grenades to his men. And wounded three times, he still somehow gave orders.

The second Canadian Division had been given the task of breaking through the fanatically fortified Hochwald Forest defence line covering the very last German bastion west of the Rhine, protecting the vital Wesel Bridge escape route.

The Essex Scottish Regiment had to breach the defence line north-east of Udem, and to clear the northern part of the forest, through which the balance of the brigade would pass.

On I March 1945, they set in motion the attack, but the ground was so soft that tanks could not support the Canadian infantry, as had been planned. The vehicles would have sunk into the ground and been sitting targets for the Nazis.

Across approximately 500 yards of flat open country, in the terrifying teeth of trails of bullets, Tilston personally led his company in the attack, keeping dangerously close to the Canadians' own splitting shells in order to extract the maximum amount of cover from their barrage. In exposed terrain like that such tactics were vital.

Tilston was wounded in the head.

He continued to lead his men forward, through a belt of barbed wire ten feet in depth that threatened to trap them. He shouted encouragement to urge them on to the enemy trenches, and his Sten sprayed fire over the trenches in question. The platoon on the left then came under heavy fire from a machine-gun post, so he darted forward, and silenced it with a grenade. He was the first to reach the enemy position, and took the first prisoners.

Determined to maintain the momentum of the attack, Tilston ordered the reserve platoon to mop up the position, and then, with great gallantry, he crept on with his main force to the second line of enemy defences, which were on the edge of the woods; the bristling Hochwald Forest.

As he approached the woods he was once again wounded, but more seriously this time. He grabbed his hip and fell to the ground. But Tilston did not give in. He shouted to his men to carry on without him for the time being, and urged them into the wood.

His hip hurt terribly, but he struggled to his feet, and actually rejoined the Canadians as they reached the trenches on their objective.

An elaborate system of underground dugouts and trenches here were manned in strength, and vicious hand-to-hand fighting to a finish followed. Despite his two wounds —in head and hip —the major's unyielding will enabled him to close with the German defenders and lead his men in the systematic clearing of this network of trenches. During the fighting two enemy company headquarters were overrun, and many casualties occurred among the desperate defenders.

But the losses were large on both sides. So grim had been the fighting, and so savage the Nazis' no-surrender struggle, that the Canadian company was now reduced to only twenty-six men. One quarter of its original strength. A tragic toll.

Before they could complete consolidation the enemy hurled repeated waves of counter-thrusts at them. These blows were supported by a stream of fire from the open flanks; mortars and machine guns. Those three words can never convey what it was like to be the target of ruthless, ear-splitting, brain-bewildering fire.

Tilston moved in the open from platoon to platoon, quickly organizing their defence, and directing fire against the advancing enemy. No man could deny the terror of feeling an enemy getting closer and closer. Now they had penetrated so near the Canadians' position that grenades could be thrown into the trenches held by Tilston's troops. Nevertheless, the major never wavered, and they held firm against odds that grew greater all the time.

When the supply of ammunition ran really low he repeatedly crossed that bullet-broken ground to the company on his right flank to carry grenades, rifles, and Bren ammunition to the troops. He also replaced a damaged radio to re-establish touch with his battalion headquarters; still with his wounds worsening.

Tilston made such hazardous trips six or more times, each single occasion crossing a road dominated by deadly fire from a number of well-sited enemy machine-gun posts.

On his last trip he was wounded for the third time —in the leg. They found him in a shell-crater beside the road. Though critically wounded, and barely conscious enough to say anything, he would not submit to medical aid until he had given complete orders for the defence plan; until he had stressed the vital necessity of holding the place; until he had ordered his one remaining officer to take over command.

'By his calm courage, gallant conduct, and total disregard for his own safety, he fired his men with grim determination, and their firm stand enabled the regiment to accomplish its task of furnishing the brigade with a solid base through which to launch further successful attacks to clear the forest.'

He lost his legs, but in the autumn of 1945 Tilston was fitted with artificial limbs. Later he married Miss Helen Adamson.

*   *   *

When he finally fell, wounded eight times in the upper part of the body, he raised his hand, and called goodbye to his comrades. It was men like Private James Stokes who won the war.

The scene was Holland, on 1 March 1945. During an attack on Kervenheim, the same day as Tilston's VC, Stokes was a member of the leading section of a platoon of the King's Shropshire Light Infantry.

While advancing, the platoon suddenly sustained sharp rifle and machine-gun outbursts from a farm building and were forced to take cover.

The platoon commander started to regroup the men, when Stokes, without waiting for any orders, got up and darted straight through the thick spray of bullets, firing from the hip as he went. He vanished inside the farm building, and the rest of the platoon held their breath and waited. The enemy guns stopped, and they saw Stokes reappear with a dozen Germans. He did not do this entirely without wounds, however, for they found that he had been hit in the neck by a bullet.

Stokes's daring enabled the platoon to proceed to its next stop, and he was ordered back to the regimental aid post. He refused to go, continuing the advance with the rest.

They were creeping up towards this second target, when they once more came under fire from a house on the left. Stokes rushed the building by himself, blazing away as before with his rifle. They saw him drop the gun and fall, groping, to the ground. But a moment later he forced himself to his feet again, picked up the rifle lying at an angle where it had fallen, and went on. The fierce fire was now covering not only Stokes but the entire platoon. He entered the house, when, as previously, all enemy shooting suddenly ceased. And, as on the last occasion also, he staggered back to the platoon, this time with five more prisoners. All due to his daring, the platoon had again been able to advance.

The climax of the whole assault was now at hand, and there was no time for discussion or dealing with wounds. Stokes by then had been really badly wounded, and was suffering severely from loss of blood. Yet, as the company was forming up for its final stab at the Germans, he did not wait, but dashed on the last sixty yards to their goal, his fingers firing instinctively, his legs carrying him on by sheer willpower. Struggling through a solid stream of gunfire, Stokes finally fell twenty yards from the enemy position, firing his rifle to the very last.

Then, as he fell, and the company passed him in the decisive charge, his hand fluttered up, and he shouted his final farewell to them. It was later that they found the eight wounds in his body. He had run those forty yards pierced with wounds and dying every second.

Private Stokes's one object throughout this action was to kill the enemy at whatever personal risk. His magnificent courage, devotion to duty, and splendid example, inspired all those round him and ensured the success of the attack at a critical time; moreover, his self-sacrifice saved his platoon and company many serious casualties.

CHAPTER SIXTY

Italian Winter and Spring

ERNEST SMITH, JOHN BRUNT,
THOMAS HUNTER, ANDERS LASSEN

Meanwhile four final VCs in Italy reflect the remorseless character of the conflict there against the elements, as well as the enemy. Yet the Allies somehow overcame both of them in that last winter and spring, with spirit such as that shown by Private Ernest Alvia Smith. Thirty feet from an enemy tank, Private Smith stood up and fired his Piat, with the vehicle viciously spitting bullets from machine guns.

On the night of 21-22 October 1944, a Canadian infantry brigade had to forge and force a way across the Savio River; one more bridgehead in the battle for Italy. The Seaforth Highlanders were selected as the spearhead of this attack. In vile weather for the operation, they somehow crossed the river, capturing their goal in spite of strong enemy efforts.

Torrential rain roared down without a pause, causing the Savio to rise six feet in five hours, and, as the soft vertical banks made it impossible to bridge the river, no tanks or anti-tank guns could be taken across the raging water to support the rifle company.

As the right forward company was consolidating its objective it suddenly received a drastic thrust from a troop of three Mark V Panther tanks, with two self-propelled guns also close at hand. Thirty infantry, added to this armour, made the whole prospect appear almost hopeless.

The three approaching tanks rattled out their machine guns at the Canadians, but Smith showed great initiative in leading his small Piat group of two men across an open field to a position from which they could deploy the weapon best. Leaving one man on the gun, he crossed the road with the other one.

One of the Panthers immediately came careering down the road, firing its machine guns along the line of ditches flanking the route. A bullet hit and wounded Smith's comrade.

At a range of exactly thirty feet —just ten yards —Smith leapt up in complete view of the machine-gunning Germans. He took aim as if they were far off, and calmly fired his Piat at the tank. Smith was not hit, but the tank was. He had put it out of action.

Ten Germans at once jumped off the back of the tank and charged him. Smith

275

made a split-second decision. He ran out on the road itself, and pointed his tommy gun fair and square at the advancing men. They were only a few feet off now. He shot and killed four of them, and drove the other six back for shelter. One against ten, and he had won.

But his battle was not yet over. Another tank started to spit out at him, and more enemy infantry began to close in on his position. All the while Smith's wounded comrade had been lying helpless nearby. Now he had to think even faster. Grabbing some abandoned tommy gun magazines from the ditch, he held the spot, fighting the new batch of Germans with his gun until they gave up and withdrew in disorder.

One tank and both the self-propelled weapons had been destroyed by this stage of the struggle, but yet a third tank started to sweep the area with fire from a longer range. This seemed comparatively harmless to Smith after surviving the earlier attacks. Still contemptuous of the fire, he helped his wounded friend to cover, and managed to get medical aid for him behind the nearest building.

Smith returned to his position beside the road to await any possible further onslaught. Fortunately, no immediate attack did develop, and so the battalion consolidated the bridgehead position on which the whole operation ultimately depended. This led to the eventual capture of San Giorgio di Cesena and an additional advance to the Ronco River.

Amid the mud and maelstrom of the Italian front on 9 December 1944, Captain John Henry Cound Brunt and his platoon of the Sherwood Foresters were holding a vital sector of the line. How often, it seems, that the Victoria Cross was won in conditions like this, when adversity brought out bravery almost beyond belief.

At dawn that day the German 90 Panther Grenadier Division struck back at the battalion's forward position powerfully. Three Mark IV tanks with supporting infantry shattered the house around which Brunt's platoon were dug in. At the same time the enemy subjected the whole area to severe mortar-fire. Two Sherman tanks lay crumpled and useless, and the anti-tank defences were destroyed.

Brunt was not outwardly dismayed, however, rallying his remaining men, and moving to an alternative position. Even so, they were outnumbered by at least three to one, yet they continued to hold off the enemy infantry. Personally using a Bren gun, Brunt killed about fourteen of the enemy.

His wireless set had been destroyed by the heavy shellfire, but Brunt did receive a message soon after by runner. This ordered him to withdraw to a company locality some 200 yards to his left and rear. While the order was being implemented, Brunt stayed behind to give covering fire for the majority of the platoon, but, before the operation could be concluded, he ran out of ammunition for his Bren gun. Instantly he looked round for a weapon, and spotted first a Piat and then a 2-inch mortar, both left by casualties, so he went on with the rearguard firing to give his men a maximum chance to complete the move. Finally, Brunt dashed over the open ground to their new position away to the left.

This aggressive defence made the enemy pause so significantly that during a quiet minute or two Brunt took a small party back to their previous advance position to try and collect the wounded they had been forced to leave there. Rifle fire and the punctuating peppering of automatics made their task harder, but they managed to bring back all the wounded.

With the winter sky already dimming slightly, the Germans put in a further counter-attack on two axes. Brunt took about five seconds to seize a spare Bren gun and set out to his forward position to rally his men. Not content with this static approach, he suddenly decided to leap on a Sherman tank supporting the company.

Brunt ordered the tank commander to drive from one fire position to another, while he sat —or stood —on the turret of the tank, directing aim at the advancing enemy. Exposed to a hail of small-arms fire, Brunt remained, regardless of the risk.

Suddenly he saw small groups of Germans, armed with bazookas, trying to approach around the left flank of the British position, so he at once jumped off the slight protection of the Sherman, and, taking a Bren gun, he forced these units well in front of the company position, killing a number of them, and making the rest evacuate the spot quickly, leaving their dead behind them.

Throughout that day Brunt was always where the fighting flared up heaviest, moving from one post to another, encouraging the men, and firing any weapon he could find at any target he could see.

The sad sequel is that about dusk he was killed by mortar-fire.

By the spring of 1945 the Allied forces —land, sea, and air —were moving northward through Italy. The Navy had played an important part in the original Sicilian and Italian invasions, the Army was on the move, and the Air Force was battering the enemy from above. In such a combined operation it is fitting that a VC commemorating this phase should have been awarded to a man combining the duties and qualities of more than one of the services.

He was Corporal Thomas Peck Hunter, of the Royal Marines, attached to Special Service Troops. He won the award posthumously for gallantry during an advance of the 43rd Royal Marine Commando troops. Hunter had charge of a Bren gun group on the attack.

The wild, towering hills of Italy swept away into the distance. Trees in the valleys were beginning to blossom. But the troops noticed none of this. The group got to within 400 yards of a canal, then halted for a minute. Suddenly, Hunter saw strong enemy forces to the south holding a row of houses. In a flash he realized that his troop behind him would be bound to be exposed to continuous fire from less than a quarter-mile range, for much of the intervening ground lay open.

He seized a Bren gun, checked it for a magazine in a moment, and hurled himself forward across 200 yards of flat open land, to attract enemy fire on him, and distract it from the rest of the troop. He ran at top speed, firing incessantly. His movement was so quick that none of the enemy could hit him. They took one or two hasty aims, then, all in a matter of seconds, became demoralized, by one man.

A hundred yards from the houses, Hunter's first magazine gave out, but by this time he had started a surge of fear through the Germans. He was too close for their comfort. Quicker than he had ever changed magazines before, he ejected the used one and reloaded, firing afresh almost before the new magazine clicked home.

He was at the houses now, but the ordeal went on. Through them he ran at full speed, still firing, the stream of bullets sounding louder in the empty rooms.

As his boots thudded up to one landing, six Germans ran out to meet him, their hands high over their heads. The rest had already clattered away round the back of the houses and fled across a footbridge to the north bank of the canal.

He accepted the surrender of the six soldiers, motioning them to meet two or three of his troops advancing on the houses. He could wait no longer. Many men had to be got across that flat 400 yards, and the enemy could still fire on them from the north bank of the canal.

For a second time Hunter offered himself as a target. He rushed round to the south of the canal, and flung himself on a heap of rubble. The Germans had reached a couple of concrete pillboxes. Hunter took out another magazine, slotted it into place in the black Bren gun, and ran his eyes along the sights. The gun gave him hardly any shelter. A frenzy of German fire from the pillboxes was again turned on to him. He returned it accurately. Several Germans succumbed, and chips of concrete fell from their stronghold. This was short-range war with a vengeance: the enemy near the north bank, Hunter on the south, only 100 yards away, and his troop advancing to the houses behind his covering fire. The enemy never had a chance to set their sights on the troops for more than a moment. They decided their best chance was to concentrate on Hunter first, then go for his troops.

The troops tore towards the houses, where half of them remained. Still Hunter was firing from just off the crest of his heap of rubble. Two-thirds of the troops crossed to safety, though a few fell to the enemy fire.

Hunter felt for another magazine, but he had none. In that instant bullets burst over the rubble, hit him in the head, and he was killed.

Without his self-sacrifice, the troops would never have crossed that 400 yards, or if they had, their casualties would have been infinitely heavier.

The last VC on the Italian front followed soon after Hunter's heroism.

Even as he fell wounded, Major Anders Frederick Emil Victor Schau Lassen lobbed a grenade at the enemy. This was the climax of an action in Italy on the night of 8–9 April 1945, when Major Lassen was ordered to take out a patrol of one officer and seventeen men to raid the north shore of Lake Comacchio.

His task was to cause as many casualties and as much confusion as possible, to give the impression of a major landing there. He also wanted to capture prisoners for interrogation purposes. The command could not offer Lassen any previous reconnaissance information, and the party found itself on a narrow road flanked on both sides by water.

Preceded by two scouts searching for anything suspicious, Lassen led his men along the road towards the town. After they had advanced about 500 yards, uneventfully, they were suddenly challenged from a position on the side of the road. The sentry's voice seemed all the more unnerving at night. They tried to allay suspicion by answering that they were local fishermen returning home, but this failed, for, as they moved forward to try and overpower the sentry, machine-gun fire opened up from the position, and also from two other block-houses to the rear.

Lassen himself then attacked the point with grenades, annihilating it and its contents of four Germans and two machine guns. Each grenade burst brilliantly for a moment, silhouetting tortured men and metal before the dark engulfed them again.

Then, ignoring a hail of trail-blazing bullets from further positions, Lassen scurried towards the next one. An additional post had now opened rasping, repeating fire from 300 yards down the road. Lassen relied on covering fire from his men to allow him to race for the second enemy entrenchment. He hurled in more grenades, causing it to go suddenly silent, before being overrun by his patrol. Two Germans were killed, two captured, and two more machine guns neutralized.

But by now Lassen's force had met murderous losses, with proportionate reduction in fire power. So, still under a heavy cone of fire, Lassen rallied and re-organized them, and turned what fire they could towards the third position. He did not wait for further developments: there was no time. With his head well down, he flung grenade after grenade at the post.

'Kamerad! Kamerad!'

The cry was wrung from the Germans in a fit of fear.

Lassen then went forward to within three or four yards of the position, to order them outside, and to take their surrender. They clearly wanted to stop resistance.

But, at the exact second he was calling to them to come out, he was hit by a burst of Spandau-fire from the left of the position.

Mortally wounded, Lassen flung a grenade at the post even as he fell, enabling his patrol to dash in and capture this final place.

Lassen was still alive, and refused to be evacuated, as he insisted that it would impede their withdrawal and endanger further lives. As ammunition had nearly run out, they had to do as he wished, and withdraw.

So Lassen died, and by the end of the month the war was over in Italy.

CHAPTER SIXTY-ONE

111 Bomber Missions

ROBERT PALMER

After Guy Gibson's fabulous record for the number of operations undertaken, Palmer ranks next among the air VCs. Acting Squadron Leader Robert Anthony Maurice Palmer, DFC, RAFVR No. 109 Squadron, completed no less than 111 bombing missions. Nothing more need really be said about a pilot with that century of sorties to his credit, except to fill in the facts of his life.

How did it begin?

His father recalled: 'We were a family of airmen. I myself joined the RFC in the last war, and have held my interest in aeroplanes ever since, joining up again as an ATC officer in this war.

'On winter evenings I used to entertain Rob and Douglas (his younger brother, an RAF officer cadet) round the fireside with stories of my last war flying. It became the very life-blood to the boys.'

Robert Palmer followed in his father's footsteps so successfully that he won the DFC in June 1944, and a Bar to it on 8 December the same year. But his record of 111 missions went a long way back before then. His very first 'op' was in January 1941. Then there was the first 1,000-bomber raid against Cologne the next year. He was one of the first pilots to drop a 4000lb bomb on the Reich. It was known even in those comparatively early days that he could be relied on to get through whatever opposition and to bomb with great accuracy. So he was always selected to take part in special operations against vital targets.

Two tours of operations. Over 100 missions behind him. The DFC and Bar.

He went on his 111th mission on 23 December 1944, when he led a formation of Lancasters to attack the marshalling yards at Cologne - in daylight.

A Pathfinder pilot, his was the job of marking the target. And Palmer's plane was the first Pathfinder. So Palmer led the whole dangerous raid. He was used to such responsibility, even at his youthful age of twenty-four. His formation was ordered to attack as soon as the bombs had gone from Palmer's plane.

The leader's duties during the final bombing run were very exacting, calling for coolness and complete resolution. To achieve the accuracy the raid must have, he had to fly at a precise height, an exact air speed, and on an utterly steady course – regardless of all opposition. And there was bound to be a great deal.

It came some minutes before Palmer reached the target. Cologne was scarcely in sight on the horizon when shells scorched the air all around the Lancaster. It was the same tragic tale: two engines set on fire, and flames and smoke swirling in the nose and the bomb bay, and the target still not sighted.

Then the fighters attacked in force.

He was flying into death. He disdained to take any evasive action at all. He knew that if he diverged from his course, however little, the special navigational and bombing equipment he was carrying would be no use.

Palmer obviously determined that unless or until the bomber was blown out of the sky, he would go on and complete the run-in, to provide an accurate and easily seen aiming-point for the following bombers. He just ignored the double risk of fire and explosion within the aircraft, and simply kept on. Half the Luftwaffe seemed to be slashing at his flanks, but the Lancaster lurched on its way.

With his engines developing unequal power, he had an immense strain to keep the cripple on its straight-as-a-die course. Palmer did keep it true for Cologne and the maze of marshalling yards now about to spread out below him. He made a perfect approach to the very yard, and his bombs hit the target bang in the middle.

His Lancaster was last seen spiralling to earth in flames. So strong was the ground and air opposition to the raid that more than half of his formation failed to return.

That flight, two days before Christmas 1944, was an all-Lancaster strike against Field Marshal von Runstedt's supplies, stacked high at Cologne for the Ardennes offensive that proved the turning point in the fight for Europe. Its importance could not be over stressed. That was why Palmer led the raid. That was why he got through. That was why he died.

His Victoria Cross was won for four years of bravery, the prolonged, extreme endeavour of 111 missions against the enemy.

CHAPTER SIXTY-TWO

Scots VC on New Year's Day

GEORGE THOMPSON

At long last the final year of the war began: 1 January 1945. And it was on this New Year's Day that another Victoria Cross was won in a Lancaster bomber. Ironical, too, that on this national holiday a Scotsman should be the man to win it: Flight Sergeant George Thompson, RAFVR, No. 9 Squadron, Bomber Command.

After being educated at the Portmoak Public and Kinross Higher Grade Schools, Thompson became a grocer's boy for a time, for want of something better to do. As soon as he was twenty, however, he enlisted as a ground wireless operator. His father said that 'he always loved tinkering with wireless-sets'. He had to be content with ground staff at this stage as there was no great demand yet for aircrew wireless operators. The days of the big bombers with their elaborate equipment lay ahead. What else was in the future Thompson could not tell in February 1942 when he was posted to Iraq. After a seven-month spell there he went on to Teheran, and in January 1943 he was serving with a ferry control unit; but there was still no sign of what the future held for him. Then in June 1943 came the turning point, when he returned to Britain to train for aircrew. His requests for this had been persistent and were eventually rewarded. There followed the usual comprehensive course, followed by routine flying duties. The invasion came and went, and sometimes it seemed to Thompson that he would never actually get operational. It all took so long. Finally, in the autumn of 1944, he joined a bomber squadron, and for two months he became part of the vast organization bombing Hitler's Fatherland night and day.

It was at this time that he linked up with his pilot, a New Zealander. Flying Officer F. H. Denton, of Christchurch, Canterbury, NZ, found him a grand fellow, both on and off duty. They had that bond of both being from a farming community and country. Denton was the only Dominion member of the crew, and he used to spend some of his leave up in Scotland with Thompson and the family, in Kinross, where the Scotsman's father farmed a big estate.

'It was there that you saw George at his best,' Denton said. 'He was what I always thought a Highlander would be: big-boned, immensely strong in character as well as physique, and with a brusque downrightness of speech. He had a very strong

Scottish accent. He was the best wireless operator I have ever known —always right on top of his job in the air.'

This was a long way from serving in a shop, or driving the grocery delivery van. This was war on New Year's Day 1945.

It was to be another of those 'special target' attacks for which Lancasters had grown famous within the service. Thompson was the wireless operator and Denton the pilot of one of the Lancasters detailed to attack the familiar Dortmund-Ems Canal in daylight. Quite a start to the year.

Here was hell, compressed into murderous, mutilating minutes. The Lancaster swept towards the target, into the inevitable storm of shell-fire, almost as if it were coming from above and not below. Denton kept the Anzac flag flying, and took the aircraft straight down over the Canal —steady, steady.

'Bombs gone.'

The plane felt lighter. But the improvement was short-lived, for almost as soon as they had left the bomb bay —in fact, about the time they were exploding below —a heavy shell scored a hit in front of the mid-upper turret. Fire broke out, and dense smoke filled the fuselage. The nose of the aircraft was then struck as well, and the sudden stifling inrush of air cleared the smoke, but revealed a scene of wholesale devastation. Most of the 'Perspex' screen of the nose compartment had been shot away, gaping holes torn in the canopy over the pilot's head, and there was even a huge hole in the floor of the aircraft. Bedding and other equipment was either damaged beyond recognition or else actually ablaze. And one engine was on fire too.

From the first moment they were hit by the flak, Denton could not speak to any of the crew, for the simple reason that the network of intercom lay shattered and scattered all over the place.

Even when bullets started to explode in the heat of the aircraft Denton thought it was the gunner returning enemy fire. All this pilot could possibly do was concentrate on trying to get the aircraft back to their own line. At first he did not think he could manage that, because they were losing height steadily, if slowly, and were attacked again by flak near Arnhem.

Denton did not know, either, what was going on elsewhere in this scarecrow of an aircraft, with the wind and flames fanning each other, it seemed. But Thompson had started on his heroic work.

The time for wireless messages was clearly past. Thompson saw that in the shambles the gunner was unconscious in the blazing mid-upper turret. Without any hesitation at all, he went down the fuselage into the face of the fire, and to the terrifying accompaniment of exploding ammunition. Now his supreme strength could come into action. He pulled the inert gunner from his turret, and, edging his way round the hole in the floor, bore him away from the flames. With his big, bare hands, Thompson then extinguished the gunner's burning clothes. And from this and the fires roasting round the rest of the plane, he sustained serious burns on his face, hands, and legs.

To lift anything at all heavy in the confined space of a perfectly sound aircraft is extremely hard. To drag a man from his burning turret with a gale blowing in the aircraft —to put out flames with bare hands —to partly drag and partly lift this grown man over and past the many ragged, ripped holes in the fuselage, was super-human. But this was not all.

Thompson was in agony now. But he then saw that the rear gun turret was also on fire —at this critical stage. So while Denton still struggled successfully to keep them aloft, Thompson went on with his own appointed rescue work.

Despite his severe burns, he moved painfully to the rear of the fuselage, where he found the rear gunner with his clothing alight too. Overcome by the flames and fumes, his hope had gone. For the second time Flight Sergeant Thompson braved the flames. With even greater difficulty he extricated the helpless gunner, and carried him clear of the incinerator of a rear gun turret.

And again he had to use his bare hands —already badly burned —to beat out the flames on his comrade's clothes.

When the aircraft had been hit originally Thompson might have devoted his efforts solely to quelling the fire, and so have contributed to his own safety. But he chose to go through fire for his friends. He knew that he would then be in no posi-tion to hear or heed any order that might be given to abandon aircraft. He hazarded his life to save the lives of the two gunners.

By now nearly exhausted, the Scot still felt that his duty was not yet done. He had to report the fate of the crew to the captain. He made the perilous journey back through the scorching, searing fuselage, clinging to the sides with his burnt hands to get across the gap in the floor.

The flow of cold air caused still more acute agony, and frostbite developed. So pitiful was his condition that his captain failed to recognize him. Yet his only concern was still for the two burned gunners he had left in the rear of the aircraft.

Up with Denton, Thompson saw how desperate the pilot's plight had become as well. Forty more minutes passed. At one stage they were saved from destruction by a faithful Spitfire. Several Spitfire pilots had seen that they were in dire trouble, and were trying to direct them to an airfield close at hand. But Denton's endurance —or rather his aircraft's —was limited to yards rather than miles. He was just about to shove the plane down in the nearest field when a Spitfire dashed past its nose. Denton looked up to see a high-tension cable ahead. He just managed to jerk up and avoid it.

Then they crash-landed, just short of a Dutch village. Denton scrambled out through where his canopy should have been, and saw for the first time the terrible damage to his Lancaster. How it had flown for those forty minutes he would never know.

Out came Thompson as well. When he clambered free of the appalling wreckage Thompson still had no thought of himself or the frightening burns all over him. He said simply: 'Jolly good landing, skipper.'

Which, of course, it was.

Then came the job of getting them all to hospital in the quickest possible time. While Thompson was there he asked every day how the rest of the crew were getting on. One of the two gunners he saved unfortunately died, but the other one recovered, and owed his life entirely to the courage of Thompson.

And Thompson himself? He went into hospital at once, in the Low Countries. From there he was taken to the casualty air evacuation unit, to be flown home for treatment. The weather was against this, however, and although desperately ill and naturally disappointed, he was cheerful and uncomplaining, even managing to raise a smile. Instead he had to go to the RAF General Hospital. His injuries proved too bad, however, and three weeks after the crash he died, despite all the efforts of the medical and nursing services to save him.

CHAPTER SIXTY-THREE

Self-sacrifice in Burma

GEORGE KNOWLAND, WILLIAM WESTON, CLAUDE RAYMOND, REGINALD RATTEY

The year 1945 in Burma brought three supreme cases of self-sacrifice, all rewarded with the VC. By a coincidence, each of the three men was a lieutenant: George Arthur Knowland, William Basil Weston and Claude Raymond.

This is Knowland's story. With any weapons he could get hold of, he held a hill alone against the Japanese most of the time only ten yards away.

Nine years earlier fourteen-year-old George Knowland went into the Rossie House Home for Working Boys in Camberwell, London. When he left about eighteen months later they gave him a reference describing him as a boy who intended to get on. This proved to be true, for by 1945 he was a lieutenant in Burma, with the Royal Norfolks.

On 31 January 1945, near Kangaw, Knowland had command of the forward platoon of a troop positioned on the extreme north of a hill being subjected to severe and ceaseless enemy attacks all day.

The odds were 300 to 24. Three hundred of the Japanese against his platoon of a couple of dozen men. But these were men of the Fourteenth Army. In spite of the ferocity of the Japanese thrusts up the hill, Knowland skipped from trench to trench all the time, distributing ammunition, and firing his rifle, and heaving grenades, often from positions 100 per cent exposed to the enemy's sights.

This went on for some time.

When the crew of one of his forward Bren guns had all received wounds in one place or another he sent back to troop headquarters for another relief crew, running forward to man the gun himself until they came.

The enemy were then less than ten yards from him, in dead ground down the hill. Ten yards. Ten paces. To get a better field of fire, Knowland stood on top of the trench, shooting the light machine gun, and somehow successfully holding off the uncomfortably close Japs till a medical orderly had dressed and evacuated the wounded gun crew.

Later on, when a fresh attack hurtled in, he took over a 2-inch mortar, and, despite the heavy fire and proximity of the enemy, he again stood up in the open to face them, firing the mortar, and killing six of them with his first bomb.

When all the bombs were gone he went back through the nightmare of grenades, mortars, and machine guns, to get more bombs. These he fired from precisely the same spot in front of his platoon positions. And when these were finished he went back to his own trench, and, still standing up defiantly, he fired single rounds from his rifle. Pitifully inadequate, it seemed. And it looked like proving so for a minute or two.

Knowland had become really hard pressed by now. The stealthy Japs started to close in on him from the ten-yard range. He had no time to recharge his rifle magazine, so he discarded it. In a split second he snatched up the tommy-gun of a casualty and fired at the advancing enemy. By this action he stemmed the assault, killing and wounding many of the Japs, but was himself mortally wounded from only a few yards range.

So although fourteen out of the twenty-four of his platoon became casualties early on that day, and six of his positions were overrun by a horde of 300 Japanese troops, Knowland and the handful of men left held on through twelve hours of non-stop carnage, until reinforcements battled through to them.

If this northern end of the hill had fallen the rest of it would automatically have been endangered, the beachhead dominated by the enemy and other units farther inland cut off from their source of supplies. As it was, the final and successful counter-thrust was later launched from that very and vital ground that Knowland had held, and where he had died.

Lying wounded beside a bunker, he withdrew the pin from a hand grenade, and killed himself, and most of the Japanese with him. So he won his VC posthumously.

It happened in Burma on 3 March 1945, during the Green Howards' attack on the town of Meiktila. Lieutenant William Basil Weston commanded a platoon at the time, and the task of his company was to clear through the town from the north to the water's edge in the south: a distance of about 1,600 yards, the last half of which was not only very strongly held but there was also a labyrinth of minor roads and well-constructed buildings.

The company was working with tanks, and Weston's platoon was one of the two leading the attack through Meiktila. They began the final 800 yards at 13.30 hours, with orders to be completed by dusk. They did not want stray Japanese at large after that.

Practically every man in Weston's platoon was seeing active service for the first time and under most difficult conditions. From the outset, he realized that only by the best personal example could he hope to carry out the clearance by the time allotted.

As they advanced farther into that final half-mile, the Japanese rearguard intensified, until towards the end it reached the state of fanaticism. First-time troops against frenzied Japanese.

Fire from guns and light automatics grew as the afternoon wore on, especially from well-bunkered positions and concrete emplacements. They had to tackle each bunker separately, and superimposed on the enemy's fire from the front was deadly sniping from selected spots on the flanks. The Japanese were up to every trick to try and delay the clearance. Fighting got progressively closer, and even hand to hand.

Weston inspired the relatively raw platoon by his valour, personally leading them into position after position, and exterminating the enemy wherever found. He was matching the foe with their same fanatical zeal.

By sheer guts, they got to within sight of the water's edge at 17.00 hours; so near to completing their task. But then Weston was held up by an especially strong bunker. Appreciating the brief time left before nightfall, Weston quickly directed the fire of the supporting tanks on to this position. Then he led a party with fixed bayonets and grenades gripped to eliminate the enemy inside the bunker.

As at all the many times already that afternoon, Weston was the first into the bunker. At its entrance he was shot by a Japanese, and fell forward wounded.

It was as he lay there that he made his last decision. He might have tried to reach safety, but to do so would have meant endangering the lives of his men who were following him into the bunker.

So instead he slipped the pin out of the grenade in his hand. The Green Howards heard —and felt —the shattering report as its time expired . . .

Throughout the final three-and-a-half hours of battle Lieutenant Weston set an example which seldom can have been equalled. His bravery and inspiring leadership were beyond question. At no time during the day did he relax, and, inspired by the deeds of valour which he continually performed, he personally led on his men as an irresistible force.

The final supreme self-sacrifice of this gallant young officer within sight of victory was typical of the courage and bravery so magnificently displayed and sustained throughout the day's operation.

The Royal Engineers were the backbone of the Burma campaign, so it seemed only right that one of them should be recognized with the VC.

Lieutenant Claude Raymond collapsed and, while being carried away with severe wounds, smiled and made the V sign.

Now it was 21 March 1945, and the Fourteenth Army were preparing for the capture of Rangoon. A small force of men were sent ahead of the main army to try and find out about enemy strength and possible movement. They would also serve to cause a diversion.

The special D Force from which these men were drawn had been trained in India to do this precise sort of job, the small group aiming to get behind the enemy and, by their activities and special sounds, to cause as much confusion as they could to the Japanese.

D Force was composed of volunteers from various branches, and had among its adventurous ranks several officers and sappers of the Royal Engineers. Lieutenant Raymond had the position of second-in-command of this particular patrol which landed on the south bank of a river near Talaho and then headed into country thick not only with jungle but with the wily Japanese as well. He had the comforting knowledge that some of the force were sappers.

When crossing open ground the patrol was fired on by an enemy post on a low hill. Raymond immediately led a charge, He was wounded in the shoulder, but pressed on.

Nearing the enemy post, he was hit in the face by a bursting grenade thrown by a nearby Japanese. Badly wounded, he fell, but picked himself up, and continued to lead his men. Though hit again, Raymond himself killed two of the enemy and wounded another. As a result of the persistence of the attack, the enemy fled.

Though so severely wounded, Raymond refused treatment till the other wounded had been dealt with, and then started to walk back with his party to the landing-craft. After a mile he collapsed and had to be carried, but he continued to cheer on the other wounded men with his smiles. On reaching the boat he collapsed and died.

The citation, after describing the action, ends:

> The outstanding gallantry, remarkable endurance and fortitude of Lieutenant Raymond, which refused to allow him to collapse, though mortally wounded, was an inspiration to every one and a major factor in the capture of the strong-point. His self-sacrifice in refusing attention to his wounds undoubtedly saved the patrol, by allowing it to withdraw in time before the Japanese could bring back fresh forces from the neighbouring position to counter-attack.

Next day, Corporal Reginald Roy Rattey also won the VC, but did not die. Bunkers, foxholes, and trenches –Corporal Rattey took them all on, and lived. The date: 22 March 1945. The place: the Solomons.

A company of an Australian infantry battalion received orders to take a strongly-held enemy entrenchment on the Buin road, South Bougainville; an order more easily given than executed. Not unexpectedly, their attack was met by murderous fire from the advanced enemy bunkers, slit trenches, and foxholes sited on strong ground. All forward movement stopped suddenly, and the sight of reeling, agonized Australians was a poignant one.

Rattey realized how serious it would be for the advance to be delayed like this, and how the only way to avert it must be by silencing Japanese jabs from their automatic weapons in the bunkers, which dominated all lines of approach by the Aussies.

He calculated that a forward move by his section would be halted by fire with heavy losses, so he decided instead on a bold rush by himself, and no one else. This might surprise the enemy, and he reckoned it offered the best chance for success. It would also have surprised him if he made it without at least injury.

He sprang forward, firing his Bren gun into the openings under the head cover of three forward bunkers. This completely neutralized enemy fire from these dangerous positions. On gaining the nearest bunker he hurled a grenade among its garrison; thereafter all was silence from it.

Rattey was now without grenades, but he raced back to his section under a chaotic criss-cross of fire. Grabbing two more grenades, he again rushed the remaining bunkers, killed seven of the Japanese inside, and stopped all further firing from the points. This caused the rest of the Japanese to turn round and disperse, thus enabling the Australian advance to go on as planned. That was not the end, though.

A little later their advance was once more delayed by a heavy machine gun firing across the front. It was Rattey again who handled the fresh situation confronting them. He rushed the gun, and silenced it with his Bren. When he had killed one of the enemy gun crew and wounded another the rest did not wait. The Aussies captured the gun and 2,000 rounds of ammunition. A valuable haul.

So the serious situation had been turned into a brilliant coup, solely by the courage and cool planning of Rattey. The Japanese were stubborn, but he was still more so. That was the way the war would be won.

CHAPTER SIXTY-FOUR

South African Pathfinder

EDWIN SWALES

Only one South African ever flew with the Pathfinder Force of Bomber Command, and he was the third of the men from this famous force to win the Victoria Cross.

His name was Captain Edwin Swales, DFC, South African Air Force, No. 582 Squadron.

Swales's career followed the familiar pattern of a man bent on serving his country. On the outbreak of war he left the bank in which he worked at Durban to join the South African army, and as a warrant officer in an infantry regiment he fought with the Eighth Army in the desert battles of North Africa, on his own continent.

Then in June 1943 the urge to fly asserted itself, and he transferred to the SAAF. Commissioned as a reliable pilot, he came to England, and the week of the invasion he got the chance of joining the Pathfinders. He was always proud of his association with this force.

In an attack in daylight over Germany his Lancaster was badly shot about by flak, but Swales struggled on until he knew that he had reached the Allied lines, where he made a skilful crash-landing. By the evening of that day he was back in his squadron mess, and ready for the next day's operation.

His great qualities of leadership were recognized by the whole squadron. 'He was ideally suited to be a "Master Bomber",' said a friend; 'he was always cool as well as daring.'

Swales was in the attack on the railway yards at Cologne when the 'Master Bomber,' Swales's friend, Squadron Leader Palmer, won the Victoria Cross. Little did he think that two months to the very day he himself would be worthy of the same award. For his part in the Cologne attack Swales received the DFC. This award came through shortly before his Victoria Cross operation on 23 February 1945.

Here is his citation:

Captain Swales was 'Master Bomber' of a force of aircraft which attacked Pforzheim on the night of 23 February 1945. As 'Master Bomber' he had the task of locating the target area with precision and of giving aiming instructions to the main force of bombers following in his wake.

Soon after he had reached the target area he was engaged by an enemy fighter and one of his engines was put out of action. His rear guns failed. His crippled aircraft was an easy prey to further attacks. Unperturbed, he carried on with his allotted task; clearly and precisely he issued aiming instructions to the main force. Meanwhile, the enemy fighter closed the range and fired again. A second engine of Captain Swales's aircraft was put out of action. Almost defenceless, he stayed over the target area issuing his aiming instructions until he was satisfied that the attack had achieved its purpose.

It is now known that the attack was one of the most concentrated and successful of the war.

Captain Swales did not, however, regard his mission as completed. His aircraft was damaged. Its speed had been so much reduced that it could only with difficulty be kept in the air. The blind-flying instruments were no longer working. Determined at all costs to prevent his aircraft and crew from falling into enemy hands, he set course for home.

After an hour he flew into thin-layered cloud. He kept his course by skilful flying between the layers, but later heavy cloud and turbulent air conditions were met. The aircraft, by now over friendly territory, became more and more difficult to control; it was losing height steadily. Realizing that the situation was desperate, Captain Swales ordered his crew to bale out. Time was very short and it required all his exertions to keep the aircraft steady while each of his crew moved in turn to the escape-hatch and parachuted to safety. Hardly had the last crew-member jumped when the aircraft plunged to earth. Captain Swales was found dead at the controls.

Intrepid in the attack, courageous in the face of danger, he did his duty to the last, giving his life that his comrades might live.

As one of his crew put it: 'But for Ted we should not be here now.'

CHAPTER SIXTY-FIVE

Victory in Europe

FREDERICK TOPHAM, EDWARD CHAPMAN, IAN LIDDELL, EDWARD CHARLTON

The Allies had broken the Siegfried Line, and were now crossing the Rhine to race into the heart of Germany. The crossing of the famous river was part waterborne, part airborne, and a representative of the parachute force won the VC.

Paratroop first-aid man, Corporal Frederick George Topham, was shot through the nose, but went on with his job of tending the wounded.

Wearing the wings and parachute of the 1st Canadian Parachute Battalion, Topham was a medical orderly dropped on to a strongly defended area, east of the River Rhine, on 24 March 1945.

At about 11.00 hours Topham was already busy treating men with injuries sustained in the mass drop, when he heard a cry for help from a wounded man out in the open. He could not stop what he was doing for a few minutes, so watched while two medical orderlies from a field ambulance went out to this man in succession. The first got out all right, and knelt down beside the suffering paratrooper. The orderly was killed. Then the second first-aid man moved out to take his place. As he knelt down, he too was shot and killed.

This was too much for Topham to bear. Under fire, he hurried out through no man's land to the spot where the two orderlies had been killed before his eyes. The casualty was still alive, and so was Topham. But as he worked on the wounded man the Germans struck again. They shot Topham right through the nose. He was lucky not to be dead, but things were bad enough as they were. The bleeding became intense, and so did the pain. He could scarcely see what he was doing, but he managed it somehow.

Having completed immediate first aid, he carried the wounded man steadily, slowly, back through the continuous fierce fire to the shelter of a wood.

During the next two hours Topham refused all offers of medical help for his own wound. Four hours had passed since the drop. Now, for those next two hours, he worked on devotedly to bring in wounded through heavy accurate attacks from guns all around them. It was only when all the casualties had been cleared that he consented to have his own wound treated. The wound in his face was bleeding profusely by this time.

Topham was ordered to be evacuated at once, but he begged to be allowed to return to duty as soon as they had patched him up again. So strong were these pleas that he was permitted to carry on.

On his way back to his company he came across a carrier that had received a direct hit. And enemy mortar bombs were continuing to drop around the place. The carrier itself was burning hotly, and its own mortar ammunition began to explode. An experienced officer on the spot warned all the Canadians there not to approach the blazing carrier.

Topham ignored the warning, however, and at once went over to it alone, and rescued three soldiers inside it. He brought each of them back across the open ground, still the target for mortars. One died almost immediately afterwards, but Topham personally arranged for the evacuation of the other two men, who certainly owed their lives to him. Another few minutes, and nothing would have been left of the carrier or its occupants.

'This non-commissioned officer showed sustained gallantry of the highest order. For six hours, most of the time in great pain, he performed a series of acts of outstanding bravery, and his magnificent and selfless courage inspired all those who witnessed it.'

So the Allies were across the Rhine safely —thanks to men like Topham —and next came their decisive drive into Germany itself.

One man versus a battalion: in other words, Corporal Edward Thomas Chapman charging determined German officer cadets in the Dortmund-Ems Canal zone.

By 2 April 1945, with the war in Europe only five weeks from its finish, the British 11th Division crossed the Rhine, and was advancing to assault the ridge of the Teutoburger Wald, which dominates the surrounding country. This ridge is steep, thickly wooded, and ideal for defensive terrain. Moreover, it was being defended by a battalion of officer cadets and their instructors, all of them picked men and fanatical Nazis. Only the fanatical believed now that Hitler could still win the war.

A company of Monmouthshires had been ordered to assault the ridge, and Chapman was advancing with his section in single file along a narrow track, when the Nazis opened fire with machine guns from a range measurable in yards. The section sustained heavy losses which inevitably caused confusion for the moment.

Chapman at once ordered the survivors of the section to take cover, and, seizing the Bren gun, he advanced alone towards the trained battalion, firing the gun and mowing them down at literally point-blank range. The Nazis stood their ground no longer, but retired raggedly.

At this stage, however, the British company was ordered to withdraw, but as this command could not be got forward to Chapman and his section, they were still left in their advanced and very vulnerable spot.

The enemy then began to close up to Chapman and his isolated group, under strong cover of machine-gun fire, and also fixed bayonets for a grim hand-to-hand encounter. Chapman heaved his Bren gun up again to meet the assault, and each time stopped it in its tracks.

By now he had nearly run out of ammunition so, shouting to his men for more magazines, he dropped into a fold in the ground to cover their advance. To fire from this fold, he lay on his back, and fired the final rounds from the Bren over his shoulder! A group of Germans ploughed forward wildly, to try and wipe him out with grenades, but, having reloaded his magazine, Chapman closed with them, still singlehanded, and forced them back with losses.

During the withdrawal of the company its commander had been severely hit, and the men had no choice but to leave him lying in the open, just a short way from where Chapman was operating his lone war. Satisfied that his section was now relatively secure, the corporal crawled out under the constant fire, reached the company commander, and carried him for fifty yards back to comparative safety. But the two men together proved too perfect a target for the enemy, and on the way a sniper hit the officer again, and also wounded Chapman in the hip. Despite this injury, Chapman staggered on with the commander to reach the British line, where it was found that the officer had already died.

Chapman's hip wound hurt him a lot, but he would not leave his men until the whole position seemed secure two hours later. Singlehanded, he had repulsed attacks of well-led, determined troops, and given his own battalion time to re-organize on a vital piece of ground overlooking the only bridge across the canal. His courage helped in the capture of this vital ridge and in the successful development of the Allied advance.

Next day, in the same sector, to save a bridge over the river Ems, Captain Ian Oswald Liddell, Coldstream Guards, cut the wires of demolition charges while in full view of the Germans.

It happened on 3 April 1945, when he was commanding a company of the Coldstream Guards told to take the bridge over the Ems intact. The Germans were back in their own native land with a vengeance now, and this bridge spanned the river near Lingen.

The bridge was covered on the far bank by an enemy strongpoint subsequently discovered to consist of 150 entrenched infantry supported by three 88-mm and two 20-mm guns. The bridge had also been prepared for demolition with 500-lb bombs, which could clearly be seen by the Coldstream Guards as they began their approach towards it.

After directing his two leading platoons on to the near bank of the river, Liddell decided that it was up to him to tackle the wires leading to these lethal-looking bombs.

So he went forward alone to the bridge, and scaled the ten-feet high road block guarding it. There was no other way if he were to succeed in neutralizing the charges. Landing on the other exposed side of the road block, Liddell was next faced with crossing the whole length of the bridge quite by himself under heavy fire.

Liddell reached the far side of the bridge, which must have seemed endless, though it took him only a few seconds to traverse. Once across, he hurriedly disconnected the charges on the Germans' side of the vital structure. Then he turned and dashed back to his own side, and started to cut the wires on this near end.

To cut these wires he had to kneel. And all the while the enemy could see him quite plainly, and were firing at him.

Then he realized with a start that charges also existed underneath the bridge, so he had to clamber down to cope with these additional hazards. Still undeterred, he disconnected the wires leading to them – a nasty enough job without being fired on all the time. So he exposed himself to the double danger of setting off a charge by mistake and getting hit by enemy fire.

He finished the task. He climbed up on to the road block once more, in full view of the defenders, and signalled his leading platoon to advance.

So alone and unprotected, without cover and against fire spurting at him every time he was seen, Liddell achieved his objective. The Coldstream Guards captured the bridge intact, and cleared the way for the advance across the river Ems. The epic episode had a sad sequel, however, for Liddell was wounded subsequently in action, and died, with victory in Europe assured.

'One day you'll be proud of me,' said twenty-year-old Edward Colquhoun Charlton, as he left his mother to join the Irish Guards in September 1940. And one day she was, as she read:

'Guardsman V.C. with one arm fought on.'

Time was running out rapidly for the Germans, as the Panzer Grenadiers were desperately trying to retake the village of Wistedt, in their own precious fatherland.

On the morning of 21 April 1945, Charlton was the co-driver in one tank of a troop which seized Wistedt, with a platoon of infantry to support them. Shortly after this the enemy counter-attack opened under cover of an artillery barrage in surprising strength. It later transpired that this concentration comprised a battalion of the 15th Panzer Grenadiers supported by six self-propelled guns. The Germans were sparing neither themselves nor the Allies in their final fling to try and stop the snowballing advance into their land. All the British tanks were hit, including Charlton's. And the infantry seemed in dire danger of being overrun by the counter-move.

It was at this second, entirely on his own initiative, that Charlton decided to counter-attack the counter-attack. Quickly recovering his Browning from the shattered tank, he prowled up the road in full view of the enemy, firing from the hip as he went. So bold and unexpected was this move that he halted the leading enemy company completely. Many of them lay dead from his Browning. Charlton's superhuman struggle brought vital relief to the British infantry.

Minute after minute he continued to blaze away at the Nazis. Ten endless minutes passsed, before he was wounded in the left arm. The fire from the enemy grew greater. But Charlton wedged his machine gun on a nearby fence, which he used to support his wounded arm.

Ten more minutes ebbed away, with Charlton firing from the fence all the time.

He was losing blood, but kept going. Then another blow struck the same left arm. It fell away, shattered, useless.

Twice wounded, without one arm, and suffering severely from loss of blood now, Charlton again somehow lifted his Browning on to the fence from which it had fallen. Now he had only one arm for firing and reloading. Nevertheless, he went on and on hitting the enemy all the time, until finally he was hit for the third time, and collapsed.

His heroism in a self-imposed duty was beyond words, and even the Germans who captured him were amazed at his valour. Not only did his deeds retrieve his comrades of the Irish Guards from a desperate situation, it also enabled them to recapture their target.

Sergeant Gallagher, one of the Guards, said that the work he did on that day was indescribable, and he certainly saved the lives of the rest of them. But after his capture by the Germans, Charlton was too badly injured to recover, and he died later in their hands.

For a whole year afterwards his mother, Mrs Edith Charlton, heard reports of his gallantry: the courage of No. 2722614 Guardsman Charlton. She learned that he was entitled to the 1939-45 Star, the France–Germany Star, and the Defence Medal. She also learned that awards for valour, except the VC, cannot be made posthumously. His colonel, however, wrote to tell her:

'His courageous action has been brought to the notice of higher authority.'

So a year after his action, on 2 May 1946, Charlton was posthumously awarded the VC.

Charlton had the distinction of being the last Army VC of the war in Europe.

CHAPTER SIXTY-SIX

Aussies Finish it Off

JOHN MACKEY, EDWARD KENNA,
LESLIE STARCEVICH, FRANK PARTRIDGE

Within a week after victory in Europe a pair of VCs had been won by Australian soldiers out East, to be followed by another one in June and the last in July. The Aussies were evidently in a hurry to finish the war.

Helen was the name of the feature under attack by the Australians, on 12 May 1945. This lay east of Tarakan town, in Burma, where the war went on as savagely as ever.

Corporal John Bernard Mackey was in charge of a section of the 2nd/3rd Australian Pioneer Battalion. Led by Mackey, the section edged along a narrow spur with scarcely width for more than one man. The ground fell away almost sheer on each side of the track, making it almost impossible to move to a flank.

At this precise instant the section came under concentrated fire from three well-sited positions near the top of a very steep razor-backed ridge. Mackey led his men forward.

He charged the first light machine-gun position, but slipped after wrestling with one Japanese. Mackey managed to recover, however, and bayoneted him. Then the Australian surged straight on to the heavy machine gun which was firing from a bunker position six yards to his right. He rushed the post, and killed the crew with a well-aimed group of grenades.

Mackey jumped back out of the blast, and, exchanging his rifle for a sub machine gun, he attacked farther up the steep slope. This time the target was a light machine gun which was firing down on his platoon. He fired his gun as he charged the post, getting to within a few feet of it.

He shot two more Japanese, and was then himself killed, having accounted for seven of the enemy and two of their posts bristling with machine guns and ammunition. His courage inspired his whole battalion.

Bullets between his arms and his body did not disturb Private Edward Kenna —he still stood up as a human target in front of the Japanese.

The war was over in Europe, but as far as the Allied troops, or the enemy, knew, it might go on for ages out East.

In New Guinea, south-west Pacific, at Wewak, on 15 May 1945, the 2nd/4th

Australian Infantry Battalion were attacking the Wirui Mission features, and Kenna's company had to take certain enemy positions. But the only place from which observation for supporting fire could be obtained was continuously raked by rapid fire. Enemy artillery or mortars could also be brought into use if necessary.

VCs always seemed to be won in such settings as this. Kenna and his section slipped in as close as they could to the enemy bunker, to harass any Japanese they spotted, while the rest of the platoon prepared to attack from the flank. But the attacking sections immediately met accurate automatic fire from a position not already disclosed. Many Australians fell and died. The survivors could not move farther forward.

Kenna stood up in full face of the Japanese less than fifty yards away from him. Swinging his Bren up to his right hip in a split second, he fired at the bunker. It vibrated violently as the bullets left the gun. The enemy machine gun fired back. It seemed incredible that he would not be killed on the spot. The Japanese bullets tore towards him. Where would they hit? Kenna had his gun held tightly, and his arms up. Several bullets sped actually between his arms and his body.

Kenna continued pointing his Bren at the bunker, firing till its magazine was exhausted. He was still alive. And, still making a sitting target of himself, he seized a rifle, and with amazing coolness shot and killed the machine-gunner with his first round. The intense fire stopped for a second. Then a second automatic stuttered into action from a different spot. It did not succeed in hitting Kenna, who was still standing there in broad daylight. A Japanese raced over towards the machine gun, but he never got there, for Kenna raised his rifle to his shoulder a second time, aimed, squeezed the trigger. The Japanese fell.

Kenna was not killed, and he stood firm as they took the bunker without further trouble or loss. His action saved the company's attack, and also saved the lives of many Australians in that company.

On 6 January 1947 in the drawing room of Government House, Melbourne, Major General C. H. Miller read out Kenna's citation, and he was invested with the Victoria Cross by the Governor General of Australia, the Duke of Gloucester. The investiture marked the highlight of the Royal farewell visit to Melbourne.

So to the citation of Private Leslie Thomas Starcevich, 2nd/43rd Australian Infantry Battalion, the last-but-one recipient of an Army VC in the Second World War:

For most conspicuous gallantry and extreme devotion to duty during the capture of Beaufort, North Borneo, on June 28, 1945.

During the approach along a thickly wooded spur, the enemy was encountered at a position where movement off the single track leading into the enemy defences was difficult and hazardous.

When the leading section came under fire from two enemy machine-gun posts, and suffered casualties, Private Starcevich, who was Bren gunner, moved forward, and assaulted each post in turn. He rushed each post, firing his Bren gun from his hip, killed five enemy, and put the remaining occupants of the posts to flight. The advance progressed until the section came under fire from two more machine-gun posts, which halted the section temporarily.

Private Starcevich again advanced fearlessly, firing his Bren gun from the hip, and, ignoring the hostile fire, captured both posts singlehanded, disposing of seven enemy in this assault. These daring efforts enabled the company to increase the momentum of the attack and so relieve pressure on another company which was attacking from another direction.

The outstanding gallantry of Private Starcevich in carrying out these attacks single-handed with complete disregard of his own personal safety resulted in the decisive success of the action.

On 16 July 1945, an atomic bomb was exploded as a test in New Mexico, bringing the end of the war nearer. But before the two bombs were dropped operationally on Japan, one more Army VC was won.

Twice torn by Japanese fire, Private Frank John Partridge shouted out a challenge to the enemy:

'Come out and fight.'

The first Australian militiaman to win the award and the last Army VC of the war, Partridge came from Upper Newee Creek, Macksville, New South Wales, and was a banana-grower in civilian life. He was called up in March 1943, at the age of eighteen, and by the time he was twenty he had seen action with a vengeance against the Japanese.

The Aussies were still battling for Bougainville, in the Solomon Islands, south-west Pacific, on 24 July 1945.

Two fighting patrols of the 8th Australian Infantry Battalion were given the job of eliminating an enemy outpost in Bougainville, which was denying any forward movement to the troops. From well-concealed and camouflaged bunkers to their front and left, one of the Australian platoons came under fire, flaring at them from various weapons. The forward section of the platoon at once suffered seriously, and were pinned down together with two other sections.

Partridge was a rifleman in a section which, carrying out an encircling move-ment, immediately came under deadly medium machine-gun fire. This hit him twice in the left arm and once in the left thigh. The Bren gunner was killed outright, and two other soldiers were seriously hurt. This left only the section leader unwounded, but another soldier soon began to move up from a different position. Partridge grasped the gravity of their plight.

In spite of wounds, and utterly oblivious of his safety, he rushed forward under a cataclysmic burst of enemy fire, and retrieved the Bren gun lying alongside the dead gunner.

He challenged the enemy to come out and fight.

He handed the Bren gun to the newly arrived man, to provide covering fire for him while he rushed the Japanese bunker. Pitching a grenade en route, he silenced the medium machine gun. Under cover of the grenade burst, too, he dived right into the bunker, and in a hectic hand-to-hand fight killed the only living occupant with his knife. All this with three wounds.

Partridge next cleared the enemy dead from the entrance to the bunker, and attacked another bunker behind it. But a trail of lost blood told its own story, and weakness forced him to halt. With the way clear by the demise of the machine gun, the platoon advanced, and set up a defence perimeter in the vicinity of the spot where Partridge was still lying wounded. It was ironic that he grew up among the bananas of New South Wales and now he was wounded and helpless amid the banana plants of the Solomons.

Heavy enemy machine-gun and rifle fire again —both direct and enfilade from other bunkers —soon created an untenable situation for the Aussies of the platoon, who had no option but to withdraw under its own covering fire.

Yet despite his wounds and weakness due to loss of blood, Partridge propped himself up somehow, and joined in this fight to extricate the platoon, remaining actually in action until they had withdrawn after recovering all their casualties.

The serious situation during the fight of the two patrols was retrieved only by the outstanding gallantry and devotion to duty displayed by Private Partridge, which inspired his comrades to heroic action, leading to a successful withdrawal that saved the small force from complete annihilation. The subsequent successful capture of the position was due entirely to the incentive derived by his comrades from the outstanding heroism and fortitude displayed by Private Partridge.

Partridge recovered to receive the VC.

Three weeks after his action the war was over.

CHAPTER SIXTY-SEVEN

Midget Sub in Singapore

IAN FRASER, JAMES MAGENNIS

Lieutenant Ian Edward Fraser and Leading Seaman James Joseph Magennis won the Victoria Cross in Singapore Strait. A midget sub, XE3, was their craft, and noon, 26 July 1945, the time of departure for their attack on one of two 10,000-ton Japanese heavy cruisers, the *Nachi* and *Takao*, lying in the Johore Strait near Singapore Island.

Meanwhile the Japanese warships were at anchor, waiting to be attacked. Although they had not been to sea for some time, they were in a position to shell the Singapore Causeway across the Straits, which could have been dangerous to any Allied forces approaching the island by that route. XE1 would attack the *Nachi* and XE3, the subject of this chapter, the *Takao*.

Operational submarines towed the two XEs from their starting point, Brunei Bay, Borneo. HM Submarine *Stygian* towed XE3. Telephonic touch broke down, and the only means of communication between the 'parent' and 'child' was walkie-talkie sets used when the two submarines surfaced.

A passage crew occupied XE3 during the four days of the outward tow. They were lucky in having good weather, because, as the Commander-in-Chief of the British Pacific Fleet stressed afterwards, the task of the passage crew is a hard one: the towing speed at times reaches as much as eleven knots, yet all the while moisture has to be mopped up, and every scrap of equipment kept at 100 per cent efficiency. The whole operation depends on their success. Needless to say, both XE1 and XE3 were turned over to the operational crews in perfect condition.

This changeover from the passage crew was effected at 06.00 hours on the morning of 30 July. Seventeen hours later, the tow was slipped at the dead of night, leaving XE3 alone at sea in a spot forty miles from the *Takao*'s anchorage.

Operation Struggle it had been named. Now the final phase of the struggle started. With the commander of XE3 (Ian Fraser) were Sub Lieutenant W. J. L. (Kiwi) Smith of the Royal New Zealand Naval Volunteer Reserve, Engine Room Artificer Charles Reed and Leading Seaman James Magennis. Fraser fortunately stood only 5 feet 4 inches, so was much happier upright in a midget sub's five and threequarter feet headroom than a man a foot taller! He had had plenty of practice, but this was his first X-craft operation.

Throughout the rest of that night he sat on the casing looking through binoculars, as the sub slipped softly through the waters on the surface. He left the safe 'swept' channel on purpose, to avoid enemy listening posts, and navigated through a known minefield, thus avoiding the danger of being heard approaching.

In the very middle of the night, as he dangled his legs and looked through the glasses, he suddenly saw the dark outline of a tanker with an armed escort proceeding towards the Singapore Straits. He scrambled to his feet, vanished below, shut the 'lid' behind him, and uttered the one word: 'Dive.'

'The safest thing for us to do, Kiwi,' he told the First Lieutenant, 'is to sit on the bottom for as long as it takes this little Oriental procession to pass.'

Thirty minutes later he came to periscope depth to peep. They were safe from the ships, but not from the minefield; for only then did he notice that the craft had become entangled with a mine, which had not exploded.

By mid-morning on 31 July, Fraser sighted the trawler which acted as guard vessel at the submarine net boom. Magennis was preparing his gear for 'baling out' quickly and cutting a way through the wire netting.

'Don't bother, Magennis,' Fraser called. 'It looks as if the 'gate' has been left open by some kind soul.'

Even so, the navigational job was extremely difficult. Fraser had to take XE3 along the side of the guard vessel, quite close to it, shifting the sub at a snail's pace. The water was shallow, and the sun shone deep down almost to the bottom. The sub slithered through the clear water, visible to any one who might have been looking down from the enemy ship. But no one was!

The first real hazard had been beaten, but worse was to come further along the route. Fraser navigated at periscope depth through several miles of narrow channels where a steady sea-traffic came and went. Keen pilotage from Fraser, level depth-keeping by Smith, and alert steering from Reed, was necessary.

A few minutes after noon Fraser said simply:

'There she is.'

The *Takao* lay ahead, a very heavy cruiser carrying eight 8-inch guns —one shell from which would wipe out XE3.

He lowered periscope. It was not wise to keep it up for more than a second or so. Two hours passed and they got closer to the cruiser.

About 14.00 hours, just after lunch on a scorching day, he went into the attack. He took a quick peep through the periscope —then dropped it at the double! Only a cricket-pitch of water away through the lens was a cutter full of Japanese sailors —'liberty men' going ashore for the afternoon. XE3 dived. The cutter passed. Fraser continued blind. He knew where the cruiser lay, but not exactly how deep or shallow was the water. He wondered if he could get XE3 underneath her? As it transpired, *Takao* was in extremely shallow water for such a ship. XE3 went in with her keel scraping the bottom of the sea.

This was going to be difficult, the more so since the method of attack would be different from the *Tirpitz* attack. Even on the bed, Fraser could not find enough water. XE3 came to the cruiser's plating and hit it hard and true with a metallic thud. They wondered if the ship had heard it. Fraser brought the craft out astern again, and by a series of trials —and errors —he discovered that the Japanese ship lay almost aground at either end, but with some water under her amidships.

The clock ticked towards 15.00. By plying back and forth parallel to the *Takao*, and occasionally hitting her hull, XE3 at last found a spot halfway under the cruiser, not a pleasant place to be, with ten thousand tons of enemy shipping on top. Fraser wedged XE3 between the hull and the sea-bed —although he knew that she might become more tightly squeezed if the tide fell much lower.

Magennis had the job of getting outside the craft on the bottom of enemy waters to attach limpet mines to the hull of the *Takao* which would go off in due course and hole her. He went into the chamber, flooded it, and then found that the external hatch only opened a quarter of the normal amount —only a matter of inches. He deflated the breathing apparatus, breathed out until his chest was as small as possible, and squeezed through the hatch. Then he began to unload the limpet charges from the port container on the outside of the sub but as he did so a stream of oxygen bubbles escaped from his equipment, which must have been damaged while he was wrestling with the hatch. Anyone seeing them reach the surface would have at once become more than suspicious.

He took the first limpet mine from its container, and prepared to place it against the hull of the ship. It was supposed to stay there by magnetism, but the cruiser's hull was so thick with barnacles, and the ship lay at such a slope, that the magnets would not work. Magennis scraped a little patch free and then secured the charges in pairs. For half an hour he swam, scraped, carried, and tied, securing them with a line under the ship's keel. An exhausting job it was, far more so since his supply of oxygen slowly but steadily went on leaking.

He could well have placed just one or two, and then returned to XE3 but he attached the entire half a dozen over a length of forty-five feet of hull. He got back exhausted to the 'wet and dry' hatch, struggled through it, shut it, dried out the chamber, and collapsed into the control room. How he shut the hatch in his condition was a miracle, particularly as his hands had been torn to pieces with vicious lacerations from the barnacles. They brought him a drink and sat him down in a bunk, wrenching his diving apparatus off him.

XE3 had done its job. She could make her getaway. But still the hazards hung about her. All she had to do was get rid of the starboard side-cargo, the large explosive charge, and the port limpet container —and back out. But *Takao* had closed her hold on the tiny adversary and would not let her free.

For nearly an hour XE3 went full astern, full ahead, and did everything conceivable to the tanks. But it was to no avail. It looked as if they would die as soon as the charges fired: killed with their own explosives. The waiting was nerve-racking. All of them sweated, but the sub would not budge; then suddenly, without warning, she shot astern right out of control, careered towards the surface and sent a splash of sea upwards only fifty yards from the *Takao*. So quickly did it happen that somehow it was not seen. A second later the bow was tilted down and hurtled back to the bottom. Fortunately this was not far, as they lay in a mere fifteen feet of clear blue water. They bumped aground, and the water began to come in.

Fraser realized that the limpet-container had not released itself as it should, which accounted for the craft being so hard to handle. He knew that no hope of escape the way they had come could be considered until it was cleared.

Magennis must already have earned his VC, yet in spite of his exhaustion, the oxygen leak in his set, and their lying in such shallow water, he at once volunteered to leave XE3 once more and free the container —as he was an experienced diver.

Fraser said he would go, but Mick Magennis was insistent. So he set out, complete with a big spanner. Seven minutes elapsed. It was hard work to get the container free from the attachment bolts, but he managed it safely. The container rolled a bit away from the craft. Magennis groped back to the 'wet and dry' hatch and so safely aboard and into the control room for the second time. Now they could get away from this hot spot, still only yards distant from the charges laid.

Once more under control, XE3 sailed but a yard or two below the surface further, further from the scene: through the minefields, the listening hydrophone positions, the loop-detector circuit, the net boom, and everything.

Fraser glanced at his watch. It was 21.30, still the same day, and he was tiring, but they had got clear, out of range, and far beyond earshot. Had they not been, two minutes later they would have heard an explosion rend the dusk of the Singapore Straits.

The charges went off, ripping a sixty-feet-long by thirty-feet-wide hole in the hull of the *Takao*, putting her turrets out of action, damaging her range-finders, flooding several compartments, and altogether immobilizing her. Meanwhile, now that the worst was over, the whole quartet aboard XE3 were genuinely glad that Fraser had not wavered but persevered to lay the charges.

On and on they ploughed, at periscope depth now and again to check the course. Finally they sighted *Stygian*. By this time they had been on duty without sleep for fifty-two hours: two days and four hours. Reed was at the helm for thirty hours without a break, and they had been submerged during the day of the attack for sixteen-and-a-half hours non-stop.

One day some time later, the wireless telegraphist aboard the base ship *Bonaventure* received the radio message that Fraser and Magennis had won the Victoria Cross. The signal came through in the early hours of the morning, about 01.00, but as soon as the captain heard about it, a party swung into action and went on right through the warm spring night off the Australian shore. It was a wonderful end to a gallant adventure.

CHAPTER SIXTY-EIGHT

The Last Week of
the War . . .

ROBERT GRAY

T he last Victoria Cross of the air was won when Japan had really already lost the war: a tragic twist of fate. It went to Lieutenant Robert Hampton Gray, Royal Canadian Naval Volunteer Reserve, flying with the Fleet Air Arm.

He had fought right through the war, until 9 August 1945. Both atomic bombs had been dropped. Hiroshima and Nagasaki would soon have passed into history. The end of the war would come within days now. But Gray was not to see VJ day. He was born when armistice was imminent, in 1918. He died within a week of armistice 1945.

A Canadian, Gray was the son of a jeweller in Nelson, British Columbia. Before the war he studied for an Arts degree at the University of British Columbia, where he served in the Officers' Training Corps. He showed literary leanings, and became editor of the University year-book. But he never took his degree. Hitler was burning books in Europe. War broke out.

Gray joined the Navy as a rating, and came to England for his early training at HMS *Raleigh*. Then he made a momentous decision. In 1940, when invasion was expected, he joined the naval air arm. After training at HMS *St Vincent* in Gosport —across the harbour from the premier port of Portsmouth —Gray won his wings, and was promoted sub lieutenant in December 1940. He had a six-month spell back in Kingston, Ontario, for further flying.

Summer 1941 brought him his first operational squadron, No. 757, which he joined at HMS *Kestrel,* Winchester. Soon he was transferred to the East Indies command, and served most of the time from Kenya with three squadrons, Nos. 795, 803, and 877. Some of this time he spent on operations aboard HMS *Illustrious.*

He graduated to lieutenant in December 1942, and then had a short spell of leave in Canada —the last time he saw his own country —followed by a refresher course. Then he was commissioned to HMS *Formidable.* It was while operating from this aircraft-carrier that he was mentioned in despatches for undaunted courage, skill, and determination in carrying out daring attacks on the German battleship

Tirpitz — the story which had been started by two other naval VCs —Cameron and Place —in their midget submarines, far up the Norwegian fjord, ended by the eventual destruction of her through combining attacks. So the careers of yet more of the VCs were interwoven in the overall pattern of the war over, on, and under the sea.

In August 1944, exactly a year before the final phase, Gray won the Distinguished Service Cross for courage and devotion to duty in air attacks on Japan.

After the atomic bombs he launched his last attack against the enemy empire. There is always something especially sad about the losses in the final few days of hostilities, and in Gray's case, after so courageous a career, more than ever was this true. Nothing but admiration remains for the lack of regard he showed for his own safety, since it was past the eleventh hour of the war. The struggle might end any day.

A naval airman of ground staff on the flight deck of HMS *Formidable* pulled the chocks clear of Gray's Corsair plane, which was leading Squadron 1841. Gray raised a hand in usual acknowledgement, and in seconds was airborne, and gaining height over the smooth sea off Honshu, the mainland island of Japan. It was a perfectly peaceful summer's day. For a few minutes they flew in towards the coast.

'Coast ahead, sir.'

Gray glanced out and down, then saw, through the heat mists drifting across the coast, the Bay of Onagawa Wan. And he saw more than that —some five or six ships spread-eagled about the bay. Gray did not waste time. He swung the plane downward, closer and closer, till a sudden burst of anti-aircraft fire heralded a barrage from batteries based ashore, as well as concentrated shooting from five of the Japanese vessels. One shot missed narrowly, and the plane shivered, bumped, and jumped. Gray flew on.

'Taking the destroyer first,' he told the crew.

The engine vibrations rose a pitch as the plane tore sharply, steeply downward. The firing cracked and streamed up at them now from land and sea.

Everything was being telescoped into a few frantic seconds as he dived to attack. There was another outburst of fire, and a shell struck the plane, ripping its fuselage.

'Going in low.'

The firing intensified, grew more accurate. Gray jerked the plane level again, 100 feet from the destroyer straight ahead. Yet another hit was hurled into the frail fuselage as Gray straightened up.

'Fire. Port wing.'

'Fifty feet.'

'Bombs gone.'

All over in a couple of seconds. The plane had scored a direct hit before sailing clear of the ship, rising in one final desperate fling, and diving —for the last time —into the blue Bay of Onagawa Wan.

As it did so, the destroyer exploded amidships and sank.

SECOND WORLD WAR
VICTORIA CROSS HOLDERS
LISTED IN ALPHABETICAL ORDER